PRESUPPOSITION and ANAPHORA

CSLI Lecture Notes
Number 89

PRESUPPOSITION
and ANAPHORA

EMIEL
KRAHMER

CSLI
PUBLICATIONS
Center for the Study of
Language and Information
Stanford, California

Copyright © 1998
CSLI Publications
Center for the Study of Language and Information
Leland Stanford Junior University
Printed in the United States
02 01 00 99 98   5 4 3 2 1

Library of Congress Cataloging-in-Publication Data

Krahmer, Emiel, 1968–
Presupposition and anaphora / Emiel Krahmer.
p.   cm.
(CSLI lecture notes ; no. 89)
Includes bibliographical references and indexes.

ISBN 1-57586-147-X (cloth : alk. paper).
ISBN 1-57586-146-1 (pbk. : alk. paper)

1. Semantics. 2. Discourse analysis. 3. Presupposition (Logic)
4. Anaphora (Linguistics) 5. Montague grammar. I. Title. II. Series.
P325.K665   1998
401′.43—dc21   98-26092
CIP

∞ The acid-free paper used in this book meets the minimum requirements of the American National Standard for Information Sciences—Permanence of Paper for Printed Library Materials, ANSI Z39.48-1984.

CSLI was founded early in 1983 by researchers from Stanford University, SRI International, and Xerox PARC to further research and development of integrated theories of language, information, and computation. CSLI headquarters and CSLI Publications are located on the campus of Stanford University.

CSLI Publications reports new developments in the study of language, information, and computation. In addition to lecture notes, our publications include monographs, working papers, revised dissertations, and conference proceedings. Our aim is to make new results, ideas, and approaches available as quickly as possible. Please visit our web site at
http://csli-www.stanford.edu/publications/
for comments on this and other titles, as well as for changes and corrections by the author and publisher.

voor Daan en Bas

Contents

Acknowledgements   xi

1   Introduction   1
  1.1   Background   1
      1.1.1   Anaphora   1
      1.1.2   Presupposition   3
      1.1.3   Anaphora and Presupposition   13
  1.2   About this Book   19
      1.2.1   Anaphora   19
      1.2.2   Presupposition   20
      1.2.3   Anaphora and Presupposition   22
  1.3   Overview   24

2   Anaphora and Discourse Semantics   27
  2.1   Introduction   27
  2.2   Representational Theories of Discourse   30
      2.2.1   File Change Semantics   30
      2.2.2   Discourse Representation Theory   35
      2.2.3   From FCS to DRT   42
      2.2.4   DRT Interpretation Using Total Assignments   43
      2.2.5   From DRT to Predicate Logic   44
  2.3   Non-representational Theories of Discourse   46
      2.3.1   Quantificational Dynamic Logic   46
      2.3.2   Dynamic Predicate Logic   49
      2.3.3   A Dynamic Version of Montague Grammar   52
  2.4   Discussion: The Quest for *the* Theory of Discourse   58
      2.4.1   The Dynamic Cube   58
      2.4.2   Extensions and Modifications   61

3   Negation and Disjunction in DRT   65
  3.1   Introduction   65

3.2 Two Problems for DRT, and a Reduction   65
    3.2.1 The Double Negation Problem   65
    3.2.2 The Disjunction Problem   68
3.3 Double Negation DRT   74
3.4 Applications   76
3.5 The Relation with Standard DRT   80
3.6 Discussion: Uniqueness, Inference   83

4 Presupposition and Partiality   87
4.1 Introduction   87
4.2 Partial Predicate Logic   94
    4.2.1 Strong Kleene PPL   95
    4.2.2 Middle Kleene PPL   98
    4.2.3 Weak Kleene PPL   100
4.3 Presuppositions and PPL   100
    4.3.1 Determining Presuppositions   101
    4.3.2 Predictions   103
4.4 Flexibility: The Floating $\mathcal{A}$ Theory   110
4.5 Discussion   118
    4.5.1 Karttunen and Peters Revisited   118
    4.5.2 A Note on the Logic of Conventional
         Implicature   119
Appendix   122

5 Presupposition and Montague Grammar   125
5.1 Introduction   125
5.2 Partial Type Theory   127
5.3 Presuppositional Montague Grammar   130
5.4 Discussion: Extending the Fragment   137
    5.4.1 Additional Presuppositions   137
    5.4.2 Note   140
    5.4.3 Dynamifying Presuppositional Montague
         Grammar   141
    5.4.4 Implicatures and Dynamics   143
Appendix: The Fragment   144

6 Presupposition and Discourse Semantics   149
6.1 Introduction   149
6.2 Presuppositions-as-Anaphors   151
    6.2.1 Resolving Presuppositions   152
    6.2.2 What is a Presuppositional DRS?   156
    6.2.3 Procedural vs. Declarative   156
    6.2.4 Accommodating Failing Presuppositions   157

6.2.5 Disjunctions   159
6.2.6 Presupposition-Quantification Interaction   161
6.3 Presuppositional DRT   162
6.4 Applications   167
6.5 Determining Semantic Presuppositions   171
6.6 Again: Presuppositions-as-Anaphors   176
6.7 Discussion: Comparing the Two Approaches   180
   6.7.1 Does Binding Preserve Meaning?   181
   6.7.2 Does Accommodation Preserve Meaning?   183
   6.7.3 An Alternative Interpretation   184
   6.7.4 Presupposition Projection as Proof
       Construction   187
Appendix   190

7 Presupposition and Determinedness   193
7.1 Introduction   193
7.2 Is Determinedness Uniqueness?   200
   7.2.1 Restricting the Uniqueness Prediction   201
7.3 Is Determinedness Anaphoricity?   202
   7.3.1 Accommodating Missing Antecedents   204
7.4 Determinedness is Familiarity   205
7.5 Determinedness is Salience   210
7.6 Discussion: Extending the Analysis   216
   7.6.1 Dependencies and Non-identity Anaphora   217
   7.6.2 Definites and Salience   220
   7.6.3 Surroundings: The Dynamics of Pointing   221

8 Concluding Remarks   225
8.1 Summary   226
   8.1.1 Anaphora   226
   8.1.2 Presupposition   227
   8.1.3 Anaphora and Presupposition   230
8.2 Discussion: Rounding Off   233

Bibliography   235

Subject Index   249

Name Index   253

Acknowledgements

This book was written in two phases. The first phase started in the summer of 1994 and ended in the summer of 1995 when I submitted the fruits of my labour as a doctoral dissertation entitled *Discourse and Presupposition*. The second phase started in the summer of 1997 and ended in the early spring of 1998 with the book you are now holding.

The foundation was laid during the time (1991–1995) I was a Ph.D. student at the Computational Linguistics Department of the University of Tilburg, with Harry Bunt and Reinhard Muskens as supervisors. As my daily supervisor in this period, Reinhard made innumerable valuable suggestions which greatly have helped shape the contents of this book. The second phase took place at IPO, Center for Research on User-System Interaction at the Eindhoven University of Technology. It was initiated by Kees van Deemter, who suggested I should write an updated version of the aforementioned doctoral dissertation. The stimulating discussions we had actually made me feel like doing just that, and I have greatly benefitted from Kees' accurate criticism.

One of the things I have learned in the past years is that doing research is even more fun if you do it together. Therefore I consider myself lucky for having had the opportunity of collaborating with, in more or less chronological order, Reinhard Muskens, David Beaver, Jan Jaspars, Kees van Deemter and Paul Piwek, and I thank each of my confrères for the highly pleasurable and educational experience. The reader will encounter some of the results of some of the cooperations in the pages to follow. In particular, sections 4.4 and 4.5.2 are based on joined work with David Beaver, while chapter 3 is an updated version of an article written in tandem with Reinhard Muskens. I should add that none of my collaborators necessarily agrees with my view of things in *this* book.

Furthermore, I am grateful to those who made useful comments on drafts of various chapters: David Beaver, Paul Dekker, Bart Geurts, Hans Kamp, Jan Landsbergen, Leo Noordman, Paul Piwek, Gerrit Rentier, Elias Thijsse, Rob van der Sandt, Jan van Eijck, Robert van Rooij and Kees Vermeulen. Special thanks to David for setting me on the track for chapter 5.

Over the past years a great number of colleagues and friends have made comments and suggestions which somehow found their way into these pages. To all those —mentioned and unmentioned— I want to say, paraphrasing Sam & Dave just a little bit: *You didn't have to help me like you did but you did but you did and I thank you!*

Let me end on a more personal note. Without the support and trust of Annemarie it would have been a lot more difficult to finish the two versions of this work. By a fortunate coincidence, the inceptions of the two phases of writing this book were marked by the respective births of our first and second son. This made the years of writing very pleasant and it is only fitting then, that this book is dedicated to the two of them.

March 1998
Eindhoven

1

Introduction

1.1 Background

1.1.1 Anaphora

For a long time the study of meaning has been concerned with single sentences. However, sentences seldom come in isolation. For one thing, they tend to be sandwiched in between other sentences, thus forming a text, or *discourse*. In the early eighties the question arose how to determine the meaning of a discourse and, somewhat surprisingly, it turned out that this is not an easy question to answer. By and large, one could say that the main problem is not so much that sentences never come in isolation, but that sequences of sentences are sequences of sentences for an interesting reason: they are 'connected', as it were, for instance, by *cross-sentential anaphors*. Consider the following sentence.

(1)   She kissed it.

We could say that the meaning of (1) is that some female person happened to kiss something, but then we would be missing the point. Sentence (1) may be preceded by (2) or (3) —to give but two possibilities— and the meaning is rather different in each case.

(2)   Louis XIV solemnly offered his hand to a new chambermaid.
(3)   Yesterday, a beautiful princess saw a regal green frog near the creek.

Sentences like (1) cannot be interpreted correctly without taking the context into account.

Problems such as these led Karttunen to the introduction of *discourse referents*. In Karttunen 1976 it is suggested to let an indefinite noun phrase (such as *a new chambermaid* or *a regal green frog*) introduce a new discourse referent, which (under normal circumstances) has a permanent *life-span*. That is to say, these referents remain available and anaphoric phrases (such as *she* and *it*) can always pick them up later on.

Much research in the area of anaphora has been concerned with finding constraints on the occurrence of anaphoric expressions. For example, in the syntactic tradition it has been noted that a pronoun (*him*) should not have an antecedent in its minimal syntactic domain, while a reflexive (*himself*) should.[1] Thus, assuming that in both (4.a) and (4.b) the phrase in object-position is intended to be anaphoric on *Louis*, it is predicted that the former is ungrammatical (indicated by the asterisk), while the latter is not.

(4)   a.   * Louis likes him.
      b.   Louis likes himself.

However, the relation between a would-be anaphor and a would-be antecedent is not only subject to syntactic constraints, but also to semantic constraints, and in this book we focus on those. Karttunen already noted that when a discourse referent is introduced in the scope of a logical connective, its life-span is generally limited to the scope of that connective. For example, indefinites in the antecedent of a conditional sentence introduce discourse referents which may be taken up by pronouns in the consequent of the conditional, but not in sentences following it. Consider (5):[2]

(5)   a.   If a princess sees a frog, she kisses it. # In fact, it is the prince of Buganda.
      b.   It is not true that Louis XIV had a wife. # He loved her madly and smothered her with diamonds.
      c.   # Either Louis XIV had a mistress or he hid her from his wife.

Here and elsewhere, the symbol # is used to indicate *semantic* markedness, like * is used to indicate *syntactic* markedness. Thus the second sentence of (5.a) is semantically marked on the intended interpretation where the pronoun *it* refers to the indefinite *a frog*. Similar observations can be made with respect to disjunction and negation; a discourse referent introduced under the scope of a negation phrase cannot be picked up outside that scope, as demonstrated by (5.b). And a discourse referent introduced in one disjunct cannot be taken up in the other disjunct, witness (5.c).

---

[1]Numerous ways of defining a minimal syntactic domain have been proposed (see for instance Reinhart 1976 and Chomsky 1981), but for the sake of exposition we may take it to be the S or NP node immediately dominating antecedent and anaphor.

[2]The first example is a variant of the old donkey-sentence rediscussed in Geach 1962. Variants of the second and third examples can be found in for instance Groenendijk and Stokhof 1991 and Kamp and Reyle 1993.

Observing that we need discourse referents with varying life-expectations as a kind of parameters in semantics is one thing, developing a formal system which meets these requirements is quite another. Since the early eighties various systems of discourse semantics incorporating the concept of discourse referents have been proposed. Of these Heim's *File Change Semantics* (FCS, Heim 1982), Kamp's *Discourse Representation Theory* (DRT, Kamp 1981) and Groenendijk & Stokhof's *Dynamic Predicate Logic* (DPL, Groenendijk and Stokhof 1991) are generally considered to be the most important ones. A key feature of these systems is that interpreting a sentence is a *dynamic* process. When a sentence like (3) has been interpreted, something has changed: two new discourse referents (for *a beautiful princess* and *a regal green frog* respectively) have made their appearance and these can be taken-up for the subsequent interpretation of (1). The last fifteen years have shown that the dynamic approach to meaning is very useful when we want to study the meaning of anaphoric pronouns in discourse, and consequently it plays a major role in this book.

1.1.2   Presupposition

Intuitively, presuppositions differ from other 'parts of speech' in that they denote propositions of which the truth is somehow taken for granted. Suppose someone tells you:

(6)   Louis' wig is grey.

The speaker of (6) could be said to convey *two* propositions: 'Louis has a wig', and 'this wig is grey'. However, she also assigns a different status to these two propositions; the former is *presupposed*, and the latter is *asserted*. In example (6) this difference is not clearly perceptible, since both propositions are implications of (6). That there really is a difference can be shown by negating (6).

(7)   It is not the case that Louis' wig is grey.

The proposition that Louis has a wig is still implied by example (7) (after all: the presupposition is taken for granted), but the proposition that it is grey is no longer an implication; the wig in question may have any colour except for grey. The negation-phrase only seems to apply to the assertional part, while it leaves the presupposition untouched. The observation that presuppositions are insensitive to negation can already be found in the pioneering work of Frege 1892, and it provides us with a diagnostics of the presence of presuppositions: the *negation* test. This test can informally be put as follows: P is a presupposition of S if, and only if, P follows from both S and the negation of S. Following Frege, many people have used the negation test to signal the presence of presuppositions. However, the negation test should be applied with some caution. The presence of explicit *denials* may blur the picture somewhat (below we address this issue).[3] It is worth stressing that the negation test is not the *only* test available for the detection of presuppositions. Various other tests have been proposed in the literature, of which the *modality* test is perhaps the least controversial. This test is based on the observation that embedding a sentence with a presupposition trigger —such as example (6)— in the scope of a modal 'possibility' operator (*maybe*) preserves the presupposition but not the assertion of the original sentence. Thus: *Maybe Louis' wig is grey* still implies that Louis has a wig, but not that it is grey.

Presuppositions are associated with certain (kinds of) lexical elements or syntactic structures. The following list contains a number of these, together with examples and associated intuitive presuppositions.[4] Each example is given in both a positive and a negative form, separated by a slash, so that the reader can verify the presence of a presupposition trigger.

DEFINITE DESCRIPTIONS: 'the CN'

(8)   The present king of France needs/doesn't need a new chambermaid.
       presupposes: there is a present king of France

CLEFTS: 'it was X who Y-ed'

(9)   It was/it was not the butler who did it.
       presupposes: someone did it

IMPLICATIVES: 'manage', 'succeed', …

(10)   Louis managed/didn't manage to find a wig-maker.
       presupposes: it was difficult for Louis to find a wig-maker

QUANTIFIERS: 'every', 'most', …

(11)   Every/Not every girl at the ball masqué wanted to dance with Louis.
       presupposes: there was at least one girl at the ball masqué

---

[3] Another problem is that sometimes negating a sentence is not so easy, for example because the sentence in question contains a *polarity item* or is not assertional (for instance, a question). See Van der Sandt 1988 for discussion.

[4] This list is by no means complete. Levinson 1983:181–184 contains a list of thirty-one triggers due to Karttunen. See also Van der Sandt 1988, Soames 1989, or Beaver 1997:943–944 and the references cited there.

FACTIVES: 'know', 'regret', 'the knowledge that', ...

(12) Louis regrets/doesn't regret that the claret is in the decanter.
presupposes: the claret is in the decanter

CHANGE OF STATE VERBS: 'stop', 'begin', ...

(13) Louis stopped/didn't stop sipping his vermouth.
presupposes: Louis was sipping his vermouth

LEXICAL/CATEGORICAL RESTRICTIONS: 'bachelor', ...

(14) Louis is/is not a bachelor.
presupposes: Louis is an adult male

It is generally assumed that these phrases/constructions are somehow marked in the lexicon/grammar as triggers of *elementary* (or potential) presuppositions. The interesting feature of these elementary presuppositions is that they sometimes survive when embedded in complex configurations, while at other times they do not. The problem of predicting *which* elementary presuppositions survive in *which* situations is known as *the projection problem for presuppositions* (first discussed by Langendoen and Savin 1971).

We already saw one example: under normal circumstances, presuppositions survive under negation, or as Karttunen 1973 put it: negation is a *hole* for presupposition projection. Here is a different example.

(15) a. If the king of France needs a new chambermaid, then his wife will keep a close watch on the course of things.
presupposes: there is a king of France
   b. If there actually is a king of France, then the king of France needs a new chambermaid.
does NOT *presuppose: there is a king of France*
   c. If Antoinette is leaving Versailles, then the king of France needs a new chambermaid.
presupposes: there is a king of France

Intuitively, the presupposition that there is a king of France projects from both the antecedent and the consequent of the conditional, *unless* the presupposition of the consequent is asserted in the antecedent or follows from it. Further evidence for these intuitions is provided by the phenomenon of anaphoric take-up. When the presupposition that there is a king of France is projected, we can refer to the king of France with a pronoun in consecutive sentences. Thus, we can follow (15.a) and (15.c)

—but not (15.b)— with (16) where *his* is intended to refer to the king of France.[5]

(16) His bedroom is a real mess.

Thus, in (15.a) and (15.c) the presupposition is projected. To borrow some more terminology from Karttunen 1973: conditionals (like disjunctions and conjunctions) are a *filter* for presupposition projection: some, but not all, elementary presuppositions arising in conditionals project. To be complete, Karttunen 1973 distinguished a third category: the *plugs*, which block projection of elementary presuppositions arising in their scope. Examples are so-called *verbs of saying* and certain verbs of propositional attitudes. This is an example of the latter kind.

(17) Francois wants to be the king of France.

This example does *not* seem to presuppose that there actually is a king of France.

The fact that natural language provides the facilities for presupposing enhances the efficiency of communication. The possibility of making short-cuts during conversation by taking things for granted, is a very convenient one. In fact, the phenomenon of presupposing is not even restricted to natural language. Van Eijck has pointed out that a similar phenomenon is encountered in an imperative programming language such as Pascal (Van Eijck 1994b:768). Suppose x is a variable over integers. If the body of a program consists of the statement (18.a), it aborts with error in states where x has a value equal to the value of MaxInt. If the program contains (18.b), however, it never aborts.

(18) a. `x := x + 1`
     b. `IF x < MaxInt THEN x := x + 1`

In the terminology of computer science, x < MaxInt is a pre-condition for executing (18.a) but not for (18.b).

Since presuppositions and assertions display such a strikingly different behavior, we may wonder if this difference is reflected in the semantic interpretation. Consider (the positive version of) example (8). It is clear what happens when the king of France does not need a new chambermaid: in that case example (8) is false. But what happens when there is no king of France at the time of interpretation? The question what should happen when a sentence presupposes a proposition which is not true has led to a minor schism in the semantic community. On the one hand, there is the Russellian standpoint. According to Russell 1905, (8)

---

[5] We return to the relation between anaphors and presuppositions in section 1.1.3 below.

means: *there is one, and only one, present king of France, and he needs a new chambermaid.* No distinction is made between presupposed and asserted material, and consequently if there is no present king of France, or if there are two, sentence (8) is a plain falsehood. On the other hand, there is the Strawsonian point of view. Strawson 1950 claims that a sentence with a failing presupposition is neither true nor false: it simply doesn't make *sense*. When there is no present king of France the question of truth or falsity just does not arise for (8).

As with all religious disputes, there has been a lively debate about the question who is right, but no conclusive answer has emerged.[6] There does not appear to be a *knock-down* argument in favor of either the Strawsonian or the Russellian position. For that the positions are too similar,[7] the differences show up precisely when the presupposition of a sentence is not true. Nevertheless I find myself in agreement with the Strawsonian intuition, and believe that presupposition failure should somehow be distinguished from ordinary falsity. As an illustration, let us take a look at presuppositions arising in yes-no questions. Intuitively, a yes-no question is a question which seeks to find out whether some (possibly complex) proposition is true or false; if the proposition in question is true, the answer should be *yes*; if it is not, the anser is *no*. But what about a yes-no question which contains a failing presupposition? If we take a Russellian view, and make no distinction between presupposed and asserted material, a yes-no question which contains a failing presupposition is indistinguishable from a question about a false proposition. Both should simply be answered in the negative. But this may lead to some undesired inferences on the questioner's part. Suppose someone is ignorant in the theory of numbers, and asks the following two questions about the natural numbers.[8]

(19) a. Is the smallest even number greater than five?
      b. Is the largest even number greater than five?

If the addressee of these questions interprets the descriptions in a Russellian manner, she will probably answer *both* questions in the negative,

---

[6]Here, I shall not review the various arguments for the various positions. The interested reader may consult Russell 1905, Strawson 1950, Russell 1959 and Strawson 1964. A nice and representative *argument by intimidation pro Russell* is given in Neale 1990. Good discussions on this topic can be found in for instance Van der Sandt 1988, Heim 1991 and Beaver 1995. In chapter 4 of this book we return to the Russell/Strawson controversy.

[7]One could even argue that Strawson's standpoint is essentially a refinement of the position of Russell.

[8]The proposition *The largest even number is greater than five* is given by Larson and Segal 1995:322 as an example of a 'straightforwardly false' proposition due to the fact that the description fails to denote.

which would be at the very least misleading. Only an explicit denial of the presupposition that the largest even number exists (*What do you mean? There is no such thing as the largest even number!*), can take away the tacit assumption on the questioner's part that there exists a largest even number; a simple *yes* or *no* will not suffice to do that.[9] But this trades on the assumption that we make a distinction between presuppositions and assertions. If we take the Strawsonian point of view, we can indeed say that neither *yes* nor *no* is a good answer to the question in (19.b), since the question itself does not make 'sense'.[10]

According to Strawson 1950, a sentence containing a description which does not refer to an existing individual cannot be interpreted. It cannot be true and it cannot be false. The question of truth and falsity just does not arise. In general, the Strawsonian spirit is caught by the following informal notion of presupposition:

π is a presupposition of φ if, and only if,
whenever π is not true, φ is neither true nor false

Or, put differently, π is a presupposition of φ if, and only if, whenever φ is either true or false, π is true. If we want to take the above notion of presupposition seriously, we have to leave the realm of classical logic. In classical, two-valued logic the *principle of the excluded middle* is valid, which says that for any ψ, the disjunction $\psi \vee \neg \psi$ is a tautology. In other words: *every* classical formula ψ is either true or false, there is no such thing as a ψ which is neither true nor false as a result of presupposition failure. So, to make sense of the Strawsonian concept of presupposition we need to give up the principle of the excluded middle. This is what is done in the field of partial logic, and consequently there is a long tra-

---

[9] A defender of Russell might object that the negative answer is ambiguous between a 'narrow scope' reading ('there is a smallest/largest even number and it is *not* greater than five') and a 'wide scope' reading ('it is *not* the case that there is smallest/largest even number that is greater than five'). But that would not be very informative for the questioner either. Consider another, 'real life' example (due to Kees van Deemter): in the Spicos automatic question answerring system a user could ask things like "*Has x read any of the files labelled 'urgent'?*". If there are in fact no files labelled urgent, the system would respond with "*No, x has not read any of the files labelled 'urgent'*". We may assume that this will confuse the user. It would be much more informative if the system would respond to the false presupposition, for instance by : "*None of the files in the database is labeled 'urgent'*". But, again, this is only possible if the system is able to *distinguish* presuppositions from assertions.

[10] In fact, Strawson 1950:52 also presents questions to illustrate the benefits of his view over the one ventured in Russell 1905: *A literal minded and childless man asked whether all his children are asleep will certainly not answer 'Yes' on the ground that he has none; but nor will he answer 'No' on this ground. Since he has no children the question does not arise.*

dition of using partial logics for the analysis of presupposition.[11] From the partial perspective the projection problem reduces to the problem of defining the truth conditions of the logical connectives in the right way. Once we have a set of truth tables which meet the demands posed by our intuitions, the projection facts come for free. It is as easy as shelling peas.

Unfortunately things are not *that* simple. The problem is this: as soon as a connective gets a partial interpretation its predictions concerning presupposition projection are fixed. But, as we have seen in connection with (15), in natural language, presupposition projection is *flexible*. To illustrate this point, let us (informally) discuss a three-valued propositional logic $\mathcal{L}$, only containing two binary operators, an implication and a presupposition operator, plus a set of propositional constants P. Following the usual convention we use lower case letters $p, q, r, \ldots$ to represent the propositional constants, while lower case Greek symbols $\varphi, \psi, \pi \ldots$ are used to represent arbitrary formulae. In general, a formula $\varphi \in \mathcal{L}$ can be True, False and Neither (True nor False), abbreviated as T, F and N respectively. Let us assume for the sake of simplicity that the partiality only arises due to presupposition failure, and that atomic propositions are either True or False. Thus, a valuation function V maps all the propositional constants in P to { T, F }. Given a valuation function V, the interpretation function $[\![.]\!]_V$ sends each formula $\varphi \in \mathcal{L}$ to { T, F, N }.

We started our discussion of presuppositions with example (6), and noted that this sentence actually conveys two propositions, but with a different status: one proposition is asserted and one is presupposed. Such simple sentences containing presuppositions are represented using the presupposition operator: $\varphi_{\langle \pi \rangle}$ (intuition: π is an 'elementary presupposition' associated with φ). The presupposition operator receives the following truth table.[12]

---

[11]It should be noted that there are two kinds of logic which may be labelled 'partial': (*i*) truely partial logics, so to speak, in which a formula can be true or false or fall in what Quine called a *truth value gap* ('undefined') and (*ii*) total logics with three or more values (so-called *many-valued logics*, for our purposes three values are generally enough). Even though there are important philosophical differences between partial and multi-valued logics (for which the reader may consult, for instance, Blamey 1986 and Urquhart 1986), they are often lumped together in the context of presupposition, which seems justified in the light of Blamey's observation that monotonic three-valued (total) functions can be taken to represent two-valued partial functions (Blamey 1986:9). Throughout this book, we loosely use the term 'partial logic' in the broad sense, and treat the truth value gap as a third truth value.

[12]This truth table is due to Blamey 1986, who refers to it as *transplication*. Notice that, given our assumption that atomic proposition are either True or False, an

$\varphi_{\langle \pi \rangle}$		π		
		T	F	N
	T	T	N	N
φ	F	F	N	N
	N	N	N	N

This truth table nicely reflects the Strawsonian intuition; when the presupposition π is not True ($[\![\pi]\!]_V \neq$ T), the entire formula is neither True nor False ($[\![\varphi_{\langle \pi \rangle}]\!]_V =$ N). The second connective of $\mathcal{L}$ is the implication, represented here as $\rightarrow$, which is given the following three-valued truth table.[13]

$\varphi \rightarrow \psi$		ψ		
		T	F	N
	T	T	F	N
φ	F	T	T	T
	N	N	N	N

Now, let us reconsider the examples in (15), with their associated schematic representations ($S \rightsquigarrow \phi$ should be read as 'sentence S is represented by formula ϕ'). We use the following key: p represents the proposition that there is a king of France, q the proposition that he needs a new chambermaid, w represents the proposition that his wife keeps a close watch on the course of things, and v that Antoinette is leaving Versailles.

(20) a. If the king of France needs a new chambermaid, then his wife will keep a close watch on the course of things.

$\rightsquigarrow q_{\langle p \rangle} \rightarrow w$

b. If there actually is a king of France, then the king of France needs a new chambermaid.

$\rightsquigarrow p \rightarrow q_{\langle p \rangle}$

c. If Antoinette is leaving Versailles, then the king of France needs a new chambermaid.

$\rightsquigarrow v \rightarrow q_{\langle p \rangle}$

Assume that we evaluate these three respective formulae with respect to some valuation function V which maps the p to False ($[\![p]\!]_V = V(p) =$ F). Thus, the elementary presupposition that there is a king of France is not satisfied by V. Given the aforementioned, Strawsonian notion of presupposition and according to the intuitions given in (15), this means that we would expect the formulae in (20.a), (20.b) and (20.c) to be Neither, True or False, and Neither respectively. Let us check this by

---

elementary presupposition can only be Neither if it contains an embedded elementary presupposition which is not True.

[13] This truth table is due to Peters 1979, we also refer to it as the *middle Kleene* interpretation of implication.

inspecting the truth tables, beginning with (20.a) Given the truth table for the presupposition operator, we find that the antecedent of the conditional is neither True nor False with respect to V ($[\![q_{\langle p \rangle}]\!]_V = \mathrm{N}$). It is easily seen that this means that the formula in (20.a) is indeed Neither given V: $[\![q_{\langle p \rangle} \to w]\!]_V = \mathrm{N}$. This is in accordance with the Strawsonian definition of presupposition given above: intuitively example (20.a) presupposes the existence of a king of France, and indeed: when this proposition is not True, (the representation in $\mathcal{L}$ of) sentence (20.a) is neither True nor False.

Also for (20.b) we get the required result. We know (by assumption) that the consequent of this conditional is Neither and that the antecedent of the conditional is False, hence the entire formula is True. Unfortunately, the same applies to (20.c). If we assume that Antoinette is not leaving Versailles, then we predict that (20.c) is True in spite of the fact that the presupposition that there is a king of France is not satisfied: using $\to$ as representation of *if ... then ...*, we predict, contrary to our intuitions, that (20.c) does not presuppose the existence of a king of France.[14] Thus, choosing $\to$ as our representation of the implication, we make wrong predictions concerning presupposition projection in the case of presuppositions which arise in the consequent of a conditional. Essentially, the problem is this: when we translate *if ... then ...* in terms of $\to$ the prediction is that *every* presupposition from the antecedent and *no* presupposition from the consequent of a conditional sentence is projected. Using the truth table given above, the predictions concerning presupposition projection are fixed. Unfortunately, the projection behavior of presuppositions in conditionals is not. Even though presuppositions arising in the antecedent of a conditional tend to project[15], the projection of presuppositions which arise in the consequent depends on the information present in the antecedent, and the truth table of $\to$ does not capture this. In fact, *no* three-valued truth table for implication captures the projection behavior illustrated by (20).

As one would expect, the situation is no different for other logical connectives. Above we noted that presuppositions tend to project from negations, and it is not difficult to add a negation $\neg$ to $\mathcal{L}$ which does justice to this observation:

---

[14]To be precise, a *weaker* presupposition is predicted, namely $v \to p$, or in words: *If Antoinette is leaving Versailles, then there is a king of France.* We return to the issue of weak presuppositions in chapter 4.

[15]But even here, there are counterexamples. For example, in a sentence like *If the king of France is bald, then fried icecream is a reality: there is no king of France*, the presupposition that there is a king of France is, intuitively, not projected.

φ	$\neg\varphi$
T	F
F	T
N	N

It is easy to see that every presupposition of a formula φ is also a presupposition of $\neg\varphi$ (if φ is Neither True nor False, so is $\neg\varphi$): every elementary presupposition arising in the scope of a negation is projected. However, in natural language we do find cases of elementary presuppositions which are not projected from a negation phrase, in particular the cases of explicit presupposition denial as in example (21).[16]

(21) It is *not* true that the king of France needs a new chambermaid, after all: there *is* no king of France.

If we translate (21) using $\neg$ we predict that this example can never be a true statement, which is clearly not the case. This seems to leave the advocate of a partial approach to presuppositions with only one option: introduce a second negation, say $-$, which acts as a 'black hole' (or plug): every presupposition in its scope vanishes:

φ	$-\varphi$
T	F
F	T
N	T

However, introducing a second negation, and thereby committing oneselves to the claim that natural language negation is truely ambiguous, seems undesirable. First, there is no independent motivation for postulating such an ambiguity (but see Seuren 1985 for discussion). Second, and more important, it would solve only part of the problem anyway. It is not difficult to come up with examples where some presuppositions which arise in the scope of a negation phrase are projected and some are not. Consider:

(22) It is not the case that the king of France kissed the queen of England, because there is no king of France.

Intuitively, this example presupposes that England has a queen, but not that France has a king. However, neither $\neg$ nor $-$ captures this intuition. Moreover, it has been argued convincingly in Soames 1979 that other logical connectives are ambiguous in essentially the same way.

---

[16]Notice that examples like (21) undermine the status of the negation test somewhat. It has been argued that such examples are exceptional (see Blok 1993 and Van der Sandt n.d.). For instance, (21) is typically used when *someone else* just claimed (the positive version of) (8.a). Horn 1985 has noticed that such 'rectifications' are accommpanied by an 'appropriate fall-rise intonation'.

For instance, disjunction would require a four-way ambiguity, *only* to account for presupposition projection.

However, we shall see that there is another option, which creates the required flexibility without postulating *ad hoc* ambiguities for the logical connectives. In general, we give partial logics a central place in this book, not only because we want to do justice to the Strawsonian intuition, but also because —as we shall see— certain techniques from partial logic are really useful, for the treatment of anaphora *and* presupposition.

1.1.3   Anaphora and Presupposition

While partial approaches to presupposition seem to have lost most of their appeal during the seventies, the *phenomenon* of presupposition was able to rejoice in a renewed interest due to the simultaneous shift of attention from sentence to discourse semantics. In Van der Sandt 1992 it is observed that there is a striking correspondence between the behavior of anaphora in discourse and the projection of presuppositions in complex sentences. Consider the following example from Karttunen 1973.

(23)   If Jack has children, then all of Jack's children are bald.

The consequent presupposes that Jack has children. But the conditional as a whole does not presuppose this: the presupposition is not projected. The antecedent conditionalizes the existence of Jack's children, in the same way in which the existence of a king of France was conditionalized in (15.b). As a result, we cannot refer to Jack's children in consecutive sentences: continuing (23) with (24), where *they* is intended to refer to Jack's children, is not possible.

(24)   # They wear grey wigs.

The same situation arose for the frog-sentence, as we saw in (5.a). Hence Van der Sandt argues: why not treat elementary presuppositions as anaphors looking for an antecedent? Then we can say that the presupposition that Jack has children is *bound* in the antecedent of (23), just like the pronouns *she* and *it* are bound by the indefinites *a princess* and *a frog* in the antecedent of (5.a). In a nutshell this is the crux of the *presuppositions-as-anaphors* theory.[17] In terms of empirical predictions, Van der Sandt's approach is the pick of the bunch in presupposition theory: no other theory has been able to deal successfully with the same range of data (see Beaver 1997:983).

Van der Sandt characterizes his approach as a combination of pragmatic and semantic features. But the semantic approaches to presupposition, that is: approaches in which the interpretations of the logical

---

[17]See Van der Sandt 1989, 1992 and Van der Sandt and Geurts 1991.

connectives determine the predictions about the projection behavior, have also benefited from the rise of dynamic/discourse semantics. Here the emphasis is primarily on the interaction between quantifiers and presuppositions. This is a heritage of Karttunen and Peters 1979, one of the most discussed accounts of presupposition from the pre-discourse era. It can be seen as the 'Montagovian crown' on the treatment of presuppositions developed by Karttunen and by Peters in the seventies. Its basic idea is simple: each sentence is associated with *two* representations: one for the asserted and one for the presupposed material. This works nicely for simple examples but, as Karttunen and Peters themselves observe in a by now notorious note to their paper, things go pear-shaped when examples are considered in which quantifiers and presuppositions interact. Their example is (25).

(25) Somebody managed to succeed George V on the throne of England.

Karttunen and Peters remark that example (25) sounds funny. George VI, the actual successor of George V, is the only person for whom the succession was *not* difficult, as it was his birthright. So, on a historically correct interpretation, (25) should be a case of presupposition failure. Karttunen and Peters' system generates two representations for (25), one for the 'assertional' meaning (26.a) and one for the 'presuppositional' meaning (26.b) of example (25). Schematically:

(26) a. $\exists x(succeed(x, g))$
      b. $\exists x(difficult\text{-}to\text{-}succeed(x, g))$

In words: the assertional meaning states that somebody succeeded George V, and the presuppositional meaning says that somebody found it difficult to succeed George V. But this presupposition can hardly fail: succeeding George V was a non-trivial accomplishment for everyone *except* George VI. The problem is that the assertive and the presuppositional representation should be about the same person. But the two separate representations make it difficult to express this: a quantifier in one formula simply cannot bind a variable in another formula. For this reason Karttunen and Peters' problem is also known as the *binding problem*.

Various attempts have been undertaken to solve the binding problem, often from the dynamic perspective. One of the first and most influential studies of presupposition from this perspective is Heim 1983b. Heim shows that the separate representation of presupposition and assertion is not necessary. She argues that the presuppositional predictions can be derived from the independently motivated dynamic meanings of the logical connectives. Thereby she immediately counters Gazdar's 1979 criticism of Karttunen and Peters that they merely describe the projection facts and do not explain them. For this purpose, she essentially uses a trimmed down, partially valued version of her File Change Semantics (Heim 1982). She shows that the File Change Semantics interpretations of the logical connectives determine the projection behavior of presuppositions arising in their scope. Since Heim abandons separate representations, her proposal sure enough solves the binding problem. Nevertheless, her solution is not without its own problems.

Given the influence of Heim's work on recent presupposition research it is worthwhile to digress a little and discuss her approach in some more detail. In doing so, we closely follow Heim 1983b. This digression is of a somewhat more technical nature than the rest of this introductory chapter. Readers who do not care for the technicalities can jump ahead to section 1.2. On the other hand, readers who want to know *more* about the technical details can consult the original work of Heim 1983b and also, for instance, Beaver 1995, 1997.

In Heim's approach *context change potential* is the key notion. Each sentence is represented by a *Logical form*, which is derived from the surface syntactic structure.[18] Interpreting such a Logical form is a dynamic process; each new Logical form leads to an *update* of the context of interpretation. Heim constructs a context as a set of assignment-world pairs. That is: pairs of the form $\langle g, w \rangle$ where w is a possible world and g is a finite assignment function mapping variables into the domain of individuals. As a simple example, consider interpreting a (simplified) Logical form like [Louis walks] in a context Γ. The update of Γ with this Logical form, designated here as $\Gamma[\![$ [Louis walks] $]\!]$, yields a new context, say Γ', consisting of those pairs $\langle g, w \rangle$ from Γ such that the proposition 'Louis walks' is true in w. Logical forms containing free variables are treated analogously. Thus, $\Gamma[\![$ [x walks] $]\!]$ equals the context Γ' consisting of those pairs $\langle g, w \rangle$ from Γ such that $g(x)$ walks in w (assuming that x is a member of $\mathsf{Dom}(g)$, the domain of g).

Now consider a Logical form like [Louis (is a) bachelor]. Above we saw that *bachelor* is associated with a lexical presupposition to the effect that the subject (in this case, Louis) is an adult male. Following Karttunen 1974, Heim takes it that *admittance* plays an important role for presupposition projection. In general, a context admits a Logical form φ if it entails the presuppositions of φ. Thus, a context Γ *admits* the Logical form [Louis (is a) bachelor] only if Γ entails that Louis is

---

[18]Many of the issues which are presented here briefly and informally (the way Logical forms are derived from the surface syntactic structure, the way they are subsequently interpreted, the determination of local context, etc.) are discussed in detail in the next chapter.

an adult male. That is: only if for every pair $\langle g, w \rangle$ in Γ the proposition 'Louis is an adult male' is true in w. Admittance is a necessary condition for an update to be *defined*. If a context does not admit a sentence (or more precisely, its Logical form), the update is not defined. This is where the partiality comes into play.

So far, we have only considered 'atomic' sentences. For complex sentences, admittance is relative to *local contexts* (Karttunen 1974). For example, when *if A, then B* is interpreted in a context c, then c is the local context of A, and $c[\![A]\!]$ (the result of updating c with A) is the local context of B. This leads to the following general statement in Heim 1983b:117.

A context Γ admits a sentence S just in case each of the constituent sentences of S is admitted by the corresponding local context.

Things get more complicated when variables come into play. Consider the following example from Heim 1983b:116.

(27) Every nation cherishes its king.

The Logical form for example (27) consists of three parts, and looks essentially as follows:

(28) [every x [x (is a) nation] [x cherishes x's king]]

Heim requires x to be a fresh variable (discourse referent). The third component of this Logical form, [x cherishes x's king], triggers the presupposition 'x has a king'. The projection behavior of this presupposition is determined by the context change potential of universally quantified sentences, which Heim claims to be independently motivated by "the truthconditions to be captured" (Heim 1983b:121). Heim defines this context change potential essentially as follows. Suppose $i = \langle g, w \rangle$ and $j = \langle h, v \rangle$ are assignment-world-pairs. The notation $i\{x\}j$ abbreviates 'worlds w and v are equal and assignment g and h only differ in that h assigns a value to x'.[19] We say that j is an x-extension of i.

$$\Gamma[\![\text{ [every } x \text{ [A][B]] }]\!] =$$
$$\{i \in \Gamma \mid \forall j((i\{x\}j \ \& \ j \in \Gamma[\![[A]]\!]) \Rightarrow j \in (\Gamma[\![[A]]\!])[\![[B]]\!])\}$$

In words: updating a context Γ with a Logical form [every x [A][B]] yields a new context which consists of those pairs i from Γ such that every x-extension of i which is an element of $\Gamma[\![[A]]\!]$ is also an element

---

[19]Formally, $i\{x\}j$, with $i = \langle g, w \rangle$ and $j = \langle h, v \rangle$, abbreviates $w = v$ & $\forall y \in \mathsf{Dom}(g)$: $g(y) = h(y)$ & $\mathsf{Dom}(h) = \mathsf{Dom}(g) \cup \{x\}$.

of $(\Gamma[\![[A]]\!])[\![[B]]\!]$ (the result of first updating Γ with [A], and updating the result with [B]).[20]

Now what about the admittance conditions? A context Γ admits (28) if, and only if, Γ admits [x (is a) nation] and $\Gamma[\![[x$ (is a) nation] $]\!]$ admits [x cherishes x's king]. The second condition is the interesting one for our present purposes, since here the presupposition 'x has a king' is triggered. This means that $\Gamma[\![[x$ (is a) nation] $]\!]$ must entail that x has a king in order to admit [x cherishes x's king]. Updating Γ with [x (is a) nation] yields a new context which consist of those pairs $\langle g, w \rangle$ from Γ such that $g(x)$ is a nation in w. In order for the presupposition 'x has a king' to be satisfied in its local context, the following entailment should hold:

for every $\langle g, w \rangle \in \Gamma$ such that $g(x)$ is a nation in w,
$g(x)$ has a king in w.

In words: in every world in Γ, every nation has to have a king. This means that Γ only admits the Logical form (28) if Γ entails that every nation has a king. Hence: example (27) is predicted to presuppose that every nation has a king (this presupposition is also predicted for sentence (27) by Karttunen and Peters 1979).

There has been much discussion in the literature about the question what is presupposed by examples like (27) in which presuppositions and quantifiers interact. The consensus seems to be that *if* such quantificational examples presuppose anything, they have *weak* presuppositions, thus: do not suffer easily from presupposition failure.[21] Intuitively, if there is a nation which does not cherish its king, example (27) appears to be false, independent of the issue whether or not other nations have kings.

Let us look at some other examples which are discussed in Heim 1983b.

(29) a. Everyone who serves his king will be rewarded.
     b. No nation cherishes its king.
     c. A fat man pushes his bicycle.

According to Karttunen and Peters 1979, example (29.a) presupposes nothing. Heim's model predicts a universal presupposition, for the same reason her model predicts a universal presupposition for example (27),

---

[20]This is not precisely Heim's definition (see definition 5 of chapter 2), but it suffices for the present purposes.

[21]Heim was well aware of these problems, and she also offered a solution to them: *local accommodation* (the presupposition is added to the relevant local context). This works all right for the present examples in that the strong, universal presupposition vanishes. But it remains unclear why the strong presupposition should arise in the first place and later be smoothed away by an accommodation mechanism.

which is paraphrasable as 'everyone has a king'. Similarly, she predicts that example (29.b) presupposes that every nation has a king. Her predictions for (29.c) are probably the most striking; according to Heim's model this example presupposes that every fat man has a bicycle.

Heim argues that indefinites are not quantificational, and assigns the following Logical form to (29.c).

(30) $[[x \text{ (was a) fat man}] [x \text{ was pushing } x\text{'s bicycle}]]$

Again, we assume that x is a fresh variable. Here, the second open sentence triggers a presupposition, namely that 'x has a bicycle'. If we want to evaluate the Logical form in (30) given some context Γ we first update Γ with the first open sentence, and then update the result with the second one. Thus, the context change potential of (30) is as follows:

(31) $(\Gamma[\![[x \text{ (was a) fat man }]\,]\!])[\![[x \text{ was pushing } x\text{'s bicycle}]\,]\!]$

What happens is the following: first the introduction of a new variable x leads to a new context Γ in which x may be mapped to any individual. Subsequently, all those pairs $\langle g, w \rangle$ from Γ where $g(x)$ does not refer to a fat man in w are removed. This results in a new context, say Γ'. This new context only admits $[x \text{ was pushing } x\text{'s bicycle}]$ if the presupposition 'x has a bicycle' is entailed by it. However, since all the worlds w which are present in Γ' are associated with all the possible assignment functions mapping x to a fat man in w, this means that the presupposition is only entailed if in every world w every individual which is a fat man in w also has a bike in w. Thus, contrary to intuition, it is predicted that (29.c) presupposes that every fat man has a bicycle.

In recent years much attention has been paid to the interaction between presuppositions and quantifiers. There appears to be consensus that these examples should be associated with weak, non-universal presuppositions. By now there are various systems in which presuppositions and quantifiers can interact, and which do not suffer from the binding problems of Karttunen and Peters or Heim. For example, Van Eijck's *Error-state Semantics* for Dynamic Predicate Logic is a modification of DPL which allows for presupposition failure by distinguishing separate interpretations for success, failure and error abortion, thereby turning DPL into a combined partial and dynamic system (see Van Eijck 1993, 1994b, 1996). Beaver, on the other hand, sticks more closely to Heim's approach, and proposes to either modify the interpretation of quantifiers and indefinites (in Beaver 1993) or to add a special, unary presupposition operator (in Beaver 1992). In all cases, the technical problems Heim has to face up to can be avoided and weak presuppositions are predicted for the examples discussed above.

1.2 About this Book

1.2.1 Anaphora

Above we noted that discourse referents introduced in the scope of a logical connective only survive inside the scope of that connective. However, Karttunen himself remarked that exceptions do exist. For instance, even though a discourse referent cannot outlive a single negation, it returns to life under a double negation. Contrast (5.b) with (32).

(32) It is not true that Louis XIV did not have a wife. He loved her madly and smothered her with diamonds.

It has been noted on various occasions that examples such as (32) are problematic for the standard theories of discourse semantics. One could say that these theories treat single negations as a 'plug' for anaphoric binding.[22] The discourse referent associated with the indefinite *a wife* in the first sentence of (5.b) cannot escape from the scope of the negation, and this is as it should be. But by the same token they treat a double negation as a *double* plug, and not as a plug unplugged as required for examples like (32). Similar problems arise in the case of disjunction. Example (5.c) illustrated that an indefinite in one disjunct cannot serve as the antecedent of a pronoun in the other disjunct. However, in (33) the pronoun *her* is naturally linked to the indefinite *a mistress*, even though the two occur in different disjuncts.[23]

(33) Either Louis XIV didn't have a mistress or he hid her from his wife.

Once again, the standard dynamic theories cannot account for this link. It will be shown that the second problem can be reduced to the first and, moreover, a general solution is presented in the guise of *Double Negation* DRT (Krahmer & Muskens 1994, 1995). This system treats single negations as is usual in discourse semantics and desired for examples like (5.b). But *double* negations get a different treatment: since in Double Negation DRT the classic law of double negation is restored in a dynamic setting, double negations can be canceled, thus allowing directly for the anaphoric link in (32) and indirectly for the one in (33). The negation in Double Negation DRT does not *fire* a discourse referent from the interpretation process, it merely places it on half-pay. A second negation brings the referent back to active service again. To accommodate the distinction between 'active' and 'passive' discourse referents the

---

[22] Analogously to the presupposition triggered by the definite description *the king of France* which is not projected from the scope of the verb *to want* in (17).

[23] Examples such as (33) can be found in Evans 1977 or Roberts 1989, who attributes it to Partee.

semantics needs to be modified, and for this some standard techniques from partial logic are used.

1.2.2 Presupposition

Partial logic also plays a central role in our studies of presupposition. From Heim 1983b we may already conclude that the combination of dynamics with a whiff of partiality is a fruitful one. And the work of Beaver and Van Eijck shows even more clearly that it pays off to combine partiality and dynamics in the analysis of presupposition. Nevertheless, in all three approaches the dynamics plays first fiddle. Of the aforementioned approaches, the partiality of interpretation is most prominent in Van Eijck 1994b. Still, one of Van Eijck's aims is to '(...) *get a clear sense of the role of the dynamics of context change in the account of the phenomenon* [of presupposition, EK]' (Van Eijck 1994b:768).

We address a different question, namely what the role of *partiality* is in the treatment of presuppositions. To do this we shall consider various interpretations of ordinary, first-order *Partial Predicate Logic* enriched with a static presupposition operator. We shall see that all the versions of Partial Predicate Logic we discuss can deal with example (25) from Karttunen and Peters, without running into the binding problem. Perhaps more surprisingly, it will be shown that they can also deal with the examples in (27) and (29), without generating Heimian universal presuppositions. This means that for the examples we discussed above —and which play such a central role in dynamic semantic approaches to presuppositions— there is no need to go dynamic; we can deal with them in a standard partial logic.

This raises a number of questions which we shall discuss in some depth. First of all, if one argues for 'a new wave of partiality' in the treatment of presupposition, one should spend some time on the question why the old wave broke down. After all, the seventies were times of plenty for 'partial' presuppositional logics, but in the eighties they quietly left the stage. By the mid-eighties Link called himself *stubborn* for taking partial logic as the foundation of Link 1986 (still one of the most amusing publications on the subject). One explanation of the rise, and in particular, fall of partial approaches to presuppositions is that people expected too much of them. The argument from Soames 1979 shows that no single, partial interpretation of disjunction can deal with *all* the relevant projection facts. From this it was concluded that a partial approach to presuppositions is not useful for the analysis of presupposition, and this brings us to a second, related explanation of the decreasing popularity of partiality, namely that there were, and still are, a number of obstinate misconceptions about the usage of partial logic.

We already touched on one particularly persistent point of critique on the partial approach to presupposition: that it lacks the required *flexibility*. We discuss an argument (from Beaver and Krahmer 1995) which shows that it *is* possible for a semantic/partial approach to make flexible projection predictions without postulating undesired, *ad hoc* ambiguities for the logical connectives. At the core of this argument lies a semantic *presupposition wipe-out device*, with its roots in the work of Frege and, in particular, Bochvar. Besides, if we share Strawson's intuition, we simply *need* a form of partiality. In other words: we shall argue that there still is, or at least should be, a place for partial logics in the treatment of presuppositions.

A second question which we shall discuss is the following. If Karttunen and Peters' binding problem can be solved inside an essentially standard partial logic, then why does their system run into it? Karttunen and Peters spend a number of pages discussing the relationship between their proposal and the partial logic of Peters 1979, and they conclude that on the propositional level there are no differences in prediction whatsoever. Of course the binding problem only arises when quantification comes into the picture, but why should things go wrong there? One reason why this question does not have a straightforward answer is the opaque character of their system. Montague Grammar itself has been compared with a Goldberg machine in Barwise and Cooper 1981:204, after the complex and inscrutable machines built by the artist Rube Goldberg. Going one step further, we might compare the system of Karttunen and Peters with *two*, independent Goldberg machines. In this book we shall address the laborious relationship between presuppositions and classical Montague Grammar and claim that the difficulties can be traced back to the absence of proper partializations of Montague Grammar at the time. It has long been thought that partializing Montague Grammar in a decent way is a very difficult task. However, in Muskens 1989 a satisfactory partialization of Montague Grammar was realized. This paves the way for a presuppositional variant of classical Montague Grammar which is both technically clean and makes satisfactory predictions. The resulting *Presuppositional Montague Grammar* can be seen as a reconstruction of what the systems of Hausser 1976, Cooper 1983 and in particular Karttunen and Peters 1979 might have looked like if they could have used a good, partial version of Montague Grammar. Moreover, it will be shown that Presuppositional Montague Grammar can very easily be upgraded to the present standards: we present a simple recipe to dynamify it.[24]

---

[24]In fact, this recipe produces a system which may be compared with the dynamic,

1.2.3 Anaphora and Presupposition

In general, the objectives of formal semantics are two-fold: (i) we want to be able to assign meanings to as many natural language constructions as possible, but (ii) we also want to *understand* the meaning of language. By looking at separate systems, such as Double Negation DRT (1.2.1) or Partial Predicate Logic (1.2.2) we may hope to come to a better understanding of which aspects of a system serve which purposes (in the treatment of negation and disjunction in discourse, in the analysis of presupposition), and this may enhance our understanding of the meaning of language, as mentioned in the second objective. However, these approaches should also be compatible, thus serving the first objective. To this end, we shall extend Double Negation DRT with an additional representation for presuppositions and call the result *Presuppositional* DRT. Presuppositional DRT can be seen as a combination of Double Negation DRT and Partial Predicate Logic (a comparable combination is discussed in Krahmer 1994). As far as interpretation is concerned, Presuppositional DRT is closely related to Beaver's Kinematic Predicate Logic and, in particular, Van Eijck's Error-state Semantics for DPL.[25] The main differences reside in the interpretation of disjunction and negation, which turns out to have some nice consequences.

We believe that the resulting system is interesting for a number of reasons. To begin with, it offers a single framework in which two rather different approaches to presupposition can be modelled. Presuppositional DRT is perfectly compatible with the presuppositions-as-anaphors approach of Van der Sandt, but also with the semantic tradition initiated by Karttunen and Heim. The resulting picture enhances the formal comparison between the two approaches.[26]

However, Presuppositional DRT is not only beneficial for the sake of comparison, it actually leads to an *improvement* of Van der Sandt's theory. Above we noted that Van der Sandt's theory is the empirically most successful approach to presupposition. Still, it raises a few questions as well. For instance, Van der Sandt extends the language of

---

Montagovian fragments for pieces of discourse in which presuppositions arise, given in Bouchez et al. 1993 and Beaver 1993.

[25] In spirit, Presuppositional DRT may also be compared with the system of Zeevat 1992 in which Van der Sandt's theory is reconstructed in terms of Update Semantics (Veltman 1996) and compared with other approaches to presupposition (in particular with Heim 1983b). Different combined partial dynamic systems devised for different purposes can be found in Dekker 1993b, Van den Berg 1993, 1996a and Piwek 1993 for example.

[26] For general discussion about the similarities and differences between the two approaches the reader may also consult, for instance, Van der Sandt 1992, Zeevat 1992, Geurts 1994 and Beaver 1995.

standard DRT with presuppositional representations, but no interpretation for them is given. It is argued in this book that having an interpretation for the presuppositional representations actually *enhances* Van der Sandt's approach, and that Presuppositional DRT may be used to give such an interpretation to presuppositional representations. It is important to notice that we do not propose significant *modifications* of the presuppositions-as-anaphors theory as such: the theory is only provided with an alternative foundation (Presuppositional DRT instead of standard DRT).

Finally, we discuss a specific kind of presupposition in a dynamic framework: those triggered by definite descriptions such as *the man* or *the king of France*. It is usually assumed that such descriptions trigger an *existence* presupposition (there is a man, there is a king of France). However, many people have argued that a mere existence presupposition is too weak to do justice to the meaning of definite descriptions, and that they should presuppose existence and something else. Following Krámský 1976 we shall refer to this 'something else' as *determinedness*. The question is of course how the determinedness condition should be interpreted. One constraint on the interpretation is that it should apply to *all* definites alike, since, following Löbner 1986, we assume that the definite article is unambiguous.

The extensive literature on definite descriptions provides us with lots of clues about possible interpretations of the determinedness condition. We shall consider various suggestions which pop up every now and then in the literature. In particular, we promote the claim that definites refer to *familiar* objects (argued for by Miklosich 1874, Sweet 1898, Christopherson 1939 and others) and the suggestion that they refer to *salient* objects (put forward in for instance Lewis 1979). Formalizations of these suggestions in terms of Presuppositional DRT are presented. Both crucially depend on the dynamics of interpretation, and they turn out to be closely related. But we argue that the salience condition is our best bet, since it makes slightly better empirical predictions, is more general and easier to generalize. Of course, defining a semantic notion underlying the analysis of definite descriptions is only the beginning of a realistic treatment of the various ways in which definite noun phrases are used in discourse. It is argued that the salience approach is a good starting point for the development of such a treatment of definites in general. To that end, we shall discuss some of the more complicated uses of definites, including the *non-identity* anaphora (of which (34.a) is an example due to Heim 1982) and the *deictic* use of definites (illustrated in (34.b), where ↗ represents an 'act of pointing').

(34) a. John read a book about Schubert. He wrote a letter to *the writer*.

    b. ↗ *That frog* is actually the prince of Buganda. He is under a spell.

It is argued that the salience interpretation of the determinedness condition is perfectly compatible with such examples.

1.3 Overview

CHAPTER 2 centers around the analyses of anaphoric reference in discourse. It sketches the main problems sentence-based theories of meaning have with anaphora in discourse, and discusses a number of well-known solutions (in particular File Change Semantics, Discourse Representation Theory, Pratt's Quantificational Dynamic Logic, Dynamic Predicate Logic and Montagovian discourse grammars). Special attention is paid to the way these proposals relate to each other. For instance, it is shown that there is a fully meaning-preserving map from File Change Semantics to Discourse Representation Theory (DRT), which can be seen as an alternative Construction Algorithm for DRT.

CHAPTER 3 discusses negation and disjunction in discourse. It is shown that the double negation problem and the disjunction problem discussed above are related, and a simultaneous solution is presented in the form of *Double Negation* DRT. This system treats single negations in the standard way, but double negations obey the law of double negation. The semantics of Double Negation DRT has its roots in the traditional partial style of interpretation. The classical DRT Construction Algorithm is revised, and applied to the relevant examples. Finally, the relation with standard DRT is discussed.

CHAPTER 4 concentrates on the usage of partial logics in the analysis of presupposition. It investigates the relevance of partiality in the current dynamic treatments of presupposition. Three partial interpretations of Predicate Logic are discussed, two of which are definable in the other one. Each interpretation corresponds with a more or less classic approach to presuppositions. It is shown that all three systems make good predictions for the examples from Karttunen and Peters 1979 and Heim 1983b we discussed above. Special attention is paid to the 'presupposition wipe-out device' and its relevance for the flexibility argument.

CHAPTER 5 focuses on the relationship between presuppositions and classical Montague Grammar. Combining results from chapter 4 with Muskens' partialization of Montague Grammar results in a system which properly encompasses the Montagovian systems of Hausser 1976, Cooper

1983 and, of course, Karttunen and Peters 1979. The resulting Presuppositional Montague Grammar is both technically clean and empirically satisfactory. Various ways of bringing the system up to the present syntactic and semantic standards are discussed.

CHAPTER 6 studies presuppositions from the dynamic perspective. The system of *Presuppositional* DRT is discussed, which combines Double Negation DRT with presuppositional representations. The Revised DRT Construction Algorithm from chapter 3 is further revised and applied to several examples. We also define a Van Eijck style method to calculate the semantic presuppositions of arbitrary DRSs. It is shown that Presuppositional DRT is compatible with two different approaches to presupposition. On the semantic side there are close links with the systems of Beaver and Van Eijck, but the representations of Presuppositional DRT are also perfectly compatible with Van der Sandt's presuppositions-as-anaphors theory. We show that the latter theory as such can benefit from being defined on top of Presuppositional DRT instead of standard DRT. The fact that Presuppositional DRT can be associated with *two* different approaches to presupposition also allows for easy comparison, and some of the questions raised by the resulting perspective are discussed as well.

CHAPTER 7 is concerned with the presuppositions triggered by definite descriptions. We assume that they trigger existence and determinedness presuppositions and raise the question what determinedness is. Various suggestions found in the literature are implemented in terms of Presuppositional DRT and judged on their merits. Some are rejected (uniqueness, anaphoricity) and some are further investigated (familiarity, salience). We argue that of the last two, salience provides the most solid foundation for a unified, general theory of definite noun phrases in discourse, also when incomplete and deictic uses are considered.

CHAPTER 8, finally, summarizes our findings and discusses some lines for future research.

Readers who are familiar with discourse semantics in general and Discourse Representation Theory in particular may decide to skip chapter 2, although it is probably expedient to glance through sections 2.2.2–2.2.5 to get a grip on the terminology and notation used throughout the rest of this book.

2

Anaphora and Discourse Semantics

2.1 Introduction

The shift of attention from sentence to discourse level has caused great changes in the study of meaning. In the seventies, the paradigmatic theory of semantics could be found in the work of Richard Montague, and it had not much to say about discourse. On the face of it, it is not clear why the Montagovian approach cannot be extended to deal with sequences of sentences. After all, what is wrong with the claim that a discourse is nothing more than the conjunction of the separate sentences?

What *is* wrong with it can be illustrated when we extend classical Montague Grammar[1] with a syntactic rule (call it *text-formation*, S18) which takes two sentences and glues them together, thus forming a complex sentence (a discourse), and a corresponding translation rule (T18) which interprets the link as a classical conjunction.[2]

Text formation
S18. If φ and ψ are syntactic trees of category S, then $[_S \, \varphi \, \psi]$ is a tree.
T18. If φ and ψ are syntactic trees of category S, and φ, ψ translate into φ', ψ' respectively, then $[_S \, \varphi \, \psi]$ translates into $\varphi' \wedge \psi'$.

Now consider the following two-sentence discourse.

(1)   A man whistles. A dog follows him.

The second sentence of (1) is the problem here: what does a sentence like *A dog follows him* mean? We could say that it means that there is

---

[1] The term Montague Grammar is used here to refer to the so-called PTQ-fragment, which intends to model the *Proper Treatment of Quantification in ordinary English*, Montague 1974b. It comprises seventeen syntactic rules (S1 to S17) which are pointwise associated with seventeen translation rules (T1 to T17). See Dowty et al. 1981, Gamut 1991 or Partee with Hendriks 1997 for excellent introductions.
[2] Such a rule and its consequences are discussed in Gamut 1991:266ff.

a dog who happens to be following some male individual. But clearly the second sentence is not about an arbitrary man, it is about a specific one: the whistling man mentioned in the first sentence. If we translate this two-sentence discourse using our extended Montagovian fragment, without invoking the notorious *quantifying-in* rule (S14), we end up with a first-order representation like the following:

(2) $\exists x_1(man(x_1) \land whistles(x_1)) \land \exists x_2(dog(x_2) \land follows(x_2, x_1))$

The pronoun *him* is represented as a free variable x_1, while it should be bound by the existential quantifier representing the indefinite determiner *a* in the first sentence. If we want to establish this anaphoric link, we have to use Montague's quantifying-in rule (or some comparable rule for raising quantifiers). That is, we replace the indefinite *a man* with a syntactic variable or *trace*, say t_1, and we translate the pronoun *him* using the same t_1. This results in a structure $[_S [_S t_1 \ whistles] [_S a \ dog \ follows \ t_1]]$. Then we quantify the indefinite NP *a man* into this structure. Thus the anaphoric link is established, and in the end we get the following, correct representation of (1).

(3) $\exists x_1(man(x_1) \land whistles(x) \land \exists x_2(dog(x_2) \land follows(x_2, x_1)))$

This way of dealing with discourse is somewhat counter-intuitive, to put it mildly. It would mean for instance that a more or less *on line* interpretation is out of the question: the procedure we just sketched can only take place when no further sentences containing anaphoric references to *a man* follow. The quantifying-in procedure fails entirely when different examples are considered. Take:

(4)   Thou shalt worship only one God, and thou shalt adore Him.

Using the extended Montague Grammar to interpret this (Russian) version of the first commandment, we get a reading which allows one to worship many divine objects, as long as there is only one which is *both* worshiped and adored. And this clearly is not the reading He had in mind.[3]

A different, yet related problem concerns the ancient, so-called *donkey-sentences* (rediscussed in Geach 1962), of which (5) is the typical example:

(5)   If a farmer owns a donkey, he beats it.

The problem with this sentence is that on its most prominent reading *every* farmer beats *every* donkey he owns. However, if we represent it in the classical way (that is: indefinites are represented by existential

---

[3]This problem was noted by Paustovskij's teacher of religion (see Paustovskij 1970:119). A similar observation is made in Evans 1977:341.

quantifiers and pronouns by variables) we arrive at the following first order representation.

(6) $\exists x_1(farmer(x_1) \land \exists x_2(donkey(x_2) \land owns(x_1, x_2))) \rightarrow beats(x_1, x_2)$

What we want is the following: the quantifiers in the antecedent should bind the variables in the consequent, and with universal force. It is well-known that the universal reading of an existential quantifier in the antecedent of an implication can be obtained via the following *prenex normal form* equivalence:

$$\exists x\varphi \rightarrow \psi \text{ is equivalent with } \forall x(\varphi \rightarrow \psi),$$
$$\text{provided } x \text{ does not occur free in } \psi$$

The problem is that in (6) the variables x_1 and x_2 *do* freely occur in the consequent.[4] The translation of sentence (5) should of course be (7).

(7) $\forall x_1 \forall x_2((farmer(x_1) \land donkey(x_2) \land owns(x_1, x_2)) \rightarrow beats(x_1, x_2))$

So there *are* correct ways of representing donkey-sentences and texts in first-order logic. The problem is how we can *get* at them.

In this chapter, a number of well-known theories of discourse semantics are discussed and compared. In section 2.2, we discuss two *representational* theories: Discourse Representation Theory and File Change Semantics. Even though it is common practice to look at File Change Semantics as a variant of Discourse Representation Theory, we start with the former and give it a central place in the rest of this chapter. It is probably the most linguistically oriented one, and this linguistic foundation of File Change Semantics is used as a means to derive representations for other, less linguistically oriented systems such as the *non-representational* theories of discourse, of which we shall discuss Quantificational Dynamic Logic and Dynamic Predicate Logic in section 2.3.[5] The use of File Change Semantics as a kind of construction algorithm for other theories of discourse semantics is interesting but also harmless, since there are also Montagovian Discourse Grammars, which are discussed in section 2.3.3. In the end we are interested in *one* system

---

[4] A rule of quantifying-in/quantifier raising does not provide any solace here. If we want to account for the anaphoric relationship we have to consider the syntactic structure of the whole conditional before we can quantify the indefinites into it. This results in the non-reading *there is a farmer and there is a donkey and if the former owns the latter, he beats it.*

[5] The distinction between representational and non-representational theories, although historically correct, is becoming increasingly artificial. There are certain philosophical differences, but we will not pay much attention to them. The interested reader is invited to read the discussions in, for example, Groenendijk and Stokhof 1991, Groenendijk et al. 1996a, Kamp 1990, Kamp and Reyle 1993 and Muskens 1996.

of discourse semantics. Therefore we devote the final section (2.4) of this chapter to the quest for the ultimate model of discourse semantics.

2.2 Representational Theories of Discourse

2.2.1 File Change Semantics

In *File Change Semantics* (FCS), as developed by Heim (1982, 1983a), texts are represented using *Logical forms* (which we shall shorten to *Lfs*). To explain what these Lfs mean Heim uses a *file-metaphor*. She writes:

> Speaking metaphorically, let me say that to understand an utterance is to keep a file which (...) contains the information that has so far been conveyed by the utterance. (Heim 1983a:167)

Consider example (1) again and let us make the (implausible) assumption that the file which an interpreter keeps before she hears (1) is empty. Upon hearing the first sentence she places a *file-card* in the file, with a number on it, say '*1*'. On this card she writes '*1 is a man*' and '*1 whistles*'. The utterance of the second sentence leads to the introduction of a new file-card, say '*2*'. On this card the hearer writes '*2 is a dog*' and '*2 follows 1*'. The latter condition is also relevant to the card labeled '*1*', so the hearer *updates* this card with the condition '*1 is followed by 2*'. After processing these two sentences the file looks as follows:

(FILE 1)

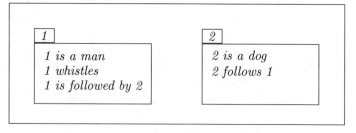

Files can be seen as a form of *score-keeping* in the sense of Lewis 1979, while the file-cards are *discourse referents* in the sense of Karttunen 1976. Karttunen observed that some discourse referents have a permanent and others have a limited *life-span*. An example of the latter is found in the donkey-sentence (5). In FCS this sentence is understood as a kind of *rule*: for every hypothetical extension of the file with the information from the antecedent, it should be possible to update the resulting file with the information conveyed by the consequent. The file is not *permanently* extended with new cards for a farmer and for a donkey owned by the farmer. Hence if the speaker would continue (5) with (8), the hearer is not be able to update the relevant cards.

(8)   # It bites him.

Heim (1983a, *ibid.*) observes the following:

> (...) with respect to their role in a model of semantics, my files are closely related to (...) the "discourse representation structures" of Kamp (1981).

But there is an important difference: Kamp's discourse representation structures function like 'real' representations, whereas Heim employs files only as a metaphor: her Lfs are always interpreted directly. Strictly speaking, the Lfs function as representations of the discourse. So let us look at them in more detail. After a discourse has undergone a syntactic analysis, three rules suffice to turn it into an Lf.

Definition 1 (Lf forming rules)

o   NP-INDEXING: Assign every *NP* a referential index.

o   NP-PREFIXING: Adjoin every non-pronominal NP_n to S, leaving behind an indexed trace t_n.

o   QUANTIFIER CONSTRUAL: Attach every quantificational determiner as a leftmost immediate constituent to S, leaving behind an indexed trace t_n.

It should be noted that Heim distinguishes the definite and indefinite determiners from quantificational ones (such as *every*), hence the definite and indefinite determiners are not subject to the rule of quantifier construal. Heim's Lfs bear a strong resemblance to the Logical Forms in the *Revised Extended Standard Theory* (the then popular branch of Chomskyan grammar). The rules all have independent linguistic motivation (see for instance part III of Van Riemsdijk and Williams 1986 for discussion). For example, her rule of NP-PREFIXING is very much like May's rule for quantifier-raising (May 1977).[6] Besides these three Lf-forming rules, Heim also uses a number of constraints on indexing. Most of these constraints work at sentence level and are now part of the binding-conditions in the *Government and Binding Theory* (a more recent branch of Chomskyan grammar). But Heim also introduces one constraint on the level of texts and this is her *Novelty/Familiarity Condition* (NFC, Heim 1983a:175). The original formulation of this syntactic constraint is a bit awkward since it makes crucial use of semantic information. The following formulation is purely syntactic, but has the

---

[6]On the other hand, Lfs can also be compared with Montague's analysis trees (see Heim 1982:131 and chapter 5 of this book for discussion).

same effect. We assume that a definite NP is labeled [+ def] at the level of Logical form, while an indefinite NP is marked as [− def].

Definition 2 (Novelty/Familiarity Condition)
A Logical form φ is *well-formed* iff for every NP_n in φ it holds that

- if NP_n is [+ def], it is preceded by an NP_n

- if NP_n is [− def], it is not preceded by an NP_n

The distinction between novelty and familiarity has a long tradition in linguistics, and we return to it in chapter 7. Heim's version of it can be paraphrased as follows: an indefinite NP should not be preceded by an NP with which it is co-referential, while a definite NP should. In our Lfs we only mark the indefinite NPs, all other NPs (including the traces) are understood to be definite.[7]

It is not difficult to see that an Lf of a sentence in its most general form has a *tripartite* structure: a number of quantifiers (possibly none), followed by a number of restrictive terms (possibly none), and finally the rest of the sentence (the predicate). Heim analyses conditionals as containing a(n implicit) universal quantifier (represented here as *all*), where the antecedent acts as the restrictive term, and the consequent is the predicate. A sequence of sentences is turned into an Lf whose root-node is labeled S, with the Lfs of the respective sentences as its daughters. Furthermore we replace occurrences of t_n, a_n, he_n and the_n in the Lfs with x_n. Example (1) results in (LF 1).

(LF 1)

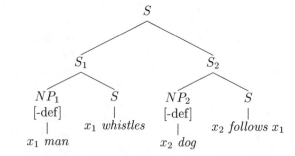

And the conditional in (5) is turned into (LF 2).

---

[7] Heim argues that the NFC should be extended by requiring definite NPs to trigger an existential presupposition. For our purposes in this chapter the NFC is sufficient.

(LF 2)

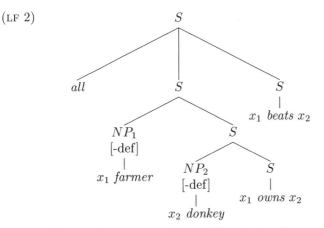

We can also put these trees in labeled bracketing format. The following is the labeled bracketing version of (LF 2):

$$[_S \ all$$
$$[_S \ [^{[-\text{def}]}_{NP_1} \ x_1 \ farmer][_S \ [^{[-\text{def}]}_{NP_2} \ x_2 \ donkey][_S \ x_1 \ owns \ x_2]]]$$
$$[_S \ x_1 \ beats \ x_2]]$$

Summarizing, the set of Lfs can be defined as follows. Assume that Var $= \{x_1, x_2, x_3, \ldots\}$ is a non-empty set of variables (the discourse referents).

Definition 3 (FCS syntax)

1. If R is an n-ary predicate ($n \leq 2$), and $x_i, x_j \in$ Var, then $[_S \ x_i \ R \ x_j]$ is an Lf.
2. If R is a unary predicate, and $x_i \in$ Var, then $[^{[\pm\text{def}]}_{NP_i} \ x_i \ R]$ is an Lf.
3. If $[_S \ \varphi]$ and $[_S \ \psi]$ are Lfs, then $[_S \ [_S \ \varphi] \ or \ [_S \ \psi]]$ and $[_S \ not \ [_S \ \varphi]]$ are Lfs.
4. If $[_{\{NP,S\}} \ \varphi]$ and $[_S \ \psi]$ are Lfs, then $[_S \ all \ [_{\{NP,S\}} \ \varphi][_S \ \psi]]$ is an Lf.
5. If $[_X \ \varphi]$ and $[_Y \ \psi]$ are Lfs, then $[_Y \ [_X \ \varphi][_Y \ \psi]]$ is an Lf.

In the first clause, x_j only appears when $n = 2$. The fourth clause gives the Lf for both conditionals and universally quantified sentences. In the former case the restrictor is an S, in the latter case it is an NP. The fifth clause can be read as follows: Lfs obey the *Right-Hand Head Rule* of Williams 1981. We suppress the syntactic labels when they can be determined from the context.

The meaning of these Lfs is determined using a first-order model $M = \langle D, I \rangle$, where D is a non-void set (the domain of individuals) and I is the interpretation function, with $I(R^n) \subseteq D^n$. Furthermore, F is the set of *finite* assignments such that $g : V \rightarrow D$, for $g \in F$ and V

some finite subset of Var. A special element of F is Λ, the assignment with the empty domain: $\mathsf{Dom}(\Lambda) = \emptyset$. We use the following respective abbreviations for 'assignment g is extended by assignment h' (notation: $g \leq h$) and 'assignment g is extended by assignment h exactly with $\vec{x}$' (notation: $g\{\vec{x}\}h$).[8]

Definition 4 ((Domain-)extension)

1. $g \leq h$ iff $\forall y \in \mathsf{Dom}(g) : g(y) = h(y)$
2. $g\{\vec{x}\}h$ iff $g \leq h$ & $\mathsf{Dom}(h) = \mathsf{Dom}(g) \cup \{\vec{x}\}$

The semantics of FCS takes sets of assignments to sets of assignments. Formally $\Gamma[\![.]\!]_M^{\mathrm{FCS}} = \Gamma'$, where $\Gamma, \Gamma' \subseteq F$, is defined as follows.[9,10] Throughout this book we drop sub- and superscripts whenever this can be done without creating confusion.

Definition 5 (FCS semantics)

1. $\Gamma[\![\, [x_i \ R \ x_j]\,]\!] = \{g \in \Gamma \mid x_i, x_j \in \mathsf{Dom}(g) \ \& \ \langle g(x_i), g(x_j)\rangle \in I(R)\}$

2. $\Gamma[\![\, [^{[+\mathrm{def}]}x_i \ R]\,]\!] = \{g \in \Gamma \mid x_i \in \mathsf{Dom}(g) \ \& \ g(x_i) \in I(R)\}$

3. $\Gamma[\![\, [^{[-\mathrm{def}]}x_i \ R]\,]\!] = \{h \mid \exists g \in \Gamma(g\{x_i\}h \ \& \ h(x_i) \in I(R))\}$

4. $\Gamma[\![\, [[\varphi] \ or \ [\psi]]\,]\!] = \{g \in \Gamma \mid \exists h(g \leq h \ \& \ (h \in \Gamma[\![\, [\varphi]\,]\!] \vee h \in \Gamma[\![\, [\psi]\,]\!]))\}$

5. $\Gamma[\![\, [not \ [\varphi]]\,]\!] = \{g \in \Gamma \mid \neg \exists h(g \leq h \ \& \ h \in \Gamma[\![\, [\varphi]\,]\!])\}$

6. $\Gamma[\![\, [all \ [\varphi][\psi]]\,]\!] = \{g \in \Gamma \mid \forall h((g \leq h \ \& \ h \in \Gamma[\![\, [\varphi]\,]\!]) \Rightarrow$
   $\exists k(h \leq k \ \& \ k \in \Gamma[\![\, [[\varphi][\psi]]\,]\!]))\}$

7. $\Gamma[\![\, [[\varphi][\psi]]\,]\!] = (\Gamma[\![\, [\varphi]\,]\!])[\![\, [\psi]\,]\!]$

---

[8] Here and elsewhere $\vec{x}$ abbreviates $x_1, \ldots, x_n$.

[9] This definition may seem different from the one given in Heim 1982 or Heim 1983a but it is basically equivalent. Heim uses a different notation and terminology. She does not speak of finite assignments, but of finite *sequences* of elements of D. She talks about the *satisfaction set* of a file F, which is a set of such sequences (a set of assignments). Heim gives a single clause for the first three clauses of definition 5. There is one 'addition' in definition 5, namely disjunction, which Heim does not discuss. We have assumed that disjunction is treated in the standard way.

[10] We assume that only well-formed Lfs are admitted to the interpretation. Thus an Lf which violates the NFC is not be interpreted (compare Heim 1983a:186). In this sense it could be argued that FCS is a partial logic: Lfs which are well-formed can be either true or false, but those which are less lucky disappear in a *truth-gap*; they are neither true nor false. See Muskens et al. 1997 for a different version of FCS where the NFC is interpreted semantically. The only difference with the present definition is that the domains of the Γ's are calculated separately.

We say that an Lf φ is supported by a set of assignments Γ and a model M (notation: $M, \Gamma \models_{\text{FCS}} \varphi$) iff $\Gamma[\![\varphi]\!]_M^{\text{FCS}} \neq \emptyset$.

Definition 6 (Truth)
A well-formed Lf φ is *true* in a model M iff $M, \{\Lambda\} \models_{\text{FCS}} \varphi$.

Using definition 5 we see that (LF 1) and (LF 2) receive interpretations which have the same truth-conditions as the following Predicate Logical formulae.[11]

(9) $\exists x_1 (man(x_1) \wedge whistles(x_1) \wedge \exists x_2 (dog(x_2) \wedge follows(x_2, x_1)))$

(10) $\forall x_1 \forall x_2 ((farmer(x_1) \wedge donkey(x_2) \wedge owns(x_1, x_2)) \rightarrow beats(x_1, x_2))$

Hence FCS indeed gets the required co-reference for example (1) in the case of (9) and the universal reading for example (5) in the case of (10); FCS succeeds in getting the right interpretation for the crucial examples.

2.2.2 Discourse Representation Theory

In the early eighties another formal system for discourse semantics was developed: Kamp's *Discourse Representation Theory* (DRT). In DRT, as it is described in Kamp 1981 and Kamp and Reyle 1993, a discourse is represented using a *Discourse Representation Structure* (DRS). Such a DRSis a box split in two by a horizontal line. Above the line we find the *universe* of the DRS, which is a set of discourse referents. Below the line, we find conditions on these referents. For example, the DRSfor (1) looks as follows:

(DRS 1)

x_1, x_2
$man(x_1)$
$whistles(x_1)$
$dog(x_2)$
$follows(x_2, x_1)$

The relation between (DRS 1) and (FILE 1) is obvious: the universe of (DRS 1) contains the set of file cards/discourse referent in (FILE 1), and the set of conditions sums up the conditions found on the two cards. But there are important differences as well. For one thing, files are only a way of speaking, whereas DRSs have a formal status. As a result, there are also formal, representational counterparts for implications, disjunctions etc. An advantage of DRSs (which should not be underestimated) is that they are *visually appealing*. A disadvantage is that they take up a lot of space. Therefore we introduce DRSs in a less spacious, linear format.

---

[11]Below we shall discuss a systematic method to derive such Predicate Logical formulae from Lfs.

Throughout this book we use the pictorial representation of DRSs when considering actual examples, and the linear ones when we are interested in the formalities of DRT.

The following definition specifies what a DRS may look like. Assume that we have a set Var of variables (discourse referents) and a set Con of constants, here and elsewhere both are assumed to be non-void. Elements of the union of Con and Var are called terms as usual.[12]

Definition 7 (DRT syntax)

1. If R is an n-ary predicate and $t_1, \ldots, t_n$ are terms, then $R(t_1, \ldots, t_n)$ is a condition.

2. If t_1, t_2 are terms, then $t_1 \equiv t_2$ is a condition.

3. If Φ, Ψ are DRSs, then $\neg\Phi, (\Phi \vee \Psi), (\Phi \Rightarrow \Psi)$ are conditions.

4. If $x_1, \ldots, x_n$ are variables ($n \geq 0$) and $\varphi_1, \ldots, \varphi_m$ are conditions ($m \geq 0$), then $[x_1, \ldots, x_n \mid \varphi_1, \ldots, \varphi_m]$ is a DRS.

5. If Φ and Ψ are DRSs, then $(\Phi \,; \Psi)$ is a DRS.

Throughout this book, we adopt the following notation convention. When discussing (variants of) DRT we use lower case Greek letters as meta-variables for conditions and upper case Greek letters for DRSs. Clauses 1–4 correspond with the original DRT fragment as it is described in Kamp 1981. We sometimes refer to this system as *classical* DRT. Clause 5 adds the *merge* or *sequencing* of two DRSs. It represents the way DRSs are updated with new information in classical DRT. $\Phi \,; \Psi$ may be read as: DRS Φ is extended with the information conveyed by DRS Ψ, in such a way that for example:

$$[x \mid P(x)] \,; [y \mid Q(y)] \text{ is equivalent with } [x, y \mid P(x), Q(y)].$$

Nowadays, it is common practice to add some form of sequencing to classical DRT, hence we refer to the entire system generated by definition 7 as *standard* DRT.

Now that we know what DRSs look like the first question to ask is where they come from. In DRT a discourse is turned into a DRS via the *construction algorithm*. Each sentence, or rather its syntactic analysis, of the discourse is placed in a DRS-under-construction (a so-called *proto-DRS*), and part by part it is broken down and turned into a normal DRS.[13] In comparison with the way Lfs are built up in FCS, the construction

---

[12] Not all DRSs from Kamp and Reyle 1993 fit in this format: it does not contain DRSs with duplex conditions or plural referents. Nevertheless, the 'first-order fragment of DRT' given in this definition can be seen as the *logical core* of DRT (see Fernando 1994c for discussion).

[13] A version of this algorithm is sketched in the next chapter.

algorithm is rather complex. Here an alternative from Krahmer 1993 is explored; a translation function σ is defined (which is meaning preserving in a way to be specified below) turning Lfs into DRSs and which thus can be seen as a kind of construction algorithm for DRT.[14]

Definition 8 (Translating FCS into DRT: constructing DRSs)

1. $\sigma([x_i\ R\ x_j])$ $=$ $[\ |\ R(x_i, x_j)]$

2. $\sigma([^{[+\text{def}]}\ x_i\ R])$ $=$ $[\ |\ R(x_i)]$

3. $\sigma([^{[-\text{def}]}\ x_i\ R])$ $=$ $[x_i\ |\ R(x_i)]$

4. $\sigma([[\varphi]\ or\ [\psi]])$ $=$ $[\ |\ \sigma([\varphi]) \vee \sigma([\psi])]$

5. $\sigma([not\ [\varphi]])$ $=$ $[\ |\ \neg\sigma([\varphi])]$

6. $\sigma([all\ [\varphi][\psi]])$ $=$ $[\ |\ \sigma([\varphi]) \Rightarrow \sigma([\psi])]$

7. $\sigma([[\varphi][\psi]])$ $=$ $(\sigma([\varphi])\ ;\ \sigma([\psi]))$

It is not difficult to check that $\sigma(\text{LF}\ 2)$ results in the following DRS:[15]

$$[\ |\ [x_1, x_2\ |\ farmer(x_1), donkey(x_2), owns(x_1, x_2)] \Rightarrow [\ |\ beats(x_1, x_2)]]$$

Or, in the pictorial format:

(DRS 2)

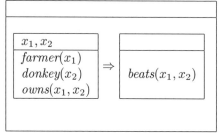

The reader may also check that σ applied to the Lf of example (1) results in (DRS 1). Using σ sweeps a number of interesting parts of the DRT construction algorithm under the carpet. In FCS no special treatment is given for proper names (PNs), while they do have a special status in

---

[14]The DRT Construction Algorithm is much more explicit than Heim's construction of Logical forms. For computational means, it is probably easiest to implement the DRT method of construction DRSs. It should also be noted that in recent compositional versions of DRT (such as Muskens 1994b, Van Eijck and Kamp 1997) the construction algorithm has become superfluous, because the DRSs are built up in the Montagovian way from the relevant lexical entries. For the purposes of this chapter, Heim's Lfs are more than adequate however. A comparable translation function mapping Lfs to DRSs is given in Chierchia 1995:59.

[15]Modulo the Merging Lemma (fact 1 below).

the DRT construction algorithm.[16] What distinguishes PNs from other NPs is that they always introduce a discourse referent with a permanent life-span, that is: in the main DRS. The motivation behind this rule is that PNs have a tendency to remain accessible for future anaphoric reference, which brings us to a second interesting aspect of the construction algorithm. In Heim's Lfs anaphora resolution is taken care of by the co-indexing rules, with the NFC as the central condition. In other words, in FCS anaphora resolution takes place on the level of Logical Form. In DRT anaphora resolution is done when the DRSs are constructed. In a sense, Heim's NFC is built into the DRT construction algorithm. When an indefinite NP is processed in a certain proto-DRSΦ, a *new* discourse referent is introduced in the universe of Φ; and when the construction algorithm hits upon a pronoun it is replaced for a *suitable, accessible* discourse referent (Kamp 1981:32). Whether a referent is suitable depends on features such as focus, as well as number and gender, and is in general not further specified. Whether a discourse referent is accessible at a certain point is determined by the *structure* of a DRS. In other words: the *life-span* of a discourse referent is dependent on the structure it occurs in. Consider some main DRS Φ'. A discourse referent x is still 'alive' in a condition φ (of Φ') iff x is accessible from φ (in Φ'). The set of accessible discourse referents for an occurrence of a sub-DRS Φ (of Φ') we call $\mathsf{ACC}(\Phi)$.[17] In $\mathsf{ACC}(\Phi)$ there is a hidden argument: it is the set of accessible discourse referents for an occurrence of Φ *in some* DRS Φ'. Since this DRS Φ' can be determined from the context (and to keep things simple), we leave it implicit. The set $\mathsf{ACC}(\Phi)$ is built up in the following top-down way: as an initialization we set $\mathsf{ACC}(\Phi') = \emptyset$.[18] It is useful to define $\mathsf{ADR}(\Phi)$ (the *active discourse referents* of a DRS Φ):

$$\mathsf{ADR}([x_1, \ldots, x_n \mid \varphi_1, \ldots, \varphi_m]) = \{x_1, \ldots, x_n\}, \text{ and}$$
$$\mathsf{ADR}(\Phi \,;\, \Psi) = \mathsf{ADR}(\Phi) \cup \mathsf{ADR}(\Psi).$$

Accessibility is defined in the following way:

Definition 9 (Accessibility)

   1. If $\mathsf{ACC}(\neg\Phi) = X$, then $\mathsf{ACC}(\Phi) = X$.

---

[16]It should be noted that Kamp & Reyle are not entirely satisfied with this situation, see Kamp and Reyle 1993, chapter 3. See also chapter 6 of the present work for some discussion.

[17]The restriction to occurrences is important. Consider the DRS $[\ \mid\ R(x)]$; $[\ \mid\ [x \mid P(x)] \Rightarrow [\ \mid\ R(x)]]$. The sub-DRS $[\ \mid\ R(x)]$ occurs twice in it, and clearly the two occurrences have different sets of accessible discourse referents.

[18]This way of defining accessibility is used in Krahmer and Muskens 1994. It differs from the usual DRT method of determining accessibility in that it is defined top down. However, the two methods make identical predictions.

2. If $\mathsf{ACC}(\Phi \vee \Psi) = X$, then $\mathsf{ACC}(\Phi) = X$ and $\mathsf{ACC}(\Psi) = X$.

3. If $\mathsf{ACC}(\Phi \Rightarrow \Psi) = X$, then $\mathsf{ACC}(\Phi) = X$ and $\mathsf{ACC}(\Psi) = X \cup \mathsf{ADR}(\Phi)$.

4. If $\mathsf{ACC}([x_1, \ldots, x_n \mid \varphi_1, \ldots, \varphi_m]) = X$, then $\mathsf{ACC}(\varphi_i) = X \cup \{x_1, \ldots, x_n\}$ (for $1 \leq i \leq m$).

5. If $\mathsf{ACC}(\Phi \, ; \Psi) = X$, then $\mathsf{ACC}(\Phi) = X$ and $\mathsf{ACC}(\Psi) = X \cup \mathsf{ADR}(\Phi)$.

By way of digression, and looking ahead a little, consider the following parallel drawn in Krahmer and Muskens 1995. In Karttunen 1974 a set of rules is given which calculate when a context (a set of sentences) C' satisfies the presuppositions of a sentence S'. When S' is a complex sentence, each of its subsentences is associated with a *local context*. The local context of some (occurrence of a) (sub)sentence S (of S') is given by $\mathsf{LC}(S)$. This local context is defined in the following top-down way: as an initialization we set $\mathsf{LC}(S') = C'$ and proceed to define:[19]

Definition 10 (Local contexts)

1. If $\mathsf{LC}(not \ S) = C$, then $\mathsf{LC}(S) = C$.
2. If $\mathsf{LC}(S \ or \ S') = C$, then $\mathsf{LC}(S) = C$ and $\mathsf{LC}(S') = C \cup \{ \ not \ S \ \}$.
3. If $\mathsf{LC}(if \ S \ then \ S') = C$, then $\mathsf{LC}(S) = C$ and $\mathsf{LC}(S') = C \cup \{ \ S \ \}$.
4. If $\mathsf{LC}(S \ and \ S') = C$, then $\mathsf{LC}(S) = C$ and $\mathsf{LC}(S') = C \cup \{ \ S \ \}$.

C' satisfies the presuppositions of the corresponding sentence S' if the local context of each subclause of S' entails all the presuppositions of that subclause. In a nutshell this is the influential theory of presuppositions developed by Karttunen in the early seventies. Notice that there is strong correspondence between ACC and LC: both display the same formal structure, except for the clause of disjunction (but see the definition of ACC for the version of DRT defined in the next chapter (Double Negation DRT), definition 2). This suggests that there is an interesting correspondence between anaphora and presupposition, an analogy which has been been observed by Kripke n.d. and in particular Van der Sandt 1992. In chapter 6 we discuss Van der Sandt's *presuppositions-as-anaphors* theory in more detail. There we briefly return to the similarities between ACC in Double Negation/Presuppositional DRT and Karttunen's LC. End of digression. Back to the accessibility-calculus. As an example: suppose (DRS 2) is updated with sentence (8), and that *it* is intended to refer to *a donkey* and *him* to *a farmer*. The resulting DRS would look as follows:

---

[19]This format of defining local contexts is due to Muskens et al. 1997.

(DRS 3)

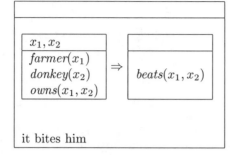

Can we replace *it* with x_2 and *him* with x_1? The answer is *yes* when both x_1 and x_2 are elements of ACC(*it bites him*). By definition, ACC(DRS 3) = ∅. Rule 4 of definition 9 implies that ACC(*it bites him*) = ∅, hence the referents x_1 and x_2 are not accessible for this condition.[20] So, in accordance with Karttunen's generalization, discourse referents introduced inside a conditional are not accessible outside that conditional.

When a referent x occurs in some atomic condition φ (of Φ) from which x is not accessible we say that x occurs *free* in Φ. An occurrence of x in some atomic condition φ in a condition ψ is free in ψ iff it is free in $[\,|\psi]$. A DRS is called *proper* when it does not contain any free occurring referents. We also introduce the following notion: a proper DRS Φ is called *totally proper* when it does not contain a variable which was introduced twice. Formally: for all sub-DRSs Ψ of Φ it holds that ACC(Ψ) ∩ ADR(Ψ) = ∅. Notice that every well-formed Lf φ results in a totally proper DRS $\sigma(\varphi)$. Similarly, every DRS which is built up using the standard DRT construction algorithm is totally proper as well.

Now we know what DRSs look like and where they come from, we address the question what they mean. Using the same first-order models $M = \langle D, I \rangle$ and set of finite assignments F as for FCS, we define $[\![.]\!]_M^{\text{DRT}} \subseteq F$ for conditions and $[\![.]\!]_M^{\text{DRT}} \subseteq F^2$ for DRSs. For terms the interpretation is defined as follows: $[\![t]\!]_{M,g} = g(t)$ if $t \in$ Var and $t \in$ Dom(g), and $[\![t]\!]_{M,g} = I(t)$ if $t \in$ Con. If $g(x)$ is undefined, $[\![x]\!]_g$ is undefined as well.[21]

---

[20]By comparison, the use of x_1 and x_2 in the consequent of the implicational condition *was* warranted: ACC($[x_1, x_2 \mid farmer(x_1), donkey(x_2), owns(x_1, x_2)]$) = ACC(DRS 3) = ∅, moreover ADR($[x_1, x_2 \mid farmer(x_1), donkey(x_2), owns(x_1, x_2)]$) = $\{x_1, x_2\}$. Combining these, clause 3 says that ACC($[\,\mid beats(x_1, x_2)]$) = ∅ ∪ $\{x_1, x_2\}$ = $\{x_1, x_2\}$. So by rule 4, x_1 and x_2 are indeed accessible for the two pronouns in *he beats it*.

[21]Definition 11 may seem different from the one presented in Kamp 1981 or Kamp and Reyle 1993, although in fact it is equivalent (modulo our addition of the merging operator). The format used here goes back to Groenendijk and Stokhof 1991, definition 26. The present version is closer to standard DRT in that it (*i*) uses finite assignments instead of total ones and (*ii*) disallows re-assignments. Extra motivation for the use of finite assignments can be found in

Definition 11 (DRT semantics)

1. $[\![R(t_1,\ldots,t_n)]\!]$ $=$ $\{g \mid [\![t_i]\!]_g \text{ defined } \& \langle [\![t_1]\!]_g, \ldots, [\![t_n]\!]_g \rangle \in I(R)\}$
$(1 \leq i \leq n)$

2. $[\![t_1 \equiv t_2]\!]$ $=$ $\{g \mid [\![t_1]\!]_g, [\![t_2]\!]_g \text{ defined } \& [\![t_1]\!]_g = [\![t_2]\!]_g\}$

3. $[\![\neg\Phi]\!]$ $=$ $\{g \mid \neg\exists h\langle g, h\rangle \in [\![\Phi]\!]\}$

4. $[\![\Phi \vee \Psi]\!]$ $=$ $\{g \mid \exists h(\langle g, h\rangle \in [\![\Phi]\!] \text{ or } \langle g, h\rangle \in [\![\Psi]\!])\}$

5. $[\![\Phi \Rightarrow \Psi]\!]$ $=$ $\{g \mid \forall h(\langle g, h\rangle \in [\![\Phi]\!] \Rightarrow \exists k\langle h, k\rangle \in [\![\Psi]\!])\}$

6. $[\![\,[\vec{x} \mid \varphi_1, \ldots, \varphi_m]\,]\!] =$ $\{\langle g, h\rangle \mid g\{\vec{x}\}h \ \& \ h \in ([\![\varphi_1]\!] \cap \ldots \cap [\![\varphi_m]\!])\}$

7. $[\![\Phi \,;\, \Psi]\!]$ $=$ $\{\langle g, h\rangle \mid \exists k(\langle g, k\rangle \in [\![\Phi]\!] \ \& \ \langle k, h\rangle \in [\![\Psi]\!])\}$

A DRS Φ is supported in a model M with respect to an assignment g (notation: $M, g \models_{\mathrm{DRT}} \varphi$) iff $\exists h\langle g, h\rangle \in [\![\Phi]\!]_M^{\mathrm{DRT}}$. In other words, g has to be an element of the domain of the relation given by $[\![\Phi]\!]_M^{\mathrm{DRT}}$.

Definition 12 (Truth)
A proper DRS Φ is true in M iff $M, \Lambda \models_{\mathrm{DRT}} \Phi$

Two DRSs Φ and Ψ are *equivalent* iff for all M $[\![\Phi]\!]_M = [\![\Psi]\!]_M$. The merge operator is interpreted using relational composition. It is easily seen that it supports the following fact.[22]

Fact 1 *(Merging Lemma)*
$[\vec{x} \mid \vec{\varphi}] \,;\, [\vec{y} \mid \vec{\gamma}]$ *is equivalent with* $[\vec{x}, \vec{y} \mid \vec{\varphi}, \vec{\gamma}]$,
provided no referent in $\vec{y}$ is free in any of $\vec{\varphi}$.

The definition of merging given here is close, yet not identical, to the one given in Zeevat 1989. An important feature is that

$$[x \mid P(x)] \,;\, [x \mid Q(x)] \text{ is equivalent with } [x \mid P(x)] \,;\, [\,\mid Q(x)].$$

This means that once a discourse referent is introduced and assigned a value, it is not possible to re-assign it a possibly different value. A less desired consequence of the Merging Lemma is that it is not always possible to merge two DRSs into a single DRS. A very simple example is $[\,\mid P(x)] \,;\, [x \mid \,]$. Of course, the construction algorithm forbids this as well as the previous case we discussed.[23]

Fernando 1992. The Groenendijk & Stokhof interpretation of DRT in terms of total assignments is discussed below.

[22]We let $\vec{y}$ abbreviate $y_1, \ldots, y_m$, and similarly $\vec{\varphi}$ and $\vec{\gamma}$ abbreviate respectively $\varphi_1, \ldots, \varphi_k$ and $\gamma_1, \ldots, \gamma_l$ (with $m, k, l \geq 0$). By our convention (see footnote 8), $\vec{x}$ abbreviates $x_1, \ldots, x_n$.

[23]More sophisticated (and more complex) definitions of the merging operator are

2.2.3 From FCS to DRT

DRT and FCS are often lumped together in the literature. But even though there are obvious similarities, there are also some important differences. Not only are Lfs rather different from DRSs, their interpretations are also couched in different terms; $[\![.]\!]^{FCS}$ takes a set of assignments and returns a set of assignments, $[\![.]\!]^{DRT}$ has a relation between assignments as its interpretation. This gap can be bridged by defining an operation which takes a set and a relation and returns a set:[24]

Definition 13
$$R * A = \{j \mid \exists i (\langle i, j \rangle \in R \,\&\, i \in A)\}$$

Now the following fact (Krahmer 1993) can be proven:

Fact 2 *(From FCS to DRT)*
For all models M and sets of assignments $\Gamma \subseteq F$:
$$\Gamma [\![\varphi]\!]_M^{FCS} = [\![\sigma(\varphi)]\!]_M^{DRT} * \Gamma$$

So, modulo the operation $*$ it can be shown that FCS can be reduced to DRT. This is the sense in which the function σ is meaning preserving. Notice that it not so clear whether DRT can be reduced to FCS.[25] If ς were to be a function from DRSs to Lfs, it would have to face up to various problems of which the 'invention' of syntactic structure is just one. In a metaphor: σ turns oranges into orange-juice while ς would have to face up to the non-trivial task of doing the opposite. One possibility would be to give Heim's files a formal, non-metaphorical status (thus: define a

---

given in Van Eijck and Kamp 1997 and Fernando 1994c, both using a kind of renaming of bound variables. Roughly speaking, this guarantees that the merging applies to disjoint DRSs, thus avoiding the aforementioned cases. Using such a renaming strategy for merging, we would have that:

$$[x \mid P(x)] \,;\, [x \mid Q(x)] \text{ is equivalent with } [x \mid P(x)] \,;\, [y \mid Q(y)].$$

And these disjoint DRSs can be merged straightforwardly. Vermeulen studies a merging operator using *referent systems*. This gives rise to a number of interesting choices. For more details the reader is referred to Vermeulen 1994, 1995. Although we have no principled objections to other ways of merging DRSs we stick to the simple definition in terms of relational composition here.

[24]This operation also arises in theoretical computer science, where it is called the strongest existential postcondition (**SEP**); $R * A$ is equivalent with $\mathsf{SEP}(A, R)$. It is closely related to a well-known operation called the *Peirce product*, as it originated from Peirce 1870, defined as follows:

$$R : A = \{i \mid \exists j (\langle i, j \rangle \in R \,\&\, j \in A)\}.$$

See for instance Brink and Schmidt 1992:331 or De Rijke 1993:71. This operation is also known as the weakest existential precondition ($\mathsf{WEP}(R, A)$). We shall encounter this concept on various occasions in this book (see definition 16 below, to begin with).
[25]Even disregarding the fact that the syntax of DRT includes constants and term-equivalence, which are absent from the FCS definition we gave above.

language of files), and let ς translate DRSs into such files, but we refrain from doing so here. The differences between DRT and FCS are mostly related to the general 'architecture' of the respective theories. Fact 2 shows that it is not really essential for the current purposes whether the representations are interpreted in a functional way (as in FCS) or in a relational way (as in DRT).

2.2.4 DRT Interpretation Using Total Assignments

Above we mentioned the interpretation Groenendijk & Stokhof give to DRT in terms of total assignments (footnote 21). Here we briefly discuss this interpretation. The total interpretation of DRT is derived from the interpretation in definition 11 by replacing all finite assignment for total ones. That is: assignments g such that $g : \mathsf{Var} \to D$ for all $g \in G$ (the set of total assignments). Notice that the switch from finite to total assignments entails that $[\![x]\!]_g$ is defined for any x and g: the definedness condition in the interpretation of atomic conditions is always satisfied. Furthermore we replace the notion $g\{\vec{x}\}h$ for its total counterpart $g[\vec{x}]h$, which abbreviates: 'assignment h differs at most from assignment g in the values it assigns to $\vec{x}$'. Formally:

Definition 14

$g[\vec{x}]h$ iff $\forall y(y \notin \{\vec{x}\} \Rightarrow h(y) = g(y))$

We shall refer to the resulting interpretation as $[\![.]\!]_M^{\mathrm{DRT}t}$. Support of a DRS Φ in a model M with respect to a total assignment g ($M, g \models_{\mathrm{DRT}t} \Phi$) is now defined as $\exists h\langle g, h\rangle \in [\![\Phi]\!]_M^{\mathrm{DRT}t}$. Since there is no longer an empty assignment, we have to define truth with respect to some assignment $g \in G$.

Definition 15 (Truth)

A DRS Φ is true in M with respect to g iff $M, g \models_{\mathrm{DRT}t} \Phi$

The switch from finite to total assignments has a number of small, but important consequences. Consider a DRS such as $[\ |x \equiv x]$. Clearly, x occurs free in this DRS, and as a result it is not a proper one. In standard DRT such a non-proper DRS is never supported. In DRTt however, $[\ |x \equiv x]$ is supported in all models M, with respect to any assignment g. Another difference concerns complex DRSs such as the following:

$$[x \mid P(x)] \, ; [x \mid \neg[\ |P(x)]]$$

This DRS is proper, but not totally so. In standard DRT the second introduction of x has no effect; there is no possibility of re-assigning a value to a variable. As a result the DRS is contradictory. This is different in DRTt however, where the notion of $g\{\vec{x}\}h$ is replaced for $g[\vec{x}]h$, and as a consequence the second introduction of x *does* amount to a re-assignment. The result is just as contradictory as $\exists x P(x) \wedge \exists x \neg P(x)$ is in standard Predicate Logic: not at all. It is important to notice that these differences only arise when we consider DRSs which are not (totally) proper. For the DRSs as they are derived by the construction algorithm it does not matter whether we interpret them in terms of finite or total assignments.

2.2.5 From DRT to Predicate Logic

It shall be clear that DRT is a radical departure from classical Predicate Logic (PL), both *qua* notation and *qua* interpretation. This raises the obvious question how the two relate to each other. In Kamp and Reyle 1993 a direct mapping from DRT into PL is given, which is proven to be truth-preserving. Here we use another construction found in the literature, which has its roots in Dynamic Logic (see section 2.3.1), and which calculates the 'weakest existential preconditions' (WEP) of a DRS.[26] We define the notions $\mathsf{WEP}(\Phi, \chi)$, where Φ is a DRS and χ is a formula of PL, and $\mathsf{TR}(\varphi)$, where φ is a condition. The intuition behind $\mathsf{WEP}(\Phi, \chi)$ is that it gives the set of states (assignments) from which we can 'execute' Φ in such a way that we may end up in a state where χ holds. We shall see below that $\mathsf{WEP}(\Phi, \top)$ gives a PL formula which is true precisely when Φ is. Here $\top$ is the tautological PL formula, defined as $c \equiv c$, for some $c \in \mathsf{Con}$ (which by assumption is non-empty). The following WEP-calculus is given in Muskens et al. 1997.

Definition 16 (WEP-calculus)

1. $\mathsf{TR}(\varphi) = \varphi$, if φ is atomic

2. $\mathsf{TR}(\neg\Phi) = \neg\mathsf{WEP}(\Phi, \top)$

3. $\mathsf{TR}(\Phi \vee \Psi) = \mathsf{WEP}(\Phi, \top) \vee \mathsf{WEP}(\Psi, \top)$

4. $\mathsf{TR}(\Phi \Rightarrow \Psi) = \neg\mathsf{WEP}(\Phi, \neg\mathsf{WEP}(\Psi, \top))$

5. $\mathsf{WEP}([\vec{x} \mid \varphi_1, \ldots, \varphi_m], \chi) = \exists\vec{x}(\mathsf{TR}(\varphi_1) \wedge \ldots \wedge \mathsf{TR}(\varphi_m) \wedge \chi)$

6. $\mathsf{WEP}(\Phi \, ; \Psi, \chi) = \mathsf{WEP}(\Phi, \mathsf{WEP}(\Psi, \top))$

As an example, let us calculate $\mathsf{WEP}((\text{DRS } 2), \chi)$:

$$\mathsf{WEP}([\,\mid [x_1, x_2 \mid F(x_1), D(x_2), O(x_1, x_2)] \Rightarrow [\,\mid B(x_1, x_2)]], \chi) \Leftrightarrow$$

$$\mathsf{TR}([x_1, x_2 \mid F(x_1), D(x_2), O(x_1, x_2)] \Rightarrow [\,\mid B(x_1, x_2)]) \wedge \chi \Leftrightarrow$$

---

[26]For the origin of such WEP-calculi, see Segerberg 1982. For discussion in the context of discourse semantics see for instance Van Benthem 1991, Van Eijck and De Vries 1992 (where the method is extended to include generalized quantifiers and a description operator), Van Eijck 1994a and Muskens et al. 1997.

$$\neg\text{WEP}([x_1, x_2 \mid F(x_1), D(x_2), O(x_1, x_2)], \neg\text{WEP}([\mid B(x_1, x_2)], \top)) \wedge \chi \Leftrightarrow$$

$$\neg(\exists x_1 \exists x_2(F(x_1) \wedge D(x_2) \wedge O(x_1, x_2)) \wedge \neg B(x_1, x_2)) \wedge \chi \Leftrightarrow$$

$$\forall x_1 \forall x_2((F(x_1) \wedge D(x_2) \wedge O(x_1, x_2)) \to B(x_1, x_2)) \wedge \chi$$

If we substitute $\top$ for χ (and given that $\varphi \wedge \top$ is equivalent with φ), we end up with the intended PL representation of the donkey-sentence, which —as discussed in the introduction— could not be achieved in a natural way in PL. In general, the following fact holds.[27]

Fact 3 *(From* DRT*t to* PL*)*
For all models M and assignments g:

1. $g \in [\![\text{TR}(\varphi)]\!]^{\text{PL}}_M \Leftrightarrow g \in [\![\varphi]\!]^{\text{DRT}t}_M$

2. $g \in [\![\text{WEP}(\Phi, \chi)]\!]^{\text{PL}}_M \Leftrightarrow \exists h(\langle g, h\rangle \in [\![\Phi]\!]^{\text{DRT}t}_M \ \& \ h \in [\![\chi]\!]^{\text{PL}}_M)$

Given what we know about the relation between DRTt and DRT, it is not difficult to relate fact 3 to standard DRT. Fact 3 is proven by an easy simultaneous induction. $[\![\varphi]\!]^{\text{PL}}_M$ is the standard Tarskian interpretation of PL, in the format of Groenendijk & Stokhof 1991:72. As a reminder: given a first-order model $M = \langle D, I\rangle$, the set of total assignments G and the usual interpretation of terms ($[\![t]\!]_{M,g} = I(t)$ for $t \in \text{Con}$ and $[\![t]\!]_{M,g} = g(t)$ for $t \in \text{Var}$), $[\![.]\!]^{\text{PL}}_M \subseteq G$ is defined as follows:

Definition 17 (PL semantics)

1. $[\![R(t_1, \ldots, t_n)]\!] \quad = \quad \{g \mid \langle[\![t_1]\!]_g, \ldots, [\![t_n]\!]_g\rangle \in I(R)\}$

2. $[\![t_1 \equiv t_2]\!] \quad = \quad \{g \mid [\![t_1]\!]_g = [\![t_2]\!]_g\}$

3. $[\![\neg\varphi]\!] \quad = \quad \{g \mid g \notin [\![\varphi]\!]\}$

4. $[\![\varphi \wedge \psi]\!] \quad = \quad \{g \mid g \in [\![\varphi]\!] \ \& \ g \in [\![\psi]\!]\}$

5. $[\![\exists x\varphi]\!] \quad = \quad \{g \mid \exists h(g[x]h \ \& \ h \in [\![\varphi]\!])\}$

Universal quantification, disjunction and implication are defined in the standard way. That is: $\forall x\varphi =_{\text{def}} \neg\exists x\neg\varphi$, $\varphi \vee \psi =_{\text{def}} \neg(\neg\varphi \wedge \neg\psi)$ and $\varphi \to \psi =_{\text{def}} \neg(\varphi \wedge \neg\psi)$. A PL formula φ is true in a model M and with respect to an assignment g (notation: $M, g \models_{\text{PL}} \varphi$) iff $g \in [\![\varphi]\!]^{\text{PL}}_M$.

Finally, there are two additional noteworthy features of this WEP-calculus. First, the reader may notice that $\text{WEP}(\sigma(\varphi), \top)$ gives the truth-conditions of any well-formed Lf φ. Second, Muskens 1996:174 proves

---

[27]Since the interpretation of PL is normally defined in terms of total assignments (and hence no variables are undefined) we relate PL with the total version of DRT (see section 2.2.4 for discussion).

an interesting fact concerning the relationship between accessibility and weakest preconditions.

Fact 4

A DRS Φ *is proper if and only if* WEP$(\Phi, \top)$ *is closed formula.*

This fact indicates that the way accessibility was defined in definition 9 is indeed correct.

2.3 Non-representational Theories of Discourse

The representational theories of discourse (FCS and DRT) raised an obvious question: do we really need an intermediate level of representation (Lfs, DRSs)? Probably the most explicit discussion of this question can be found in Groenendijk and Stokhof 1991.[28] Groenendijk & Stokhof claim that we do not need it and to make their point more clearly they show that as far as representations are concerned standard Predicate Logical formulae will do just as well as DRSs or Lfs. Of course this means that a different semantics has to be attached to Predicate Logic, and for this they employ techniques from Quantificational Dynamic Logic. This logic, developed by Pratt 1976 to deal with the semantics of computer programs, aims to describe the *changes* a program can bring about. Groenendijk & Stokhof present a dynamic interpretation of Predicate Logic, modeling the changes a sentence can bring to a certain context, and this can be seen as a first but important step towards a fully non-representational, compositional theory of discourse semantics.

In this section we discuss various alternatives to the representational theories of discourse. In 2.3.1 we briefly discuss Pratt's Quantificational Dynamic Logic. Then we turn to Groenendijk & Stokhof's Dynamic Predicate Logic in section 2.3.2. Finally, in 2.3.3 we discuss how Dynamic Predicate Logic can be turned into a fully Montagovian theory of discourse semantics.

2.3.1 Quantificational Dynamic Logic

Quantificational Dynamic Logic (QDL) is intended to reason about the changes computer programs bring about. The syntax of QDL consists of two types of expressions: *programs*, which have a dynamic interpretation, and *statements* (formulae), which have a static interpretation. This leads to the following twofold definition of the syntax of QDL:[29]

---

[28] An early discussion on this topic can be found in Zeevat 1989, where DRT is reformulated in such a way that it is compositional in Montague's sense. In Barwise 1987 the dynamics of finite assignments is discussed, and in Rooth 1987, Barwise's work is compared with both FCS and Montague Grammar.

[29] We have ignored iteration here.

Definition 18 (QDL syntax)

1. If R is an n-ary predicate and $t_1, \ldots, t_n$ are terms, then $R(t_1, \ldots, t_n)$ is a formula.
2. If t_1, t_2 are terms, $t_1 \equiv t_2$ is a formula.
3. $\perp$ is a formula.
4. If Φ is a program and ψ is a formula, then $[\Phi]\psi$ is a formula.
5. If x is a variable and t is a term, then $x :=?$ and $x := t$ are programs.
6. If φ is a formula, then $\varphi?$ is a program.
7. If Φ and Ψ are programs, then $(\Phi \, ; \Psi)$ and $(\Phi \cup \Psi)$ are programs.

We may think of these constructions as having the following intuitive meanings (Goldblatt 1982):

$[\Phi]\psi$	after every terminating execution of Φ, ψ holds
$x :=?$	assign some arbitrary value to x
$x := t$	assign the current value of t to x
$\varphi?$	test φ; if φ is true continue, else fail
$\Phi \, ; \Psi$	do Φ and then Ψ
$\Phi \cup \Psi$	do either Φ or Ψ non-deterministically

Notice that $[\Phi]\psi$ is a *modal* statement. In fact, QDL is a modal logic with labeled modalities. Negation can be defined as follows:

Definition 19

$$\neg\Phi = [\Phi]\perp \qquad \text{there is no terminating execution of } \Phi$$

Let us now focus on the semantics of QDL. We use standard first-order models $M = \langle D, I \rangle$ and the set of total assignments G. Define $[\![\varphi]\!]_M^{\mathrm{QDL}} \subseteq G$ for formulae φ, and $[\![\Phi]\!]_M^{\mathrm{QDL}} \subseteq G^2$ for programs Φ as follows:

Definition 20 (QDL semantics)

1. $[\![R(t_1, \ldots, t_n)]\!] \quad = \quad \{g \mid \langle [\![t_1]\!]_g, \ldots, [\![t_n]\!]_g \rangle \in I(R)\}$

2. $[\![t_1 \equiv t_2]\!] \quad = \quad \{g \mid [\![t_1]\!]_g = [\![t_2]\!]_g\}$

3. $[\![\perp]\!] \quad = \quad \emptyset$

4. $[\![[\Phi]\psi]\!] \quad = \quad \{g \mid \forall h(\langle g, h \rangle \in [\![\Phi]\!] \Rightarrow h \in [\![\psi]\!])\}$

5. $[\![x :=?]\!] \quad = \quad \{\langle g, h \rangle \mid g[x]h\}$

6. $[\![x := t]\!] \quad = \quad \{\langle g, h \rangle \mid g[x]h \ \& \ h(x) = [\![t]\!]_g\}$

7. $[\![\varphi?]\!] \quad = \quad \{\langle g, h \rangle \mid g = h \ \& \ g \in [\![\varphi]\!]\}$

8. $[\![\Phi ; \Psi]\!]$ $= \{\langle g, h\rangle \mid \exists k(\langle g, k\rangle \in [\![\Phi]\!] \ \& \ \langle k, h\rangle \in [\![\Psi]\!])\}$

9. $[\![\Phi \cup \Psi]\!]$ $= \{\langle g, h\rangle \mid \langle g, h\rangle \in [\![\Phi]\!] \text{ or } \langle g, h\rangle \in [\![\Psi]\!]\}$

$g[x]h$ is defined in definition 14 and abbreviates: assignment h is like assignment g except possibly in the value h assigns to x. Support and truth are defined in a similar way as for DRTt: $M, g \models_{\text{QDL}} \Phi$ iff $\exists h\langle g, h\rangle \in [\![\Phi]\!]_M^{\text{QDL}}$ and $M, g \models_{\text{QDL}} \varphi$ iff $g \in [\![\varphi]\!]_M^{\text{QDL}}$. Truth is now defined as follows:

Definition 21 (Truth)

A program Φ is true in M with respect to g iff $M, g \models_{\text{QDL}} \Phi$

A formula φ is true in M with respect to g iff $M, g \models_{\text{QDL}} \varphi$

There are a lot of interesting aspects of QDL, but for those the reader is referred to Pratt's original paper, as well as to Goldblatt 1982 and Harel 1984. For our purposes in this book it is interesting to see how we can use QDL as a model of discourse semantics.[30]

Let us use Heim's Lfs as a kind of construction algorithm to built up QDL representations, in a similar fashion as we did for DRT above.

Definition 22 (Translating FCS into QDL)

1. $\tau([x_i \ R \ x_j])$ $= R(x_i, x_j)?$

2. $\tau([[+\text{def}]\ x_i \ R])$ $= R(x_i)?$

3. $\tau([[-\text{def}]\ x_i \ R])$ $= x_i :=? ; R(x_i)?$

4. $\tau([[\varphi] \ or \ [\psi]])$ $= (\tau([\varphi]) \cup \tau([\psi]))!?$

5. $\tau([not \ [\varphi]])$ $= (\neg\tau([\varphi]))?$

6. $\tau([all \ [\varphi][\psi]])$ $= ([\tau([\varphi])]\tau([\psi])!)?$

7. $\tau([[\varphi][\psi]])$ $= (\tau([\varphi]) ; \tau([\psi]))$

Here $\Phi!$ is an abbreviation of $[[\Phi]\bot?]\bot$.[31] It is used to turn programs into formulae with the same truth-conditions. The QDL representations of our basic examples look as follows:[32]

---

[30] For more details on QDL and its use for discourse semantics, the reader may for instance consult Groenendijk and Stokhof 1991, Fernando 1992 or Muskens 1995b.

[31] Hence $[\![\Phi!]\!] = \{g \mid \exists h\langle g, h\rangle \in [\![\Phi]\!]\}$. Notice that all formulae φ are equivalent with $\varphi?!$.

[32] Since $\Phi ; (\Psi ; \Upsilon)$ is equivalent with $(\Phi ; \Psi) ; \Upsilon$, we leave out the brackets.

(11) $\tau(\text{LF } 1) =$
$x_1 :=?\,;man(x_1)?\,;whistles(x_1)?\,;x_2 :=?\,;dog(x_2)?\,;follows(x_2,x_1)?$

(12) $\tau(\text{LF } 2) =$
$([x_1 :=?\,;farmer(x_1)?\,;x_2 :=?\,;donkey(x_2)?\,;owns(x_1,x_2)?]$
$beats(x_1,x_2))?$

Although these representations do not look like DRSs, it is not difficult to see that $\tau(\text{LF } 1)$ is equivalent with $\sigma(\text{LF } 1)$ and that $\tau(\text{LF } 2)$ is equivalent with $\sigma(\text{LF } 2)$. This seems to indicate that as far as representing discourse is concerned, QDL programs are just as good as DRSs (interpreted using total assignments). This is supported by the following fact.

Fact 5

For all models M and for all Logical forms φ:
$[\![\tau(\varphi)]\!]_M^{\text{QDL}} = [\![\sigma(\varphi)]\!]_M^{\text{DRT}t}$

In words: it does not matter whether we translate Lfs into DRSs or into QDL programs, the meaning is the same. Given what we know about the relation between DRT and DRTt it is not difficult to relate fact 5 to standard DRT. A more general fact is given in Muskens 1995b, where it is shown that DRTt can be embedded in QDL.

2.3.2 Dynamic Predicate Logic

With *Dynamic Predicate Logic* (DPL), Groenendijk & Stokhof go even further and represent texts simply using standard first-order PL. The semantics of DPL is rather different from ordinary PL however. Given a first-order model $M = \langle D, I \rangle$ and the set of total assignments G, $[\![.]\!]_M^{\text{DPL}} \subseteq G^2$ is defined as follows:

Definition 23 (DPL semantics)

1. $[\![R(t_1,\ldots,t_n)]\!] \quad = \quad \{\langle g,h\rangle \mid g = h\ \&\ \langle [\![t_1]\!]_g,\ldots,[\![t_n]\!]_g\rangle \in I(R)\}$

2. $[\![t_1 \equiv t_2]\!] \quad = \quad \{\langle g,h\rangle \mid g = h\ \&\ [\![t_1]\!]_g = [\![t_2]\!]_g\}$

3. $[\![\neg\varphi]\!] \quad = \quad \{\langle g,h\rangle \mid g = h\ \&\ \neg\exists k\langle g,k\rangle \in [\![\varphi]\!]\}$

4. $[\![\varphi \wedge \psi]\!] \quad = \quad \{\langle g,h\rangle \mid \exists k(\langle g,k\rangle \in [\![\varphi]\!]\ \&\ \langle k,h\rangle \in [\![\psi]\!])\}$

5. $[\![\exists x\varphi]\!] \quad = \quad \{\langle g,h\rangle \mid \exists k(g[x]k\ \&\ \langle k,h\rangle \in [\![\varphi]\!])\}$

Again, the other constructions can be defined in the standard way. That is: $\forall x\varphi =_{\text{def}} \neg\exists x\neg\varphi$, $\varphi \vee \psi =_{\text{def}} \neg(\neg\varphi \wedge \neg\psi)$ and $\varphi \to \psi =_{\text{def}} \neg(\varphi \wedge \neg\psi)$. A DPL formula φ is supported in a model M and with respect to an assignment g (notation $M, g \models_{\text{DPL}} \varphi$) iff $\exists h\langle g,h\rangle \in [\![\varphi]\!]_M^{\text{DPL}}$.

Definition 24 (Truth)

A DPL formula φ is true in M with respect to g iff $M, g \models_{\text{DPL}} \varphi$

Two formulae φ and ψ are equivalent iff they have the same interpretation in every model M, formally, for all M: $[\![\varphi]\!]_M = [\![\psi]\!]_M$. A special kind of DPL formulae are the *tests*. The distinguishing feature of a test is that it can only be supported on the *diagonal* Δ of G^2. Δ is the set of pairs of assignments of which the input-assignment equals the output-assignment: $\Delta = \{\langle g, h \rangle \mid g = h\}$.

Definition 25 (Test)
A formula φ is a test iff in all models M: $[\![\varphi]\!]_M \subsetneq \Delta$

Existential quantification and conjunction are *not* tests: existential quantification can (randomly) assign new values to variables, while conjunction can pass these new values on. It is easily seen that the DPL tests stand in a one-to-one relationship to the DRT conditions. It is also manifest that the DPL conjunction coincides with the merge operator interpreted in DRTt (and with the sequencing operator from QDL). A much discussed feature of the relationship between conjunction and existential quantification in DPL is that quantifying more than once over the same variable may lead to loss of information. More specifically, consider:

$$\exists x P(x) \land \exists x Q(x)$$

It is easily seen that after the second quantification over x the information about possible values of x with property P is lost. This problem has been called the *downdate* problem in the literature, for obvious reasons. Groenendijk & Stokhof remark:

> We mention in passing that if one would use DPL for practical purposes, one would certainly choose active quantifiers and free variables in such a way that these troublesome cases are avoided.
> (Groenendijk and Stokhof 1991:69)

Since DPL as such is not associated with a kind of construction algorithm, we might use Heim's Lfs for that purpose, just as we did for DRT and QDL. And since Lfs use indexing to guarantee that an indefinite introduces a new variable while definites pick up an old one, no variable is quantified twice and the downdate problem does not arise. However, using these non-compositional Lfs is definitely not in the spirit of DPL, since one of the things Groenendijk & Stokhof want to show is that we do not need to

> (...) postulate a level of semantic representation, or 'logical form', in between syntactic form and meaning proper, which is supposed to be a necessary ingredient of a descriptively and explanatory adequate theory. (Groenendijk and Stokhof 1991:94)

There is no harm in using Lfs here for the time being, since in section 2.3.3 it is shown how DPL can be turned into a fully compositional Montagovian system. Of course we do get the downdate problem back then, so we have to return to it in the discussion. For now, let us define a function ρ which maps Lfs onto DPL formulae.

Definition 26 (Translating FCS into DPL)

1. $\rho([x_i \ R \ x_j]) \qquad = \qquad R(x_i, x_j)$

2. $\rho([[+\text{def}] \ x_i \ R]) \qquad = \qquad R(x_i)$

3. $\rho([[-\text{def}] \ x_i \ R]) \qquad = \qquad \exists x_i R(x_i)$

4. $\rho([[\varphi] \ or \ [\psi]]) \qquad = \qquad (\rho([\varphi]) \vee \rho([\psi]))$

5. $\rho([not \ [\varphi]]) \qquad = \qquad \neg\rho([\varphi])$

6. $\rho([all \ [\varphi][\psi]]) \qquad = \qquad (\rho([\varphi]) \rightarrow \rho([\psi]))$

7. $\rho([[\varphi][\psi]]) \qquad = \qquad (\rho([\varphi]) \wedge \rho([\psi]))$

$\rho(\text{LF 1})$ and $\rho(\text{LF 2})$ yield the following respective translations for examples (1) and (5):[33]

(13) $\exists x_1 man(x_1) \wedge whistles(x_1) \wedge \exists x_2 dog(x_2) \wedge follows(x_2, x_1)$

(14) $(\exists x_1 farmer(x_1) \wedge \exists x_2 donkey(x_2) \wedge owns(x_1, x_2)) \rightarrow beats(x_1, x_2)$

These DPL formulae are essentially the same as the intuitive translations into PL given in (2) and (6) and discussed in section 2.1. The *difference* is that the DPL formulae have a different interpretation. In particular, the following fact applies to them, *without* restrictions on the quantified variable x.

Definition 27 (DPL binding facts)

1. $\exists x\varphi \wedge \psi$ is equivalent with $\exists x(\varphi \wedge \psi)$
2. $\exists x\varphi \rightarrow \psi$ is equivalent with $\forall x(\varphi \rightarrow \psi)$

Given this fact it is easily seen that $\rho(\text{LF 1})$ and $\rho(\text{LF 2})$ are equivalent with (15) and (16) respectively.

(15) $\exists x_1(man(x_1) \wedge whistles(x_1) \wedge \exists x_2(dog(x_2) \wedge follows(x_2, x_1)))$

(16) $\forall x_1 \forall x_2((farmer(x_1) \wedge donkey(x_2) \wedge owns(x_1, x_2)) \rightarrow beats(x_1, x_2))$

And these are exactly the intended interpretations (compare (3) and (7) in the introduction). How does ρ relate to σ and τ?

---

[33]Since $\varphi \wedge (\psi \wedge \gamma)$ is equivalent with $(\varphi \wedge \psi) \wedge \gamma$ we leave out the brackets.

Fact 6

For all models M and for all Logical forms φ:
$$[\![\sigma(\varphi)]\!]_M^{\mathrm{DRT}t} = [\![\tau(\varphi)]\!]_M^{\mathrm{QDL}} = [\![\rho(\varphi)]\!]_M^{\mathrm{DPL}}$$

This means that it is immaterial whether we translate Lfs into DRSs, QDL programs or DPL formulae (or interpret the Lfs directly). They are all equally suitable as a vehicle for the first-order representation of texts. Groenendijk & Stokhof characterize the relation between DPL and QDL as follows: while QDL is intended to reason about programs, DPL is more like a programming language (Groenendijk and Stokhof 1991:83). One cannot reason about DPL formulae in DPL itself. But, Groenendijk & Stokhof observe that ordinary dynamic logic can be used to formalize reasoning about DPL, and that is basically what Van Eijck and De Vries 1992 and Van Eijck 1994a do. In general, Groenendijk & Stokhof show that DPL can be embedded into QDL and that QDL (disregarding $\cup$ and $x := t$) can be embedded into DPL (Groenendijk and Stokhof 1991:83–89). We return to the interrelations between the various models discussed so far in the discussion. First we discuss how DPL can be turned into a completely compositional, non-representational theory of discourse semantics which may bear the label 'Montagovian'.

2.3.3   A Dynamic Version of Montague Grammar

Various ways to turn DPL into a dynamic version of Montague Grammar have been proposed. One possibility is the *Dynamic Montague Grammar* (DMG) of Groenendijk & Stokhof 1990, where a version of Montague Grammar is presented which uses *Dynamic Intensional Logic* (DIL, Janssen 1986) as representation language. Other dynamic versions of Montague Grammar have been proposed in Rooth 1987, Muskens 1991, Dekker 1993b, Bouchez et al. 1993 and Beaver 1993, for example. A different method to treat anaphora in discourse in a compositional Montagovian manner is by extending DRT with lambdas, as done in for instance Bos et al. 1994 and Asher 1993. An interesting synthesis between these two strategies is presented in Muskens 1996, which generalizes the method from Muskens 1991 and applies it to DRT.

Here we focus on the system from Muskens 1991, which uses *Two-Sorted Type Theory* (abbreviated as TY_2) as intermediate representation language. TY_2 is basically the logic from Church 1940, and traces back to the work of Russell and Ramsey in the beginning of this century. Before we discuss how TY_2 can be used in a dynamic version of Montague Grammar, let us first take a closer look at the logic itself. Here is the set of TY_2 types (where t stands for truth-values, e for entities and s for states).

Definition 28 (Types)

1. e, s and t are types,
2. if α and β are types, then $(\alpha\beta)$ is a type.

A characteristic feature of the set of TY2 types is that s is an extra basic type. The TY2 expressions are defined in the following fashion. Assume that we have sets Con_α of constants of type α, and Var_α of variables of type α. An expression of type t is called a formula.

Definition 29 (TY2 syntax)

1. If φ and ψ are formulae, then $\neg\varphi$ and $(\varphi \wedge \psi)$ are formulae.
2. If φ is a formula and x is a variable of any type, then $\exists x\varphi$ is a formula.
3. If A is an expression of type $(\alpha\beta)$ and B is an expression of type α, then (AB) is an expression of type β.
4. If A is an expression of type β and x is a variable of type α, then $\lambda x(A)$ is an expression of type $(\alpha\beta)$.
5. If A and B are expressions of the same type, then $(A \equiv B)$ is a formula.

Parentheses are omitted where this can be done without creating confusion, on the understanding that association is to the left. So instead of writing $(\ldots(AB_1)\ldots B_n)$ we write $AB_1 \ldots B_n$.

So much for the language of TY2. Let us now turn to its interpretation. TY2 models are defined as $M = \langle\{D_\alpha\}_\alpha, I\rangle$. Here $\{D_\alpha\}_\alpha$ is a TY2 frame, in which each type α is associated with its own domain D_α in such a way that D_e and D_s are non-empty sets, $D_t = \{0,1\}$ (the set of truth-values) and $D_{(\alpha\beta)}$ is the set of functions from D_α to D_β. I is the interpretation function of M. It has the set of constants as its domain, and $I(c) \in D_\alpha$ for all $c \in \mathsf{Con}_\alpha$. G is the set of total assignments such that for any $g \in G$ and x a variable of type α, $g(x) \in D_\alpha$. $g[x/d]$ is the assignment which is exactly like g except that $g[x/d](x) = d$. The value $[\![A]\!]^{TY_2}_{M,g}$ of a term A in a model M with respect to assignment g is defined in the following way. First of all, the interpretation of terms of any type α goes as follows: $[\![t]\!]_{M,g} = I(t)$, if $t \in \mathsf{Con}_\alpha$, and $[\![t]\!]_{M,g} = g(t)$, if $t \in \mathsf{Var}_\alpha$.

Definition 30 (TY2 semantics)

1. $[\![\neg\varphi]\!]_g \quad = \quad 1$ iff $[\![\varphi]\!]_g = 0$

2. $[\![\varphi \wedge \psi]\!]_g \quad = \quad 1$ iff $[\![\varphi]\!]_g = 1$ and $[\![\psi]\!]_g = 1$

3. $[\![\exists x_\alpha \varphi]\!]_g \quad = \quad 1$ iff $[\![\varphi]\!]_{g[x/d]} = 1$ for some $d \in D_\alpha$

4. $[\![AB]\!]_g \quad = \quad [\![A]\!]_g([\![B]\!]_g)$

5. $[\![\lambda x_\alpha A]\!]_g \quad = \quad$ the function F such that $F(d) = [\![A]\!]_{g[x/d]}$
   for all $d \in D_\alpha$

6. $[\![A \equiv B]\!]_g \quad = \quad 1$ iff $[\![A]\!]_g = [\![B]\!]_g$

Disjunction, implication and universal quantification are defined in the standard way. The following principle holds, where $\{B/x\}A$ is the substitution of B for the free occurrences of x in A.

Fact 7 *(λ-conversion)*
$\lambda x(A)B$ *is equivalent with* $\{B/x\}A$, *provided the free variables in B are free for x in A.*[34]

TY$_2$ is an entirely static system, so it shall not be immediately clear how it can be used to deal with the semantics of discourse. The central idea is to establish a relation between states and discourse referents. Muskens introduces discourse referents as *individual concepts*, that is functions from states to entities (expressions of type (se)).[35] We use $d, d', d_1, d_2, \ldots$ to represent discourse referents. Muskens defines what it means for two states i and j to agree on all discourse referents, except possibly in the value of d, which is abbreviated as $i[d]j$.

Definition 31
$i[d]j$ iff $\forall d'((DR\,d' \wedge \neg(d \equiv d')) \to d'i \equiv d'j)$

DR is a non-logical constant of type $(se)t$ with the intuitive interpretation 'is a discourse referent'. To make this work Muskens defines three axioms. The first, and most important one, guarantees that we can always assign a new value to a discourse referent. That is: it guarantees that we have 'enough states'. The other two axioms are straightforward bookkeeping axioms.

Definition 32 (Axioms)

AX1 $\forall i \forall d \forall x (DR\,d \to \exists j(i[d]j \wedge dj \equiv x))$

AX2 $DR\,d$, for each discourse referent d

AX3 $\neg(d_1 \equiv d_2)$, for each two different discourse referents d_1 and d_2.

It is instructive to translate DPL into TY$_2$. Muskens claims that his system is

---

[34] A variable y is called free for x in A if and only if no free occurrence of x in A is within the scope of a quantifier $\exists y$, $\forall y$ or a lambda operator λy (Gamut 1991:110).

[35] Muskens uses the term *store* instead of discourse referent, in analogue with the way variables are treated in computer programs. Note that Muskens 1996 proceeds in a slightly different way. There a separate type for stores is introduced (π). Additionally, ordinary predicates take stores as arguments, and not entities, which leads to a somewhat simpler notation than the one used here.

(...) closer to DPL than Groenendijk & Stokhof's own generalization, DMG, is. Roughly, what Groenendijk and Stokhof do on the metalevel of DPL I do on the object level of type theory.
(Muskens 1991:fn9)

So let $\diamond$ be a function translating DPL formulae in TY$_2$ expressions. Any DPL formula is translated into an expression of the form $\lambda ij\varphi$, an expression which looks for two states and produces a formula φ.

Definition 33 (Translating DPL into TY$_2$)

1. $\diamond(R(t_1, \ldots, t_n)) = \lambda ij(i \equiv j \wedge R \diamond t_n \ldots \diamond t_1)$,
   where $\diamond t_k = (d_k i)$, if $t_k \in \mathsf{Var}$ &
   $\diamond t_k = t_k$, if $t_k \in \mathsf{Con}$ $(1 \leq k \leq n)$

2. $\diamond(t_1 \equiv t_2) = \lambda ij(i \equiv j \wedge \diamond t_1 \equiv \diamond t_2)$,
   where $\diamond t_k = (d_k i)$, if $t_k \in \mathsf{Var}$ &
   $\diamond t_k = t_k$, if $t_k \in \mathsf{Con}$ $(k \in \{1, 2\})$

3. $\diamond(\neg\varphi) = \lambda ij(i \equiv j \wedge \neg\exists h \diamond (\varphi)ih)$

4. $\diamond(\varphi \wedge \psi) = \lambda ij\exists h(\diamond(\varphi)ih \wedge \diamond(\psi)hj)$

5. $\diamond(\exists x_n\varphi) = \lambda ij\exists h(i[d_n]h \wedge \diamond(\varphi)hj)$

We can illustrate Muskens' claim by comparing $\diamond(\varphi)$ (the object level of type theory) with $[\![\varphi]\!]^{\mathrm{DPL}}$ (the DPL meta-level). Every $\diamond(\varphi)$ is an expression of type $s(st)$. It asks for two states, and returns a truth-value. Consider the conjunction; it anticipates two states which are connected via an intermediate state. The set of pairs of states which satisfy this requirement looks as follows:

$$\{\langle s_1, s_2\rangle \mid \exists s_3(\langle s_1, s_3\rangle \in [\![\diamond(\varphi)]\!]^{TY_2} \ \& \ \langle s_3, s_2\rangle \in [\![\diamond(\psi)]\!]^{TY_2})\}$$

Given that the axioms force states to behave like assignments to discourse markers, the relation with the DPL interpretation of conjunction will be clear.

Let us now briefly describe a fragment for natural language discourse. It uses the following categories:

Definition 34 (Categories)

1. E and S are categories.
2. If A and B are categories, then A/B and $A//B$ are categories.

A string of category A is translated into a TY$_2$ expression of $\mathsf{Type}_2(A)$ by the following correspondence:

Definition 35 (Category-to-type)

1. $\mathsf{Type}_2(E) = e$, $\mathsf{Type}_2(S) = s(st)$
2. $\mathsf{Type}_2(A/B) = \mathsf{Type}_2(A//B) = (\mathsf{Type}_2(B)\ \mathsf{Type}_2(A))$

The following table lists the categories which are used together with abbreviations and examples of basic expressions:

Category	Abbreviation	Basic Expressions
S/E	VP	whistles, walks
$S//E$	CN	donkey, farmer, man
S/VP	NP	he_n, it_n
VP/NP	TV	beats, owns
NP/CN	DET	a_n, $every_n$
S/S		not
$(S/S)/S$		or, and, . (*the stop*)
$(S/S)//S$		if

We need one rule to form texts:

Functional application:

If ξ is an expression of category A/B or $A//B$ and ϑ is an expression of category B, then $\xi\vartheta$ is an expression of category A.

We define a function $(.)^\bullet$ which maps syntactic trees onto expressions of TY_2. The basic expressions are translated as follows:[36]

$$\text{whistles}^\bullet = \lambda x \lambda i j (i \equiv j \wedge whistles\, x)$$

$$\text{donkey}^\bullet = \lambda x \lambda i j (i \equiv j \wedge donkey\, x)$$

$$\text{he}_n{}^\bullet = \lambda P \lambda i j (P(d_n i) i j)$$

$$\text{beats}^\bullet = \lambda Q \lambda x (Q \lambda y \lambda i j (i \equiv j \wedge beats\, yx))$$

$$\text{a}_n{}^\bullet = \lambda P_1 \lambda P_2 \lambda i j \exists k \exists h (i[d_n]k \wedge P_1(d_n k)kh \wedge P_2(d_n k)hj)$$

$$\text{every}_n{}^\bullet = \lambda P_1 \lambda P_2 \lambda i j (i \equiv j \wedge \forall kl((i[d_n]k \wedge P_1(d_n k)kl) \to \exists h P_2(d_n k)lh))$$

$$\text{not}^\bullet = \lambda \mathcal{P} \lambda i j (i \equiv j \wedge \neg \exists h(\mathcal{P}\, ih))$$

$$\text{or}^\bullet = \lambda \mathcal{P} \lambda \mathcal{Q} \lambda i j (i \equiv j \wedge \exists h(\mathcal{P}\, ih \vee \mathcal{Q}\, ih))$$

$$\text{and}^\bullet, .^\bullet = \lambda \mathcal{P} \lambda \mathcal{Q} \lambda i j \exists h(\mathcal{P}\, ih \wedge \mathcal{Q}\, hj)$$

$$\text{if}^\bullet = \lambda \mathcal{P} \lambda \mathcal{Q} \lambda i j (i \equiv j \wedge \forall h(\mathcal{P}\, ih \to \exists k \mathcal{Q}\, hk))$$

---

[36] In these translations h, i, j, k and l range over states (type s), x and y are variables of type e, the d_i's are discourse referents (of type se), P_i is of $\mathsf{Type}_2(VP)(= \mathsf{Type}_2(CN))$, Q of type $\mathsf{Type}_2(NP)$, $\mathcal{P}$, $\mathcal{Q}$ of $\mathsf{Type}_2(S)$. Furthermore, *donkey* and *whistles* are constants of type et, and *beats* is a constant of type $e(et)$. The translations of other basic expressions can be derived from the translations given. So, the translations of *walks, farmer, owns, ...* are alphabetical variants of the translations of *whistles, donkey, beats,...* respectively.

The relation between these translations and the function $\diamond$ from DPL to TY$_2$ is clear. The logical connectives are only different in that they abstract over their arguments, the other items are 'adapted' versions of the $\diamond$ output to allow for compositional combination. The translation of functional application goes as follows:

FUNCTIONAL APPLICATION translated:
$$([\xi\vartheta])^\bullet = \xi^\bullet\vartheta^\bullet$$

The reader is referred to Muskens 1991 for discussion and applications. Here we briefly consider the treatment of the central examples, beginning with (1). Suppose we assigned *a man* index 1 and *a dog* index 2. Applying the definitions, and writing $i[d_1, d_2]j$ for $\exists k(i[d_1]k \wedge k[d_2]j)$ gives us the following TY$_2$ translation:

(17) $\lambda ij(i[d_1, d_2]j \wedge man(d_1 j) \wedge whistles(d_1 j) \wedge dog(d_2 j) \wedge follows(d_1 j)(d_2 j))$

Example (5) is associated with the following TY$_2$ translation (once again abbreviating $\exists k(i[d_1]k \wedge k[d_2]j)$):

(18) $\lambda ij(i \equiv j \wedge$
$\forall k((i[d_1, d_2]k \wedge farmer(d_1 k) \wedge donkey(d_2 k) \wedge owns(d_2 k)(d_1 k)) \rightarrow$
$beats(d_2 k)(d_1 k)))$

These two expressions describe the *meanings* of the respective examples; to get at the truth-conditions we need something more: φ is *true* in a state i (and in a model M) iff there is a state j such that $\langle i, j \rangle$ is in the denotation of the meaning of φ (in M). The satisfaction set of φ is given by $\lambda i \exists j \varphi ij$.[37] The relation with DPL truth shall be clear. So, the satisfaction sets of (17) and (18) are:

(19) $\lambda i \exists j(i[d_1, d_2]j \wedge man(d_1 j) \wedge whistles(d_1 j) \wedge dog(d_2 j) \wedge$
$follows(d_1 j)(d_2 j))$

(20) $\lambda i \forall k((i[d_1, d_2]k \wedge farmer(d_1 k) \wedge donkey(d_2 k) \wedge owns(d_2 k)(d_1 k)) \rightarrow$
$beats(d_2 k)(d_1 k))$

Muskens proves a useful lemma which says that quantifying over a state is the same as unselectively binding all the values of discourse referents in that state. The lemma is phrased as follows:

Fact 8 *(Unselective Binding Lemma)*
Let $d_1, \ldots d_n$ be discourse referents of type se and $x_1, \ldots, x_n$ distinct variables of type e, let φ be a formula that does not contain j, then

$$\exists j(i[d_1, \ldots, d_n]j \wedge \{d_1 j/x_1, \ldots, d_n j/x_n\}\varphi) \text{ is equivalent with}$$
$$\exists x_1 \ldots \exists x_n \varphi$$

---

[37]Muskens 1991 calls it *the content* of φ.

$$\forall j (i[d_1, \ldots, d_n]j \to \{d_1 j / x_1, \ldots, d_n j / x_n\} \varphi) \text{ is equivalent with}$$
$$\forall x_1 \ldots \forall x_n \varphi$$

Given this fact, the satisfaction sets in (19) and (20) are equivalent to the following:

(21) $\lambda i \exists x_1 \exists x_2 (man\, x_1 \land whistles\, x_1 \land dog\, x_2 \land follows\, x_1 x_2)$

(22) $\lambda i \forall x_1 \forall x_2 ((farmer\, x_1 \land donkey\, x_2 \land owns\, x_2 x_1) \to beats\, x_2 x_1)$

Observe that $\diamond(\rho(\text{LF } 1))$ is equivalent with (17) and that $\diamond(\rho(\text{LF } 2))$ is equivalent with (18). This is no coincidence: it indicates that using Lfs for the construction of DPL formulae was indeed harmless.

2.4 Discussion: The Quest for *the* Theory of Discourse

In this chapter we have discussed a number of important theories of discourse semantics. We started with the pivotal theories of discourse representation: FCS and DRT. FCS rests on the assumption that we need an intermediate level of Logical form, which is required for syntactic analysis anyway. In DRT the claim is that Discourse Representation Structures should be employed as intermediate between syntax and interpretation. As a reaction to the 'representationalist' view on discourse various alternatives have been proposed. One of them is DPL; it couples a QDL-style semantics to the language of standard PL. This shows that as far as representations are concerned, it is not necessary to use DRSs; formulae of PL will do. It is not difficult to define a dynamic version of Montague Grammar on the basis of DPL which means that the use of Lfs is not essential either.

2.4.1 The Dynamic Cube

A recent trend in discourse semantics is to stress the similarities between the various theories and try to come to one general system of discourse semantics combining the niceties of the different approaches. For instance, in this chapter we have seen that FCS can be reduced to DRT, and that the reduction itself can be understood as an alternative to the standard DRT construction algorithm. But what about the relationship between DRT and DPL? If we compare classical DRT (as described in Kamp 1981) with standard DPL (as in Groenendijk and Stokhof 1991) there are essentially three dimensions along which they differ: single *vs.* collective quantification,[38] total *vs.* finite assignments and re-assignments *vs.* no re-assignments. Arguably this is overstating the differences between DRT and DPL, but it nicely serves to classify a number of alternatives 'in between' classical DRT and standard DPL, and discuss their

---

[38]The term 'collective quantification' should not be confused with the collective quantification in plural logic, for the latter see for instance Van der Does 1992.

properties and interrelations. So let us introduce three features representing these dimensions: $[\pm single]$, $[\pm total]$ and $[\pm re\text{-}ass]$. Classical DRT can be characterized by the matrix $[-single, -total, -re\text{-}ass]$; the referents are quantified over collectively, the interpretation is in terms of finite assignments and there is no possibility of re-assigning a value to a referent. DPL is on the other extreme. It can be classified using the matrix $[+single, +total, +re\text{-}ass]$; each variable is quantified separately, the interpretation is in terms of total assignments and there is the possibility to assign a new value to a variable.[39] Let us label the six other combinations a-f. Figure 1 visualizes the situation.

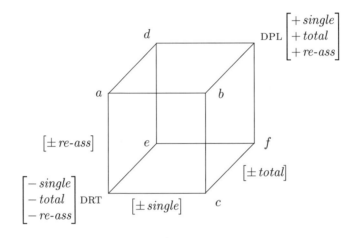

FIGURE 1 The dynamic cube

If we look at some well-known variations of classical DRT we encounter a couple of the possibilities in a-f. For example, the version of DRT we have called *standard* and which combines classical DRT with a merging-operator interpreted as relational composition corresponds with point c; it uses finite assignments and forbids re-assigning of values but does have the possibility of single quantifications.[40] The version of DRT discussed in Groenendijk and Stokhof 1991, which uses total assign-

---

[39]Besides the contrast between single and collective quantification, there is a second difference between the DRT and the DPL language; DRT distinguishes static conditions from dynamic DRSs, while DPL blurs the distinction between static conditions and dynamic formulae. The difference between conditions and DRSs is not crucial however. After all, a discourse is always represented by a DRS, which has a dynamic interpretations. Furthermore, each condition φ has the same truth-conditions as the DRS $[\,|\,\varphi]$.

[40]Since $[x_1, \ldots, x_n \mid \varphi_1, \ldots, \varphi_m]$ is equivalent with $[x_1 \mid \,]; \ldots; [x_n \mid \,]; [\,\mid \varphi_1, \ldots, \varphi_m]$.

ments, allows for re-assignment and quantifies collectively, corresponds with point d. This is essentially DRTt without merging. Groenendijk & Stokhof show that DPL can be embedded in a meaning-preserving way in (their version of) DRT, but that the opposite would only be possible if DRT had a way of quantifying over one variable at a time. This possibility is available in the system we called DRTt, and it is indeed characterized by the same matrix as DPL. It is possible to define a meaning-preserving translation from DPL into DRTt (see for instance Vermeulen 1994 or Dekker 1994 for discussion). Some vertices are not explored so-far, and sometimes with good reason. For instance, the combination of total assignments with a ban on re-assignment (points e and f) makes it impossible to treat discourse referents as variables.

If we look at the cube from the DPL perspective we can also label a number of vertices. The fact that DPL allows for re-assignments (just like classical logic does) has an undesired side-effect as we saw: the downdate-problem. Several solutions to this problem have been proposed. In Dekker 1993b, 1996 it is argued that we need to switch to finite assignments and forbid re-assignment. In other words, his *Eliminative* DPL (EDPL) can be found on angular point c; the place where we also find standard DRT. In fact, EDPL is more in the spirit of FCS. Dekker builds Heim's Novelty/Familiarity Condition into the semantics of EDPL, with the difference that when an attempt is made to re-assign a value in EDPL we end up in a state of undefinedness. Another solution for the downdate problem can be found in Fernando 1992. Fernando also argues for an interpretation in terms of finite assignments and without the possibility of re-assigning. But, his so-called *guarded quantification* cannot result in undefinedness. His proposal for the existential quantifier can be put as follows: when a variable x is quantified over in a situation in which x does not have a value, it is assigned one. But when x *has* already been assigned a value, nothing happens. This is basically the way things go in standard DRT as well, modulo the fact that in DRT it is the clause for merging which does the hard work.

An interesting question is whether the downdate problem can be solved in a system which remains faithful to DPL; in a system which can be placed on the same vertex as DPL. That this is indeed possible is shown in Vermeulen 1993, see also Vermeulen 1994. Vermeulen switches to assignments which do not map one value to a variable, but a *sequence* of values. Each time a variable is quantified over, a new value is pushed on the stack of values. This means that old values do not disappear, but just move up one place. This solves the downdate problem '*without compromising*' (Vermeulen 1994:51): this system uses total assignments and allows for re-assigning just like standard DPL does, but there is no longer the possibility of losing information, nor is there the risk of ending up in a state of undefinedness. Vermeulen presents a generalization of this idea in terms of *referent systems* (see Vermeulen 1994, 1995) and these are also used in the most recent official version of DPL; the one presented in Groenendijk et al. 1996b. Groenendijk, Stokhof and Veltman present a combination of DPL with Update Semantics (US, Veltman 1996). The DPL-part of this combination is different from the version of DPL presented in Groenendijk and Stokhof 1991 in that the semantics of the existential quantifier is defined using referent systems and in terms of finite assignments. This version of DPL is positioned at vertex b.

The use of sequence valued assignments/referent systems is the nicest solution to the downdate problem from a logical point of view. If we look at standard Predicate Logic for example there is no reason to forbid or discourage multiple quantifications over the same variable. If we look at the problem from a linguistic angle there are some complications however. It is true that the use of referent systems guarantees that we cannot lose an object nor any information about it, but the object may become 'less accessible' when different objects are pushed on top of it. If we want objects to remain accessible, we have to associate a fresh variable with each new indefinite NP, which is in accordance with Karttunen's original notion of a discourse referent. Naturally, this observation is perfectly compatible with the desire to keep the underlying language as 'classical' as possible. On the other hand, it also indicates that Heim's NFC or some comparable constraint is not without its merits either. Even though it often happens that objects become less accessible, this seems to be tied to factors like discourse structure and focus rather than to re-using variables. Our personal favorite spot on the cube is labeled c: the corner where we also find Dekker's EDPL, Fernando's guarded assignments and standard DRT. It uses finite assignments, has the possibility of quantifying over one variable at a time and has an active policy against re-assignments. Whether this is done DRT-like or DPL-style is immaterial for the purposes of this book.

2.4.2 Extensions and Modifications

Besides fundamental issues in dynamic semantics, some of which we discussed above, there are also more empirical topics of interest. These can roughly be divided into two groups: extensions and modifications. All the systems we discussed above have 'first-order expressivity' (see footnote 12), but as far as empirical applications are concerned they are primarily focussed on indefinites and anaphoric pronouns. Yet, there is more to discourse than sentence sequencing and donkey-sentences. Therefore, quite a number of *extensions* have been proposed. Some of them are attempts to combine other semantic philosophies with discourse semantics. In the introduction, the combination of dynamic semantics with theories of presupposition was discussed. This combination, and the related treatment of definite NPs in general, is the subject of the final chapters of this book. Another combination we have already encountered is the one with classical Montague Grammar. Yet another obvious combination, not mentioned before, is the one with *Generalized Quantifier Theory* (GQT). GQT arose almost at the same time as DRT/FCS, following Barwise and Cooper 1981. Attempts to combine the two semantic philosophies can be found in for instance Van Eijck and De Vries 1992, Chierchia 1992, Van der Berg 1994, 1996a, Fernando 1994a and Kamp and Reyle 1993. A related issue is the dynamic analysis of *plurals*, as discussed in, among others, Van Eijck 1983, Van den Berg 1989, 1996b, Van der Does 1994 and again Kamp and Reyle 1993 among others. A particularly interesting combination is the one with temporal elements. In the early seventies Partee noted that there are certain similarities between anaphoric pronouns and tenses (Partee 1973), and indeed the dynamic analysis of anaphora can readily be extended to a dynamic theory of tense (Kamp and Rohrer 1983 and Muskens 1995b). A final important extension is the following. The dynamic theories we have discussed can be seen as modeling a hearer interpreting a piece of text. Of course the every day dynamics of discourse is much more involved. Where there is a hearer, there usually is a speaker as well, and moreover the two tend to interact. What is needed for this is a dynamic theory of dialogues, see for instance Bunt 1988, 1990. Dekker 1993b, Van Eijck and Cepparello 1994 and Groenendijk et al. 1996c contain some observations on 'multispeaker DPL'. In Piwek 1998 the semantics and pragmatics of dialogue are studied in depth from a DRT-like, proof-theoretic perspective.

The second line of dynamic research, labeled *modifications* above, is based on questions about the predictions made by the various systems. We have seen that they essentially assign the same meanings to the core examples. So, there appears to be consensus that a donkey-sentence like (5) has a universal reading which can be paraphrased as *every farmer beats every donkey that he owns*, and that there can be no anaphoric pronoun outside the donkey-sentence referring back to either the farmer or the donkey (see the continuation of (5) with (8)). Similarly, all theories agree that indefinites embedded under a negation cannot serve as an antecedent for anaphoric pronouns outside the scope of this negation and that there can be no anaphoric links between the two parts of a disjunction. Nevertheless these generalizations are not undisputed. It has been argued by, for instance, Rooth 1987 and

Pelletier and Schubert 1989 that donkey-type sentences can also have weaker readings. Pelletier and Schubert point to the following example:

(23) If I have a coin in my pocket, I will put it in the parking-meter.

Surely the indefinite in the antecedent does not have a universal reading. The speaker will not put *every* dime he finds in his pocket into the parking-meter; he will just throw enough coins in the slot. Factors like context and world-knowledge about parking-meters seem to play an important role here, but it is fair to demand of a theory of discourse semantics that it '(...) *should provide a framework in which the range of intuitions can be modelled*' (Rooth 1987:257). And in fact, this seems to be possible as shown by Chierchia 1992 for example, who defines a weaker implication in a DPL-style framework. See also Kanazawa 1994 for extensive discussion.

Another objection, and a more fundamental one, is that there do exist counterexamples to the generalizations about anaphoric reference. Take the donkey-sentence and compare it with example (24) from Roberts 1989:683.

(24) If John bought a book, he'll be home reading it by now. It'll be a murder mystery.

The pronoun *it* in the second sentence seems to refer back to the indefinite *a book* in the antecedent of the first sentence. Roberts calls this phenomenon *modal subordination* because the presence of a modal verb (*will*) is essential. She argues that the second sentence should be interpreted as part of the consequent of the first sentence, that is: she argues that sentence (24) should be interpreted as *If John bought a book, he'll be home reading it by now and it'll be a murder mystery*. This is a problem for all the theories discussed in this chapter. To solve it, real extensions have to be developed (witness for instance Geurts 1994). There are also counterexamples to the claim about negation, like example (25), quoted from Groenendijk and Stokhof 1991:91.

(25) It is not true that John doesn't own a car. It is red, and it is parked in front of his house.

An example of anaphoric dependence between disjuncts is (26), attributed to Partee.

(26) Either there's no bathroom in this house, or it is in a strange place.

These last two sentences should be separated from the modal subordination cases; no modal verbs are involved. What seems to make the anaphoric interpretation viable in example (25) is the presence of a *second* negation; in example (26) the anaphoric pronoun seems licensed by the negation in the first disjunct. In the next chapter it is argued that the problems with sentences like (25) and (26) can be solved at one fell swoop. A modification of DRT is presented which does exactly that.

3

Negation and Disjunction in DRT

3.1 Introduction

Standard Discourse Representation Theory (DRT) predicts that an indefinite NP cannot antecede an anaphoric element if the NP is, but the anaphoric element is not, within the scope of a negation; the theory also predicts that no anaphoric links are possible between the two parts of a disjunction. However, it is well-known that these predictions meet with counterexamples. In particular, anaphora is often possible if a double negation intervenes between antecedent and anaphoric element, and also if the antecedent occurs in the first part of a disjunction and within the scope of a negation, and the anaphoric element is in the second part of the same disjunction. These recalcitrant phenomena are related and it will be shown that a solution to the double negation problem will also provide us with a solution to the disjunction problem. In this chapter we shall look at these matters from a DRT perspective. An extension of standard DRT will be offered (called *Double Negation* DRT) which validates the law of double negation. An adaptation of the standard DRT construction algorithm which transforms texts into Discourse Representation Structures (DRSs) is sketched and it is shown that the problems with negation and disjunction that led to the definition of our new version of DRT are properly dealt with in this theory.

3.2 Two Problems for DRT, and a Reduction

3.2.1 The Double Negation Problem

In a now classic paper (Karttunen 1976) Karttunen noted that while a discourse referent cannot outlive a single negation or a single verb with an inherently negative implication (such as *fail, neglect* or *forget*) it will not be blocked by a double negation. While in (1) the pronoun *it* cannot be interpreted as dependent on *a question* and in (2) the pronoun cannot depend on *an answer*, the definite in (3) may depend on the preceding indefinite and the *it* in (4) can be taken to refer to *an umbrella*. The anaphoric pronouns in (5) can likewise be interpreted as depending on the indefinite that precedes them, even though the latter is within the scope of two negations.[1]

(1) Bill didn't dare to ask a question. # The lecturer answered it.

(2) John failed to find an answer. #It was wrong.

(3) John didn't fail to find an answer. The answer was even right.

(4) John didn't remember not to bring an umbrella, although we had no room for it.

(5) It is not true that John didn't bring an umbrella. It was purple and it stood in the hallway.

Various authors[2] have pointed out that examples such as (3), (4) and (5) are a problem for the dynamic theories of discourse discussed in chapter 2. These theories correctly predict negation to be a plug with respect to anaphoric binding and thus fit the facts in (1) and (2),[3] but they also incorrectly predict a double negation to be a double plug, not a plug unplugged as the facts in (3)-(5) would suggest. In DRT for example, the discourse referent that is connected to *an umbrella* in the first sentence of (5) will land up in a DRS that is twice embedded to the main DRS and that will thus not be accessible for future anaphoric reference. An application of the standard DRT construction algorithm to the first sentence of (5) gives (DRS 1) as an output, while it is the simpler (DRS 2) that would give the right predictions here. In the latter, but not in the former, the discourse referent y, which is connected to *an umbrella*, will be accessible from conditions in the main DRS.

---

[1]Examples (1) - (4) are taken form Karttunen's original paper (Karttunen 1976:369-370). Karttunen marks the respective second sentences of (1) and (2) with a *, we follow the convention from the introduction to indicate semantic markedness with #.

[2]Chierchia 1992, Groenendijk and Stokhof 1991, Kamp and Reyle 1993.

[3]Double negations in standard English are one of out two main concerns in this chapter. Negative verbs allow for easy construction of natural examples of double negations, where it is assumed that negative verbs such as *fail* and *forget* should be analyzed with the help of a negation (thus we might treat *fail* as *not succeed*, see Karttunen and Peters 1979:52 for a similar analysis). However, such an analysis also introduces problems which are orthogonal to our present interests (for instance, *forget* and *deny* are verbs of propositional attitudes). Therefore, in the rest of this chapter we shall stick to straightforward examples such as the one in (5).

(drs 1)

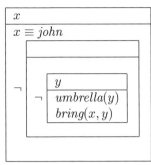

(drs 2)

x, y
$x \equiv john$
$umbrella(y)$
$bring(x, y)$

Other formulations of the dynamic perspective are confronted with essentially the same difficulty. In DPL, for example, the negation of a formula φ will act as a *test*, irrespective of the internal structure of φ, and so, since the first clause of (5) is of the form $\neg\varphi$, the anaphoric link between *an umbrella* and *it* is predicted to be impossible. In FCS, to mention a second example, we have that the first sentence in (5) does not succeed in extending the domain of the current file. The interpretation of a negation only eliminates assignments; there are no extensions with 'new cards'. Still a new card would be needed for *an umbrella* in order to establish the link between antecedent and anaphoric pronoun. In this chapter we will discuss the double negation problem (and the disjunction problem — see below) from a DRT perspective, but the reader will have no difficulty in translating our proposed solutions to her favorite dynamic semantic framework.

Before we turn to the disjunction problem, let us briefly point out one category of *prima facie* counterexamples to the double negation rule, which is formed by cases where the only plugs for anaphoric reference intervening between a possible antecedent and an anaphoric element are indeed two negations, but where the two still do not conspire to form an authentic double negation because they sandwich other material. We have in mind examples like (6), whose first sentence should be represented as (drs 3). Clearly this is as much a case of double negation as the sequence $\neg\exists x\neg$ is a case of double negation in Predicate Logic.

(6) No man didn't bring an umbrella. # It was purple and it stood in the hallway.

(DRS 3)

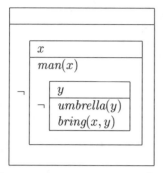

Since such apparent counterexamples on closer examination turn out to be no counterexamples at all, it seems we can take it as a general rule that as far as truth conditions and the possibility of anaphora are concerned double negations in standard English behave as if no negation at all were present.

3.2.2 The Disjunction Problem

The double negation problem seems to be related to another problem that is also generally thought to be a hard nut for DRT and related theories. In example (7) the pronoun *it* is naturally linked to *no bathroom*, while DRT and other dynamic theories predict no antecedent in one part of a disjunction to be accessible for a pronoun in the other part. If we apply the standard construction rules to this sentence we get (DRS 4), but in this DRS the pronoun *it* cannot be resolved as the referent x.

(7)   Either there's no bathroom in this house, or it's in a funny place.[4]

(DRS 4)

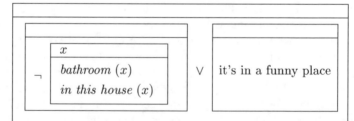

Kamp and Reyle 1993[5] remark that it is in fact the presence of a negative element in the first disjunct which seems to license the anaphora in (7), even though negations in themselves usually block the possib-

---

[4]Roberts 1987 attributes this sentence to Barbara Partee. In Evans 1977 we find *Either John does not own a donkey, or he keeps it very quiet.*

[5]For a discussion of the issue of accessibility in disjunctions see section 2.3.1 (pages 185-190) of this work. See also Asher and Wada 1989:340.

ility of linking. If there is no such negative element, as in (8) from Kamp and Reyle 1993, coreference is impossible.

(8)   # Jones owns a car or he hides it.[6]

A second observation made by Kamp & Reyle is that sentences of the form *A or B* can in general be paraphrased as *A or otherwise B* and this leads to a proposal to let the DRT construction algorithm provide for the 'other case'. In (8) the 'other case' is the case where Jones does not own a car, and thus a revised form of the construction algorithm adds a condition to this effect to the second disjunct of the DRS for the sentence. The result is shown in (DRS 5).

(DRS 5)

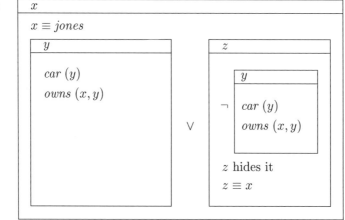

Here, since *it* cannot be resolved as y, the revised construction algorithm does not lead to predictions different from the original one, but as soon as we turn to sentences like (7) we see that Kamp & Reyle's revision pays off. The 'other case' to be considered now is the case where a bathroom is present, and if this information is added to that of the second disjunct we get (DRS 6) at a crucial stage of the DRS construction. This time it is possible to resolve *it* as x and the link between anaphor and antecedent can be established.

---

[6]Roberts 1989 gives the following example (attributed to Berman):

   Either there's a bathroom on the first floor, or it's on the second floor.

We believe that in examples such as this one the indefinite noun phrase gets a wide scope, specific reading. Intuitively the speaker is committed to the existence of a bathroom. Note that the indefinite allows for subsequent anaphoric reference: we can continue with *I keep forgetting exactly where it is, but it's easy to find*, another sign that the indefinite has wide scope here.

(DRS 6)

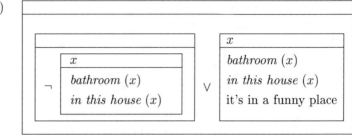

Kamp & Reyle's treatment of bathroom-sentences can perhaps be criticized for not being entirely precise, in the sense that their new construction rule does not seem to prescribe exactly what material is to be added to the second disjunct. Suppose that we take the rule to be that in construing the DRS for a disjunction we should add the negation of the DRS for the first disjunct as a condition to the DRS for the second disjunct (call this Rule A). Then the DRS associated with (8) would indeed be (DRS 5), but the DRS for (7) would be (DRS 7) instead of (DRS 6): we get a double negation where we want no negation at all.[7]

(DRS 7)

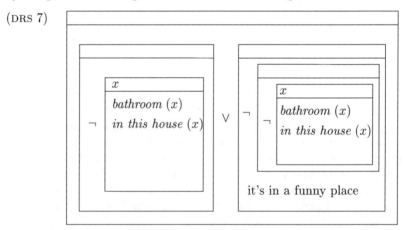

Notice that there is structural similarity between the problem how to get from (DRS 7) to (DRS 6) and our previous problem how to obtain (DRS 2) from (DRS 1). In both cases we should like to be able to erase the double negation.

---

[7]The reader may note that $\Phi \vee [\vec{x} \mid \vec{\varphi}]$ and $\Phi \vee [\vec{x} \mid \neg\Phi, \vec{\varphi}]$ are equivalent (provided none of $\vec{x}$ occurs free in Φ), and hence that (DRS 4) and (DRS 7) are equivalent as well. This means that the revised construction rule A would give an output that is not semantically different from the output we get from the standard DRT construction rules.

So, why not define a rule which allows us to do away with double negations? First of all notice that an explicit rule to this effect would be very much ad hoc and would be quite unlike all other DRT construction rules. It would have the useful property of being able to make certain referents accessible to certain pronouns (the referent x is accessible from *it* in (DRS 6) but not in (DRS 7)) but this very property would also make it be theoretically suspicious for not being meaning preserving. If meanings determine context change potentials, as the dynamic perspective has it, then a rule to erase double negations that would change (DRS 1) into (DRS 2) (and (DRS 7) into (DRS 6)) cannot be meaning preserving since (DRS 1) gives a context which does not allow reference to y while (DRS 2) gives one which does. Hence, such a rule would only make sense if the semantics of DRT is altered in such a way that wiping out double negations can be done in a meaning preserving way. Notice also that such an explicit, syntactic rule would result in loss of explanatory power. *John didn't fail to find an answer* would still entail *John found an answer*, but only because the rule turns the representation of the premiss into the representation of the conclusion by stipulation. There is another difficulty with Kamp & Reyle's proposed solution to the problem of bathroom-sentences: (DRS 6) does not seem to have the truth conditions that (7) has. Suppose there are in fact two bathrooms in the house, one of which is, and one of which is not in a strange place; then (7) is not true according to our intuitions, but (DRS 6) *is* true since its second disjunct can be verified. We therefore turn to an earlier proposal from Roberts 1987, who renders (7) as (DRS 8).

(DRS 8)

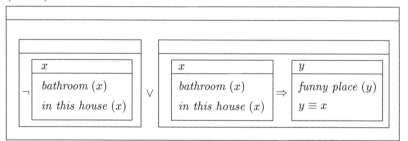

The idea here is that the material under the negation in the first disjunct is accommodated to provide an antecedent to the second disjunct. Since the first disjunct gives a negative answer to the question whether there is a bathroom in the house, it is natural to interpret the second disjunct as pertaining to the possibility that there is one. It is easy to see that $[\,|\neg\Phi]\vee[\,|\,\Phi\Rightarrow\Psi]$ is equivalent with $\Phi\Rightarrow\Psi$, and hence that Roberts'

(DRS 8) is equivalent with the simpler (DRS 9). And indeed, we feel that this is correct, since intuitively example (7) is equivalent to example (9).

(DRS 9)

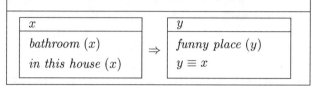

(9)   If there is a bathroom in this house, it's in a funny place.

How can we revise the DRT construction algorithm so that it gives (DRS 9) instead of (DRS 4) as an output for (7)? Here again we see that if we could but solve the double negation problem we would have a solution to the disjunction problem as well. For suppose that we would revise the construction algorithm so that at any time that a sentence disjunction *A or B* is encountered a condition of the form (DRS 10) (instead of the equivalent $\boxed{\Phi}$ ∨ $\boxed{\Psi}$) would be added to the current DRS (call this rule B);[8] then (DRS 11) would be the output for (8), but for (7) we would obtain (DRS 12).[9]

(DRS 10) $\boxed{\neg \boxed{\Phi}} \Rightarrow \boxed{\Psi}$

(DRS 11)

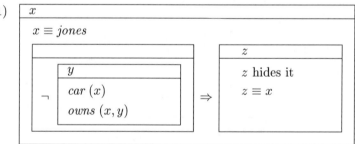

---

[8] Below we shall give a slightly different analysis of disjunctions. We shall not change the DRS construction rule for disjunctions, but the semantics for the symbol ∨ will be altered in such a way that *A or B* will be semantically equivalent to *if not A then B*. In an earlier version of Double Negation DRT our analysis was based on Kamp & Reyle's analysis plus our solution to the double negation problem. We wish to thank Paul Dekker for insisting that the equivalence between *A or B* and *if not A then B* should be retained.

[9] Notice that since [| ¬Φ] ⇒ Ψ is equivalent with Φ ∨ Ψ, adopting rule B would have no semantic effects either, compare footnote 7.

(drs 12)

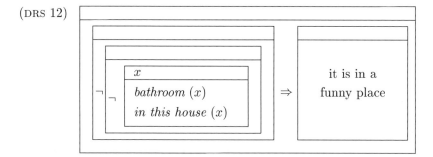

The first of these is indeed correct in the sense that the anaphoric link is predicted to be impossible, but in the second we have a double negation again where no negation at all is wanted. The problem how to get from (drs 12) to (drs 9) is formally similar to the problem how to get from (drs 7) to (drs 6) or indeed to the question how to get (drs 2) from (drs 1). In this sense it can be said that the disjunction problem reduces to the double negation problem.

It thus seems that if we can revise the drt language by adding a new negation which obeys the law of double negation (which allows for canceling double negations), we may not only solve the problems that we have encountered with umbrella-sentences, but we may also be able to deal with bathroom-sentences. An attempt to carry out such a revision will be made in the next section.

But before we turn to this revision, we would like to stress the following: it is our intention to solve the negation and the disjunction problem by sticking as close as possible to standard drt. This means that things which are problematic for drt as such, and are not directly related to double negations, will be problematic for our version of drt as well. For example, we predict that (4) is equivalent with (10).

(10) John remembered to bring an umbrella, although we had no room for it.

It has been pointed out (by Geurts 1997) that there is still a problem with this example, as it needs to be explained how a discourse entity that is introduced within the complement of an attitude verb can become accessible for subsequent anaphoric reference. However, this is a general problem for drt, for our version as well as for standard drt. While we do see ways for dealing with this question, we feel that the matter falls outside the scope of this chapter.

3.3   Double Negation DRT

The basic problem with negation in standard DRT is that it is not a flip-flop operation like its cousin in ordinary logic. Even the very DRT syntax of negation discourages flip-flop behaviour: if Φ is a DRS, $\neg\Phi$ is a condition and there is no comparable operator which takes us from conditions to DRSs again. In our variant of DRT —*Double Negation* DRT— we remedy this and let the negation $\sim\Phi$ of a DRS Φ itself be a DRS. This is our only addition and we have removed the original negation, so that the syntax of Double Negation DRT looks as follows.

Definition 1 (Double Negation DRT syntax)

1. If R is an n-ary predicate and $t_1, \ldots, t_n$ are terms, then $R(t_1, \ldots, t_n)$ is a condition.

2. If t_1 and t_2 are terms, then $t_1 \equiv t_2$ is a condition.

3. If Φ and Ψ are DRSs, then $(\Phi \Rightarrow \Psi)$ and $(\Phi \vee \Psi)$ are conditions.

4. If $x_1, \ldots, x_n$ $(n \geq 0)$ are variables and $\varphi_1, \ldots, \varphi_m$ $(m \geq 0)$ are conditions, then $[x_1, \ldots, x_n \mid \varphi_1, \ldots, \varphi_m]$ is a DRS.

5. If Φ and Ψ are DRSs, then $(\Phi \, ; \Psi)$ and $\sim\Phi$ are DRSs.

We interpret this language by borrowing a technique from partial logic. Conditions will have an extension which consists of a set of finite assignments, as in standard DRT (see the previous chapter), but with each DRS Φ *two* relations between assignments will be associated, its positive extension $[\![\Phi]\!]^+$ and its negative extension $[\![\Phi]\!]^-$. In the definition below we give the semantics of Double Negation DRT. The idea is that all conditions, except those of the form $\Phi \vee \Psi$, have a semantics that does not differ from the one given in chapter 2 and that the semantics of $\Phi \vee \Psi$ is no different from that of $\sim\Phi \Rightarrow \Psi$.[10] The positive extension of a non-negated DRS Φ is as before, but its negative extension is defined to be equal to the extension of $[\, \mid \neg\Phi]$ in standard DRT. Negation is now indeed a flip-flop operator and switches between positive and negative extensions. Let $M = \langle D, I \rangle$ be a standard first-order model, and let F be the set of finite assignments (mapping finite subsets of Var to D), with Λ as the 'empty' assignment ($\mathsf{Dom}(\Lambda) = \emptyset$). Terms are interpreted in the usual DRT way. That is: $[\![t]\!]_{M,g} = g(t)$, if $t \in$ Var and $t \in \mathsf{Dom}(g)$, and $[\![t]\!]_{M,g} = I(t)$, if $t \in$ Con. If $g(x)$ is not defined, then neither is $[\![x]\!]_{M,g}$. Define $[\![\varphi]\!]_M \subseteq F$ for conditions φ and $[\![\Phi]\!]^+_M \subseteq F^2$ and $[\![\Phi]\!]^-_M \subseteq F^2$ for DRSs Φ as follows (again, dropping subscripts when this can be done without creating confusion).

---

[10]This means that disjunction is treated asymmetrically, just as implication. This asymmetry is not forced upon us however. See below for some discussion.

Definition 2 (Double Negation DRT semantics)

1. $[\![R(t_1,\ldots,t_n)]\!] = \{g \mid [\![t_i]\!]_g \text{ defined } \& \langle [\![t_1]\!]_g,\ldots,[\![t_n]\!]_g \rangle \in I(R)\}$
   $(1 \leq i \leq n)$

2. $[\![t_1 \equiv t_2]\!] = \{g \mid [\![t_1]\!]_g, [\![t_2]\!]_g \text{ defined } \& \; [\![t_1]\!]_g = [\![t_2]\!]_g\}$

3. $[\![\Phi \Rightarrow \Psi]\!] = \{g \mid \forall h(\langle g,h \rangle \in [\![\Phi]\!]^+ \Rightarrow \exists k \langle h,k \rangle \in [\![\Psi]\!]^+)\}$

4. $[\![\Phi \vee \Psi]\!] = \{g \mid \forall h(\langle g,h \rangle \in [\![\Phi]\!]^- \Rightarrow \exists k \langle h,k \rangle \in [\![\Psi]\!]^+)\}$

5. $[\![[\vec{x} \mid \varphi_1,\ldots,\varphi_m]]\!]^+ = \{\langle g,h \rangle \mid g\{\vec{x}\}h \; \& \; h \in ([\![\varphi_1]\!] \cap \ldots \cap [\![\varphi_m]\!])\}$
   $[\![[\vec{x} \mid \varphi_1,\ldots,\varphi_m]]\!]^- = \{\langle g,g \rangle \mid \neg \exists h(g\{\vec{x}\}h \; \& \; h \in ([\![\varphi_1]\!] \cap \ldots \cap [\![\varphi_m]\!]))\}$

6. $[\![\Phi \, ; \Psi]\!]^+ = \{\langle g,h \rangle \mid \exists k(\langle g,k \rangle \in [\![\Phi]\!]^+ \; \& \; \langle k,h \rangle \in [\![\Psi]\!]^+)\}$
   $[\![\Phi \, ; \Psi]\!]^- = \{\langle g,g \rangle \mid \neg \exists k(\langle g,k \rangle \in [\![\Phi]\!]^+ \; \& \; \exists h \langle k,h \rangle \in [\![\Psi]\!]^+)\}$

7. $[\![\sim\Phi]\!]^+ = [\![\Phi]\!]^-$
   $[\![\sim\Phi]\!]^- = [\![\Phi]\!]^+$

In this definition $g\{\vec{x}\}h$ as before abbreviates $\mathsf{Dom}(h) = \mathsf{Dom}(g) \cup \{\vec{x}\}$ $\& \; \forall y \in \mathsf{Dom}(g) : g(y) = h(y)$. Two conditions are said to be equivalent iff their extensions coincide. DRSs Φ and Ψ are equivalent iff in all models M $[\![\Phi]\!]_M^+ = [\![\Psi]\!]_M^+$ and $[\![\Phi]\!]_M^- = [\![\Psi]\!]_M^-$. It is immediate that $\sim\sim\Phi$ is equivalent with Φ, whence the name *Double Negation* DRT. In the definition of accessibility a little care must be taken for the following reason. Clearly, in $[x \mid man(x)] \, ; [y \mid umbrella(y), owns(x,y)]$ the first occurrence of x should be accessible to the condition $owns(x,y)$. (Note that the DRS is equivalent to $[x,y \mid man(x), umbrella(y), owns(x,y)]$.) But in $\sim[x \mid man(x)] \, ; [y \mid umbrella(y), owns(x,y)]$ this should not be the case, yet in $\sim\sim[x \mid man(x)] \, ; [y \mid umbrella(y), owns(x,y)]$ the accessibility should be restored again. To get this right we do not only define the set of active discourse referents of a given DRS this time, we also define its set of passive discourse referents. The following clauses do the job.

Definition 3 (Active and Passive DRs)

1. $\mathsf{ADR}([x_1,\ldots,x_n \mid \varphi_1,\ldots,\varphi_m]) = \{x_1,\ldots,x_n\}$
   $\mathsf{PDR}([x_1,\ldots,x_n \mid \varphi_1,\ldots,\varphi_m]) = \emptyset$

2. $\mathsf{ADR}(\Phi \, ; \Psi) = \mathsf{ADR}(\Phi) \cup \mathsf{ADR}(\Psi)$
   $\mathsf{PDR}(\Phi \, ; \Psi) = \emptyset$

3. $\mathsf{ADR}(\sim\Phi) = \mathsf{PDR}(\Phi)$
   $\mathsf{PDR}(\sim\Phi) = \mathsf{ADR}(\Phi)$

Accessibility can now be defined as follows. Initially, we set $\text{ACC}(\Phi') = \emptyset$, where Φ' is the main DRS, and compute the accessible discourse referents of subDRSs and subconditions with the help of the following rules. (See section 2.2.2 for discussion.)

Definition 4 (Accessibility)

1. If $\text{ACC}(\Phi \Rightarrow \Psi) = X$, then $\text{ACC}(\Phi) = X$ and $\text{ACC}(\Psi) = X \cup \text{ADR}(\Phi)$.

2. If $\text{ACC}(\Phi \vee \Psi) = X$, then $\text{ACC}(\Phi) = X$ and $\text{ACC}(\Psi) = X \cup \text{PDR}(\Phi)$.

3. If $\text{ACC}([x_1, \ldots, x_n \mid \varphi_1, \ldots, \varphi_m]) = X$, then $\text{ACC}(\varphi_i) = X \cup \{x_1, \ldots, x_n\}$, for $1 \leq i \leq m$.

4. If $\text{ACC}(\Phi \,;\, \Psi) = X$, then $\text{ACC}(\Phi) = X$ and $\text{ACC}(\Psi) = X \cup \text{ADR}(\Phi)$.

5. If $\text{ACC}(\sim\Phi) = X$, then $\text{ACC}(\Phi) = X$.

Notice that now there is an even stronger connection with the Karttunen-style calculation of local contexts: see chapter 2, definition 10. Again, an occurrence of x in an atomic condition φ in Φ is said to be *free* in Φ iff $x \notin \text{ACC}(\varphi)$. An occurrence of x in an atomic condition φ in a condition ψ is free in ψ iff it is *free* in $[\,\mid \psi]$. A DRS Φ is *proper* iff no occurrence of a discourse referent in Φ is free in Φ. A DRS Φ is supported in a model M with respect to an assignment g $(M, g \models \Phi)$ iff $\exists h \langle g, h \rangle \in [\![\Phi]\!]^+_M$, and rejected in M with respect to g $(M, g =\!\mid \Phi)$ iff $\exists h \langle g, h \rangle \in [\![\Phi]\!]^-_M$. Truth and falsity are defined as follows. Let Φ be a proper DRSs, then

Definition 5 (Truth and falsity)

1. Φ is true in a model M iff $M, \Lambda \models \Phi$
2. Φ is false in a model M iff $M, \Lambda =\!\mid \Phi$

It is easily seen that every proper DRS is either true or false, and that no proper DRS is both true and false. The following fact is of practical importance (compare fact 1 in chapter 2).

Fact 1 *(Merging Lemma)*
$[\vec{x} \mid \vec{\varphi}] \,;\, [\vec{y} \mid \vec{\gamma}]$ *is equivalent with* $[\vec{x}, \vec{y} \mid \vec{\varphi}, \vec{\gamma}]$,
provided no referent in $\vec{y}$ *is free in any of* $\vec{\varphi}$.

3.4 Applications

Since we want to show in this section how our new version of DRT deals with the kind of sentences that we have encountered in the second section, we must sketch how its construction algorithm works. Fortunately we can borrow many rules from the standard approach. The basic set-up is as follows (compare the following rule for the global structure of DRS construction with that of Kamp and Reyle 1993:86).[11]

> ## Revised Construction Algorithm
>
> *Input*: a discourse $S_1, \ldots, S_n$
>
> the empty DRS $\Phi_0 = \Box$
>
> *For* $i = 1$ *to* n *do*:
>
> (i)   Let $\Phi_i^* = \Phi_{i-1}$; $\boxed{S_i}$. Go to (ii).
>
> (ii)   Keep on applying construction rules to each reducible condition of Φ_i^* until a DRS Φ_i is obtained that only contains irreducible conditions.

Applying one step of this algorithm to (5), reprinted as (11) below, gives (DRS 13) as an output.

(11) It is not true that John didn't bring an umbrella. It was purple and it stood in the hallway.

(DRS 13) $\Box$; $\boxed{\text{It is not true that John didn't bring an umbrella.}}$

In (DRS 13) we encounter a negation and a proper name. For these we have construction rules that are slightly different from their standard variants. They are formulated as follows.

> ## Negation Rule
>
> Upon encountering any form of linguistic negation, prefix the DRS that the condition containing the negation belongs to with $\sim$ and remove the linguistic negation

> ## Proper Name Rule
>
> Upon encountering a proper name α, replace α with a new discourse referent x and prefix the entire DRS under construction
>
> with $\begin{array}{|c|} \hline x \\ \hline x \equiv \alpha \\ \hline \end{array}$

This exhausts our changes to the construction algorithm. An application of the negation rule to (DRS 13) gives (DRS 14) and a subsequent application of the proper name rule (DRS 15). In the latter we may (if

---

[11] A more precise account would have the *syntactic analysis* of S_i as the contents of the new box. Compare Kamp and Reyle 1993.

we wish) merge $[x \mid john \equiv x]$ and the empty box $[\,\mid\,]$ to $[x \mid john \equiv x]$, according to the Merging Lemma of the previous section. This gives (DRS 16) and with a second application of the negation rule we obtain (DRS 17).

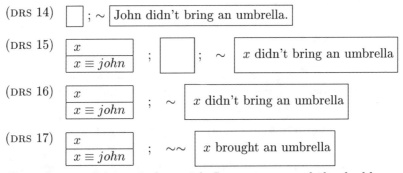

(DRS 14) $\Box$; $\sim$ | John didn't bring an umbrella. |

(DRS 15)
x
$x \equiv john$
; $\Box$; $\sim$ | x didn't bring an umbrella |

(DRS 16)
x
$x \equiv john$
; $\sim$ | x didn't bring an umbrella |

(DRS 17)
x
$x \equiv john$
; $\sim\sim$ | x brought an umbrella |

Given that $\sim\sim\Phi$ is equivalent with Φ, we may cancel the double negation, with (DRS 18) as a result. An application of the standard DRT construction rule for indefinites brings us to (DRS 19). Now the Merging Lemma can be applied, so that we get (DRS 20).

(DRS 18)
x
$x \equiv john$
; | x brought an umbrella |

(DRS 19)
x
$x \equiv john$
;
y
$umbrella(y)$
$bring(x, y)$

(DRS 20)
x, y
$x \equiv john$
$umbrella(y)$
$bring(x, y)$

Since there are no more reducible conditions now, the Revised Construction Algorithm prescribes attaching a new box with the second sentence of our discourse in it. The result is given in (DRS 21). Clearly, since y is accessible from this new condition, both occurrences of *it* can be resolved as y.

(DRS 21)
x, y
$x \equiv john$
$umbrella(y)$
$bring(x, y)$
;
| It was purple and it stood in the hallway |

This shows that our version of DRT treats double negations as holes for anaphora. That it treats single negations as plugs can be illustrated from the treatment of (12). Notice that in this respect our negation is different from the *dynamic* negations considered in Groenendijk and Stokhof 1990, Dekker 1993b and Van den Berg 1993. While these negations correctly predict that a double negation does not block anaphora, they also predict that a single negation does not.

Since the only difference between the first sentence of (11) and that of (12) is that the latter lacks a negation, it is obvious that the construction algorithm outputs (DRS 22) instead of (DRS 19) for this sentence. This DRS can no further be reduced and if the second sentence of (12) is added, as in (DRS 23), we find that the two occurrences of *it* cannot be resolved as y since the latter referent is not accessible.

(12) John didn't bring an umbrella. # It was purple and it stood in the hallway.

(DRS 22)

x
$x \equiv john$

$;\quad \sim$

y
$umbrella(y)$
$bring(x, y)$

(DRS 23)

x
$x \equiv john$

$;\sim$

y
$umbrella(y)$
$bring(x, y)$

$;$

It was purple and it stood in the hallway

This brings us to the treatment of bathroom-sentences. Supposing that the construction algorithm assigns (DRS 24) to (7) (here reprinted as (13)), we see that these sentences no longer pose a problem. Since x is an active discourse referent of $[x \mid bathroom(x), in\ this\ house(x)]$, it is a passive discourse referent of its negation. This means that it will be accessible from the second disjunct, so that we can resolve *it* as x. The result is shown in (DRS 25). Note that this last DRS is equivalent to (DRS 9) (reprinted as (DRS 26)), so that (13) is predicted to be equivalent with (14).

(13) Either there's no bathroom in this house, or it's in a funny place.

(DRS 24)

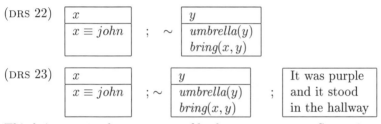

(DRS 25)

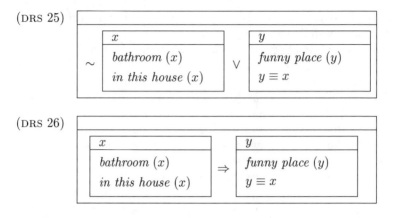

(DRS 26)

(14) If there's a bathroom in this house, it's in a funny place.

As we already noted, the treatment of disjunction is asymmetric. It has been argued that disjunction should be treated in a symmetric way, especially in light of examples such as the following.

(15) Either it's in a funny place, or there is no bathroom in this house.

On the present proposal it is predicted that the pronoun *it* cannot dependent on *no bathroom*, and we believe that this is correct since example (15) is rather strange if no previous mention of a bathroom has occurred. Nevertheless, let us note that the following semantics for disjunction treats both disjuncts in the same, symmetric way, predicting that (15) and (13) are equivalent.[12]

Definition 6 (Symmetric disjunction)

$$[\![\Phi \vee \Psi]\!] = \{g \mid \forall h(\langle g, h\rangle \in [\![\Phi]\!]^- \Rightarrow \exists k\langle h, k\rangle \in [\![\Psi]\!]^+) \text{ or }$$
$$\forall h(\langle g, h\rangle \in [\![\Psi]\!]^- \Rightarrow \exists k\langle h, k\rangle \in [\![\Phi]\!]^+)\}$$

3.5   The Relation with Standard DRT

In this chapter we have used a representation language that extends the familiar DRT language and for some discourses the DRS that we obtain after applying the Revised Construction Algorithm will not be equivalent to a DRS of the old language. Thus while the DRS for the first sentence of (11) turned out to be part of the old language, the DRS in (DRS 22) could not be so reduced. Theoretically there is no problem here, but for the sake of simplicity and comparison with the standard DRT set-up,

---

[12]See Karttunen 1973 for discussion on the symmetric/asymmetric debate.

we may nevertheless want to use the old forms. To this end we may reintroduce the 'old' DRT negation into the new language.[13]

Definition 7 (Standard Negation)

    syntax   If Φ is a DRS, then $\neg\Phi$ is a condition.

    semantics $[\![\neg\Phi]\!] = \{g \mid \neg\exists h\langle g, h\rangle \in [\![\Phi]\!]^+\}$

The notion of accessibility is extended in the obvious way. We now have the following useful fact which has a simple proof. Let Ψ be an arbitrary atomic DRS $[\vec{x} \mid \vec{\varphi}\,]$.

Fact 2 *(Single Negation Lemma)*

$\Phi \,;\sim\!\Psi$	*is equivalent with*	$\Phi \,; [\,\mid \neg\Psi]$
$\sim\!\Psi \,; \Phi$	*is equivalent with*	$[\,\mid \neg\Psi] \,; \Phi$
$\Phi \Rightarrow \sim\!\Psi$	*is equivalent with*	$\Phi \Rightarrow [\,\mid \neg\Psi]$
$\sim\!\Psi \Rightarrow \Phi$	*is equivalent with*	$[\,\mid \neg\Psi] \Rightarrow \Phi$

Since we can cancel double negations, since we can trade disjunctions for implications via the equivalence between $\Phi \vee \Psi$ and $\sim\!\Phi \Rightarrow \Psi$ and in virtue of the properties of the construction algorithm, we can now reduce our new DRSs to the old ones. The procedure is illustrated for (DRS 22) below. To this DRS the Single Negation Lemma applies, and we get (DRS 27). A last application of the Merging Lemma results in (DRS 28), the form that we are used to associate with the first sentence of (12).

(DRS 27)

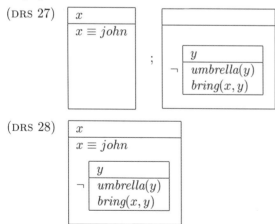

(DRS 28)

Another way to relate our proposal to standard DRT is to define a WEP-calculus for Double Negation DRT, as we did for DRT in chapter 2, section

---

[13]In fact, the 'old' negation is definable in terms of Double Negation DRT. Let $\top$ abbreviate $[\,\mid c \equiv c]$, for some $c \in$ Con (which by assumption is non-empty), and let $\bot$ abbreviate $\sim\!\top$, then $\neg\Phi$ abbreviates $\Phi \Rightarrow \bot$.

2.2.5. Since we have split up the interpretation for DRSs into positive and negative extensions, we also have to distinguish between positive and negative WEPs. We define $\mathrm{WEP}^+(\Phi, \chi)$ and $\mathrm{WEP}^-(\Phi, \chi)$, where Φ is a DRS and χ a PL formula. $\mathrm{WEP}^+(\Phi, \top)$ will be a PL formula which is true whenever Φ is true, and $\mathrm{WEP}^-(\Phi, \top)$ will be a PL formula which is true whenever Φ is false.[14]

Definition 8 (WEP-calculus)

1. $\mathrm{TR}(\varphi) = \varphi$, if φ atomic

2. $\mathrm{TR}(\Phi \Rightarrow \Psi) = \neg\mathrm{WEP}^+(\Phi, \neg\mathrm{WEP}^+(\Psi, \top))$

3. $\mathrm{TR}(\Phi \vee \Psi) = \neg\mathrm{WEP}^-(\Phi, \neg\mathrm{WEP}^+(\Psi, \top))$

4. $\mathrm{WEP}^+([\vec{x} \mid \varphi_1 \ldots \varphi_m], \chi) = \exists \vec{x}(\mathrm{TR}(\varphi_1) \wedge \ldots \wedge \mathrm{TR}(\varphi_m) \wedge \chi)$
   $\mathrm{WEP}^-([\vec{x} \mid \varphi_1 \ldots \varphi_m], \chi) = \neg\mathrm{WEP}^+([\vec{x} \mid \varphi_1 \ldots \varphi_m], \top) \wedge \chi$

5. $\mathrm{WEP}^+(\Phi \,;\, \Psi, \chi) = \mathrm{WEP}^+(\Phi, \mathrm{WEP}^+(\Psi, \chi))$
   $\mathrm{WEP}^-(\Phi \,;\, \Psi, \chi) = \neg\mathrm{WEP}^+(\Phi \,;\, \Psi, \top) \wedge \chi$

6. $\mathrm{WEP}^+(\sim\Phi, \chi) = \mathrm{WEP}^-(\Phi, \chi)$
   $\mathrm{WEP}^-(\sim\Phi, \chi) = \mathrm{WEP}^+(\Phi, \chi)$

This calculus relates the interpretation of Double Negation DRT in terms of total assignments (the interpretation achieved by letting g, h and k in definition 2 range over total assignments and replacing $g\{\vec{x}\}h$ with $g[\vec{x}]h$; see section 2.2.4 for discussion) to the Groenendijk & Stokhof version of PL given in definition 17 from chapter 2). In general, the following fact can be proven.

Fact 3
For all models M and assignments g:

1. $g \in [\![\mathrm{TR}(\varphi)]\!]_M^{\mathrm{PL}} \Leftrightarrow g \in [\![\varphi]\!]_M$

2. $g \in [\![\mathrm{WEP}^+(\Phi, \chi)]\!]_M^{\mathrm{PL}} \Leftrightarrow \exists h(\langle g, h \rangle \in [\![\Phi]\!]_M^+ \ \& \ h \in [\![\chi]\!]_M^{\mathrm{PL}})$
   $g \in [\![\mathrm{WEP}^-(\Phi, \chi)]\!]_M^{\mathrm{PL}} \Leftrightarrow \exists h(\langle g, h \rangle \in [\![\Phi]\!]_M^- \ \& \ h \in [\![\chi]\!]_M^{\mathrm{PL}})$

The proof of this fact is a straightforward extension/modification of the standard proof of fact 3 for DRT.[15] If we compare this calculus with the

---

[14]Warning: $\top$ does double duty. The $\top$ used here is the tautological PL formula, which should be contrasted with the $\top$ introduced in footnote 13 as an abbreviation of $[\,\mid c \equiv c]$.

[15]By way of example, here is one of the more interesting cases.

$g \in [\![\mathrm{WEP}^-([\vec{x} \mid \varphi_1, \ldots, \varphi_m], \chi)]\!]^{\mathrm{PL}} \Leftrightarrow$
$g \in [\![\neg\mathrm{WEP}^+([\vec{x} \mid \varphi_1, \ldots, \varphi_m], \top) \wedge \chi]\!]^{\mathrm{PL}} \Leftrightarrow$
$g \in [\![\neg\mathrm{WEP}^+([\vec{x} \mid \varphi_1, \ldots, \varphi_m], \top)]\!]^{\mathrm{PL}} \ \& \ g \in [\![\chi]\!]^{\mathrm{PL}} \Leftrightarrow$

one for standard DRT, we see a couple of unsurprising differences, in particular where disjunction and negation are involved. It is easily seen that the only differences with standard DRT arise when we encounter double negations or negated disjuncts, and that was exactly the intention.

3.6 Discussion: Uniqueness, Inference

In this chapter we have discussed two related problems for DRT (and for the other theories of anaphora in discourse discussed in the previous chapter), the negation problem and the disjunction problem, and we have offered a simultaneous solution for both of them in the framework of Double Negation DRT. The key-property of Double Negation DRT is that it supports the law of double negation, both with respect to truth-conditions and with respect to the possibilities of anaphoric take-up. One difference with the 'dynamic' negations proposed by Groenendijk and Stokhof 1990, Dekker 1993b and Van den Berg 1993 is that in Double Negation DRT a *single* negation still acts as a plug for anaphoric binding. Interestingly, the resulting notion of accessibility for Double Negation DRT is very similar to the Karttunen-style calculation of local contexts for presupposition satisfaction (see chapter 2, definition 10). In chapter 6 we will discuss an extension of Double Negation DRT, in which partiality will play a more substantial role. As we shall see, the treatment of negation and disjunction has some useful properties for the study of presuppositions.

As said in section 3.2, it was our intention to solve the negation and disjunction problem by sticking as close as possible to standard DRT, and we feel that this resulted in a simple and intuitive system. But this selfimposed restriction also has its limitations; what is problematic for standard DRT (except, of course, where double negations and disjunctions are concerned) remains problematic for Double Negation DRT. Consider the following examples:

(16) It's ludicrous to pretend that this palace doesn't have a bathroom. You showed it to me, remember? (Geurts 1997)

(17) It is possible that John does not own a donkey, but it is also possible that keeps it very quiet. (Van Rooy 1997b)

Standard DRT does not say anything about the interpretation of *ludicrous*

$g \in [\![\neg\exists\vec{x}(\mathsf{TR}(\varphi_1) \wedge \ldots \wedge \mathsf{TR}(\varphi_m) \wedge \top)]\!]^{\mathrm{PL}} \;\&\; g \in [\![\chi]\!]^{\mathrm{PL}} \Leftrightarrow$
$\neg\exists k(g[\vec{x}]k \;\&\; k \in ([\![\mathsf{TR}(\varphi_1)]\!]^{\mathrm{PL}} \cap \ldots \cap [\![\mathsf{TR}(\varphi_m)]\!]^{\mathrm{PL}})) \;\&\; g \in [\![\chi]\!]^{\mathrm{PL}} \Leftrightarrow [\mathrm{IH}]$
$\neg\exists k(g[\vec{x}]k \;\&\; k \in ([\![\varphi_1]\!]^{\mathrm{DRT}} \cap \ldots \cap [\![\varphi_m]\!]^{\mathrm{DRT}})) \;\&\; g \in [\![\chi]\!]^{\mathrm{PL}} \Leftrightarrow$
$\exists h(g = h \;\&\; \neg\exists k(g[\vec{x}]k \;\&\; k \in ([\![\varphi_1]\!]^{\mathrm{DRT}} \cap \ldots \cap [\![\varphi_m]\!]^{\mathrm{DRT}})) \;\&\; h \in [\![\chi]\!]^{\mathrm{PL}}) \Leftrightarrow$
$\exists h(\langle g, h \rangle \in [\![[\vec{x} \mid \varphi_1, \ldots, \varphi_m]]\!]^- \;\&\; h \in [\![\chi]\!]^{\mathrm{PL}})$

to pretend or *possible*, and neither does Double Negation DRT, even though these examples appear to be related to the umbrella- and the bathroom-examples. It does not seem too farfetched to interpret *ludicrous to pretend* as a negation, with the additional information that the speaker has particularly strong feelings about this, but we will not pursue this line any further here.

Another issue relates to uniqueness. Van Rooy 1997b argues that double negations in general act like a plug for anaphoric binding, *unless* it is understood between speaker and hearer that the indefinite in the scope of the double negation refers to a unique object. Consider:

(18) It is not the case that Louis does not own a book. It is lying on the table.

Van Rooy proposes to treat the anaphoric pronoun *it* in (18) as an E-type pronoun (Evans 1977, Heim 1990) standing for 'the book that Louis owns'. This means that according to Van Rooy's analysis this example is only correct if Louis has a unique book. But while Van Rooy 1997b treats the pronoun *it* in (18) as an E-type pronoun (and is thus committed to a uniqueness prediction for this example), he treats the pronoun *it* in an example like (19) as usual in discourse semantics.

(19) Louis has a book. It is lying on the table.

In other words: he seems to be committed to the claim that (18) is about the unique book owned by Louis, while (19) is not. However, we feel that (18) is just as good (or bad) as its counterpart (19), and this is in accordance with the analysis in Double Negation DRT. Kadmon 1990 claims that standard DRT is wrong here, and that pronouns (and definites in general) refer to the unique object satisfying the descriptive content. If Kadmon is right (which we feel is not the case, see chapter 7 for some discussion), then Double Negation DRT has precisely the same problem as standard DRT; after all, it is just a small variation of standard DRT.

It has been suggested, among others by Geurts 1997 that the double negation problem is essentially a problem of *inference*. One might claim, for example, that the relation between (DRS 1) and (DRS 2), and between (DRS 7) and (DRS 6) should be one of inference, and that this is what makes discourse referents introduced in the scope of two negations available for subsequent anaphoric reference. On such a proposal the construction algorithm would be extended with an inference mechanism (for instance as in Saurer 1993), in such a way that drawing conclusions is an admissable processing rule. And the rule of double negations would be a prima example. As noted by Saurer, the main problem for such an approach is to restrict overgeneration. Consider Partee's 'marble' sentences:

(20) a. I dropped ten marbles and found only nine of them. # It is probably under the sofa.
  b. I dropped ten marbles and found all of them, except for one. It is probably under the sofa.

On a natural account of inference the first sentence of (20.b) would follow from the first sentence of (20.a). So a theory which allows inference as an acceptable processing rule will have to explain the difference in acceptability between (20.a) and (20.b). Even though there may be ways in which such problems can be circumvented, it will be clear that this approach will be a significant departure from standard DRT. As a final remark, even if we would allow inferencing to erase double negations, then we *still* would want this to be a meaning preserving operation (compare the argument on page 71).

4

Presupposition and Partiality

In chapters 2 and 3 we have primarily been concerned with anaphora in discourse. Let us now focus on the second pillar of this book: presupposition.

4.1   Introduction

We begin with a bit of history. Presupposition has played a central role in the study of meaning from the early days. In Frege 1892 it is argued that 'names', to which Frege counts both proper names and definite descriptions, presuppose the existence of a unique object with the relevant properties; the name *Kepler* is presupposed to designate someone. Frege observes that presuppositions differ from assertions in that they are insensitive to negation. His example is (1), Frege 1892:131.

(1)   Kepler did not die in misery.

Frege remarks that the negation cannot get a grip on the presupposition; (1) presupposes that the name Kepler designates someone, just as its positive counterpart (*Kepler died in misery*) does. If the presupposition would be just as sensitive to negation as assertions are, then —Frege argues— we should be able to read (1) as *Kepler did not die in misery, or the name 'Kepler' has no reference*, which we cannot.

Frege was well aware of the fact that natural language sentences may contain presuppositions which are not satisfied, but he thought of this as a defect of natural language. Consider the most classic of classical examples (due to Russell 1905).

(2)   The present king of France is not bald.

This sentence presupposes the current existence of a king of France, a presupposition which was not true in the days of Frege and Russell, and has not been true ever since. In other words: the presupposition of (2) is not satisfied. Yet since Frege 'strives for truth', he 'fills up' the truth-value gap which might be created by presupposition-failure. In this way, his logical set-up (in Frege 1879) is able to obey *the principle of the excluded middle*, that is: every formula is either true or false.

Russell agreed with Frege that proper names and definite descriptions intend to refer to unique individuals, but he objected to the *ad-hoc* stuffing of the truth-value gap. Russell's main claim, put forward in Russell 1905, is that there is no such gap and that definite descriptions merely differ from 'non-presuppositional' phrases in their *scoping behavior*. The suggestions from Russell 1905 are formalized in the theory of descriptions (Whitehead and Russell 1927), in which definite descriptions are represented using so-called *iota terms*. Thus, (3) is the representation of (2).

(3) $\neg bald(\iota x.king\text{-}of(x, f))$

In fact, a iota term is nothing but an abbreviation, and the context it occurs in determines what it abbreviates. This is handled by the famous ∗14.01 from the theory of descriptions. Paraphrasing a little:

[∗14.01]: $\vartheta(\iota x \varphi)$ abbreviates $\exists x(\varphi \wedge \forall y(\{y/x\}\varphi \to x \equiv y) \wedge \vartheta(x))$

$\vartheta(t)$ represents a formula with an occurrence of a term t, where t has to occur free when it is a variable. $\{y/x\}\varphi$ is again the substitution of all free occurrences of x in φ for y. Unfolding the expression in (3) with the help of ∗14.01 gives us two options: we can either equate ϑ with $\neg bald$ or merely with $bald$. The first option leads to (4.a), the second to (4.b).

(4)   a. $\exists x(king\text{-}of(x, f) \wedge \forall y(king\text{-}of(y, f) \to y \equiv x) \wedge \neg bald(x))$
       b. $\neg \exists x(king\text{-}of(x, f) \wedge \forall y(king\text{-}of(y, f) \to y \equiv x) \wedge bald(x))$

In the first case the description has *primary* occurrence (as Russell 1905 puts it). This is the 'presuppositional' reading: it entails the existence of a (unique) present king of France. But according to Russell, example (2) has a second reading, given in (4.b), in which the description has *secondary* occurrence. This is a 'non-presuppositional' reading; it does not entail the existence of a French king. This reading is favored in an example such as (5).

(5)   The king of France is not bald, since there is no king of France.

If we do not want (5) to be contradictory, the description *the king of France* should not have a primary occurrence in the representation. Conjoining (4.a) with the proposition that there is no king of France will inevitably be a contradiction. On the other hand, conjoining it with (4.b) produces a perfectly contingent expression.

Strawson differed with Russell, and agreed with Frege that presupposition failure is a common phenomenon in natural language. But where Frege wanted to maintain bivalence, Strawson took the gap resulting from presupposition failure very seriously. In Strawson 1950 it is argued that a sentence containing a description which does not refer to an existing individual cannot be interpreted. It cannot be true and it cannot be false, the question of truth and falsity just doesn't arise. In general, this leads to the following semantic notion of presupposition.[1]

π is a *presupposition* of φ if, and only if,
whenever π is not true, φ is neither true nor false.

Put differently: π is a presupposition of φ if, and only if, whenever φ is either true or false, π is true. Karttunen and Peters 1979 observe that we can equate π with $\varphi \vee \neg\varphi$: φ is either true or false whenever $\varphi \vee \neg\varphi$ is true. This means that the Strawsonian notion of presupposition only makes sense when we leave the realm of classical logic. After all in classical logic the *principle of the excluded middle* is valid, which says that for any φ, the disjunction $\varphi \vee \neg\varphi$ is a tautology: it is *always* true. So if we want the Strawsonian concept of presupposition to have any body, we need to give up the principle of the excluded middle. This is what is done in the field of *partial logic*, and consequently there is a long tradition in using partial logics for the analysis of presuppositions. In all partial logics there is more amidst truth and falsity. For instance, there may be a *gap* between the two, as Quine 1952 puts it. But we can also consider this gap to be a *third* truth-value, call it the *neither* (true-nor-false)-value, and that is what we do here.

The development of partial logics for the treatment of presupposition reached its zenith in the seventies. Also around that time the first attempts were made to define compositional, Montagovian grammars for fragments of natural language in which presuppositions arise. The one presented in Karttunen and Peters 1979 is without a doubt the most important of those. It is still one of the most explicit and comprehensive studies of presuppositions around (and certainly the most reviled one). Its characteristic property is the strict separation of asserted and presupposed material. Every sentence is associated with *two* compositionally derived representations: one for the assertion and one for the presupposition of the sentence in question. As Karttunen and Peters note in a well-known note to their paper, this separation causes problems when presuppositions arise in the scope of quantifiers, as in the following example.

---

[1] In Soames 1989 it is argued that this approach to presuppositions follows Strawson in spirit, but not in letter. It is labeled 'semantic' since the concept of presupposition is defined purely in terms of truth and falsity conditions.

(6)   Somebody managed to succeed George V on the throne of England.

The rules of Karttunen and Peters 1979 derive two representation for this sentence: one saying that there is someone who succeeded George V (the assertion) and one saying that there is someone who found it difficult to succeed George V (the presupposition). The problem with this analysis is that it entirely fails to account for the odd flavor of example (6), the oddity being that the successor of George V (which was George VI) did not have any difficulty with his accession to the throne: it was his birthright. In other words, intuitively example (6) is a case of a failing presupposition. Nevertheless, the presupposition derived by Karttunen and Peters' system will not fail easily; there are lots of people for whom succeeding George V would be an enormous attainment.

One of the most influential attempts to repair this *binding problem* can be found in Heim 1983b. In this short paper, also discussed in chapter 1, Heim uses a trimmed down, partially valued version of her File Change Semantics as a dynamic improvement of Karttunen and Peters' approach.[2] She gives up the separation between presuppositions and assertions, and argues that the solution to the projection problem for presuppositions[3] can be *derived* from the dynamic meaning. Heim specifies what the dynamic meaning —or *context change potential*, as she calls it— of words like *if* and *not* is, and shows that these meanings determine the projection behavior of presuppositions arising in their scope. As a result of the integrated representations Heim uses, her proposal does not suffer from the binding-problem. Still the analysis of sentences in which presuppositions and quantifiers interact, such as (6), is not entirely satisfactory. Heim discusses the following example, which is structurally similar to (6).

(7)   A fat man pushes his bicycle.

Heim treats definite NPs like *his bicycle* using a free variable, which has to be defined; essentially a consequence of Heim's Novelty/Familiarity Condition (see chapter 2). This means that for any choice of fat man, a bicycle has to be present. Hence, Heim's system predicts that (7) presupposes that *every* fat man has a bicycle, a presupposition which is generally not associated with this sentence. Suppose that there are some fat men who do *not* have a bicycle while there is also at least one fat man who *does* own a bicycle which he pushes as well. Intuitively, example

---

[2]See Heim 1983b:118 and Van der Sandt 1989:275 for discussion.

[3]Langendoen and Savin 1971:54: *"how [are] the presupposition and assertion of a complex sentence (...) related to the presupposition and assertion of the clauses it contains?"*

(7) is just a true statement in that case. Since the strong presupposition which Heim's system predicts derives from the use of free variables in presuppositions we would expect similar universal presuppositions in the context of quantifiers like *every*, and this is indeed what we see. Heim discusses examples (8) and (9).

(8)   Every fat man pushes his bike.[4]

(9)   Every man who serves his king will be rewarded.

In both cases Heim's system predicts universal presuppositions: for example (8) that it shares its presupposition with example (7), for (9) that every man has a king.[5] Although the universal presuppositions sound better for examples (8) and (9) than they do for (7), they are still considered to be too strong. Suppose there are two fat men: one who has a bicycle which he does not push and another one who does not have a bicycle. In such a situation, (8) does not seem to be a case of presupposition failure, intuitively the sentence is just false in that case. In general, it takes just one fat man who has bike and does not push it to falsify the proposition expressed by (8). Now consider (9) and suppose that there are ten men in a given room: nine Belgians and one Dutchman. The nine Belgians all serve their king loyally and will be rewarded accordingly. The Dutchman does not serve his king, since he does not have one. With respect to the men in this room, (9) seems intuitively true and not, as Heim predicts, undefined due to presupposition failure. To solve these problems, Heim proposes a mechanism of local accommodation, which amounts to adding the presupposition in the required local context (here: in the scope of the universal quantifier). Even though this works for the present examples, it is also a bit odd. For one thing, it is unclear why the strong presupposition should arise in the first place and later be disguised by an accommodation mechanism.

Exactly what is presupposed by quantified examples such as these is still an open question since intuitions seem to vary (but see Beaver 1994 for a first systematic attempt to answer this question). Nevertheless, there is consensus that the universal Heimian predictions are too strong (as Heim herself acknowledges). In general, the intuition seems to be that if such sentences presuppose anything at all, the presupposition should be as weak as possible. These requirements are met in the systems of Beaver and van Eijck. Both can be seen as extensions of Heim's system, without the technical problems Heim has and both use a version of Dynamic Predicate Logic with a source of partiality added. Beaver

---

[4]Heim's actual example is *Every nation cherishes its king.*

[5]Compare: Karttunen and Peters 1979 predict that example (8) presupposes that every fat man has a bike, while (9) is predicted to presuppose nothing.

1992, 1995 extends *Eliminative* DPL (due to Dekker 1993b) with a unary presupposition operator called ∂. Updating with $\partial\phi$ yields undefined in any context in which ϕ is not true. In Beaver's system there is also a distinction between presupposed and asserted material (the former occur under the scope of an occurrence of ∂, while the latter do not), but the separation is not strict: one single formula represents both aspects of meaning. In Beaver 1992 it is shown that in this way the binding-problem can be avoided, without predicting universal presuppositions for examples (7), (8) or (9). Van Eijck defines an Error-State Semantics for DPL, and the intuition behind this is that a formula with a failing presupposition can be seen as a program that cannot be executed; it will end up in the error-state (see Van Eijck 1993, 1994b, 1996). Thus: a(n atomic) formula which contains a presupposition trigger can only be 'executed' when the presupposition is satisfied: if not, the formula 'aborts with error'. The way errors are handled in constructions like sequencing and implication determines the presuppositional predictions for complex sentences. Since only a single representation is used the binding-problem does not arise. Moreover, no Heimian predictions are made either (see Van Eijck 1994b for discussion).

As noted in the introductory chapter: we may already conclude from Heim 1983b that it is useful to combine a dynamic semantics with a limited form of partiality when we want to deal with presuppositions. And the work of Beaver and van Eijck shows even more clearly that combining partiality and dynamics pays off. Still, in all three systems it is the dynamics which plays first fiddle. In Heim 1983b the partiality only is present in the periphery of the context change potential. In Beaver's set-up the partiality is interweaved in the update formulation of DPL. When a presupposition is not satisfied, the update becomes undefined and the interpretation process stops.[6] Finally, in van Eijck's system the error-state can be considered a third (dynamic) truth-value besides truth and falsity. Still, one of van Eijck's aims is to '*get a clear sense of the role of the dynamics of context change in the account of phenomenon*' (of presuppositions) (Van Eijck 1994b:768).

Here we want to ask ourselves a different question, namely what the role is of *partiality* in the analysis of presuppositions. To answer this question we forget about the dynamics of meaning for now (and return to it in chapters 6 and 7), and focus only on the partiality of meaning. In this chapter we look at three static systems of *Partial Predicate Logic* extended with a presupposition operator. Each interpretation corresponds

---

[6]It should be noted that both Beaver 1992 and Beaver 1995 pay a lot of attention to more sophisticated analyses for cases of 'presupposition failure'.

with a 'classical' analysis of semantic presuppositions. We pay special attention to the interaction between presuppositions and quantifiers.[7] It will be shown that none of the three versions of Partial Predicate Logic runs into the binding problem for examples like (6). Perhaps more surprisingly, they can also deal with examples (7), (8) and (9), and without predicting universal presuppositions. In other words, for the examples discussed above, and which play such a central role in dynamic semantic approaches to presuppositions, there is no need to go dynamic.

This outcome raises a number of questions, some of which are addressed in this chapter as well. First of all, if 'a new wave of partial approaches to presuppositions' is something we advocate, we should spend a little time on the question why the old wave broke down. After all, in the sixties and seventies a great amount of partial and multi-valued logics for presuppositions have been proposed, but in the eighties the interest in them rapidly vanished. By the mid-eighties, Link was crying in the wilderness and called his own defense of partial logic for presuppositions 'stubborn' (Link 1986). Perhaps one explanation of the rise and, in particular, fall of partial approaches to presuppositions was that one expected too much of the partiality. Another explanation is that there were, and still are, some stubborn misconceptions about partial approaches to presuppositions.[8] We discuss one particularly obstinate point of criticism: that partial logics lack *flexibility*. That is to say: the partial approach is rigid in its predictions, while presupposition projection in natural language is a flexible phenomenon. In Beaver and Krahmer 1995 it is shown that this argument does not hold. In particular it is shown that using techniques which date back to some of the earliest work on presuppositions and on partial logic (Frege 1879, Bochvar 1939) a flexible semantic account of presuppositions can be given, which, in fact, seems comparable with the analyses in Link 1986 and Van der Sandt 1992. In section 4.4 we discuss these issues.

Another issue is the following. If the binding problem does not arise in a more or less standard logic, albeit a partial one, the question arises why Karttunen and Peters run into this binding problem. After all, they themselves spend several pages comparing the predictions of their Montagovian system with those generated by the partial approach to presuppositions from Peters 1979 and conclude that on the propositional level there are no differences. Of course it is on the quantificational level

---

[7]Classical partial logics for the analysis of presuppositions are also central in Kracht 1994, but he focuses on the propositional part. Kracht discusses four partial propositional logics with different *control structures*, including the propositional parts of the three Partial Predicate Logics discussed in this chapter.

[8]For a discussion on a lot of these misconceptions, see Martin 1979.

that the interesting things start to happen, but why should things go wrong there? This question is addressed in section 4.5 and, more in general, in chapter 5.

The reader may notice at this point that we have said nothing of substance about Van der Sandt's theory of *presupposition as anaphora*, which is arguably the best theory of presuppositions to date with respect to empirical predictions. We will make up for this in chapter 6 where presuppositions are studied on the level of discourse.

4.2 Partial Predicate Logic

In this section we discuss a number of static interpretations of *Partial Predicate Logic* (PPL). We focus on three well-known partial logics, which will be seen to correspond with three equally well-known approaches to presuppositions in section 4.3. The syntax of PPL extends the classical Predicate Logical syntax with the following construct:

If φ, π are formulae, then $\varphi_{\langle \pi \rangle}$ is a formula.

The intuition behind it is that π is an *elementary* (or potential) presupposition associated with φ. The subscript notation plus the 'elementary presupposition' terminology is used in Van der Sandt 1989. Here $\varphi_{\langle \pi \rangle}$ gets the same interpretation as Blamey's transplication (represented as π/φ, see Blamey 1986:5). Elementary presuppositions can be seen as presuppositions which arise in the lexicon/grammar. As we have seen in the introductory chapter, not all presuppositions which are triggered in a sentence are *projected* to become presuppositions of the sentence as a whole.

Consider the standard example:

(10) The king of France is bald.

This sentence presupposes the (unique) existence of a king of France and asserts that he is bald.[9] The presupposition is said to be *triggered* by the definite determiner, and we assume that this trigger is marked in the lexicon. The sentence in (10) is represented by a formula of the form $\varphi_{\langle \pi \rangle}$, where π is the representation of the presupposition 'there is a king of France' and φ of the assertion 'there is a king of France and he is bald'.[10] In this chapter we focus on the presuppositions triggered by

---

[9]Exactly *what* is presupposed by a definite NP is still a matter of debate. Here we simply assume that they presuppose existence and uniqueness. In chapter 7 we will address this issue in more detail, and present various alternatives.

[10]In this chapter, we do not discuss the question how the translations into the logical representation language are derived from the natural language examples. We will make up for this in chapter 5, where a fully compositional Montague Grammar

definite descriptions, possessives and the verb *to manage*. Of course the set of presupposition triggers under discussion can be extended at will.

In chapter 1 we have discussed the well-known phenomenon that elementary presuppositions do not always 'project'. An example is (11):

(11) If France has a king, then the king of France is bald.

Intuitively this sentence does not presuppose the existence of a king of France, even though the consequent contains an elementary presupposition to this effect. In PPL, example (11) is represented schematically as $\pi \rightarrow \varphi_{\langle \pi \rangle}$. The interpretation of the implication determines whether or not it is predicted that the presupposition of the consequent projects. In this section we discuss various interpretations and review their predictions in section 4.3.

4.2.1 Strong Kleene PPL

In Predicate Logic every formula is either true or false, where the disjunction is read exclusively. In other words, for any formula φ, the disjunction $\varphi \vee \neg\varphi$ is a tautology (this is known as the principle of the excluded middle or *tertium non datur*). As a result of this there is a close correspondence between truth and falsity. When a formula φ is true, it is not false. And when φ is not true, it has to be false. In partial logics this correspondence between truth and falsity is given up; truth and falsity need to be calculated separately. Assuming that no formula can be both true and false, three possible *truth combinations* arise: 'true (and not false)', 'false (and not true)', and 'neither (true nor false)'.[11] In Belnap 1979 (and Muskens 1989) these combinations are abbreviated as T(rue), F(alse), and N(either) respectively.

In a sense the so-called *strong Kleene* system is *the mother of partial logics*, since it is possible to define a great number of other partial logics in terms of it (see for instance Thijsse 1992, chapter 1).[12] Kleene 1945's strong interpretation of the propositional connectives using these three values looks as follows:

---

will be developed for a fragment of English which properly includes the examples discussed in this chapter.

[11] If we give up the assumption that a formula cannot be true and false at the same time, we allow for a fourth truth combination: 'both (true and false)'. For theory and application of four-valued logics, the reader may consult Muskens 1989.

[12] In particular, Thijsse shows that every trivalent truth function is definable in terms of strong Kleene $\neg$ and $\wedge$, plus # (the undefined formula) and − (a second, so-called external negation; see below). Apart from Blamey's transplication (to be defined below), the propositional connectives we are interested in are all *monotonic*, as well as *classically closed* (truth-functions over classical truth values yield a classical truth value), and these are all definable in terms of strong Kleene negation and conjunction, plus T.

Definition 1 (Strong Kleene)

$\land$	T	F	N
T	T	F	N
F	F	F	F
N	N	F	N

$\to$	T	F	N
T	T	F	N
F	T	T	T
N	T	N	N

$\lor$	T	F	N
T	T	T	T
F	T	F	N
N	T	N	N

	$\neg$
T	F
F	T
N	N

As said, the language of PPL contains Blamey's transplication, which we represent as $\varphi_{\langle\pi\rangle}$. Here is the truth table for $\varphi_{\langle\pi\rangle}$, picture π across and φ down:

Definition 2 (Transplication)

	T	F	N
T	T	N	N
F	F	N	N
N	N	N	N

Compare this truth table with the Strawsonian notion of presupposing discussed in section 4.1. Blamey characterizes transplication as follows: $\varphi_{\langle\pi\rangle}$ is True when $\pi \land \varphi$ is True, and $\varphi_{\langle\pi\rangle}$ is False when $\pi \to \varphi$ is False. It is easily seen that when π is not True, $\varphi_{\langle\pi\rangle}$ is Neither. There is an interesting alternative for a Blamey-style binary presupposition connective, namely the introduction of a *unary* presupposition operator: the static version of Beaver's unary presupposition construction (first used in Beaver 1992). Its syntax is defined as follows:

If π is a formula, then $\partial\pi$ is a formula.

Definition 3 (Unary presupposition operator)

	∂
T	T
F	N
N	N

The intuition behind $\partial\pi$ is that it says of π that it is presupposed. Thus $\partial\pi$ is True if π is True (the presupposition is satisfied), and otherwise $\partial\pi$ is Neither. It is easily seen that the two presuppositional operators are interdefinable in the context of strong Kleene PPL.

Fact 1

$(\partial\pi \land \varphi) \lor (\partial\pi \land \neg\partial\pi)$ *has the same truth table as* $\varphi_{\langle\pi\rangle}$

Let us now turn to the full definition of the semantics of strong Kleene based PPL in terms of assignments (in the same way in which Groenendijk & Stokhof define the semantics of standard first-order PL in Groenendijk and Stokhof 1991, see definition 17 in chapter 2). The semantics consists of two parts: $[\![\varphi]\!]^+$ (the positive extension of φ) is the set of assignments which *support* φ, and $[\![\varphi]\!]^-$ (the negative extension) is the set of assignments which *reject* φ. Models are standard; $M = \langle D, I \rangle$, where D is a non-empty set and I an interpretation function. Furthermore, G is the set of total assignments. Terms are interpreted as follows: for $t \in \mathsf{Var}$, $[\![t]\!]^+_{M,g} = [\![t]\!]^-_{M,g} = g(t)$ and for $t \in \mathsf{Con}$, $[\![t]\!]^+_{M,g} = [\![t]\!]^-_{M,g} = I(t)$. As a result, terms are polarity insensitive ($[\![t]\!]^+ = [\![t]\!]^-$), so there is no harm in dropping the superscript in the interpretation of terms. For formulae φ, we define $[\![\varphi]\!]^+_M \subseteq G$ and $[\![\varphi]\!]^-_M \subseteq G$ as follows, dropping subscripts when possible.

Definition 4 (Strong Kleene based interpretation of PPL)

1. $[\![R(t_1, \ldots, t_n)]\!]^+ \quad = \quad \{g \mid \langle [\![t_1]\!]_g, \ldots, [\![t_n]\!]_g \rangle \in I(R)\}$
    $[\![R(t_1, \ldots, t_n)]\!]^- \quad = \quad \{g \mid \langle [\![t_1]\!]_g, \ldots, [\![t_n]\!]_g \rangle \notin I(R)\}$

2. $[\![t_1 \equiv t_2]\!]^+ \quad = \quad \{g \mid [\![t_1]\!]_g = [\![t_2]\!]_g\}$
    $[\![t_1 \equiv t_2]\!]^- \quad = \quad \{g \mid [\![t_1]\!]_g \neq [\![t_2]\!]_g\}$

3. $[\![\neg\varphi]\!]^+ \quad = \quad [\![\varphi]\!]^-$
    $[\![\neg\varphi]\!]^- \quad = \quad [\![\varphi]\!]^+$

4. $[\![\varphi \wedge \psi]\!]^+ \quad = \quad \{g \mid g \in [\![\varphi]\!]^+ \ \& \ g \in [\![\psi]\!]^+\}$
    $[\![\varphi \wedge \psi]\!]^- \quad = \quad \{g \mid g \in [\![\varphi]\!]^- \ \text{or} \ g \in [\![\psi]\!]^-\}$

5. $[\![\varphi \vee \psi]\!]^+ \quad = \quad \{g \mid g \in [\![\varphi]\!]^+ \ \text{or} \ g \in [\![\psi]\!]^+\}$
    $[\![\varphi \vee \psi]\!]^- \quad = \quad \{g \mid g \in [\![\varphi]\!]^- \ \& \ g \in [\![\psi]\!]^-\}$

6. $[\![\varphi \rightarrow \psi]\!]^+ \quad = \quad \{g \mid g \notin [\![\varphi]\!]^- \Rightarrow g \in [\![\psi]\!]^+\}$
    $[\![\varphi \rightarrow \psi]\!]^- \quad = \quad \{g \mid g \in [\![\varphi]\!]^+ \ \& \ g \in [\![\psi]\!]^-\}$

7. $[\![\exists x \varphi]\!]^+ \quad = \quad \{g \mid \exists h (g[x]h \ \& \ h \in [\![\varphi]\!]^+)\}$
    $[\![\exists x \varphi]\!]^- \quad = \quad \{g \mid \forall h (g[x]h \Rightarrow h \in [\![\varphi]\!]^-)\}$

8. $[\![\forall x \varphi]\!]^+ \quad = \quad \{g \mid \forall h (g[x]h \Rightarrow h \in [\![\varphi]\!]^+)\}$
    $[\![\forall x \varphi]\!]^- \quad = \quad \{g \mid \exists h (g[x]h \ \& \ h \in [\![\varphi]\!]^-)\}$

9. $[\![\varphi_{\langle \pi \rangle}]\!]^+ \quad = \quad \{g \mid g \in [\![\pi]\!]^+ \ \& \ g \in [\![\varphi]\!]^+\}$
    $[\![\varphi_{\langle \pi \rangle}]\!]^- \quad = \quad \{g \mid g \in [\![\pi]\!]^+ \ \& \ g \in [\![\varphi]\!]^-\}$

Here, as before, $g[x]h$ stands for 'assignment h is like assignment g, except possibly for the value h assigns to x'. A PPL formula φ is *supported* in a model M with respect to an assignment g (notation: $M, g \models_{\text{PPL}} \varphi$) when $g \in [\![\varphi]\!]^+_M$. Similarly, φ is *rejected* in M with respect to g (notation: $M, g \dashv_{\text{PPL}} \varphi$) when $g \in [\![\varphi]\!]^-_M$. On the basis of these two notions we can define the three truth combinations as follows.

Definition 5 (Truth combinations)

In a model M and with respect to an assignment g we say that

φ is True $\qquad$ iff $\qquad M, g \models \varphi$

φ is False $\qquad$ iff $\qquad M, g =\!\!\mid \varphi$

φ is Neither $\qquad$ iff $\qquad M, g \not\models \varphi$ and $M, g \not=\!\!\mid \varphi$

We say that a formula φ is *defined* in M with respect to g —abbreviated as $\mathrm{def}_{M,g}(\varphi)$— iff φ is either True or False in M with respect to g. Two formulae φ and ψ are *equivalent* iff in all models M $[\![\varphi]\!]^+_M = [\![\psi]\!]^+_M$ and $[\![\varphi]\!]^-_M = [\![\psi]\!]^-_M$. It is easily seen that the following equivalences hold:

Fact 2 *(Equivalences)*

1. $\varphi \lor \psi$ *is equivalent with* $\neg(\neg\varphi \land \neg\psi)$
2. $\varphi \to \psi$ *is equivalent with* $\neg(\varphi \land \neg\psi)$
3. $\forall x\varphi$ *is equivalent with* $\neg\exists x\neg\varphi$

Concerning embedded presuppositions: the following fact in essence says that we do not have to bother with more than one presuppositional embedding.

Fact 3

$\left(\varphi_{\langle\pi_1\rangle}\right)_{\langle\pi_2\rangle}$ *is equivalent with* $\varphi_{\langle\pi_2\land\pi_1\rangle}$

Finally, as the reader may verify, no formula is both True and False, and every presupposition-free (classical) formula is either True or False. This means that the partiality only arises in the case of elementary presuppositions. For any assignment g such that $g \notin [\![\pi]\!]^+$ it holds that $g \notin [\![\varphi_{\langle\pi\rangle}]\!]^+$ *and* $g \notin [\![\varphi_{\langle\pi\rangle}]\!]^-$. The properties of $\varphi_{\langle\pi\rangle}$ are discussed in more detail below.

4.2.2 Middle Kleene PPL

There is a second partial logic which deserves our attention here. This is the system from Peters 1979, to which we shall also refer as *middle Kleene*, because, in an intuitive sense, it lies in between the strong Kleene system we just discussed and the weak Kleene system which is the subject of the next subsection. Its characteristic property is that it is *asymmetric*. Consider the conjunction. According to the table Peters 1979 defines, the right-hand conjunct only has to be considered when the left-hand conjunct is True, in the other cases the conjunction as a whole gets the same value as the left conjunct. Similar observations can be made with respect to disjunction and implication. Here are the Peters/middle Kleene truth tables for the propositional connectives. We shall indicate that a connective has a middle Kleene interpretation by placing one dot above it.

Definition 6 (Middle Kleene)

$\dot\wedge$	T	F	N		$\dot\rightarrow$	T	F	N		$\dot\vee$	T	F	N			$\neg$
T	T	F	N		T	T	F	N		T	T	T	T		T	F
F	F	F	F		F	T	T	T		F	T	F	N		F	T
N	N	N	N		N	N	N	N		N	N	N	N		N	N

Obviously the middle Kleene conjunction is not commutative (that is: $\varphi \wedge \psi$ is not equivalent with $\psi \wedge \varphi$), a property it shares with the dynamic interpretation of conjunction.[13] With these observations in the back of our mind, we can define the middle Kleene connectives *in terms of* the strong Kleene connectives presented in definition 4:

Definition 7 (Middle Kleene connectives in terms of strong Kleene)

1. $\varphi \mathbin{\dot\wedge} \psi = (\varphi \wedge \psi) \vee (\varphi \wedge \neg\varphi)$
2. $\varphi \mathbin{\dot\vee} \psi = (\varphi \vee \psi) \wedge (\varphi \vee \neg\varphi)$
3. $\varphi \mathbin{\dot\rightarrow} \psi = (\varphi \rightarrow \psi) \wedge (\varphi \vee \neg\varphi)$[14]

It is not difficult to check that the following holds:

Fact 4 *(Equivalences)*

1. $\varphi \mathbin{\dot\vee} \psi$ is equivalent with $\neg(\neg\varphi \mathbin{\dot\wedge} \neg\psi)$
2. $\varphi \mathbin{\dot\rightarrow} \psi$ is equivalent with $\neg(\varphi \mathbin{\dot\wedge} \neg\psi)$

We can write out the resulting interpretations of these connectives in the fashion of definition 4:[15]

Fact 5 *(Middle Kleene based interpretation of* PPL*)*

1. $[\![\varphi \mathbin{\dot\wedge} \psi]\!]^+ = \{g \mid g \in [\![\varphi]\!]^+ \ \& \ g \in [\![\psi]\!]^+\}$
   $[\![\varphi \mathbin{\dot\wedge} \psi]\!]^- = \{g \mid (g \in [\![\varphi]\!]^+ \Rightarrow g \in [\![\psi]\!]^-) \ \& \ \mathrm{def}_g(\varphi)\}$

2. $[\![\varphi \mathbin{\dot\vee} \psi]\!]^+ = \{g \mid (g \in [\![\varphi]\!]^+ \text{ or } g \in [\![\psi]\!]^+) \ \& \ \mathrm{def}_g(\varphi)\}$
   $[\![\varphi \mathbin{\dot\vee} \psi]\!]^- = \{g \mid g \in [\![\varphi]\!]^- \ \& \ g \in [\![\psi]\!]^-\}$

3. $[\![\varphi \mathbin{\dot\rightarrow} \psi]\!]^+ = \{g \mid (g \in [\![\varphi]\!]^+ \Rightarrow g \in [\![\psi]\!]^+) \ \& \ \mathrm{def}_g(\varphi)\}$
   $[\![\varphi \mathbin{\dot\rightarrow} \psi]\!]^- = \{g \mid g \in [\![\varphi]\!]^+ \ \& \ g \in [\![\psi]\!]^-\}$

These are just the strong Kleene interpretations from definition 4 plus some definedness conditions.

---

[13] Compare Groenendijk and Stokhof 1988:467: *A semantics is dynamic if and only if its notion of conjunction is dynamic, and hence non-commutative.*

[14] Or, equivalently: $\varphi \mathbin{\dot\rightarrow} \psi =_{\mathrm{def}} (\varphi \rightarrow \psi) \wedge (\varphi \rightarrow \varphi)$.

[15] Notice that $g \notin [\![\varphi]\!]^- \ \& \ \mathrm{def}_g(\varphi)$ entails $g \in [\![\varphi]\!]^+$.

4.2.3 Weak Kleene PPL

A final alternative we discuss is the *Bochvar* interpretation (from Bochvar 1939), which is also known as *weak Kleene*. The Bochvar/weak Kleene system differs from the strong and the middle Kleene systems in that it has a different philosophy underlying the N value. In the two Kleene systems discussed above N means that the relevant formula is Neither true nor false, in the weak Kleene system the underlying intuition is that it is Nonsense (or meaningless). The intuition behind Nonsense is that it is a *disease* (as Martin 1979 puts it): when one part of a formula is infected, the whole formula is. The truth tables of weak Kleene are built up in such a way that when a subformula is Nonsense, the entire formula is Nonsense. We indicate that a connective has a weak Kleene interpretation by placing two dots above it. The weak Kleene truth tables for the propositional connectives look as follows.

Definition 8 (Weak Kleene)

$\ddot{\wedge}$	T	F	N		$\ddot{\rightarrow}$	T	F	N		$\ddot{\vee}$	T	F	N		$\neg$	
T	T	F	N		T	T	F	N		T	T	T	N		T	F
F	F	F	N		F	T	T	N		F	T	F	N		F	T
N	N	N	N		N	N	N	N		N	N	N	N		N	N

Even though in weak Kleene the third value has a different underlying philosophy than it has in the strong Kleene system, we can define the weak Kleene connectives in terms of the strong Kleene ones:

Definition 9 (Weak Kleene connectives in terms of strong Kleene)

1. $\varphi \ddot{\wedge} \psi = (\varphi \wedge \psi) \vee (\varphi \wedge \neg\varphi) \vee (\psi \wedge \neg\psi)$
2. $\varphi \ddot{\vee} \psi = (\varphi \vee \psi) \wedge (\varphi \vee \neg\varphi) \wedge (\psi \vee \neg\psi)$
3. $\varphi \ddot{\rightarrow} \psi = (\varphi \rightarrow \psi) \wedge (\varphi \vee \neg\varphi) \wedge (\psi \vee \neg\psi)$

Here again the following holds:

Fact 6 *(Equivalences)*

1. $\varphi \ddot{\vee} \psi$ is equivalent with $\neg(\neg\varphi \ddot{\wedge} \neg\psi)$
2. $\varphi \ddot{\rightarrow} \psi$ is equivalent with $\neg(\varphi \ddot{\wedge} \neg\psi)$

Writing out the resulting interpretations is a straightforward extension of fact 5.

4.3 Presuppositions and PPL

In this section we look more closely at the behavior of $\varphi_{\langle\pi\rangle}$ in the three versions of PPL described. As said, the intended interpretation of this construction is that π is an *elementary presupposition* of φ. The intruiging thing about elementary presuppositions is that they sometimes survive when they occur embedded under one or more logical operations, but at other times they do not. We say that an *arbitrary* formula φ presupposes π iff whenever φ is defined, π is True. More formally:

Definition 10 (Presuppose)
φ *presupposes* π iff for all models M and assignments g:

$$\text{if } M, g \models \varphi \text{ or } M, g \dashv \varphi, \text{ then } M, g \models \pi$$

Put differently: if $M, g \not\models \pi$, then $M, g \not\models \varphi$ and $M, g \not\dashv \varphi$, and this is just the Strawsonian definition given in the introduction (*whenever π is not true, φ is neither true nor false*). Also notice that we can derive from this definition what it means for φ *not* to presuppose π. Then there should be a model M and an assignment g such that π is not True in M with respect to g while φ is still defined with respect to these parameters.

4.3.1 Determining Presuppositions

There is a long tradition in semantic approaches to presupposition to equate the presupposition of a formula with the disjunction of its truth and falsity conditions (see for example Karttunen and Peters 1979, or Cooper 1983), and this is probably no surprise in light of the definition of *presuppose* we just gave. It is not difficult to see that the definition of *presuppose* can also be put as follows: φ presupposes π iff for all models M and assignments g:

$$\text{if } M, g \models \neg\varphi \vee \varphi, \text{ then } M, g \models \pi$$

Karttunen and Peters 1979:45 remark that the disjunction of truth and falsity conditions can be called *the* presupposition of a formula, since this disjunction gives the *strongest* presupposition of the relevant formula (that is: it entails all presuppositions). Of course, it would be desirable if the maximal presupposition of a formula is itself devoid of elementary presuppositions. For this purpose, we use two translations of PPL into standard (that is: presupposition-free) PL: TR^+, which maps a PPL formula φ to a PL formula φ' which is true iff φ is True, and TR^-, which maps a PPL formula φ to a PL formula φ' which is true whenever φ is False. These translations are variants of well-known embeddings of partial logics into standard Predicate Logic found in Gilmore 1974, Feferman 1984 and Langholm 1988. We let φ_{at} be an atomic formula; either a predication or an identity.

Definition 11 (Strong Kleene based TR^+ and TR^-)

$$
\begin{aligned}
\mathsf{TR}^+(\varphi_{at}) &= \varphi_{at} & \mathsf{TR}^+(\varphi_{\langle\pi\rangle}) &= \mathsf{TR}^+(\pi) \wedge \mathsf{TR}^+(\varphi) \\
\mathsf{TR}^-(\varphi_{at}) &= \neg\varphi_{at} & \mathsf{TR}^-(\varphi_{\langle\pi\rangle}) &= \mathsf{TR}^+(\pi) \wedge \mathsf{TR}^-(\varphi)
\end{aligned}
$$

$$
\begin{aligned}
\mathsf{TR}^+(\neg\varphi) &= \mathsf{TR}^-(\varphi) & \mathsf{TR}^+(\varphi \wedge \psi) &= \mathsf{TR}^+(\varphi) \wedge \mathsf{TR}^+(\psi) \\
\mathsf{TR}^-(\neg\varphi) &= \mathsf{TR}^+(\varphi) & \mathsf{TR}^-(\varphi \wedge \psi) &= \mathsf{TR}^-(\varphi) \vee \mathsf{TR}^-(\psi)
\end{aligned}
$$

$$
\begin{aligned}
\mathsf{TR}^+(\exists x\varphi) &= \exists x\mathsf{TR}^+(\varphi) & \mathsf{TR}^+(\varphi \vee \psi) &= \mathsf{TR}^+(\varphi) \vee \mathsf{TR}^+(\psi) \\
\mathsf{TR}^-(\exists x\varphi) &= \forall x\mathsf{TR}^-(\varphi) & \mathsf{TR}^-(\varphi \vee \psi) &= \mathsf{TR}^-(\varphi) \wedge \mathsf{TR}^-(\psi)
\end{aligned}
$$

$$
\begin{aligned}
\mathsf{TR}^+(\forall x\varphi) &= \forall x\mathsf{TR}^+(\varphi) & \mathsf{TR}^+(\varphi \to \psi) &= \mathsf{TR}^-(\varphi) \vee \mathsf{TR}^+(\psi) \\
\mathsf{TR}^-(\forall x\varphi) &= \exists x\mathsf{TR}^-(\varphi) & \mathsf{TR}^-(\varphi \to \psi) &= \mathsf{TR}^+(\varphi) \wedge \mathsf{TR}^-(\psi)
\end{aligned}
$$

An easy induction (given in the appendix) proves the following fact, where $[\![.]\!]^{\mathrm{PL}}$ is once again the Tarskian definition of PL given in definition 2.17.

Fact 7 *(From PPL to PL)*
For all PPL formulae φ and all models M:

1. $[\![\mathsf{TR}^+(\varphi)]\!]_M^{\mathrm{PL}} \Leftrightarrow [\![\varphi]\!]_M^+$
2. $[\![\mathsf{TR}^-(\varphi)]\!]_M^{\mathrm{PL}} \Leftrightarrow [\![\varphi]\!]_M^-$

These two functions allow us to calculate the presupposition of an arbitrary PPL formula.[16] Let $\mathsf{PR}(\varphi)$ be the (strongest) presupposition of φ, then $\mathsf{PR}(\varphi)$ is defined as $\mathsf{TR}^+(\varphi) \vee \mathsf{TR}^-(\varphi)$. Given fact 7 the following has an easy proof. For all formulae φ, all models M and assignments g:

$$M, g \models_{\mathrm{PPL}} \varphi \vee \neg\varphi \text{ if, and only if, } M, g \models_{\mathrm{PL}} \mathsf{PR}(\varphi) \text{ }^{17}$$

It is important to note that since $\mathsf{PR}(\varphi)$ is a classical formula (does not contain elementary presuppositions) it is true in PL whenever it is True in PPL. That is:

$$M, g \models_{\mathrm{PL}} \mathsf{PR}(\varphi) \text{ if, and only if, } M, g \models_{\mathrm{PPL}} \mathsf{PR}(\varphi)$$

From this we immediately derive fact 8.

Fact 8
φ *presupposes* $\mathsf{PR}(\varphi)$, *for any PPL formula φ.*

The middle Kleene based version of PPL was defined in terms of the strong Kleene system, and differs only with respect to conjunction, im-

---

[16] An interesting alternative is discussed in Kracht 1994, where an algorithm is presented which brings propositional formulae into *presuppositional normal form*.

[17] Suppose M, g are an arbitrary model and assignment respectively, then $M, g \models_{\mathrm{PPL}}$ $\varphi \vee \neg\varphi \Leftrightarrow (g \in [\![\varphi]\!]_M^+ \text{ or } g \in [\![\neg\varphi]\!]_M^+) \Leftrightarrow (g \in [\![\mathsf{TR}^+(\varphi)]\!]_M^{\mathrm{PL}} \text{ or } g \in [\![\mathsf{TR}^+(\neg\varphi)]\!]_M^{\mathrm{PL}}) \Leftrightarrow$ $(g \in [\![\mathsf{TR}^+(\varphi)]\!]_M^{\mathrm{PL}} \text{ or } g \in [\![\mathsf{TR}^-(\varphi)]\!]_M^{\mathrm{PL}}) \Leftrightarrow (M, g \models_{\mathrm{PL}} \mathsf{TR}^+(\varphi) \text{ or } M, g \models_{\mathrm{PL}} \mathsf{TR}^-(\varphi)) \Leftrightarrow$ $M, g \models_{\mathrm{PL}} \mathsf{TR}^+(\varphi) \vee \mathsf{TR}^-(\varphi) \Leftrightarrow M, g \models_{\mathrm{PL}} \mathsf{PR}(\varphi)$.

plication and disjunction.[18] If we apply TR^+ and TR^- to the middle Kleene definitions of these three connectives we get:

Fact 9 *(Middle Kleene based* TR^+ *and* TR^- *)*

1. $\mathsf{TR}^+(\varphi \mathbin{\dot{\wedge}} \psi) = \mathsf{TR}^+(\varphi) \wedge \mathsf{TR}^+(\psi)$
   $\mathsf{TR}^-(\varphi \mathbin{\dot{\wedge}} \psi) = \big(\mathsf{TR}^-(\varphi) \vee \mathsf{TR}^-(\psi)\big) \wedge \big(\mathsf{TR}^+(\varphi) \vee \mathsf{TR}^-(\varphi)\big)$

2. $\mathsf{TR}^+(\varphi \mathbin{\dot{\vee}} \psi) = \big(\mathsf{TR}^+(\varphi) \vee \mathsf{TR}^+(\psi)\big) \wedge \big(\mathsf{TR}^+(\varphi) \vee \mathsf{TR}^-(\varphi)\big)$
   $\mathsf{TR}^-(\varphi \mathbin{\dot{\vee}} \psi) = \mathsf{TR}^-(\varphi) \wedge \mathsf{TR}^-(\psi)$

3. $\mathsf{TR}^+(\varphi \mathbin{\dot{\rightarrow}} \psi) = \big(\mathsf{TR}^-(\varphi) \vee \mathsf{TR}^+(\psi)\big) \wedge \big(\mathsf{TR}^+(\varphi) \vee \mathsf{TR}^-(\varphi)\big)$
   $\mathsf{TR}^-(\varphi \mathbin{\dot{\rightarrow}} \psi) = \mathsf{TR}^+(\varphi) \wedge \mathsf{TR}^-(\psi)$

By complete analogy with the middle Kleene case we come to the following for the weak Kleene system.

Fact 10 *(Weak Kleene based* TR^+ *and* TR^- *)*

1. $\mathsf{TR}^+(\varphi \mathbin{\ddot{\wedge}} \psi) = \mathsf{TR}^+(\varphi) \wedge \mathsf{TR}^+(\psi)$
   $\mathsf{TR}^-(\varphi \mathbin{\ddot{\wedge}} \psi) = \big(\mathsf{TR}^-(\varphi) \vee \mathsf{TR}^-(\psi)\big) \wedge \big(\mathsf{TR}^+(\varphi) \vee \mathsf{TR}^-(\varphi)\big) \wedge$
   $\big(\mathsf{TR}^+(\psi) \vee \mathsf{TR}^-(\psi)\big)$

2. $\mathsf{TR}^+(\varphi \mathbin{\ddot{\vee}} \psi) = \big(\mathsf{TR}^+(\varphi) \vee \mathsf{TR}^+(\psi)\big) \wedge \big(\mathsf{TR}^+(\varphi) \vee \mathsf{TR}^-(\varphi)\big) \wedge$
   $\big(\mathsf{TR}^+(\psi) \vee \mathsf{TR}^-(\psi)\big)$

   $\mathsf{TR}^-(\varphi \mathbin{\ddot{\vee}} \psi) = \mathsf{TR}^-(\varphi) \wedge \mathsf{TR}^-(\psi)$

3. $\mathsf{TR}^+(\varphi \mathbin{\ddot{\rightarrow}} \psi) = \big(\mathsf{TR}^-(\varphi) \vee \mathsf{TR}^+(\psi)\big) \wedge \big(\mathsf{TR}^+(\varphi) \vee \mathsf{TR}^-(\varphi)\big) \wedge$
   $\big(\mathsf{TR}^+(\psi) \vee \mathsf{TR}^-(\psi)\big)$

   $\mathsf{TR}^-(\varphi \mathbin{\ddot{\rightarrow}} \psi) = \mathsf{TR}^+(\varphi) \wedge \mathsf{TR}^-(\psi)$

4.3.2 Predictions

In this paragraph we discuss the predictions of the various versions of PPL with respect to presupposition projection. We first mention a useful little fact:

Fact 11

For all φ *without elementary presuppositions:* $\mathsf{PR}(\varphi) \Leftrightarrow \top$.

$\top$ is defined as $c \equiv c$, for some $c \in \mathsf{Con}$ (which was stipulated to be non-empty). Fact 11 says that when φ contains no source of partiality (no elementary presuppositions) $\varphi \vee \neg\varphi$ is a tautology. In that case we say that φ presupposes nothing. A basic prediction we would like to make is that $\varphi_{\langle \pi \rangle}$ at least presupposes π. And this is exactly what is predicted

---

[18]To clear a possible confusion. With middle Kleene (weak Kleene) based PPL the subsystem of strong Kleene based PPL is meant in which the propositional connectives are defined as in definition 7 (definition 9).

(observe that when π itself does not contain elementary presuppositions, π is True iff $\mathsf{TR}^+(\pi)$ is true (fact 7)).

$$\mathsf{PR}(\varphi_{\langle\pi\rangle}) \Leftrightarrow \mathsf{TR}^+(\pi) \wedge \mathsf{PR}(\varphi)^{19}$$

When φ presupposes nothing ($\mathsf{PR}(\varphi) \Leftrightarrow \top$), $\varphi_{\langle\pi\rangle}$ presupposes π. This means that all three versions of PPL predict that example (10) indeed presupposes the existence of a king of France. Another characteristic property of presuppositions is that they tend to survive under negation. It is immediately seen that

$$\mathsf{PR}(\neg\varphi) \Leftrightarrow \mathsf{PR}(\varphi).$$

In other words, all three logics predict that, conform intuitions, the following two sentences presuppose the same, namely that France has a king.

(12) a. The king of France is bald.
      b. The king of France is not bald.

The three logics are not always so at one in their predictions, especially not when the projection of presuppositions in complex formulae is at stake. First let us briefly review the intuitions. We focus on the conditional sentences here, but these predictions carry over to the other cases easily. It is generally accepted that presuppositions arising in the antecedent of a conditional project, as do presuppositions which arise in the consequent but are not entailed by the antecedent. Thus, people tend to read the classic examples (13.a) and (13.b) as presupposing the existence of a king of France, while such a presupposition is not attributed to (11), here repeated as (13.c).

(13) a. If the king of France is bald, then baldness is hereditary.
          intuitively presupposes that there is a king of France
      b. If baldness is hereditary, then the king of France is bald.
          intuitively presupposes that there is a king of France
      c. If France has a king, then the king of France is bald.
          intuitively doesn't *presuppose that there is a king of France*

The respective schematic representations of these sentences in PPL are:

$$\delta_{\langle\pi\rangle} \xrightarrow{*} \xi,$$

$$\xi \xrightarrow{*} \delta_{\langle\pi\rangle}, \text{ and}$$

$$\pi \xrightarrow{*} \delta_{\langle\pi\rangle}.$$

---

[19]A simple calculation shows this. $\mathsf{PR}(\varphi_{\langle\pi\rangle}) \Leftrightarrow (\mathsf{TR}^+(\varphi_{\langle\pi\rangle}) \vee \mathsf{TR}^-(\varphi_{\langle\pi\rangle})) \Leftrightarrow ((\mathsf{TR}^+(\pi) \wedge \mathsf{TR}^+(\varphi)) \vee (\mathsf{TR}^+(\pi) \wedge \mathsf{TR}^-(\varphi))) \Leftrightarrow (\mathsf{TR}^+(\pi) \wedge (\mathsf{TR}^+(\varphi) \vee \mathsf{TR}^-(\varphi))) \Leftrightarrow (\mathsf{TR}^+(\pi) \wedge \mathsf{PR}(\varphi))$

Here $\overset{*}{\to}$ ranges over the three implications discussed in the previous section. π represents the proposition that there is a king of France, δ represents the proposition that the king of France is bald and ξ represents the proposition that baldness is hereditary. δ, π and ξ themselves presuppose nothing ($\mathrm{PR}(\delta) \Leftrightarrow \mathrm{PR}(\pi) \Leftrightarrow \mathrm{PR}(\xi) \Leftrightarrow \top$).

Above we defined $\mathrm{PR}(\varphi)$ as the disjunction of $\mathrm{TR}^+(\varphi)$ and $\mathrm{TR}^-(\varphi)$. In the case of a non-atomic φ, it is useful to write out this definition. Here are the cases of the strong Kleene propositional connectives.[20]

$$\mathrm{PR}(\varphi \wedge \psi) \quad \Leftrightarrow \quad \left(\mathrm{PR}(\varphi) \vee \mathrm{TR}^+(\neg\psi)\right) \wedge \left(\mathrm{TR}^+(\neg\varphi) \vee \mathrm{PR}(\psi)\right)$$

$$\mathrm{PR}(\varphi \vee \psi) \quad \Leftrightarrow \quad \left(\mathrm{PR}(\varphi) \vee \mathrm{TR}^+(\psi)\right) \wedge \left(\mathrm{TR}^+(\varphi) \vee \mathrm{PR}(\psi)\right)$$

$$\mathrm{PR}(\varphi \to \psi) \quad \Leftrightarrow \quad \left(\mathrm{PR}(\varphi) \vee \mathrm{TR}^+(\psi)\right) \wedge \left(\mathrm{TR}^+(\neg\varphi) \vee \mathrm{PR}(\psi)\right)$$

(Compare Karttunen and Peters 1979:45.) Using this rewriting, we see that strong Kleene based PPL predicts the following presuppositions for the examples in (13):[21]

$\delta_{\langle\pi\rangle} \to \xi$ presupposes $\pi \vee \xi$,

$\xi \to \delta_{\langle\pi\rangle}$ presupposes $\neg\xi \vee \pi$, and

$\pi \to \delta_{\langle\pi\rangle}$ presupposes $\neg\pi \vee \pi (\Leftrightarrow \top)$.

So, if we look at the natural language examples again, we see that strong Kleene predicts that (13.a) presupposes *either there is a king of France or baldness is hereditary*, (13.b) is predicted to presuppose *if baldness is hereditary, then there is a king of France* and (13.c) comes out presupposing nothing. Strong Kleene based PPL gets the intuitions right for the third example, but for the other two examples it predicts presuppositions which are too weak. Of course weak presuppositions are not *wrong*, they are just not strong enough compared with the natural language intuitions. The issue of weak presuppositions is one of the central issues in semantic approaches to presuppositions, and we will return to it below. In Hausser 1976 it is argued that the strong Kleene predictions are the best as far as the natural language facts are concerned. In Karttunen and Peters 1979:39–40/44–45, there is some discussion on this issue.

---

[20] As an example: $\mathrm{PR}(\varphi \to \psi) \Leftrightarrow (\mathrm{TR}^+(\varphi \to \psi) \vee \mathrm{TR}^-(\varphi \to \psi)) \Leftrightarrow ((\mathrm{TR}^-(\varphi) \vee \mathrm{TR}^+(\psi)) \vee (\mathrm{TR}^+(\varphi) \wedge \mathrm{TR}^-(\psi))) \Leftrightarrow ((\mathrm{TR}^-(\varphi) \vee \mathrm{TR}^+(\psi) \vee \mathrm{TR}^+(\varphi)) \wedge (\mathrm{TR}^-(\varphi) \vee \mathrm{TR}^+(\psi) \vee \mathrm{TR}^-(\psi))) \Leftrightarrow ((\mathrm{PR}(\varphi) \vee \mathrm{TR}^+(\psi)) \wedge (\mathrm{TR}^+(\neg\varphi) \vee \mathrm{PR}(\psi)))$.

[21] As an example: $\mathrm{PR}(\delta_{\langle\pi\rangle} \to \xi) \Leftrightarrow (\mathrm{PR}(\delta_{\langle\pi\rangle}) \vee \mathrm{TR}^+(\xi)) \wedge (\mathrm{TR}^+(\neg\delta_{\langle\pi\rangle}) \vee \mathrm{PR}(\xi)) \Leftrightarrow ((\mathrm{TR}^+(\pi) \wedge \mathrm{PR}(\delta)) \vee \mathrm{TR}^+(\xi)) \wedge (\mathrm{TR}^+(\neg\delta_{\langle\pi\rangle}) \vee \top) \Leftrightarrow (\mathrm{TR}^+(\pi) \vee \mathrm{TR}^+(\xi))$. It is easily seen that this PL formula is true if and only if $\pi \vee \xi$ is True (fact 7).

How does the middle Kleene version of PPL fare? In general the presuppositions of the middle Kleene based propositional formulae can be reduced to the following patterns:

$$PR(\varphi \wedge \psi) \quad \Leftrightarrow \quad PR(\varphi) \wedge (TR^+(\neg\varphi) \vee PR(\psi))$$

$$PR(\varphi \dot\vee \psi) \quad \Leftrightarrow \quad PR(\varphi) \wedge (TR^+(\varphi) \vee PR(\psi))$$

$$PR(\varphi \dot\rightarrow \psi) \quad \Leftrightarrow \quad PR(\varphi) \wedge (TR^+(\neg\varphi) \vee PR(\psi))$$

For the examples under consideration this means the following:

$\delta_{\langle \pi \rangle} \dot\rightarrow \xi$ presupposes π,

$\xi \dot\rightarrow \delta_{\langle \pi \rangle}$ presupposes $\neg\xi \vee \pi$, and

$\pi \dot\rightarrow \delta_{\langle \pi \rangle}$ presupposes $\top$.

Thus, looking back at (13), we see that middle Kleene predicts that (13.a) presupposes *there is a king of France*, that (13.b) presupposes *if baldness is hereditary, then there is a king of France* and that (13.c) presupposes nothing. Middle Kleene PPL still predicts a weak presupposition for example (13.b). On the propositional level, Peters/middle Kleene based PPL essentially makes the predictions argued for in in Karttunen 1974 (as well as Karttunen and Peters 1979). Of course this is no surprise since Peters 1979 proposed the middle Kleene connectives as 'a truth conditional formulation of Karttunen's account of presupposition'.

The weak Kleene version of PPL *does* predict that (13.b) presupposes the existence of a king of France. But, weak Kleene gets the facts right for the wrong reason: it is predicted that *every* presupposition projects, no matter where it originates. So, at the risk of confusing the reader, we can observe that weak Kleene uniformly predicts presuppositions which are too strong, whereas strong Kleene uniformly predicts presuppositions which are too weak. Here are the general rules:

$$PR(\varphi \ddot\wedge \psi) \quad \Leftrightarrow \quad PR(\varphi) \wedge PR(\psi)$$

$$PR(\varphi \ddot\vee \psi) \quad \Leftrightarrow \quad PR(\varphi) \wedge PR(\psi)$$

$$PR(\varphi \ddot\rightarrow \psi) \quad \Leftrightarrow \quad PR(\varphi) \wedge PR(\psi)$$

Applying this to the three examples in (13) gives the following:

$\delta_{\langle \pi \rangle} \ddot\rightarrow \xi$ presupposes π,

$\xi \ddot\rightarrow \delta_{\langle \pi \rangle}$ presupposes π, and

$\pi \ddot\rightarrow \delta_{\langle \pi \rangle}$ presupposes π.

So, translating the conditionals in (13) in terms of the weak Kleene implication entails predicting that all three examples presuppose that *there is a king of France*. The hypothesis that presuppositions always project is known as the *cumulative hypothesis* ('the presuppositions of the whole equal the sum of the presuppositions of the parts'), and was first discussed by Langendoen and Savin 1971. It is not difficult to come up with counterexamples to the pure cumulative hypothesis (example (13.c) is one).[22]

Quantification

Above we noted that as far as the propositional connectives are concerned, middle Kleene makes the same predictions about projection as the system of Karttunen and Peters 1979 does. Let us now see how middle Kleene based PPL deals with the notorious example (6) due to Karttunen and Peters 1979, here repeated (in curtailed form) as (14).

(14) Somebody managed to succeed George V.

Like the system from Karttunen and Peters 1979, PPL distinguishes presupposed from asserted material, but PPL *does* have the possibility of interaction between quantifiers and elementary presuppositions. Consider the following translation in PPL of (14):[23]

(15) $\exists x (S(x)_{\langle D(x) \rangle})$

For all three logics we have the following:

$$\mathsf{PR}(\exists x \varphi) \Leftrightarrow \exists x \mathsf{TR}^+(\varphi) \vee \forall x \mathsf{TR}^-(\varphi)$$

All three PPL systems predict that the formula in (15) presupposes:

$$\exists x (D(x) \wedge S(x)) \vee \forall x (D(x) \wedge \neg S(x))$$

In words: (15) presupposes that either someone had difficulty to succeed George V but did so anyway, or everyone found it difficult to follow up George V and no one actually did. Notice that the first disjunct gives the conditions under which (15) is True, while the second disjunct gives the conditions under which (15) is False. That is: these two conditions tell us —in the Strawsonian fashion— when 'the question of truth and

---

[22]Still the weak Kleene system certainly can be useful in the treatment of presupposition. For example, in Gazdar 1979 the 'potential presuppositions' of a sentence amount to the union of the potential presuppositions of the sub-sentences and for the calculation of these potential presuppositions a weak Kleene logic may be used. In Gazdar's system, the unwanted presuppositions are later thrown away by a canceling mechanism.

[23]Here S represents 'succeed George V', while D represents 'had difficulty to succeed George V'; we have not bothered to deal with the internal structure of the VP (which is beyond first-order logic anyway). We make up for this lack of concern in chapter 5.

falsity' *does* arise for example (14); compare the Strawsonian definition of presupposing on page 89. Notice that the alleged oddity of example (14) is explained: both possibilities are contradicted by the actual 'way of the world': it is a historic fact that the accession of George VI to the throne went smoothly. So as far as example (14) is concerned, any version of PPL does better than Karttunen and Peters 1979.

The inability of Karttunen and Peters to deal with examples like (14) is one of the issues Heim discusses in her influential Heim 1983b. In that article, she gives an example which is similar to (14), namely (16).

(16) A fat man pushes his bicycle.

Heim's system predicts that this example presupposes that every fat man has a bicycle. Obviously, sentence (16) does not give rise to any intuitive presuppositions to that effect. It should be noted here that it is a matter of debate what the intuitive presuppositions of (16) and other sentences involving presupposition-quantification interaction are. Nevertheless, there is consensus that (16) does not give rise to the Heimian, universal presupposition, but that it presupposes something 'weaker'. Given that PPL can deal with examples like (14) it is interesting to see what it predicts for example (16). Consider the following translation of (16) in middle Kleene based PPL.[24]

(17) $\exists x(FM(x) \mathbin{\dot\wedge} \exists y(B\text{-}of(y,x) \mathbin{\dot\wedge} P(x,y))_{\langle\exists!z B\text{-}of(z,x)\rangle})$

Calculating PR (17), we get the following result:

$$\exists x(FM(x) \wedge \exists!z B\text{-}of(z,x) \wedge \exists y(B\text{-}of(y,x) \wedge P(x,y)))\vee$$
$$\forall x(FM(x) \rightarrow (\exists!z B\text{-}of(z,x) \wedge \forall y(B\text{-}of(y,x) \rightarrow \neg P(x,y))))$$

In words: either there is a fat man who has a (unique) bicycle which he pushes or every fat man has a (unique) bike which he doesn't push. Again, the first disjunct gives the Truth condition of (17) while the second gives the condition under which it is False. This presupposition is much weaker than the universal one predicted by Heim, and the binding problem from Karttunen and Peters does not arise either.[25] In the situation discussed in the introduction (there is a fat man who has a bicycle which he pushes and there is another fat man who does not

---

[24]Since PPL is a static logic, the variable x in $P(x)$ cannot be bound in a formula like $P(x)_{\langle\exists!xQ(x)\rangle}$. The quantifier in the presupposed material cannot bind the variable in the asserted part. To circumvent this problem we systematically translate such presuppositions as: $\exists x(Q(x) \mathbin{\dot\wedge} P(x))_{\langle\exists!xQ(x)\rangle}$. And this has the desired effect. Again, the next chapter will present a compositional derivation of this formula.

[25]Roughly the same holds for the strong and weak Kleene versions. Strong Kleene makes the same predictions as middle Kleene based PPL for this example. According to weak Kleene based PPL, example (16) presupposes that either someone has a bike or everyone does.

have a bicycle), the predicted presupposition is satisfied and the entire formula is True. Let us now see how PPL does with the other examples Heim discusses, beginning with (18) and its associated middle Kleene based PPL translation in (19).

(18) Every fat man pushes his bicycle.

(19) $\forall x (FM(x) \dot\to \exists y (B\text{-}of(y,x) \dot\wedge P(x,y))_{\langle \exists!z B\text{-}of(z,x) \rangle})$

Heim's system predicts that (18) presupposes that every fat man owns a bicycle, just as it did for (16), and that prediction is too strong as argued before. PPL does not predict such a presupposition. In general, the following holds:

$$\mathsf{PR}(\forall x \varphi) \Leftrightarrow \forall x \mathsf{TR}^+(\varphi) \vee \exists x \mathsf{TR}^-(\varphi)$$

So, it is predicted that the presupposition of (18) comes very close to the presupposition of (16). Namely:

$$\forall x (FM(x) \to (\exists!z B\text{-}of(z,x) \wedge \exists y (B\text{-}of(y,x) \wedge P(x,y)))) \vee$$
$$\exists x (FM(x) \wedge \exists!z B\text{-}of(z,x) \wedge \forall y (B\text{-}of(y,x) \to \neg P(x,y)))$$

In words: either every fat man has a (unique) bicycle which he pushes or some fat man has a (unique) bicycle which he does not push. Finally consider another example which Heim 1983b discusses in some detail:

(20) Every man who serves his king will be rewarded

If we represent (20) in (middle Kleene based) PPL we get the following formula:

(21) $\forall x ((M(x) \dot\wedge \exists y (K\text{-}of(y,x) \dot\wedge S(x,y))_{\langle \exists!z K\text{-}of(z,x) \rangle}) \dot\to R(x))$

In Heim's system it is predicted that this sentence presupposes that every man has a king. In PPL again a weaker, disjunctive presupposition is derived. This is PR(21):

$$\forall x (M(x) \wedge \exists!z \ K\text{-}of(z,x) \wedge \exists y (K\text{-}of(y,x) \wedge S(x,y)) \to R(x)) \vee$$
$$\exists x (M(x) \wedge \exists!z \ K\text{-}of(z,x) \wedge \exists y (K\text{-}of(y,x) \wedge S(x,y)) \wedge \neg R(x))$$

In words: either every man who has a king and serves him is rewarded, or there is a man who has a king which he serves but is not rewarded. Notice that this presupposition is satisfied in the scenario with the nine Belgians and one Dutchman discussed in section 4.1.

Where does this leave us? We have seen that to deal with example (14) from Karttunen and Peters 1979 there is no need to 'go dynamic'. As long as we have a representation in which presupposed and asserted material can interact with each other we do not run into the problems Karttunen and Peters have to face up to. We have also seen that when we have such an integrated representation we can deal with the quantificational examples (16), (18) and (20) from Heim 1983b, without predicting the strong presuppositions Heim's system gives rise to.

Statics

This is of course not to say that ultimately we do not want a combination of partiality and dynamics to deal with presuppositions. It *does* mean that for the examples discussed so far it is not necessary. It is not difficult to come up with examples which really need both partiality and dynamics. First consider (22), which extends example (16). Here the *it* in the second sentence refers to the bicycle owned by the fat man, which was introduced in the first sentence. The intuitive PPL representation is given in (23).

(22)   A fat man pushes his bicycle. It is broken.

(23) $\exists x(FM(x) \,\dot{\wedge}\, \exists y(B\text{-}of(y,x) \,\dot{\wedge}\, P(x,y))_{\langle \exists ! z B\text{-}of(z,x)\rangle}) \,\dot{\wedge}\, Br(z)$

Since PPL is a static system there is no way in which a quantifier can bind variables which occur outside its scope, hence the z in the last conjunct will remain unbound.

Another example which cannot be dealt with in PPL is (24), which extends example (20). The intended reading is that every man who serves his king is rewarded *by his king*. A PPL representation which tries to reflect this reading is given in (25).

(24)   Every man who serves his king will be rewarded by him.

(25) $\forall x((M(x) \,\dot{\wedge}\, \exists y(K\text{-}of(y,x) \,\dot{\wedge}\, S(x,y))_{\langle \exists ! z K\text{-}of(z,x)\rangle}) \,\dot{\to}\, R(x,z))$

Again, the fact that PPL is a static system is responsible for the fact that the co-reference between *his king* and *him* cannot be accounted for. Note, however, that these problems are simply a specific instance of the problems *any* static logic has with *sentence sequencing* and *donkey-type sentences* (as discussed in section 2.1), and which are the main motivation for dynamic semantics anyway. Put differently: the problems for PPL posed by (22) and (24) have nothing to do with the treatment of presuppositions as such, but everything with the treatment of anaphora in discourse. In chapter 6, where presuppositions are studied from the dynamic perspective, we shall return to these examples.

4.4   Flexibility: The Floating $\mathcal{A}$ Theory

The foregoing illustrates that partiality in the semantic analysis of presuppositions is still as relevant as ever. As a consequence, so is the critique on it. One major point of criticism is that the partial approach lacks *flexibility*. However, as argued in Beaver and Krahmer 1995, this flexibility argument does not hold. Before we discuss this argument, let us first look at the flexibility criticism itself in more detail.

As an example consider the negation. As soon as negation is given a truth table, as we did for ¬ in definition 1, the predictions concerning the projection behavior of presuppositions arising in the scope of negation are fixed. So, given the PPL truth table, negation is predicted to be a hole for presupposition projection, and this is indeed the way negation in natural language often behaves. But often is not always; there are cases in which negation displays a different behavior. A classic example is (26).

(26) The king of France is *not* bald, since there is no king of France.

Example (26) intuitively does not presuppose that France has a king; this is explicitly denied by the *since* sentence. Still, the first sentence of (26) triggers an elementary presupposition which says that France does have a king. If negation usually is a hole for presupposition projection, then the negation in example (26) behaves as a *black hole*; the presupposition in its scope simply vanishes. Sticking to a single negation (¬), entails predicting that (26) can never be a true statement, which is obviously not the case. Therefore it has been argued that we need to introduce a second, 'black hole' (or in more conventional terminology, 'plug') negation (represented here as −).

Definition 12 (Black hole negation)

> *syntax*   If φ is a formula, then $-\varphi$ is a formula.
>
> *semantics* $[\![-\varphi]\!]^+ = \{g \mid g \notin [\![\varphi]\!]^+\}$
> $[\![-\varphi]\!]^- = [\![\varphi]\!]^+$

This definition gives rise to the following truth table:

	−
T	F
F	T
N	T

Although this negation is interesting from a logical point of view (see footnote 12), the introduction of a second negation only motivated to deal with so-called canceling cases like (26) is a highly undesirable move.[26] For one thing, examples like (26) can only be used in certain restricted contexts. Moreover, supposing that we have two negations (¬ and −): which one should be the representation of the negation-phrase in example (27)?

(27) It is not true that the queen of England courts the king of France, since France has no king.

---

[26] But see Seuren 1985:260-266 for independent motivation for this second negation.

Intuitively, the presupposition that there is a queen of England is projected, while the presupposition that there is a king of France is not, since this presupposition is explicitly denied by the *since* sentence. Translating *it is not true that* as ¬ entails wrongly presupposing that France has a king, while translating it as − entails wrongly *not* presupposing that England has a queen. Even more problematic is that the phenomenon of vanishing presuppositions is not restricted to negation at all. We have already encountered an example involving implication: intuitively, the presupposition that France has a king projects in the first example but not in the second one:

(28) a. If baldness is hereditary, then the king of France is bald.
　　 b. If France has a king, then the king of France is bald.

As we have seen, writing down a PPL truth table for the implication entails not predicting the right analysis for one of these examples. Middle and strong Kleene capture the intuitions for the b-sentence but not for the a-sentence, and for weak Kleene the opposite holds. Hence, none of these interpretations captures the projection facilities of natural language implication. Yet we do not want to commit ourselves to an ambiguity view on implications merely to account for the presupposition projection facts. And, even if we would consider postulating such an ambiguity for implications, one look at the discussion in Soames 1979 should convince us that this is not the way to go. Soames discusses the case of disjunction. Consider:

(29) Either *the king of France* is bald, or baldness isn't hereditary.
(30) Either baldness isn't hereditary, or *the king of France* is bald.
(31) Either *the king of France* is bald, or *the queen of England* was confused when she told me she saw no hair on his head.
(32) Either *the king of France* is bald, or France is a republic.
(33) Either France is a republic, or *the king of France* is bald.
(34) Either *the king of France* is bald, or *the president of France* is.

Intuitively, in (29) the elementary presupposition triggered by the definite description projects from the left disjunct, in (30) it projects from the right disjunct and in (31) the elementary presuppositions project from both disjuncts. However, in (32) presupposition projection from the left disjunct is blocked by the right disjunct, and *vice versa* in (33). In the last example no elementary presupposition projects from either disjunct: they are incompatible. Clearly no single, partial interpretation of disjunction can account for all these facts, and here we would need to postulate a four-way ambiguity for the word *or*, just to account for presupposition projection. The upshot of this discussion is the following.

There is no single partial logic which can account for all the projection data, and there is no independent motivation to assume that the logical connectives are multiply ambiguous (two partial interpretations for negation, four for disjunction etc.) merely to account for the projection facts (as pointed out by, for example, Van der Sandt 1989 and Soames 1979).

What are we to do about this? The previous examples show clearly that we cannot entirely solve the projection problem by defining some partial truth tables and hope for the best. There is more to it than that. In Beaver and Krahmer 1995 it is argued that it is nevertheless possible for an approach to presuppositions based on partial logic to make flexible projection predictions, without postulating any *ad hoc* ambiguities for the logical connectives. Let us discuss this argument. Its main ingredient goes back to the early days of partial logic: Bochvar's *assertion* operator (introduced in Bochvar 1939, compare also the *horizontal* in Frege 1879). It is defined as follows:

Definition 13 (Assertion operator)

syntax   If φ is a formula, then $\mathcal{A}\varphi$ is a formula.

semantics $[\![\mathcal{A}\varphi]\!]^+ = [\![\varphi]\!]^+$
$[\![\mathcal{A}\varphi]\!]^- = \{\ g\ \mid\ g \notin [\![\varphi]\!]^+\}$

This definition gives rise to the following truth table:

	$\mathcal{A}$
T	T
F	F
N	F

$\mathcal{A}\varphi$ is True iff φ is True, and False otherwise. Bochvar introduces this operator to relate his so-called *internal matrices* (the ones which are presently also known as weak Kleene) with the classical, external matrices. For the present purposes, the $\mathcal{A}$-operator can be thought of as an *elementary-presupposition wipe-out device*. Whatever is presupposed by some formula φ, it is easily seen that $\mathcal{A}\varphi$ presupposes nothing.[27] Here are some characteristic properties of $\mathcal{A}$.

Fact 12 *($\mathcal{A}$ equivalences)*

1. $\mathcal{A}(\varphi_{\langle\pi\rangle})$ *is equivalent with* $\mathcal{A}\pi \wedge \mathcal{A}\varphi$
2. $\mathcal{A}\mathcal{A}\varphi$ *is equivalent with* $\mathcal{A}\varphi$
3. $\mathcal{A}\varphi$ *is equivalent with* φ, *if* φ *is defined*
4. $-\varphi$ *is equivalent with* $\neg\mathcal{A}\varphi$

---

[27] Recall the Strawsonian definition of 'presuppose' (φ presupposes π iff whenever π is not true, φ is neither true nor false) and observe that $\mathcal{A}\varphi$ is *always* either true or false.

The first equivalence says that the *presupposition wipe-out device* indeed wipes out presuppositions. As a corollary, note that $\mathcal{A}(\top_{\langle\pi\rangle})$ (or $\mathcal{A}\partial\pi$) is equivalent with $\mathcal{A}\pi$. The second equivalence illustrates that multiple $\mathcal{A}$'s have the same effect as a single one; you can't wipe-out presuppositions which are not there any more. The third equivalence is related to this: if φ is defined (always either True or False) and hence does not contain presuppositions, $\mathcal{A}\varphi$ is equivalent with φ. The fourth and final equivalence shows that we can define the 'black hole' negation $(-)$ in terms of $\neg$ and $\mathcal{A}$. This means that in the presence of the $\mathcal{A}$-operator we can translate negation unambiguously using $\neg$, and allow for the possibility that (under certain conditions) an occurrence of $\mathcal{A}$ may wipe-out presuppositions in the scope of the negation. This would do justice to the observation that the canceling/black hole-negation is only used in certain specific contexts. But there is an additional advantage: there is no reason whatsoever to limit occurrences of $\mathcal{A}$ to propositions directly under the scope of negation. Why not let them float around freely? This is the essence of a *Floating $\mathcal{A}$ theory*. Instead of postulating any ambiguities we take one logical system as basic; say, weak Kleene based PPL (which, as we have seen, embodies the cumulative hypothesis: every elementary presupposition projects). If we let $\mathcal{A}$'s float around freely, then we can represent the first sub-sentence of (27) schematically as $\neg(\mathcal{A}(\varphi_{\langle\pi'\rangle})_{\langle\pi\rangle})$,[28] the implications in (28) can be modeled as $\varphi \dot{\rightarrow} \psi$ and $\varphi \dot{\rightarrow} \mathcal{A}\psi$ respectively, and for the disjunctions we have $\varphi \ddot{\vee} \psi$, $\mathcal{A}\varphi \ddot{\vee} \psi$, $\varphi \ddot{\vee} \mathcal{A}\psi$ and $\mathcal{A}\varphi \ddot{\vee} \mathcal{A}\psi$ thus covering all cases in (29) – (34).

How can we employ this flexibility in a floating $\mathcal{A}$ theory? For that, we need the following ingredients:

- o each sentence is associated with a *set* of translations,
- o over this set a *preference order* is defined, and
- o the translations have to satisfy certain *constraints*.

Without particularly wanting to commit ourselves to a specific version of a floating $\mathcal{A}$ theory, let us look at one possible interpretation of it.

First, we associate each (syntactically disambiguated) sentence with a set of translations. Consider some sentence S and suppose that φ

---

[28]Or, equivalently, $\neg(\top_{\langle\pi\rangle} \ddot{\wedge} \mathcal{A}(\top_{\langle\pi'\rangle}) \ddot{\wedge} \varphi)$. Where π represents the proposition that England a queen and π' that France has a king. As noted below fact 12: $\mathcal{A}(\top_{\langle\pi'\rangle})$ is equivalent with π' (the presupposition is wiped-out).

is an $\mathcal{A}$-free, weak Kleene based PPL formula representing S.[29] The translation-set of S, designated as $\mathsf{TS}(S)$, is the minimal set such that:[30]

1. $\varphi \in \mathsf{TS}(S)$

2. Any formula η that results from replacing all occurrences of one or more formulae χ which are of the form $\psi_{\langle \pi \rangle}$ by $\mathcal{A}\chi$ is an element of $\mathsf{TS}(S)$.

Thus, for example, if some sentence S is initially represented by a formula of the form $\gamma_{\langle \pi_1 \rangle} \ \ddot{\vee} \ \delta_{\langle \pi_2 \rangle}$, then:

$$\mathsf{TS}(S) = \{ \ \gamma_{\langle \pi_1 \rangle} \ \ddot{\vee} \ \delta_{\langle \pi_2 \rangle},$$
$$\mathcal{A}(\gamma_{\langle \pi_1 \rangle}) \ \ddot{\vee} \ \delta_{\langle \pi_2 \rangle},$$
$$\gamma_{\langle \pi_1 \rangle} \ \ddot{\vee} \ \mathcal{A}(\delta_{\langle \pi_2 \rangle}),$$
$$\mathcal{A}(\gamma_{\langle \pi_1 \rangle}) \ \ddot{\vee} \ \mathcal{A}(\delta_{\langle \pi_2 \rangle}) \}$$

Second, we need to define a preference order over the translation set. How to do this? The intention is to keep the usage of the $\mathcal{A}$ operator as limited as possible; the default is that presuppositions project. We can interpret this as follows: if γ and δ are both elements of $\mathsf{TS}(S)$, then γ is preferred over δ if the number of $\mathcal{A}$ operators occurring in γ is lower then the number of $\mathcal{A}$ occurrences in δ.[31]

The net effect of defining the order in this way is that the preferred element of $\mathsf{TS}(S)$ will be φ itself. When φ violates one of the constraints, a formula which is lower on the ordering than φ (and which contains $\mathcal{A}$'s) may turn out to be the most preferred one. This brings us to the third and last ingredient: the constraints. For now, let us follow Van der Sandt 1992 and just require *consistency* and *informativity*. Informativity essentially says that no (sub-)formula should be redundant, consistency amounts to: no (sub)formula should be inconsistent.[32]

---

[29]The reader may think of φ as the representation derived for (one of the readings of) S by the fragment discussed in the next chapter.

[30]For the sake of clarity, we do not let $\mathcal{A}$-operators float around *entirely* free, since this would create a lot of redundancy, and does not add anything to the main argument.

[31]Needless to say this is a simplification, but it will do for the present purposes. It would be interesting to (further) investigate the possibility of defining the ordering in terms of logical strength (as done in Beaver and Krahmer 1995), but here we refrain from doing so.

[32]The conditions can be defined analogously to the Van der Sandtian condition. For example, a formula φ is consistent if there is a model M such that φ is True in M. A formula φ is informative if it contains no subformula ψ such that φ is equivalent with $\{\top/\psi\}\varphi$ (compare Beaver's version of Van der Sandtian informativity in Beaver 1997). As in Van der Sandt's approach, the assumption is that informativity applies at the level of (sub-)sentences.

Now, consider example (26) again. Schematically, this sentence is represented by a formula of the form

$$\neg(\varphi_{\langle\pi\rangle}) \,\ddot{\wedge}\, \neg\pi,$$

and this is also, by definition, the most preferred element of the translation set of example (26). However, it is easily seen that this formula is not consistent: the second conjunct explicitly denies the presupposition of the first conjunct. This means that the first element of the translation set is rejected, and the next (and only remaining) element is considered, which is:

$$\neg\mathcal{A}(\varphi_{\langle\pi\rangle}) \,\ddot{\wedge}\, \neg\pi$$

This formula is the most preferred element of the translation set which does not violate any of the constraints, and coincides with the intuitive interpretation for example (26) given above.

Next consider the following example.

(35) If John is married, then his wife is a lucky woman.

Schematically, this sentence would be represented by the following formula:

$$\pi \,\ddot{\rightarrow}\, \varphi_{\langle\pi\rangle}$$

where π represents the proposition that John has a wife/is married, and φ the proposition that John's wife is a lucky woman. This formula violates the informativity condition; it contains a subformula (the antecedent of the conditional) which is redundant: $\pi \,\ddot{\rightarrow}\, \varphi_{\langle\pi\rangle}$ is equivalent with $\top \,\ddot{\rightarrow}\, \varphi_{\langle\pi\rangle}$. The next element of the translation set of (35) is:

$$\pi \,\ddot{\rightarrow}\, \mathcal{A}(\varphi_{\langle\pi\rangle})$$

This interpretation does not violate any of the constraints. The presupposition that John has a wife is wiped out (not projected) and intuitively this is correct.

Discussion

Let us recapitulate. We have seen that it is possible for a partial account of presuppositions to be given the required flexibility without postulating unmotivated ambiguities for the logical connectives, namely by adding the $\mathcal{A}$ operator to the language of PPL. We presented a very rudimentary sketch of such a flexible 'floating $\mathcal{A}$ theory'. Such a theory contains three important ingredients: each sentence is associated with a set of representations, this set is ordered, and a number of independently motivated, pragmatic constraints apply to the elements of this set.[33] We

---

[33]It seems to us that these ingredients are also, at least conceptually, present in Link 1986, a somewhat cryptic but rather funny defense of partial logic in the analysis

have seen that this allows us to give an account of cancelation of pre-suppositions under the scope of negation by throwing away readings which are not consistent, and we gave one illustration of canceling in conditionals by throwing away readings which violate the informativity condition. We believe that sentences involving other logical connectives, can be dealt with along similar lines, although we leave such matters for future research. There is a lot of room for fine-tuning, in particular with respect to the preference order and the constraints. Remember also that the approach, as all the work in this chapter, is fully static. For a discussion of the restrictions this brings about we refer back to the part on 'statics' of section 4.3 and forward to chapter 6 in which we discuss an approach to presupposition which combines a version of DRT with techniques from partial logic. In chapter 6 we also briefly describe a dynamic version of the floating $\mathcal{A}$ theory. We have also said nothing about the role of *accommodation* in a partial setting. For that we refer to Beaver and Krahmer 1995 in which it is shown how a Stalnakerian model of common ground maintenance (Beaver 1995) can serve as a kind of shell around the partial approach to presupposition.

In the end, the constraints may turn out to play a rather important role in the theory. Not only are the constraints as they are preliminar-ily defined above, open for improvements, other constraints will have to be added. To give but one example, presupposition cancelation in the scope of negations, as in example (26), is not only related to consistency, but also to more general discourse/dialogue factors. Examples like (26) are typically uttered when someone else has just claimed that the king of France is bald (see Blok 1993 and Van der Sandt n.d. for discussion). This rather specific context should certainly be an important factor in the treatment of such examples. How to account for the influence of such more general pragmatic properties by formulating constraints on possible readings is still an open question. It should be stressed, however, that in this respect the partial approach discussed here is not different from other current theories of presupposition (such as the presuppositions-as-anaphors approach of Van der Sandt). Even though the influence of such diverse factors as world-knowledge, intonation and discourse structure (to name but a few) on presupposition projection is currently a cent-ral theme in presupposition research (see, for example, Bos et al. 1995, Asher and Lascarides 1997, Krahmer and Piwek 1997, Geurts and Van der Sandt 1997), there is to the best of our knowledge no theory of pre-

---

of presupposition. Link's work is a prime example of the combination of partial logic with pragmatic principles. He seeks to connect partial logic with theories of context change, and ends with a plea to "*both the semanticist and the pragmaticist camp (. . .) to strive for mutual cooperation*" (Link 1986: 116).

supposition which can account for the restricting influence of all these factors on the possibilities of presupposition projection.

For our current purposes, however, the lack of a full-fledged set of pragmatic constraints, entails that the role of the underlying partial logic in the ultimate version of the floating $\mathcal{A}$ theory cannot be fully estimated. What we have shown, however, is that contrary to popular belief, it is possible to give a flexible account of presupposition based on partial logics, and that there are still a number of very promising lines for future research from the partial perspective.

4.5 Discussion

4.5.1 Karttunen and Peters Revisited

We have looked at three standard (static) versions of PPL, each with its own predictions about the projection behavior of presuppositions, called strong Kleene, Peters/middle Kleene and Bochvar/weak Kleene based PPL respectively. The first system can be seen as the underlying logic of Hausser's Montagovian analysis of presuppositions. It uniformly predicts symmetric, weak presuppositions. The second system is – as far as the propositional connectives are concerned – essentially the logic underlying the analysis of presuppositions argued for by Karttunen, Peters and Karttunen and Peters in various publications. The key feature is the asymmetry of presupposition projection: the elementary presuppositions in left-hand subexpressions project, while those in right-hand subexpressions give rise to weak presuppositions. The third system corresponds with the cumulative analysis of presuppositions discussed by Langendoen & Savin. Here every presupposition projects, no matter where it originates. Furthermore, we have discussed one main, traditional point of criticism on the partial approach to presuppositions, namely that it is too rigid. In the previous section we have seen that this objection can be overcome.

Our main motivation for this enterprise was to see what the role of partiality is in the recent interest in combined partial/dynamic approaches to presupposition. Here the central body of examples involves interaction between elementary presuppositions and quantifiers. The standard examples are Karttunen and Peters' (14), and Heim's (16), (18) and (20). It turns out that no version of PPL we discussed suffers from the Karttunen and Peters binding-problem. Since Karttunen and Peters keep presupposed and asserted material strictly separated, there is no way in which quantifiers in one component can bind variables in the other one. In the versions of PPL we discussed, there is also a division between presuppositions and assertions (the former are 'subscripts' on the latter), but PPL uses an integrated representation; there is room for interaction. As far as Heim's examples are concerned: none of the PPL versions results in the undesired universal presuppositions, irrespective of the quantificational force in which the elementary presupposition is embedded. So as far as the standard examples are concerned, there is no immediate need to 'go dynamic'. Of course, PPL cannot deal with examples like (22) and (24), but as we noted above, these problems are totally independent of the analysis of presupposition as such: examples (22) and (24) are just presuppositional variants of the type of examples which prompted the shift to dynamic semantics in the first place.

Above we mentioned the relation between the middle Kleene propositional connectives and Karttunen and Peters' Montagovian analysis of presuppositions. In fact, this relationship is not as clear as Karttunen and Peters suggest it is. To begin with, middle Kleene is a three-valued logic, while Karttunen and Peters' system is either classical or four-valued, depending on your point of view. More interestingly, middle Kleene PPL, with transplication, does not suffer from the binding-problem, while Karttunen and Peters' system of Conventional Implicatures does. Some reflection (as we do below) shows that it is not so much the complex Montagovian architecture which causes the problems; it is the underlying two-dimensional approach of strictly separating between presupposed and asserted representations which makes trouble. The system of Karttunen and Peters 1979 is not the only attempt to add presuppositions to classical Montague Grammar, a similar intention can be found in Hausser 1976 and Cooper 1983. However, neither of these is entirely satisfactory either. In the next chapter we shall discuss the difficult relationship between classical Montague Grammar and presupposition theory in more detail. Before we do that, however, let us say something more about the 'Logic of Conventional Implicature'.

4.5.2 A Note on the Logic of Conventional Implicature

In an attempt to get a clearer view of what is going on in the system of Karttunen and Peters 1979, Beaver and Krahmer 1995 strip the system of Karttunen and Peters of everything which is a Montagovian artefact. The result is a non-standard but handy first-order logic which might be called the *Logic of Conventional Implicatures* (abbreviated as CIL). CIL is best understood as a *two-dimensional* logic (Herzberger 1973, Karttunen and Peters 1979:fn7). With each formula, *two* interpretations are connected: $[\![\varphi]\!]^A_{M,g}$ gives the *assertive meaning* of φ in a model M with respect to an assignment g while $[\![\varphi]\!]^P_{M,g}$ gives the *presuppositional meaning* of φ in M with respect to g. The *interpretation* of φ in M with respect to g, $[\![\varphi]\!]^{CIL}_{M,g}$, is equated with $\langle [\![\varphi]\!]^A_{M,g}, [\![\varphi]\!]^P_{M,g} \rangle$. Both the assertive and the presuppositional meaning of a formula are standard: both map formulae to either 1 (true) or 0 (false). This gives rise to four possibilities: $\langle 1,1\rangle$, $\langle 0,1\rangle$, $\langle 1,0\rangle$ and $\langle 0,0\rangle$. We abbreviate these combinations as T, F, t and f respectively. In words: a formula is interpreted as T when both the presuppositional and the assertive meanings are true, as F when the presuppositional meaning is true and the assertive one is false, as t when the presuppositional meaning is false and the assertive meaning is true and as f when both the presuppositional and the assertive meanings are false. Now, given the semantic parameters used in this chapter, $[\![.]\!]^{\mathrm{CIL}}_{M,g}$ is defined as follows (where $\bigvee x[\varphi,\psi]$ is the notation employed by Karttunen and Peters as a binary version of existential quantification).

Definition 14 (CIL semantics)

1. $[\![R(t_1,\ldots,t_n)]\!]^A_g = 1$ iff $\langle [\![t_1]\!]_g,\ldots,[\![t_n]\!]_g\rangle \in I(R)$
   $[\![R(t_1,\ldots,t_n)]\!]^P_g = 1$

2. $[\![\neg\varphi]\!]^A_g = 1$ iff $[\![\varphi]\!]^A_g = 0$
   $[\![\neg\varphi]\!]^P_g = 1$ iff $[\![\varphi]\!]^P_g = 1$

3. $[\![\varphi \wedge \psi]\!]^A_g = 1$ iff $[\![\varphi]\!]^A_g = [\![\psi]\!]^A_g = 1$
   $[\![\varphi \wedge \psi]\!]^P_g = 1$ iff $[\![\varphi]\!]^P_g = 1$ & $([\![\varphi]\!]^A_g = 1 \Rightarrow [\![\psi]\!]^P_g = 1)$

4. $[\![\varphi_{\langle\pi\rangle}]\!]^A_g = 1$ iff $[\![\varphi]\!]^A_g = 1$
   $[\![\varphi_{\langle\pi\rangle}]\!]^P_g = 1$ iff $[\![\pi]\!]^P_g = [\![\pi]\!]^A_g = [\![\varphi]\!]^P_g = 1$

5. $[\![\bigvee x[\varphi,\psi]]\!]^A_g = 1$ iff $\exists d : [\![\varphi]\!]^A_{g[x/d]} = [\![\psi]\!]^A_{g[x/d]} = 1$
   $[\![\bigvee x[\varphi,\psi]]\!]^P_g = 1$ iff $\exists d [\![\varphi]\!]^P_{g[x/d]} = 1$ & $\exists d [\![\varphi]\!]^A_{g[x/d]} = [\![\psi]\!]^P_{g[x/d]} = 1$

In general, the assertive meaning of a formula is as it is in standard Predicate Logic. The novelties are found in the presuppositional meanings. The presuppositional interpretation of a predicate is always 1: an atomic formula can only be True or False, atomic predicates do not trigger presuppositions. The presuppositional interpretation of $\neg\varphi$ is true iff the presuppositional meaning of φ is true; the negation of a formula shares its presuppositions with the formula itself, negation is a hole for presupposition projection. From clause 2 of definition 14 we can distil the interpretation of $\neg$ itself: negation changes the assertive truth-value, but leaves the presuppositional one untouched. For example, if $[\![\varphi]\!]^{\mathrm{CIL}} = \langle 1,1\rangle$ (= T), then $[\![\neg\varphi]\!]^{\mathrm{CIL}} = \langle 0,1\rangle$ (= F). Of course, we can do the same exercise for conjunction and transplication.[34] The reader may verify that this gives rise to the following truth tables:

Fact 13 (CIL *negation, conjunction and transplication*)

¬	
T	F
F	T
t	f
f	t

∧	T	F	t	f
T	T	F	t	f
F	F	F	F	F
t	t	f	t	f
f	f	f	f	f

	T	F	t	f
T	T	t	t	t
F	F	f	f	f
t	t	t	t	t
f	f	f	f	f

In accordance with Visser 1984 let us call this the *extended middle Kleene system*. Some reflection shows that when all t's and f's (cases where the presuppositional meaning is not true) are replaced for N's, we immediately arrive at the middle Kleene truth table. That CIL is indeed the underlying first-order logic of Karttunen and Peters 1979 can be checked by inspecting the appendix of their article: $[\![.]\!]^A$ gives the interpretation of extensional phrases, while $[\![.]\!]^P$ gives the interpretation of implicational phrases. As an example let us once more re-discuss Karttunen and Peters' example, repeated here as (36.a), with the CIL translation given in (36.b).[35]

(36) a. Somebody managed to succeed George V.

b. $\bigvee x[human(x), succeed\,(x,g)_{\langle difficult\text{-}to\text{-}succeed(x,g)\rangle}]$

Calculating $[\![(36.b)]\!]^{CIL}$ shows that the assertional meaning of this formula is true if there is somebody who succeeded George V. The presuppositional meaning is true if there is somebody who had difficulty succeeding George V. Hence the representation in (36.b) is T in a model where somebody succeeded George V and somebody had difficulty succeeding George V. And this is exactly the —wrong— analysis predicted by the Montagovian system of Karttunen and Peters 1979. So CIL shows that it is not so much the Montagovian architecture of

---

[34]Karttunen and Peters do not use transplication. Rather they specify for a presupposition trigger what it asserts and what it presupposes. In CIL terms:

$[\![bachelor(x)]\!]_g^A = [\![\neg married(x)]\!]_g^A$, while
$[\![bachelor(x)]\!]_g^P = [\![male(x) \wedge adult(x)]\!]_g^A$.

Obviously, $[\![bachelor(x)]\!]_g^{CIL}$ and $[\![(\neg married(x))_{\langle male(x) \wedge adult(x)\rangle}]\!]_g^{CIL}$ are equivalent.

[35]We assume that *somebody* is translated as an existential quantifier over human beings. Since CIL is a first-order logic we can not express the higher-order property of having difficulty with something. Hence we treat 'difficult-to-succeed' as an atomic first-order predicate.

Karttunen and Peters 1979 which cause them; their underlying two-dimensional philosophy is to be blamed.[36]

Appendix

In this appendix we give a proof of fact 7, repeated below.

Fact 7 *(From* PPL *to* PL*)*
For all PPL *formulae φ and models M:*

1. $[\![\mathsf{TR}^+(\varphi)]\!]^{\mathrm{PL}}_M \Leftrightarrow [\![\varphi]\!]^+_M$
2. $[\![\mathsf{TR}^-(\varphi)]\!]^{\mathrm{PL}}_M \Leftrightarrow [\![\varphi]\!]^-_M$

Proof. By a simple induction. We let $\mathsf{TR}^\pm(\varphi) = \mathsf{TR}^\pm(\psi)$ abbreviate $\mathsf{TR}^+(\varphi) = \mathsf{TR}^+(\psi)$ and $\mathsf{TR}^-(\varphi) = \mathsf{TR}^-(\psi)$.

1. $[\![\mathsf{TR}^+(R(t_1,\ldots,t_n))]\!]^{\mathrm{PL}} \Leftrightarrow [\![R(t_1,\ldots,t_n)]\!]^{\mathrm{PL}} \Leftrightarrow$
   $\{g \mid \langle [\![t_1]\!]_g,\ldots,[\![t_n]\!]_g \rangle \in I(R)\} \Leftrightarrow [\![R(t_1,\ldots,t_n)]\!]^+$
   $[\![\mathsf{TR}^-(R(t_1,\ldots,t_n))]\!]^{\mathrm{PL}} \Leftrightarrow [\![\neg R(t_1,\ldots,t_n)]\!]^{\mathrm{PL}} \Leftrightarrow$
   $\{g \mid \langle [\![t_1]\!]_g,\ldots,[\![t_n]\!]_g \rangle \notin I(R)\} \Leftrightarrow [\![R(t_1,\ldots,t_n)]\!]^-$

2. $[\![\mathsf{TR}^+(t_1 \equiv t_2)]\!]^{\mathrm{PL}} \Leftrightarrow [\![t_1 \equiv t_2]\!]^{\mathrm{PL}} \Leftrightarrow \{g \mid [\![t_1]\!]_g = [\![t_2]\!]_g\} \Leftrightarrow [\![t_1 \equiv t_2]\!]^+$
   $[\![\mathsf{TR}^-(t_1 \equiv t_2)]\!]^{\mathrm{PL}} \Leftrightarrow [\![\neg t_1 \equiv t_2]\!]^{\mathrm{PL}} \Leftrightarrow \{g \mid [\![t_1]\!]_g \neq [\![t_2]\!]_g\} \Leftrightarrow [\![t_1 \equiv t_2]\!]^-$

3. $[\![\mathsf{TR}^+(\neg\varphi)]\!]^{\mathrm{PL}} \Leftrightarrow [\![\mathsf{TR}^-(\varphi)]\!]^{\mathrm{PL}} \Leftrightarrow [\mathrm{IH}] \ [\![\varphi]\!]^- \Leftrightarrow [\![\neg\varphi]\!]^+$
   $[\![\mathsf{TR}^-(\neg\varphi)]\!]^{\mathrm{PL}} \Leftrightarrow [\![\mathsf{TR}^+(\varphi)]\!]^{\mathrm{PL}} \Leftrightarrow [\mathrm{IH}] \ [\![\varphi]\!]^+ \Leftrightarrow [\![\neg\varphi]\!]^-$

4. $[\![\mathsf{TR}^+(\varphi \wedge \psi)]\!]^{\mathrm{PL}} \Leftrightarrow [\![\mathsf{TR}^+(\varphi) \wedge \mathsf{TR}^+(\psi)]\!]^{\mathrm{PL}} \Leftrightarrow$
   $\{g \mid g \in [\![\mathsf{TR}^+(\varphi)]\!]^{\mathrm{PL}} \ \& \ g \in [\![\mathsf{TR}^+(\psi)]\!]^{\mathrm{PL}}\} \Leftrightarrow [\mathrm{IH}]$
   $\{g \mid g \in [\![\varphi]\!]^+ \ \& \ g \in [\![\psi]\!]^+\} \Leftrightarrow [\![\varphi \wedge \psi]\!]^+$
   $[\![\mathsf{TR}^-(\varphi \wedge \psi)]\!]^{\mathrm{PL}} \Leftrightarrow [\![\mathsf{TR}^-(\varphi) \vee \mathsf{TR}^-(\psi)]\!]^{\mathrm{PL}} \Leftrightarrow$
   $\{g \mid g \in [\![\mathsf{TR}^-(\varphi)]\!]^{\mathrm{PL}} \ \text{or} \ g \in [\![\mathsf{TR}^-(\psi)]\!]^{\mathrm{PL}}\} \Leftrightarrow [\mathrm{IH}]$
   $\{g \mid g \in [\![\varphi]\!]^- \ \text{or} \ g \in [\![\psi]\!]^-\} \Leftrightarrow [\![\varphi \wedge \psi]\!]^-$

5. $\varphi \vee \psi$ is equivalent with $\neg(\neg\varphi \wedge \neg\psi)$

6. $\varphi \to \psi$ is equivalent with $\neg(\varphi \wedge \neg\psi)$

7. $[\![\mathsf{TR}^+(\exists x\varphi)]\!]^{\mathrm{PL}} \Leftrightarrow [\![\exists x\mathsf{TR}^+(\varphi)]\!]^{\mathrm{PL}} \Leftrightarrow$
   $\{g \mid \exists h(g[x]h \ \& \ h \in [\![\mathsf{TR}^+(\varphi)]\!]^{\mathrm{PL}})\} \Leftrightarrow [\mathrm{IH}]$
   $\{g \mid \exists h(g[x]h \ \& \ h \in [\![\varphi]\!]^+)\} \Leftrightarrow [\![\exists x\varphi]\!]^+$
   $[\![\mathsf{TR}^-(\exists x\varphi)]\!]^{\mathrm{PL}} \Leftrightarrow [\![\forall x\mathsf{TR}^-(\varphi)]\!]^{\mathrm{PL}} \Leftrightarrow$
   $\{g \mid \forall h(g[x]h \Rightarrow h \in [\![\mathsf{TR}^-(\varphi)]\!]^{\mathrm{PL}})\} \Leftrightarrow [\mathrm{IH}]$

---

[36]In Van Rooy 1995, see also Van Rooy 1997a, the two-dimensional approach is re-animated however. Van Rooy allows for truth-conditional material to occur in the representation of the presupposition. In a sense, he generalizes Karttunen and Peters' fragment by separately calculating the semantic content, and three presuppositional representations, the disjunction of which gives the presupposition of the sentence.

$$\{g \mid \forall h(g[x]h \Rightarrow h \in [\![\varphi]\!]^-)\} \Leftrightarrow [\![\exists x \varphi]\!]^-$$

8. $\forall x \varphi$ is equivalent with $\neg \exists x \neg \varphi$

9. $[\![\mathsf{TR}^+(\varphi_{\langle \pi \rangle})]\!]^{\mathrm{PL}} \Leftrightarrow [\![\mathsf{TR}^+(\pi) \wedge \mathsf{TR}^+(\varphi)]\!]^{\mathrm{PL}} \Leftrightarrow$
   $\{g \mid g \in [\![\mathsf{TR}^+(\pi)]\!]^{\mathrm{PL}} \ \& \ g \in [\![\mathsf{TR}^+(\varphi)]\!]^{\mathrm{PL}}\} \Leftrightarrow [\mathrm{IH}]$
   $\{g \mid g \in [\![\pi]\!]^+ \ \& \ g \in [\![\varphi]\!]^+\} \Leftrightarrow [\![\varphi_{\langle \pi \rangle}]\!]^+$
   $[\![\mathsf{TR}^-(\varphi_{\langle \pi \rangle})]\!]^{\mathrm{PL}} \Leftrightarrow [\![\mathsf{TR}^+(\pi) \wedge \mathsf{TR}^-(\varphi)]\!]^{\mathrm{PL}} \Leftrightarrow$
   $\{g \mid g \in [\![\mathsf{TR}^+(\pi)]\!]^{\mathrm{PL}} \ \& \ g \in [\![\mathsf{TR}^-(\varphi)]\!]^{\mathrm{PL}}\} \Leftrightarrow [\mathrm{IH}]$
   $\{g \mid g \in [\![\pi]\!]^+ \ \& \ g \in [\![\varphi]\!]^-\} \Leftrightarrow [\![\varphi_{\langle \pi \rangle}]\!]^-$

$\square$

5

Presupposition and Montague Grammar

5.1 Introduction

In the late seventies several Montagovian grammars have been proposed for fragments of English in which presuppositions arise. Prime examples are Hausser 1976, Cooper 1983 and, of course, Karttunen and Peters 1979. However none of these grammars is technically and empirically satisfactory.[1] How come? Perhaps an explanation can be found in the lack of proper partializations of Montague Grammar at that time. Semantic approaches to presuppositions almost all involve one form of partiality or other. Still, it has long been thought that partializing Montague Grammar was a highly non-trivial task (see for instance Barwise and Perry 1985), and only relatively recently a satisfactory partialization has been achieved in Muskens 1989. Karttunen and Peters 1979 do not need partiality since they switch to an essentially *two-dimensional* approach (see Herzberger 1973) in which each sentence of the fragment is translated into *two* expressions of Montague's Intensional Logic: one representing what is *expressed* (asserted) and one what is *conventionally implicated* (presupposed). However, it has been observed on numerous occasions —first of all by Karttunen and Peters themselves— that this strict separation does not work for sentences involving presupposition-quantification interaction. In the previous chapter we concluded that standard Partial Predicate Logic (PPL) is a suitable vehicle for the semantic treatment of presuppositions, even

---

[1]The binding-problem from Karttunen and Peters was discussed in the previous chapter. When presupposition-triggers arise in the scope of universal quantifiers, Cooper 1983 predicts the Heimian presuppositions we also discussed in the previous chapter. Hausser 1976's partialization of Intensional Logic is problematic from a technical point of view. See below for some discussion.

when they occur under the scope of quantifiers. Combined with the Partial Montague Grammar developed in Muskens 1989 this paves the way for a presuppositional extension of classical Montague Grammar, which combines technical clarity with a decent analysis of presupposition. In this chapter we give such a fragment, once again with the emphasis on presupposition-quantification interaction. It can be seen as a reconstruction of what Hausser 1976, Karttunen and Peters 1979 and Cooper 1983 might have looked like if they had access to a good partialization of Montague Grammar.[2]

The reader may well wonder if this does not come a bit too late in the afternoon. I believe that it does not, and that the fragment is more than a nice exercise in classical formal semantics with some historical significance. It is true that the syntactic analysis of orthodox Montague Grammar does not stand up to present day standards, but the Montagovian approach to semantics is without a doubt as influential as ever (see for instance the discussion in Partee with Hendriks 1997). Moreover, there are nowadays various ways to overcome certain traditional 'limitations' of classical Montague Grammar. For example. Montague Grammar can be reformulated in such a way that notorious concepts such as quantifying-in (or Cooper storage) and generalizing to the worst-case in the type assignments are no longer needed, as shown in Hendriks 1993. We can also replace Montague's syntactic component by more contemporary grammar formalisms. In Muskens 1994a, for example, type-theoretical formulae are built up in a Montagovian fashion on the basis of *Categorial Grammar* (see also Morrill 1994 for a comparison of classical Montague Grammar with extended versions of categorial grammar), while in Verschuur 1994 *Head-Driven Phrase Structure Grammar* fulfills this role. In this chapter we remain neutral as to what the syntactic component looks like and concentrate on the semantic side of the story. Another relevant observation in this context concerns the compatibility of the fragment presented in this chapter with the dynamic view on meaning. As discussed in chapter 2, Muskens 1991 shows how type theory can be used as a classical vehicle for dynamic semantics. Muskens' method for this is independent of our use of type theory in the present chapter, and hence nothing blocks a combination of these two uses of type theory. In fact, section 5.4.3 contains a recipe for such a combination. The result of cooking this recipe is comparable with the Montagovian discourse fragments which include presuppositions discussed in Bouchez et al. 1993 and Beaver 1995. So both the syntactic

---

[2]The fragment developed here is also discussed in Beaver and Krahmer 1995.

as well as the semantic side of the *Presuppositional Montague Grammar* we discuss here can easily be upgraded to the present day standards.

In section 5.2 we look at the representation language of the fragment: Muskens' partialization of two-sorted type-theory. The section thereafter presents a gradual trip through the fragment of Presuppositional Montague Grammar. Section 5.4 discusses extensions of the fragment with additional presupposition triggers, and gives the aforementioned recipe for dynamification. The chapter ends with an appendix containing the relevant formalities.

5.2 Partial Type Theory

Before we turn to the actual fragment and discuss a number of examples, we first consider the representation language in more detail. Muskens 1989 starts from *two-sorted type theory* (TY_2) and presents various 4-valued partializations of it. Here we restrict our attention to TY_2^3, three-valued two-sorted type-theory.[3] To begin with, any TY_2 type is a TY_2^3 type. That is:

Definition 1 (Types)

1. e, s and t are types,
2. if α and β are types, then $(\alpha\beta)$ is a type.

The syntax of TY_2^3 differs in only one respect from standard TY_2, namely the addition of $\star$, the undefined expression. We again have sets Var_α and Con_α of variables and constants of type α. Recall from chapter 2 that a *formula* is an expression of type t.

Definition 2 (TY_2^3 syntax)

1. If φ and ψ are formulae, then $\neg\varphi$ and $(\varphi \wedge \psi)$ are formulae.
2. If φ is a formula and x is a variable of any type, then $\exists x \varphi$ is a formula.
3. If A is an expression of type $(\alpha\beta)$ and B is an expression of type α, then (AB) is an expression of type β.
4. If A is an expression of type β and x is a variable of type α, then $\lambda x(A)$ is an expression of type $(\alpha\beta)$.
5. If A and B are expressions of the same type, then $(A \equiv B)$ is a formula.
6. $\star$ is a formula.

---

[3]It has been argued on various occasions that TY_2 is preferable over Montague's *Intensional Logic* (IL) for independent reasons (see for instance Gallin 1975 or Groenendijk and Stokhof 1984).

Again parentheses are omitted where this can be done without creating confusion, on the understanding that association is to the left. So instead of writing $(\ldots(AB_1)\ldots B_n)$ we write $AB_1 \ldots B_n$.

The semantics is defined over a distributive lattice on {T,F,N} (called L3), in which the meet $\cap$ corresponds with conjunction, the join $\cup$ with disjunction and the complement $-$ with negation. This gives rise to the following Hasse diagram.

T

N

F

For instance, to find the value of a conjunction of T and N, we look at T $\cap$ N, which amounts to the minimum of the two with respect to the ordering, which is N. On the other hand, the disjunction of T and N is given by T $\cup$ N, which is the maximal element of the two and that is T. The negation of T, given by $-$ T, is F, while the negation of N is N again.

To turn a TY_2 model $M = \langle\{D_\alpha\}_\alpha, I\rangle$ into a TY_2^3 one, it suffices to add N to D_t such that $D_t = \{\mathrm{T,F,N}\}$. Otherwise nothing changes: so D_e and D_s are non-empty disjoint sets and $D_{(\alpha\beta)}$ is $D_\beta{}^{D_\alpha}$; the set of (total) functions from D_α to D_β. As usual, D_s is a set of *states*, which in classical Montague Grammar are *world-time pairs*. Elements of D_s are ordered by $<$ and $\approx$, which have the following intuitive meanings: $i < j$ expresses that state i precedes state j on the time axis and $i \approx j$ has the intuitive meaning that states i and j agree on the world dimension.[4] I is the interpretation function of M; specified as $I(c) \in D_\alpha$, for all $c \in \mathsf{Con}_\alpha$. G is the set of total assignments mapping elements of Var_α to the corresponding domain D_α. $g[x/d]$ is the assignment which differs from g at most in that $g[x/d](x) = d$. We define $[\![A]\!]_{M,g}$ (the value of a term A in a model M with respect to an assignment g) in the following way. First of all, the interpretation of terms goes as follows: $[\![t]\!]_{M,g} = I(t)$, if $t \in \mathsf{Con}_\alpha$, and $[\![t]\!]_{M,g} = g(t)$, if $t \in \mathsf{Var}_\alpha$.

Definition 3 (TY_2^3 semantics)

1. $[\![\neg\varphi]\!]_g \qquad = \quad -[\![\varphi]\!]_g$

---

[4]For the axioms which force $<$ and $\approx$ to behave in this intended way, see Muskens 1989:14.

2. $\quad [\![\varphi \wedge \psi]\!]_g \quad = \quad [\![\varphi]\!]_g \cap [\![\psi]\!]_g$

3. $\quad [\![\exists x_\alpha \varphi]\!]_g \quad = \quad \bigcup_{d \in D_\alpha} [\![\varphi]\!]_{g[x/d]}$

4. $\quad [\![AB]\!]_g \quad = \quad [\![A]\!]_g([\![B]\!]_g)$

5. $\quad [\![\lambda x_\alpha A]\!]_g \quad = \quad$ the function F such that $F(d) = [\![A]\!]_{g[x/d]}$
   for all $d \in D_\alpha$

6. $\quad [\![A \equiv B]\!]_g \quad = \quad$ T, iff $[\![A]\!]_g = [\![B]\!]_g$
   $\qquad\qquad\quad = \quad$ F, iff $[\![A]\!]_g \neq [\![B]\!]_g$

7. $\quad [\![\star]\!]_g \quad = \quad$ N

Here $-, \cap$ and $\bigcup$ are operations on L3. If we only consider the values
T and F (and thus ignore $\star$) it is readily seen that the definition is
exactly the same as definition 2.30. The propositional connectives of
TY_2^3 follow the strong Kleene pattern, which the reader can easily verify
by writing down the truth tables. The existential quantifier also has a
Kleene interpretation: $\exists x \varphi$ is True iff for some assignment to x, φ is
True; $\exists x \varphi$ is False iff for all assignments to x, φ is False. On the level
of λ-free formulae, TY_2^3 is the same logic as strong Kleene based PPL
(modulo $\star$).[5] This has a nice consequence: if we want to calculate the
presuppositions of a certain fully-reduced, extensional TY_2^3 formula (that
is: a formula without lambdas), we can use the method of the previous
chapter. Similarly, we define:

Definition 4 (Abbreviations)

$\varphi \vee \psi$	abbreviates	$\neg(\neg\varphi \wedge \neg\psi)$
$\varphi \rightarrow \psi$	abbreviates	$\neg(\varphi \wedge \neg\psi)$
$\forall x \varphi$	abbreviates	$\neg\exists x \neg\varphi$
$\varphi \dot\wedge \psi$	abbreviates	$(\varphi \wedge \psi) \vee (\neg\varphi \wedge \varphi)$
$\varphi \ddot\wedge \psi$	abbreviates	$(\varphi \wedge \psi) \vee (\neg\varphi \wedge \varphi) \vee (\neg\psi \wedge \psi)$
$\top$	abbreviates	$\star \equiv \star$
$\partial\pi$	abbreviates	$(\pi \equiv \top) \vee \star$
$\varphi_{\langle\pi\rangle}$	abbreviates	$\partial\pi \dot\wedge \varphi$

As in the previous chapter, $\dot\wedge$ is the Peters/middle Kleene conjunction,
while $\ddot\wedge$ is the Bochvar/weak Kleene conjunction. The corresponding
notions of disjunction and implication are defined in the obvious way.
Via the last two abbreviations elementary presuppositions are introduced in the system of TY_2^3. In the context of this chapter, the reader
may think of ∂ as the formal counterpart to Cooper's meta-predicate

---

[5] See Muskens 1989, chapter 5 for discussion on the relationship between strong
Kleene and partial Type Theory.

PRESUPPOSE (see Beaver 1992 for discussion). Finally, we want to observe that TY_2^3 supports the following fact (like TY_2).[6]

Fact 1 *(Equivalences)*

1. $\lambda x(A)B$ *is equivalent with* $\{B/x\}A$, *provided B is free for x in A.*
2. $\lambda x(A\ x)$ *is equivalent with* A, *provided x doesn't occur free in A.*
3. $\lambda x A$ *is equivalent with* $\lambda y\{y/x\}A$, *provided y is free for x in A.*

The first of these facts is known as lambda-conversion (or beta-reduction), the second as eta-conversion and the third as alpha-conversion. TY_2^3 is a clean, well-behaved logic, with lots of nice meta-theoretical results as shown in Muskens 1989, chapter 5. An additional advantage over Montague's IL is that TY_2^3 is 'Church-Rosser'; it has the *diamond-property* (see Muskens 1989:15–16).

5.3   Presuppositional Montague Grammar

The fragment we present is an extension of Muskens' streamlined version of Montague Grammar (see Muskens 1989, 1990), where Montague Grammar refers to the so-called PTQ-fragment of Montague 1974b (see also chapter 2). As a result of the replacement of IL for (a partial version of) TY_2, the translations can be simplified to begin with. The main difference with Montague's IL is the absence of the intensional $^\wedge$- and extensional $^\vee$-operators, as well as the tense-operators F and P and the universal modality $\square$. All these operations are definable in terms of two-sorted type-theory. For example, the IL-expression $^\wedge\varphi$ corresponds with $\lambda i \varphi$ (abstraction over states), while $^\vee\varphi$ corresponds with φi, where i is some fixed variable of type s (see the embedding of IL into TY_2 of Gallin 1975). $^{\vee\wedge}$-elimination is now simply lambda-conversion. In general, a formula such as *push xbi* should be read as: in state i entity b pushes entity x. So, in this set-up *push* is not a two-place but a tree-place predicate, looking for a state and two entities.[7]

Presuppositional Montague Grammar extends the basic PTQ fragment by including presuppositions. As said, the emphasis is on the interaction of presuppositions and quantifiers, and as a result we concentrate on the examples discussed in the previous chapter, repeated here as (1), (2), (3) and (4).

(1)   Somebody managed to succeed George V on the throne of England.

(2)   A fat man pushes his bicycle.

---

[6]Again, $\{B/x\}A$ is the substitution of B for all free occurrences of x in A.

[7]None of these changes mark true departures from standard Montague Grammar: Muskens' version of PTQ makes exactly the same predictions as the version of PTQ found in Dowty et al. 1981.

(3) Every man who serves his king will be rewarded.

(4) Every fat man pushes his bicycle.

This requires the following additions. First of all, presupposition triggers are added to the lexicon of basic expressions. *Manage to* is treated as a presuppositional variant of *try to*, which *is* part of the PTQ-fragment. The possessive *'s* requires a real extension: it is assigned the category *DET/NP*; it looks for an *NP* and produces a determiner. Furthermore, adjectives like *fat* are not in the PTQ fragment either. Here we follow the analysis from Gamut 1991 and assign adjectives the category *CN/CN*. In section 5.4 various other extensions are discussed.

In this section, we gradually go through the fragment. More details are given in the appendix. Let us begin by re-discussing (1) from Karttunen and Peters 1979. Here is its syntactic analysis tree (ignoring the PP *on the throne of England*).[8] The syntactic labels are defined in the usual categorical fashion; see the appendix.

(5)

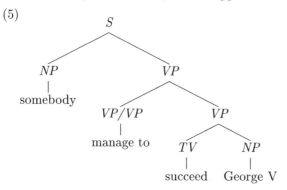

We define a function $(.)^\bullet$ which translates syntactic trees into TY_2^3 expressions. These are the translations of the relevant lexical entries:[9]

$$\text{somebody}^\bullet = \lambda P \lambda i \exists y (P\, yi)$$
$$\text{manage to}^\bullet = \lambda P \lambda x \lambda i (P\, xi_{\langle (\text{difficult } P)\, xi \rangle})$$
$$\text{succeed}^\bullet = \lambda Q \lambda y (Q \lambda x (\text{succeed } xy))$$
$$\text{George V}^\bullet = \lambda P (P\, g)$$

We use one syntactic operation here, namely functional application. The

---

[8] In orthodox Montague Grammar (as described in the PTQ fragment of Montague 1974b) this would be an analysis tree which employs (in top-down order) rules 4, 8 and 5.

[9]Here and elsewhere we let p, q range over propositions (type st), P over properties (type $e(st)$), Q over quantifiers (type $(e(st))(st)$), x, y over individuals (type e) and i, j over states (type s). Constants are typed in the appendix. There the reader will see that *difficult* is a constant of type $(e(st))(e(st))$ and *succeed* is a constant of type $e(e(st))$.

syntactic details can be found in the appendix. The corresponding translation rule looks as follows:

Definition 5 (Functional application translated)
$([[\alpha]^{A/^m B} [\beta]^B]^A_{\text{fa}})^\bullet = \alpha^\bullet\beta^\bullet$, for $m \in \{1, 2\}$.

We assume that functional application is the default syntactic operation, and hence we omit the 'fa' subscript. Here is the (step-by-step) derivation of $(5)^\bullet$.

1. $([\ \text{succeed George V}])^\bullet =$
   $\text{succeed}^\bullet\ \text{George V}^\bullet$
   $\lambda Q\lambda y(Q\lambda x(succeed\ xy))\lambda P(P\ g) \Longrightarrow_\lambda$
   $\lambda y(succeed\ gy) \Longrightarrow_\eta$
   $succeed\ g$

2. $([\ \text{manage to }[\ \text{succeed George V}]\ ])^\bullet =$
   $\text{manage to}^\bullet\ (\text{succeed George V})^\bullet$
   $\lambda P\lambda x\lambda i(P\ xi_{\langle(difficultP)\ xi\rangle})succeed\ g \Longrightarrow_\lambda$
   $\lambda x\lambda i(succeed\ gxi_{\langle(difficult(succeed\ g))\ xi\rangle})$

3. $([\ \text{somebody }[\ \text{manage to }[\ \text{succeed George IV}]\ ]\ ])^\bullet =$
   $\text{somebody}^\bullet\ (\text{manage to succeed George V})^\bullet$
   $\lambda P\lambda i\exists y(P\ yi)\lambda x\lambda i(succeed\ gxi_{\langle(difficult(succeedg))\ xi\rangle}) \Longrightarrow_\alpha$
   $\lambda P\lambda i\exists y(P\ yi)\lambda x\lambda j(succeed\ gxj_{\langle(difficult(succeedg))\ xj\rangle}) \Longrightarrow_\lambda$
   $\lambda i\exists y(succeed\ gyi_{\langle(difficult(succeed\ g))\ yi\rangle})$

Here $\Longrightarrow_{\lambda,\alpha,\eta}$ indicates that one or more lambda, alpha or eta-conversions have been carried out. The meaning of the resulting proposition can be paraphrased as follows: it is a function from states to truth values, and given a state s the function produces True if there is someone of which it is asserted that he succeeded George V in s and presupposed that he (and not just any person) had difficulty to succeed George V in s. This means that the system here does not run into the binding problem of Karttunen and Peters. Let me point out that the binding problem does not arise in the Montagovian fragments of Cooper 1983 and Hausser 1976 either, see section 5.4.1 below. In other words: the binding problem is really typical of Karttunen and Peters' two-dimensional approach.

All this does not tell us what *is* the predicted presupposition associated with the proposition we just derived. For that we need to (re-)define the *presuppose* notion. The main difference between TY_2^3 translations and PPL ones is of course that the former are intensional while the latter are not. In the present set-up propositions are no longer True or False, they are True or False with respect to some state s. So we need to define when an expression φ_{st} presupposes an expression π_{st}. The following definition is a straightforward generalization of the Strawsonian notion of 'presupposing' in definition 10 of chapter 4.

Definition 6 (Presuppose)
Let φ and π be expressions of type st. φ *presupposes* π iff for all models M, assignments g and for all states s:

$$\text{if } [\![\varphi s]\!]_{M,g} = \text{T or } [\![\varphi s]\!]_{M,g} = \text{F, then } [\![\pi s]\!]_{M,g} = \text{T}$$

Put differently: if $[\![\pi s]\!]_{M,g} \neq \text{T}$, then $[\![\varphi s]\!]_{M,g} = \text{N}$. By analogy with the previous chapter we can define $\text{PR}(\varphi)$, the (maximal) presupposition of φ, as follows. If φ is of the form $\lambda i\psi$ and ψ is a λ-free formula[10] (without free occurrences of j), then the presupposition of φ is given by:

$$\text{PR}(\varphi) = \lambda j(\text{TR}^+(\varphi\, j) \vee \text{TR}^-(\varphi\, j))$$

When φj is reduced we end up with a formula without lambdas and, as we observed above, now we can use the TR^+- and TR^--functions from definition 4.11. Using this method, we find that the presupposition of the type-theoretical formula we just derived is the following:

(6) $\lambda j(\exists y((\textit{difficult}(\textit{succeed}\; g))\; yj \wedge \textit{succeed}\; gyj) \vee$
   $\forall y((\textit{difficult}(\textit{succeed}\; g))\; yj \wedge \neg \textit{succeed}\; gyj))$

This is just the intensional version of the presupposition we discussed previously and once more the first disjunct gives the conditions under which (1) is True and the second under which (1) is False. Again this presupposition can be understood as an explanation of the odd flavor of (1): any state which satisfies one of these disjuncts is in conflict with history.

Next, let us turn to the first example from Heim 1983b, given here as (2). Its syntactic analysis is given in (7). The reader is invited to verify that this is essentially the Lf which Heim's FCS would produce for sentence (2) (see chapter 2). The pronoun *his* is analyzed as a combination of *he* and the possessive *'s*. The occurrence of *he* is replaced for a free, indexed trace to achieve co-reference.[11]

---

[10]Thus, **PR** cannot be applied to formulae containing representations of intensional verbs (such as *regret* and *look for*, see section 5.4.1).

[11]In chapter 2 it was noted that Heim compares her Lfs with both Chomskyan Logical Forms and Montagovian Analysis Trees. That this comparison is justified can be illustrated nicely by looking at the tree in (7). As said, this is almost the Lf which Heim's Lf forming rules would produce for example (2). The non-pronominal NP *a fat man* is prefixed to S, leaving behind a trace t_0 (rule for NP-PREFIXING, definition 2.1). It would be exactly Heim's Lf if we replaced the indefinite determiner and the traces t_0 for free variables x_0. On the other hand, the tree is also a Montagovian analysis tree, namely

$$[[\text{a [fat man]}^b]^3[\text{he}_0 [\text{push} [[\text{he}_0 \text{ 's]}^a \text{ bicycle]}^3]^5]^4]^{14,0}$$

(7)

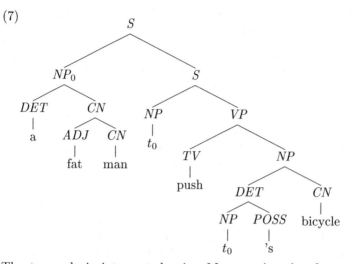

The top-node is interpreted using Montague's rule of quantifying-in $(14,n)$, which is needed to allow the indefinite *a fat man* to bind the possessive pronoun *his*. As said in the introduction, nothing hinges on the use of quantifying-in; any alternative will do. All other syntactic rules used here are translated using the functional application pattern given in definition 5. The translation rule for quantifying-in goes as follows (again, the syntactic rule is given in the appendix):

Definition 7 (Quantifying-in translated)

$([[\xi]^{NP} [\vartheta]^S]_{qi}^{S,n})^\bullet = \xi^\bullet \lambda x_n (\vartheta^\bullet)$, for $n \in \mathbb{N}$.

In the case of (7), ξ is the NP *a fat man*, and ϑ the sub-sentence t_0 *pushes t_0's bicycle*. The following translations of basic lexical items are required:

$$
\begin{aligned}
\text{a}^\bullet &= \lambda P_1 \lambda P_2 \lambda i \exists y (P_1\, yi \,\dot\wedge\, P_2\, yi) \\
\text{fat}^\bullet &= fat \\
\text{man}^\bullet &= man, \text{bicycle}^\bullet = bike \\
\text{push}^\bullet &= \lambda Q \lambda y (Q \lambda x (push\, xy)) \\
t_n{}^\bullet &= \lambda P (P\, x_n) \\
\text{'s}^\bullet &= \lambda Q \lambda P_1 \lambda P_2 \lambda i \\
&\quad (\exists x (P_1\, xi \,\dot\wedge\, Q \lambda y (of\, yx)i \,\dot\wedge\, P_2\, xi)_{\langle \exists! x (P_1\, xi \,\dot\wedge\, Q\lambda y (of\, yx)i) \rangle})
\end{aligned}
$$

Notice that in these translations we have used the middle Kleene conjunction $\dot\wedge$. It is worth pointing out that the use of $\dot\wedge$ is by no means

---

Where 14,0/Montague's *quantifying-in* rule is the counterpart to quantifier raising, and *a* and *b* are rules of functional application added to the present fragment to deal with adjectives and possessives. The occurrences of he$_0$ are Montague's syntactic variables.

essential for Presuppositional Montague Grammar; we could also follow Hausser 1976, for example, and employ the strong Kleene connectives. Of course, this would mean that the predicted presuppositions are somewhat weaker (although for quantificational sentences the differences are rather small, see the previous chapter). The predicate *of* is used to represent the possessive relation. For *of* we introduce a harmless notation convention:

Definition 8 (Notation Convention 1)

$\forall x \forall y \forall i((\gamma\, xi \wedge of\, yxi) \dot{\to} \gamma\text{-}of\, yxi)$, where γ is *man, bike* or *king*

This gives us all the machinery we need to determine $(7)^{\bullet}$. In the following calculation all reductions are carried out immediately; the relevant translation rule is the one for functional application unless otherwise indicated.

1. $([\text{ fat man}])^{\bullet} \Longrightarrow fat\ man$

2. $([\text{ a }[\text{ fat man}]])^{\bullet} \Longrightarrow \lambda P_3 \lambda i \exists z((fat\ man)\ zi \wedge P_3\ zi)$

3. $([t_0\text{ 's }])^{\bullet} \Longrightarrow$
   $\lambda P_1 \lambda P_2 \lambda i (\exists x (P_1\ xi \wedge of\, x_0 xi \wedge P_2\ xi)_{\langle \exists! x (P_1\ xi\ \wedge\ of\, x_0 xi) \rangle})$

4. $([[t_0\text{ 's }]\text{ bicycle}])^{\bullet} \Longrightarrow$
   $\lambda P_2 \lambda i (\exists x (bike\text{-}of\, x_0 xi \wedge P_2\ xi)_{\langle \exists! x (bike\text{-}of\, x_0 xi) \rangle})$

5. $([\text{ push }[[t_0\text{ 's }]\text{ bicycle}]])^{\bullet} \Longrightarrow$
   $\lambda y \lambda i (\exists x (bike\text{-}of\, x_0 xi \wedge push\ xyi)_{\langle \exists! x (bike\text{-}of\, x_0 xi) \rangle})$

6. $([t_0\ [\text{ push }[[t_0\text{ 's }]\text{ bicycle}]]])^{\bullet} \Longrightarrow$
   $\lambda i (\exists x (bike\text{-}of\, x_0 xi \wedge push\ xx_0 i)_{\langle \exists! x (bike\text{-}of\, x_0 xi) \rangle})$

7. $([[\text{ a }[\text{ fat man}]]\ [t_0\ [\text{ push }[[t_0\text{ 's }]\text{ bicycle}]]]]_{qi}^{S,0})^{\bullet} \Longrightarrow$
   $\lambda i \exists z ((fat\ man)\ zi \wedge \exists x (bike\text{-}of\, zxi \wedge push\ xzi)_{\langle \exists! x (bike\text{-}of\, zxi) \rangle})$

By NC1, *bike-of* zxi should be read as in state i object x is the bicycle of object z. This translation differs only marginally from the PPL one we discussed in the previous chapter,[12] but here the translation is build up in a fully compositional way. If we calculate the presupposition, we arrive at essentially the same presupposition as we did for middle Kleene PPL. We once more find a disjunction of an existential truth-condition and a universal falsity-condition, which is again weaker than Heim's predicted presupposition:

$$\lambda j (\exists z ((fat\ man)\ zj \wedge \exists! x (bike\text{-}of\, zxj) \wedge \exists x (bike\text{-}of\, zxj \wedge push\ xzj)) \vee$$
$$\forall z ((fat\ man)\ zj \to (\exists! x (bike\text{-}of\, zxj) \wedge \forall x (bike\text{-}of\, zxj \to \neg push\ xzj))))$$

The reader is invited to compare this predicted presupposition with its middle Kleene based PPL counterpart on page 108.

The other examples from Heim 1983b, (3) and (4), are also captured

---

[12]It is intensional and contains higher-order predicates (such as *fat*).

by the fragment. Example (4) differs from (2) only in the initial determiner. As a result, its syntactic analysis tree is structurally isomorphic with (7). The corresponding translation is built up in a completely analogous way and results in the following expression.

(8) $\lambda i \forall z((fat\ man)zi \dot\to \exists x(bike\text{-}of\ zxi \wedge push\ xzi)_{\langle\exists!x(bike\text{-}of\ zxi)\rangle})$

As in the previous chapter, the presupposition of this formula is very close to the one associated with (4), as the reader can easily verify. The syntactic analysis tree for example (3) is (9). For the sake of simplicity we leave the *VP be rewarded* unanalyzed. It is treated as a simple intransitive verb.

(9)

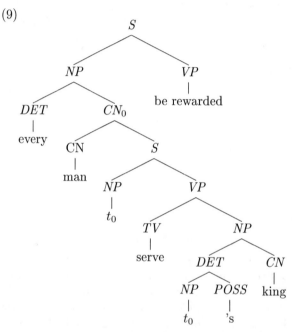

The rule for relative clause formation (rcf, Montague's 2,n) is used to combine the *CN man* with the relative-*S* t_0 *serves* t_0 *'s king* to form the complex *CN man who serves his king*. Rcf is interpreted as follows:

Definition 9 (Relative clause formation translated)
$([[\xi]^{CN}\ [\vartheta]^{S}]_{\mathrm{rcf}}^{CN,n})^{\bullet} = \lambda x_n \lambda i(\xi^{\bullet}\ x_n i \wedge \vartheta^{\bullet}\ i)$, for $n \in I\!N$.

Applying the (.)$^{\bullet}$ function (which contains no more surprises on the level of lexical elements) and reducing a lot we find the following:

$([[\ every\ [\ man\ [\ t_0\ [\ serve\ [[\ t_0\ 's]\ king]]]]_{\mathrm{rcf}}^{CN,0}]\ be\ rewarded\ ])^{\bullet} \Longrightarrow$
$\lambda i \forall x((man\ xi \wedge \exists y(king\text{-}of\ xyi \wedge serve\ yxi)_{\langle\exists!yking\text{-}of\ xyi\rangle}) \dot\to reward\ xi)$

As the reader may verify, once again a suitably weak presupposition is predicted, consisting of a disjunction of a universal truth-condition and an existential falsity-condition. So again, the only crucial difference with PPL is the way the semantic representation is built up.

5.4 Discussion: Extending the Fragment

So much for the basics, let us now discuss a number of possible extensions of the fragment.

5.4.1 Additional Presuppositions

By now the reader probably is under the impression that there is nothing more to presuppositions than some fat men with their bicycles and a little bit of royalty watching. Of course that is not the case. In fact, in both Karttunen and Peters 1979 and Hausser 1976 the emphasis is on other kinds of presuppositional phenomena. To do justice to these predecessors of the current version of Presuppositional Montague Grammar and to show that it really subsumes both of them, let us now discuss these additional presuppositions.

Hausser argues that certain quantificational determiners (in particular *every* and *some*) are what he calls *existential P-inducers*.[13] In other words: *every* and *some* trigger an existential presupposition leading to a scope restriction (as discussed in Keenan 1972).[14] The examples from Hausser 1976:252 are (10.a) and (10.b).

(10) a. Bill kissed every girl at the party.
     b. Bill didn't kiss every girl at the party.

Both the a. and the b. sentence intuitively presuppose that there was at least one girl at the party. This can be modeled in Presuppositional Montague Grammar by defining the lexical translation of *every* as follows:

$$\text{every}^\bullet = \lambda P_1 \lambda P_2 \lambda i (\forall x (P_1 \ xi \dot{\to} P_2 \ xi)_{\langle \exists y (P_1 \ yi) \rangle})$$

Presuppositional Montague Grammar produces the following two representations for (10.a) and (the wide-scope reading of the negation in) (10.b) respectively.

---

[13]More recently this assumption has been generalized in various ways. Several people, for example, De Jong 1987 and Zucchi 1995, have argued that all NPs with a *strong* determiner (in the sense of Milsark 1977) are presupposition triggers. In Krahmer and Deemter 1997 this has been further generalized to an *NP presupposition scheme* which assigns uniform, existential presuppositions to NPs with a strong or accented determiner.

[14]In fact, Hausser notes that Kleene 1938 introduced his three-valued logic to deal with scope-restrictions triggered by functions which are defined only for a subset of a certain mathematical domain. See Rescher 1969:34 and Hausser 1976:255.

(11) a. $\lambda i(\forall x(girl\ xi \overset{.}{\to} kiss\ xbi)_{\langle \exists y(girl\ yi)\rangle})$
      b. $\lambda i\neg(\forall x(girl\ xi \overset{.}{\to} kiss\ xbi)_{\langle \exists y(girl\ yi)\rangle})$

It is easily seen that both formulae presuppose that there was a girl at
the party. This analysis is not entirely faithful to Hausser for two reasons. First, it uses the middle Kleene connectives instead of the strong
Kleene ones. Obviously, replacing $\overset{.}{\to}$ for $\to$ removes this minor discrep-
ancy. What is more: the predicted presuppositions do not differ (since
the inner structure of the assertional part of the respective translations is
not relevant for the predicted presupposition). A second, but important
difference is that Hausser does not use an explicit presupposition operator; rather he builds presuppositions *into* the definition of functional
application (roughly as follows: the interpretation of (AB) is undefined
if the presuppositions of B are not satisfied (see Hausser 1976:277). This
leads to a serious complication of the interpretation of functional application, but on the other hand, since Hausser uses a single representation,
the binding problem does not arise.[15] This is also clear from Hausser's
treatment of the verb *stop*, which can be seen as a variant of *manage*.
(A slight variation of) Hausser's example is (12) (Hausser 1976:276).

(12) Somebody stopped dating Mary.

Hausser's analysis of the verb *stop* can be phrased in terms of Presuppositional Montague Grammar by defining (stop to)$^\bullet$ as follows:

$$stop\ to^\bullet = \lambda P \lambda x \lambda i(\neg(P\ xi)_{\langle \exists j(j<i\ \wedge\ i\approx j\ \wedge\ P\ xj)\rangle})$$

In words: stop doing X in a state s presupposes having done X before
and asserts not doing X any more in s. The syntactic structure of (12)
is structurally similar to that of example (1), as given in (5). Hence the
translation is built up in an analogous way, and produces the following
representation.

(13) $\lambda i \exists x(\neg(date\ mxi)_{\langle \exists j(j<i\ \wedge\ i\approx j\ \wedge\ date\ mxj)\rangle})$

In words: given a state s, it is asserted that there is someone who doesn't
date Mary in s, and it is presupposed that there is a state s' which
precedes s on the time-axis in which that *same* someone dates Mary.
The predicted presupposition for this formula can be paraphrased in

---

[15]Karttunen and Peters 1979:44 write about Hausser's approach:

> We should briefly point out (...) how close the so-called "strong projection
> method" incorporated in Kleene's three-valued truth tables is to the treatment
> of connectives in Karttunen 1974 and in this paper. Unfortunately, the far-
> reaching similarities have eluded most people who have written on this topic
> (e.g., Hausser 1976).

This may be so, but on the other hand, the partiality serves Hausser well: his approach does not suffer from the binding problem.

extensional terms as: either somebody has been dating Mary before and now no longer dates her, or everybody dated Mary before and still dates her at the moment.

Finally, Hausser discusses two more verbs triggering presuppositions, namely the extensional *regret that* and the intensional *look for*. Example (14) is based on Hausser 1976:277.

(14)   a.   Bill regrets that no unicorn exists.
       b.   Bill is looking for a unicorn.

According to Hausser, example (14.a) presupposes that no unicorns exist, and (14.b) that Bill believes that unicorns exist. The interaction between presuppositions and attitudes is notoriously difficult and Hausser's analysis is not as sophisticated as more recent proposals (like Heim 1992, Zeevat 1992 and Geurts 1994), but let us discuss it anyway. In terms of Presuppositional Montague Grammar, the relevant translations are defined as follows.[16]

$\text{regret}^\bullet = \lambda \mathcal{P} \lambda x \lambda i ((\text{regret } \mathcal{P} \ xi)_{\langle \mathcal{P} \ i \rangle})$
$\text{look for}^\bullet = \lambda Q \lambda y \lambda i ((\text{look for } Q \ yi)_{\langle B \ (Q \ exist) \ yi \rangle})$

Syntactically, *regret* is assigned the category VP/S, and *look for* is assigned the category VP/NP. Example (14.a) is translated into the following TY_2^3 formula (on the *de dicto* reading of *regret*):

$\lambda i ((\text{regret } \lambda j \neg \exists x (\text{unicorn } xj \ \wedge \ \text{exists } xj) \ bi)_{\langle \neg \exists x (\text{unicorn } xi \ \wedge \ \text{exist } xi) \rangle})$

In words: given a state s in which Bill regrets the fact (proposition) that there are no unicorns, it is presupposed that there actually are no unicorns in s. For example (14.b) the following formula is produced (on the non-specific reading of *a unicorn*).

$\lambda i ((\text{look for}$
$\lambda P_2 \lambda j \exists x (\text{unicorn } xj \ \wedge \ P_2 \ xj) \ bi)_{\langle B \lambda j \exists x (\text{unicorn } xj \ \wedge \ \text{exist } xj) \ bi \rangle})$

In words: given a state s where Bill is looking for a unicorn, Bill presupposedly believes the proposition that unicorns exist.

A presuppositional example which plays a central role in Karttunen and Peters 1979 is (15).

(15)   Bill loves Mary too.

According to Karttunen and Peters focus sensitive particles like *too* and *even* are different from 'real' presuppositions, such as the ones triggered by descriptions and factives, in that they can be cancelled. Hence, they

---

[16]The constants B (believe) and *regret* both have type $(st)(e(st))$, *exist* is a constant of type $e(st)$ and *look for* of type $((e(st)(st))(e(st))$, $\mathcal{P}$ is a variable of type st. The other variables are typed according to the convention of this chapter.

claim that *too* and *even* give rise to *conventional implicatures* and from there they 'overgenerate' (as Soames 1989 puts is) and treat *all* presuppositions as conventional implicatures.[17]

Be that as it may, Karttunen and Peters treat *too* (and *even*) as a special kind of quantifying-in, in which the combination of *too* and an NP is quantified into the first syntactic variable with the right index. The NP in question is assumed to be in focus, but they abstract over the issue of focus assignments (for that, see for example Rooth 1985, 1992 and Krifka 1992). The translation corresponding with this Too-rule is defined in Presuppositional Montague Grammar as follows:

Definition 10 (Too rule translated)

$$([[\xi]^{NP}[\vartheta]^S]_{too}^{S,n})^\bullet = \lambda i(\xi^\bullet \lambda x_n(\vartheta^\bullet)i_{\langle too\ \xi^\bullet \vartheta^\bullet i\rangle})$$

For example (15), ξ is the NP *Mary* and ϑ is the sentence *Bill loves t_0*. Applying the Too-rule produces the following expression (where the translation of *too* is governed by a meaning-postulate given in the appendix).

(16) $\lambda i(love\ mbi_{\langle\exists x(\neg(x\equiv m)\ \wedge\ love\ xbi)\rangle})$

In (extensional) words, it is predicted that example (15) asserts that Bill loves Mary and presupposes that there is someone other than Mary whom Bill loves as well.[18]

5.4.2 Note

One problem with the rules of Presuppositional Montague Grammar is that they do not assign the correct presuppositions to sentences such as *A fat man pushes his bicycle. It is broken* or *Every man who serves his king is rewarded by him.* But this will hardly come as a surprise in light of the objective of this chapter to present a Presuppositional version of *classical* Montague Grammar. Nevertheless, it is interesting to see what is needed to include these examples in the fragment. Consider the text

---

[17]It is interesting to note that Hausser comes to the opposite conclusion, and argues that words like *too* and *only* are not 'presuppositional' at all (Hausser 1976:250/1). Recently, both Beaver 1997:944 and Geurts and Van der Sandt 1997 come to a similar conclusion, but for rather different reasons.

[18]As Kripke has argued convincingly, this presupposition is not specific enough. Karttunen and Peters require the 'someone other than Mary whom Bill loves' to be contextually relevant, but this is not what Kripke has in mind. Consider the following example, which is based on an example from Kripke n.d.

If Bill loves Mary, then the boss loves Mary too.

According to Kripke the presupposition of the consequent is that Bill is not the boss, and obviously we cannot derive this presupposition without the antecedent. Hence, Kripke argues, here we really need an 'anaphoric' account of presuppositions. The relation between anaphora and presupposition is the subject of the next chapter.

we mentioned first. Of course, the fragment as we presented it does not include analysis trees for texts. Let us tentatively add the following rule.[19]

Definition 11 (Text formation)
If $[\xi]^S$ and $[\vartheta]^S$ are trees then $[[\xi]^S [\vartheta]^S]^S_{tf}$ is a tree, and
$([[\xi]^S [\vartheta]^S]^S_{tf})^\bullet = \xi^\bullet \dot{\wedge} \vartheta^\bullet$

If we add this rule to the fragment, we can derive a syntactic analysis for the aforementioned text, but it would not be a particularly satisfactory one. For one thing, it would crucially require quantifying-in (or some alternative mechanism) to account for the co-reference between *his bicycle* and *it*. And when we have applied the quantifying-in rule, further anaphoric reference to the bicycle is no longer viable.

This problem will look familiar for the dynamically trained reader. For reasons discussed in the introduction of chapter 2, a classical Montagovian analysis of texts is doomed to failure. This means that the problems connected with the two sentences mentioned above are not tied to the analysis of presuppositions *at all*. They are merely instances of the well-known problems all static logics have with *sentence-sequencing* and *donkey*-sentences. Moreover, in the present context, these limitations can be overcome quite easily and without touching on the essence of the fragment: we just have to *dynamify* Presuppositional Montague Grammar.

5.4.3 Dynamifying Presuppositional Montague Grammar

There is a surprisingly simple way to replace the above fragment for a dynamic one, following Muskens 1991, see also chapter 2. Here is the recipe.

Ingredients: TY^3_2, $DR_{(se)t}$, $\mapsto$, $i[d]j$, plus three axioms.

Step 1. Add discourse referents $d_1, d_2, \ldots$ to our main ingredient, TY^3_2. Identify discourse markers with individual concepts, that is: functions from states to entities (type se). Add the non-logical constant DR of type $(se)t$ to the language, with the intuitive interpretation 'is a discourse referent'. It receives a total interpretation; every expression of type se either is a discourse referent or it is not. Furthermore, use Muskens' classical implication $\mapsto$ which is defined as follows:

Definition 12 (Another abbreviation)
$\varphi \mapsto \psi$ abbreviates $\varphi \wedge \psi \equiv \varphi$

---

[19]This rule essentially comprises S18 and T18, discussed in the introduction of chapter 2.

That this implication is classical is a direct consequence of the use of $\equiv$.

Step 2. Next, take $i[d]j$ and define it in such a way that it can be understood as 'states i and j agree on all discourse referents except possibly in the value of d':[20]

Definition 13

$i[d]j$ iff $\forall d'((DR\ d' \wedge \neg(d \equiv d')) \mapsto d'i \equiv d'j)$

Add three axioms to make this work:

Definition 14 (Axioms)

AX1 $\forall i \forall d \forall x(DR\ d \mapsto \exists j(i[d]j \wedge dj = x))$

AX2 $DR\ d$, for each discourse referent d

AX3 $\neg(d_1 \equiv d_2)$, for each two different discourse referents d_1 and d_2.

It is easily seen that the axioms do not create partiality either. This means that the modeling of dynamics in TY_2^3 is exactly like the modeling of dynamics in TY_2.

Step 3. Build the discourse fragment on top of the construction resulting from steps 1 and 2. The essential difference with the fragment discussed in this chapter is that sentences are now translated into expressions of type $s(st)$; they are interpreted as a relation between states. This has direct consequences for the types and translations of analysis trees. Here we will not spell out the obvious details (see section 2.3.3). Adding the rule for text-formation gives us a dynamic variant of Presuppositional Montague Grammar.

This solves the problem we mentioned in the note, by modeling the dynamic behavior of discourse assignments in a static system. Notice that this means that the classical intensionality of Montague Grammar is lost, since in Muskens' set-up states are forced to behave as assignments to discourse referents, and not as world-time pairs as in classical Montague Grammar. There are some ways to regain the traditional intensionality; for example we can complicate the notion of state, or we can introduce a fourth basic category so that both notions of state can live next to each other. We do not touch on these issues here.

---

[20]Since no partiality arises here, it is immaterial whether we use strong, middle or weak Kleene connectives.

5.4.4 Implicatures and Dynamics

We have seen how a version of Presuppositional Montague Grammar can be constructed which does not run into the binding-problem of Karttunen and Peters and does not predict overly strong, universal presuppositions like Heim does. The fragment presented here copies the predictions made by Partial Predicate Logic, but arrives at them in a fully compositional fashion. The present fragment is entirely compatible with the fragments discussed in Karttunen and Peters 1979 and Hausser 1976; so it can indeed be seen as a reformulation of what these systems might have looked like if there had been satisfactory partial versions of Montague Grammar around in the seventies.

Karttunen and Peters might object that the fragment in this chapter is concerned with presuppositions and not with conventional implicatures, and that failing implicatures (our presuppositions) should not necessarily result in undefinedness (interpreted as N). But (as we saw in the discussion section of chapter 4) the N value can also be split up into 'true (in spite of presupposition failure)' and 'false (in spite of presupposition failure)'. TY_2^3 can easily be turned into TY_2^4, *four-valued*, two-sorted type theory (see Muskens 1989). In fact, the only (syntactic) change is the addition of a second formula besides $\star$, say $\#$. The interpretation of TY_2^4 is defined as the interpretation of TY_2^3 was defined, but with $D_t = \{$ T,F,t,f $\}$, where $[\![\star]\!] = $ t and $[\![\#]\!] = $ f and L3 is replaced for L4 (with F at the bottom, T at the top and t and f in between). In this system the 'extended middle Kleene' connectives become definable,[21] and the choice between *presuppositions* and *conventional implicatures* is just a matter of names.

We encountered some (expected) limitations of the present fragment when looking at texts and donkey-sentences, and we also saw how they can be circumvented by teaming Presuppositional Montague Grammar with Muskens' Montagovian discourse grammar based on TY_2. The resulting system combines the partial and the dynamic view on meaning in a Montagovian context. In the next two chapters we look at the combination of partiality and (real) dynamics in more detail. In the following chapter we define a partial version of Double Negation DRT (with presuppositional representations added). The resulting system can be seen as a kind of intermediate between the dynamic semantic approaches to presuppositions as put forward by Heim, Beaver, Van Eijck and others, and the combined semantic/pragmatic approach of Van der Sandt. Finally, in chapter 7 we look at a specific family of presuppositions triggers:

---

[21]This follows from theorem 4 of Muskens 1989, which says that his four-valued propositional logic (which is subsumed by TY_2^4) is functionally complete.

definite NPs. We shall argue that for those definite presuppositions the dynamics of finite assignments is essential.

Appendix: The Fragment

This appendix lists all the relevant definitions which together form Presuppositional Montague Grammar. *As in the main text, the emphasis is on the semantics. For an extensive presentation of both the syntax and the semantics of classical Montague Grammar in terms of type theory the reader is referred to Muskens 1989. The set of categories is defined as follows:*

Definition 15 (Categories)

1. E is a category; S is a category;
2. If A and B are categories, then A/B and $A//B$ are categories.

The following table lists the categories that we shall actually use in the fragment.

Category	Abbreviation	Basic Expressions
S		
S/E	VP	whistle, be rewarded
$S//E$	CN	man, bicycle, king
S/VP	NP	Bill, Mary, George V, somebody, t_n
VP/VP		try to, manage to
VP/NP	TV	succeed, push, love, serve
NP/CN	DET	every, a, the
CN/CN	ADJ	fat
DET/NP	$POSS$	's

We only use three of Montague's syntactic rules (besides the basic rule): functional application, quantifying-in *and* relative clause formation.

Definition 16 (Syntactic Trees)

1. BASIC:
   If α is a basic expression of category A, then $[\,\alpha\,]^A$ is a tree.
2. FUNCTIONAL APPLICATION:
   If $[\,\alpha\,]^{A/^m B}$ and $[\,\beta\,]^B$ are trees, then $[[\,\alpha\,]^{A/^m B}\,[\,\beta\,]^B]^A_{\text{fa}}$ is a tree $(m \in \{1,2\})$.
3. QUANTIFYING-IN:
   If $[\,\xi\,]^{NP}$ and $[\,\vartheta\,]^S$ are trees, then $[[\,\xi\,]^{NP}\,[\,\vartheta\,]^S]^{S,n}_{\text{qi}}$ is a tree, for $n \in I\!N$.
4. RELATIVE CLAUSE FORMATION:
   If $[\,\xi\,]^{CN}$ and $[\,\vartheta\,]^S$ are trees, then $[[\,\xi\,]^{CN}\,[\,\vartheta\,]^S]^{CN,n}_{\text{rcf}}$ is a tree, for $n \in I\!N$.

The first rule corresponds with rule 1 (in Montague 1974b). The rule for functional application subsumes Montague's rules 3 to 10 and here also deals with adjectives and possessives. The quantifying-in rule is labeled 14,n in PTQ, *while the rule for relative clauses has number 2,n.*

This concludes the brief overview of the syntactic part of Presuppositional Montague Grammar. Let us now focus on the semantics. The following definition maps (syntactic) categories to (semantic) types.

Definition 17 (Category-to-type Rule)

1. $\mathsf{Type}_2(E) = e; \mathsf{Type}_2(S) = (st);$
2. $\mathsf{Type}_2(A/B) = \mathsf{Type}_2(A//B) = (\mathsf{Type}_2(B)\mathsf{Type}_2(A)).$

This gives the following types for the categories employed in the fragment:

Category A		$\mathsf{Type}_2(A)$	
S		st	Proposition
S/E	(VP)	$e(st)$	Property
$S//E$	(CN)	$e(st)$	Property
S/VP	(NP)	$(e(st))(st)$	Quantifier
VP/VP		$(e(st))(e(st))$	
VP/NP	(TV)	$((e(st))(st))(e(st))$	
NP/CN	(DET)	$(e(st))((e(st))(st))$	
CN/CN	(ADJ)	$(e(st))(e(st))$	
DET/NP	$(POSS)$	$((e(st))(st))((e(st))((e(st))(st)))$	

We use the following terms in the representations:

Definition 18 (Terms)

Let b, m, g, *whistle, reward, man, bike, king, succeed, push, love, serve, of, try, difficult* and *fat* be constants and let x, y, i, j, $\mathcal{P}$, P_i, and Q_i be variables with types as indicated in the following table.

Type	Constants	Variables
e	b, m, g	x, y
s		i, j
st		$\mathcal{P}$
$e(st)$	*whistle, reward*	P_i
$e(st)$	*man, bike, king*	P_i
$e(e(st))$	*succeed, push, love, serve, of*	
$(e(st))(st)$		Q_i
$(e(st))(e(st))$	*try, difficult*	
$(e(st))(e(st))$	*fat*	

Finally, the function (.)$^\bullet$ gives us the translation of the syntactic trees in partial type-theory.

Definition 19 (Translation)

For each tree $[\,\xi\,]$ define its translation $\xi^\bullet$ as follows:

1. **BASIC**

    whistle$^\bullet$ = *whistle*, be rewarded$^\bullet$ = *reward* ;

    man$^\bullet$ = *man*, bicycle$^\bullet$ = *bike*, king$^\bullet$ = *king*;

    Bill$^\bullet$ = $\lambda P(P\ b)$, George V$^\bullet$ = $\lambda P(P\ g)$, Mary$^\bullet$ = $\lambda P(P\ m)$,
    somebody$^\bullet$ = $\lambda P \lambda i \exists x(P\ xi)$, $t_n{}^\bullet$ = $\lambda P(P\ x_n)$;

    try to$^\bullet$ = *try*; manage to$^\bullet$ = $\lambda P \lambda x \lambda i(P\ xi_{\langle(difficult\ P)\ xi\rangle})$;

    succeed$^\bullet$ = $\lambda Q \lambda y(Q \lambda x(succeed\ xy))$, push$^\bullet$ = $\lambda Q \lambda y(Q \lambda x(push\ xy))$,
    love$^\bullet$ = $\lambda Q \lambda y(Q \lambda x(love\ xy))$, serve$^\bullet$ = $\lambda Q \lambda y(Q \lambda x(serve\ xy))$;

    every$^\bullet$ = $\lambda P_1 \lambda P_2 \lambda i \forall x(P_1\ xi \to P_2\ xi)$,
    a$^\bullet$ = $\lambda P_1 \lambda P_2 \lambda i \exists x(P_1\ xi \wedge P_2\ xi)$,
    the$^\bullet$ = $\lambda P_1 \lambda P_2 \lambda i(\exists x(P_1\ xi \wedge P_2\ xi)_{\langle \exists! x P_1\ xi\rangle})$;

    's$^\bullet$ = $\lambda Q \lambda P_1 \lambda P_2 \lambda i$
    $\quad (\exists x(P_1\ xi \wedge Q \lambda y(of\ yx)i \wedge P_2\ xi)_{\langle \exists! x(P_1\ xi\ \wedge\ Q \lambda y(of\ yx)i)\rangle})$;

    fat$^\bullet$ = *fat*;

2. **FUNCTIONAL APPLICATION**

    $([\xi\vartheta]_{\text{fa}})^\bullet = \xi^\bullet \vartheta^\bullet$;

3. **QUANTIFYING-IN**

    $([\xi\vartheta]_{\text{qi}}^n)^\bullet = \xi^\bullet \lambda x_n(\vartheta^\bullet)$;

4. **RELATIVE CLAUSE FORMATION**

    $([\xi\vartheta]_{\text{rcf}}^n)^\bullet = \lambda x_n \lambda i(\xi^\bullet\ x_n i \wedge \vartheta^\bullet\ i)$.

Definition 20 (Notation Convention 1)

$\forall x \forall y \forall i((\gamma\ xi \wedge of\ yxi) \to \gamma\text{-}of\ yxi)$, where γ is *man*, *bike* or *king*

ADDITIONAL PRESUPPOSTIONS

From Hausser: Add the following basic categories.

Category	Abbreviation	Basic Expressions
VP/VP		stop to
NP/CN	DET	some
VP/NP		look for
VP/S		regret

We add constants believe *and* regret *of type* $(st)(e(st))$, exist *of type* $e(st)$ *and* look for *of type* $((e(st)(st))(e(st)))$. *Furthermore, we use the constants* $<$ *and* $\approx$, *which represent the two orderings on* D_s, *and both have type* $s(st)$. *The basic translation of* every *is modified, and otherwise the set of basic translations is extended with the following lexical entries.*

stop to$^\bullet = \lambda P \lambda x \lambda i (\neg (P\ xi)_{\langle \exists j (j<i\ \wedge\ i \approx j\ \wedge\ P\ xj) \rangle})$;

some$^\bullet = \lambda P_1 \lambda P_2 \lambda i (\exists x (P_1\ xi\ \wedge\ P_2\ xi)_{\langle \exists y (P_1\ yi) \rangle})$;

every$^\bullet = \lambda P_1 \lambda P_2 \lambda i (\forall x (P_1\ xi \rightarrow P_2\ xi)_{\langle \exists y (P_1\ yi) \rangle})$;

regret$^\bullet = \lambda P \lambda x \lambda i ((regret\ P\ xi)_{\langle \mathcal{P}\ i \rangle})$;

look for$^\bullet = \lambda Q \lambda y \lambda i ((look\ for\ Q\ yi)_{\langle believe\ (Q\ exist)\ yi \rangle})$.

Karttunen and Peters' analyses of even *and* too *can be cast in terms of Presuppositional Montague Grammar as follows.*

Definition 21 (More Syntactic Trees)

    5. TOO:

        If $[\, \xi\,]^{NP}$ and $[\, \vartheta\,]^S$ are trees, then $[[\, \xi\,]^{NP} [\, \vartheta\,]^S]^{S,n}_{\text{too}}$ is a tree, for $n \in I\!N$.

    6. EVEN:

        If $[\, \xi\,]^{NP}$ and $[\, \vartheta\,]^S$ are trees, then $[[\, \xi\,]^{NP} [\, \vartheta\,]^S]^{S,n}_{\text{even}}$ is a tree, for $n \in I\!N$.

Add constants even *and* too, *of type* $((e(st))(st))((st)(st))$, *as well as* $*$ *('contextually relevant'), of type* $e(st)$.

Definition 22 (More Translations)

    5. TOO

        $([\xi\vartheta]^n_{\text{too}})^\bullet = \lambda i (\xi^\bullet \lambda x_n (\vartheta^\bullet) i_{\langle too\ \xi^\bullet \vartheta^\bullet i \rangle})$;

    6. EVEN

        $([\xi\vartheta]^n_{\text{even}})^\bullet = \lambda i (\xi^\bullet \lambda x_n (\vartheta^\bullet) i_{\langle even\ \xi^\bullet \vartheta^\bullet i \rangle})$.

Even and too obey the following meaning-postulates.

Definition 23 (Axioms)

1. $too \equiv \lambda Q \lambda \mathcal{P} \lambda i \exists x (*\ xi\ \wedge\ \neg (\lambda P (P\ x) \equiv Q)\ \wedge\ \lambda x_n (\mathcal{P})\ xi)$

2. $even \equiv \lambda Q \lambda \mathcal{P} \lambda i \exists x (*\ xi\ \wedge\ \neg (\lambda P (P\ x) \equiv Q)\ \wedge\ \lambda x_n (\mathcal{P})\ xi)\ \wedge\ \forall x (*\ xi$
   $\wedge\ \neg (\lambda P (P\ x) \equiv Q) \rightarrow exceed(likelih(\lambda x_n (\mathcal{P})\ xi), likelih(Q \lambda x_n (\mathcal{P})i)))$

The non-logical constants exceed *and* likelih(ood) *have obvious intended interpretations and are discussed in Karttunen and Peters 1979.*

6

Presupposition and Discourse Semantics

6.1 Introduction

There are currently two rather different dynamic approaches to presupposition in vogue. On the one hand, there is the *semantic* approach to presupposition, which might also be dubbed the *contextual satisfaction* approach. It has its roots in Karttunen 1974 and modern (dynamic) versions can be found in the work of, among others, Heim, Beaver and Van Eijck. These theories have in common that they all incorporate a form of partiality in a dynamic semantic framework, and determine the presupposition of an expression purely in terms of the (dynamic) meaning. A rather different approach to presupposition is due to Van der Sandt 1992. The crux of Van der Sandt's approach is the idea that, in many respects, presuppositions behave as anaphors. A consequence of his *presuppositions-as-anaphors* view is that the projection problem for presuppositions can be reduced to the problem of resolving anaphoric pronouns. More concretely, Van der Sandt argues that presuppositions can be handled using the same mechanism which resolves anaphoric pronouns in DRT. There is one important difference between pronouns and 'real' presuppositions: when no suitable, accessible antecedent can be found for a presupposition, and the presupposition has sufficient descriptive content, it can be *accommodated* and, so to speak, create its own antecedent. The flexible combination of binding and accommodation yields the empirical strength of Van der Sandt's presuppositions-as-anaphors theory.

In this chapter a version of DRT is discussed which can be seen as a kind of bridge between these two approaches to presupposition. We extend the system of Double Negation DRT from chapter 3 with presuppositional DRSs. The resulting system, to which we shall refer as

Presuppositional DRT, can be seen as a combination of Double Negation DRT with the Peters/middle Kleene based version of PPL. As far as the *interpretation* is concerned, Presuppositional DRT is closely related to Beaver 1992's *Kinematic Predicate Logic* and Van Eijck 1993's *Error-state Semantics for* DPL (both incorporating a form of partiality in a DPL(-like) framework), although the Presuppositional DRT treatment of negation and disjunction is different. On the other hand, the *representations* of Presuppositional DRT show great resemblance to those employed by Van der Sandt in his presuppositions-as-anaphors theory.

Thus, Presuppositional DRT may be associated with *two* different approaches to presuppositions: on the one hand, the approach in the tradition of Karttunen, Heim, Beaver, Van Eijck and others, and on the other hand the presuppositions-as-anaphors approach of Van der Sandt. The resulting picture obviously enhances comparison between the two approaches, but in this chapter we also discuss an additional advantage: taking Presuppositional DRT as an alternative foundation (instead of DRT) enhances the presuppositions-as-anaphors theory. We do not propose any significant *changes* to Van der Sandt's theory, rather we show that defining Van der Sandt's presupposition resolution algorithm on top of Presuppositional DRT instead of standard DRT has a number of advantages.[1]

The rest of this chapter contains the following sections. In section 6.2 we discuss Van der Sandt's theory in more detail. In sections 6.3, 6.4 and 6.5 we present Presuppositional DRT (the formal system, the applications and a method to calculate the semantic presupposition of arbitrary DRSs). In section 6.6 we re-discuss Van der Sandt's theory, but now in terms of Presuppositional DRT. Finally, section 6.7 discusses some of the questions raised by the present perspective. In particular, we take a closer look at the differences in predictions between the two approaches, propose a different interpretation of Presuppositional DRT and discuss a different view on accommodation, namely as abductive inference.

---

[1]In spirit, Presuppositional DRT can also be compared with the system of Zeevat 1992. Zeevat proposes a reformulation of Van der Sandt's theory in terms of Update Semantics and compares this reformulation with other approaches to presupposition, in particular the one found in Heim 1983b. But where Zeevat re-defines Van der Sandt's theory in the formalism of Update Semantics, we leave Van der Sandt's representational theory essentially untouched and show how it can be employed on top of the system of Presuppositional DRT. Another relevant, alternative approach can be found in Fernando 1994b, where *syntactic translations* are used to produce the presuppositions of dynamic formulae.

6.2 Presuppositions-as-Anaphors

Van der Sandt's theory[2] rests on the assumption that presuppositions are nothing more than anaphors looking for an antecedent. More concretely, Van der Sandt proposes to 'resolve' presuppositions, just like anaphoric pronouns are resolved in standard DRT. For this purpose, Van der Sandt uses a slightly modified version of DRT, which differs from standard DRT only in the way DRSs are constructed. In standard DRT, the construction algorithm turns (the syntactic tree of) a sentence into a DRS, and pronouns are resolved *en route*. In the presuppositions-as-anaphors approach a curtailed version of the construction algorithm (which does not resolve anaphors) produces a so-called S-DRS for a sentence:

If $x_1, \ldots, x_n$ are variables, $\varphi_1, \ldots, \varphi_m$ are conditions, and $\Phi_1, \ldots, \Phi_k$ are S-DRSs, then $[x_1, \ldots, x_n \mid \varphi_1, \ldots, \varphi_m \mid \Phi_1, \ldots, \Phi_k]$ is an S-DRS. $(n, m, k \geq 0)$

In a pictorial format an S-DRS looks as follows:[3]

(DRS 1)

So, an S-DRS can be seen as a standard DRS with embedded DRSs Φ_i added, each representing an elementary presupposition, awaiting resolution. Notice that since the presuppositional Φ_i are S-DRSs as well, they may themselves contain embedded presuppositions. Below we often use the term 'DRS' to refer to an S-DRS, trusting that this will not lead to confusion.

As an example, consider (1), and its associated Van der Sandtian representation, (DRS 2).

(1)   If France has a king, then the king of France is bald.

---

[2]As developed in Van der Sandt 1989, 1992, Van der Sandt and Geurts 1991, and further extended in for example Geurts 1994 and Sæbø 1996.

[3]This DRS is not *entirely* faithful to Van der Sandt: he represents presuppositional DRSs using *dashed* lines.

(DRS 2)

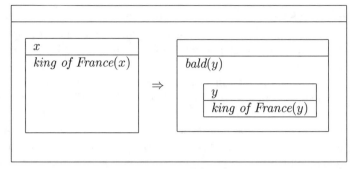

The consequent DRS contains a presuppositional DRS representing the presupposition, triggered by the definite description, that there is a king of France.

6.2.1 Resolving Presuppositions

After an S-DRS has been constructed, the presuppositional representations (if any) are resolved in the context of the representation of the discourse so far. In Van der Sandt's theory, resolving a presupposition amounts to either *binding* or *accommodating* it. For this purpose, a *presupposition resolution algorithm* is developed, consisting of three consecutive stages. Here we loosely follow Van der Sandt's so-called *anaphoric loop*; one of the two versions of the presupposition resolution algorithm discussed in Van der Sandt 1992. Nothing hinges on this (see section 6.2.3 for some discussion).[4] The first thing we do is the following:

ONE: *Try to* bind *the presuppositional* DRS *as low as possible.*

Since it is assumed that presupposition is just a species of anaphora, we look for a *suitable, accessible* antecedent. As usual, accessibility is determined by the structure of the relevant DRS, and here we can simply look at the set of accessible antecedents (given by ACC, see chapters 2 and 3) as we have been doing so far. But now we can also say something about the *suitability* of the antecedent: it has to satisfy the conditions of the presuppositional DRS. In fact, Van der Sandt also allows for *partial matches* between presupposition and antecedent, but for now we ignore this possibility.[5] Consider (DRS 2). To resolve the presuppositional DRS, we look for an accessible, suitable antecedent, and obviously the discourse referent introduced by the indefinite *a king* (x) in the antecedent-DRS is the ideal candidate. So, the presuppositional DRS can indeed be bound. Binding goes as follows: the presuppositional DRS is removed

---

[4]For formal details on the resolution process we refer to the references cites in footnote 2.

[5]See footnote 28.

from the DRS where it originates (the *source* DRS, for short) in this case the consequent-DRS, and 'moved into' the DRS where the antecedent was introduced to which the presupposition is bound (henceforth the *target* DRS), in this case the antecedent-DRS. To round things off, all free occurrences of y are replaced by its newly found antecedent, x. In this way the anaphor is 'absorbed' by the antecedent (Van der Sandt 1992:349). This results in the following DRS:

(DRS 3)

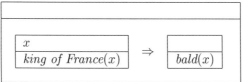

Notice that (DRS 3) is also the standard DRT representation for example (2). In fact, the parallel between examples like (1) and (2) is one of the suggestive facts discussed by Van der Sandt to motivate his presuppositions-as-anaphors approach.

(2)   If France has a king, then he is bald.

In this case, we easily succeeded in finding an antecedent, and hence in binding the presupposition: there was only one possibility. If there is more than one possible antecedent for a presupposition, Van der Sandt's algorithm prefers binding to the *lowest* antecedent. That is, if we find two accessible antecedents with the right properties, we bind the presupposition to the closest one (where closeness is defined in terms of the number of intervening (sub-)DRSs between source- and target-DRS). For this purpose, Van der Sandt defines the *projection line* of a presuppositional DRS Φ, which is just the list of (sub-)DRSs encountered in calculating the accessible antecedents, ACC(Φ). If there are two or more closest, suitable antecedents, an unresolvable ambiguity is predicted.

It is also possible that we have checked every accessible DRS without finding a possible antecedent for the presupposition, not even on the highest possible landing-site: the main DRS. Then we go the next phase of the resolution algorithm:

TWO: *If binding a presuppositional* DRS *fails, try to* accommodate *it as high as possible.*

Accommodation of a presuppositional DRS Φ in some target-DRS Ψ simply amounts to adding Φ to Ψ: we replace Ψ with the merge of the two DRSs Φ ; Ψ. When attempting to accommodate a presuppositional DRS, we once again follow the projection line, but now in the opposite direction: we first try to accommodate in the main DRS ('global accommodation'), before we attempt accommodation in (sub-)DRSs lower on the projection line ('intermediate accommodation'). The last option is to accommodate the presupposition in the sub-DRS where the presupposition was triggered in the first place: the source-DRS ('local accommodation'). Consider example (3), with its DRT representation (DRS 4) added.

(3)   If a farmer owns a donkey, he gives it to the king of France.

(DRS 4)

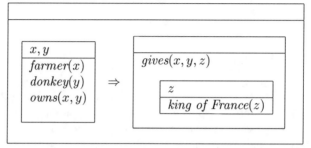

To be precise, this DRS is already partially resolved; the representations of the pronouns *he* and *it* have been bound to the antecedents *a farmer* and *a donkey* respectively. One presuppositional DRS remains, expressing the elementary presupposition that there is a king of France. Obviously, binding this presupposition is out of the question, since none of the accessible discourse referents satisfies the condition that it is a king of France. So, we attempt to accommodate the presupposition. That is: we remove the presuppositional DRS $[z \mid king\ of\ France(z)]$ from the consequent, and merge it with what is left of (DRS 4) after the removal of the presuppositional DRS. After applying the Merging Lemma this results in (DRS 5).

(DRS 5)

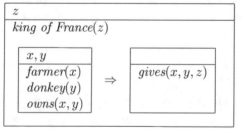

Accommodation is a very strong mechanism, and therefore Van der Sandt requires the result of accommodation to satisfy certain constraints. One obvious constraint is that variables may not end up being free after accommodation, this is the so-called *trapping constraint*. Moreover, the result of accommodation must satisfy certain general, independently motivated constraints: it has to be both *informative*

and *consistent*. Roughly, accommodating Ψ in Φ with Φ' as output is (i) informative if the set of models which support Φ' is a proper subset of the set of models supporting Φ and (ii) consistent if there is at least one model satisfying Φ'. These conditions are originally due to Stalnaker 1979, but Van der Sandt 1988 discusses these constraints in detail for the purpose of presupposition and generalizes them to apply at the level of sub-DRSs as well (for formal details we again refer to the references cited in footnote 2). If accommodating a presuppositional DRS at a certain level violates one or more of the constraints, we try to accommodate it on a lower level of the projection line. If no accommodation is possible, we come to the last phase of the resolution algorithm.

THREE: *If both binding and accommodation fail: Give up*

This would happen with an example like (4).

(4)   There is no king of France. # The king of France is bald.

If the reader constructs a mental DRS for this example, she may easily verify that binding the presupposition that there is a king France (triggered by the definite description in the second sentence) does not succeed since there are no accessible antecedents, and similarly any accommodation violates the consistency condition.

Van der Sandt's presuppositions-as-anaphors theory has several attractive features. It uses a single mechanism for presuppositions and 'ordinary' anaphors, and it has an integrated analysis which treats binding and accommodation as two sides of the same coin. Moreover, on the empirical side it does very well (see Beaver 1997:983). The previous sketch illustrates the observation made above that Van der Sandt's theory is flexible by nature: each presuppositional DRS gives rise to various possible resolutions which are ordered by the underlying principles. Moreover, no weak presuppositions are predicted. For example: the presuppositional DRS in (DRS 4) is accommodated at top-level; the predicted presupposition for example (3) is that there is a king of France. By comparison: the Peters/middle Kleene based version of PPL (which may be seen as a representative of the semantic, Karttunen-style approach to presuppositions) predicts that (3) presupposes the weaker *either it is not true that a farmer owns a donkey, or there is a king of France* (see chapter 4). For extensive discussion on the differences between the two approaches, as well as on the similarities, the reader is referred to Van der Sandt 1992, Zeevat 1992, Geurts 1994 and Beaver 1995. Some of the relevant issues are also discussed in section 6.7. In general, it is fair to say that there is no other theory (static or dynamic) which deals in a successful way with quite the same range of data as the presuppositions-as-anaphors approach. Nevertheless it raises a few questions as well.

6.2.2 What is a Presuppositional DRS?

To begin with, Van der Sandt modifies the syntax of DRT so as to include presuppositional DRSs in it. But, there is no interpretation for these new S-DRSs. One can argue that representations such as (DRS 2) are in fact *proto-DRSs* in the sense that they are still 'under construction'. To some extent this position can be defended: the representation *is* under construction since some anaphoric elements are still to be resolved. And, when they are all resolved, the net-result is a standard DRS which has a perfectly normal interpretation. On the other hand: one would like to have an interpretation for *any* expression of the DRS language. By comparison, the proto-DRSs which occur in Kamp and Reyle 1993 are *not* elements of the DRT language; they are just partly dismantled syntactic trees with a box around them. So we have two options: either representations like (DRS 2) are indeed proto-DRSs, and hence they are not elements of the proper DRT language (and thus do not require interpretation). Or, we do not treat them like proto-DRSs but like ordinary DRSs, and then they do require an interpretation. Here we argue for the second option. We shall see that Presuppositional DRT can be used to give an interpretation to S-DRSs. Moreover, it will be shown that having such an interpretation actually has several positive effects.

6.2.3 Procedural vs. Declarative

For example, Van der Sandt has observed that his (procedural) way of resolving presuppositions we just sketched '(...) *obviously leads to problems when we check for logical properties such as consistency or entailment. For interpretation and determination of these logical properties can only ensue after full resolution of all anaphoric expressions.*' (Van der Sandt 1992:362). After all, S-DRSs do not have an interpretation, ordinary DRSs without embedded presuppositions do. Hence in more complex cases, the procedural version of the algorithm involves '*a substantial amount of backtracking*' (Van der Sandt 1992, *ibid.*). Therefore, Van der Sandt discards the procedural 'anaphoric loop' and opts for a more declarative approach: for an unresolved S-DRS Φ a set of all *logically possible* resolutions for Φ is constructed. That is, every possible resolution is carried out and interpreted. By the underlying principles we discussed above (binding as low as possible, accommodation as high as possible, binding preferred over accommodation), this set of logical possibilities is partially ordered,[6] and the resolution which occupies the first place in the ordering —the preferred reading— will also be the output of the procedural version of the resolution algorithm. For simple sentences the difference between the procedural and the declarative approach is not so dramatic, but when considering longer stretches of text the set of all logically possible resolutions may turn out to be rather big, and computing all of them may take a significant amount of time. If there is an interpretation for presuppositional DRSs we can check the logical properties on the spot, and the procedural algorithm will not run into problems; we can stop when we have found *one* satisfactory resolution.[7] Of course this does not mean that we *have* to stop: if we wanted to, we could continue searching for less preferred resolutions as long as we like.

6.2.4 Accommodating Failing Presuppositions

Consider example (5).

(5) It is not the case that the king of France is bald.

On Van der Sandt's approach this sentence is represented by (DRS 6).

(DRS 6)

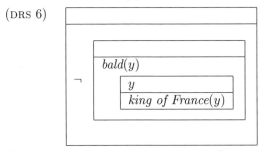

Once this representation is constructed we apply the presupposition resolution mechanism to it. That is: we first attempt to bind the presuppositional DRS. This does not succeed since there are no antecedents, let alone suitable ones. Thus we try to accommodate the presupposition at top level in the main DRS. This obviously does not violate any constraints. So, after resolution (accommodation) and an application of the DRT Merging Lemma we end up with the following representation.

---

[6]It is not a total order in general, since ambiguities may arise, for instance if there are *two* closest, suitable antecedents.

[7]Although having an interpretation for presuppositional DRSs leads to a substantial reduction of the search space, some amount of backtracking is inevitable. See note 23 below.

(DRS 7)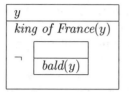

Now suppose we interpret (DRS 7) in a model in which France has no king. In such a model (DRS 7) is false. Thus, for this example Van der Sandt essentially follows the Russellian analysis of example (5) discussed in chapter 4.

Kracht 1994 objects to this way of accommodating presuppositions —or *re-allocation* as he calls it— by observing that an accommodated presupposition should still be a presupposition. However, in Van der Sandt's theory a presupposition loses its *presuppositionhood* when it is resolved. If a presupposition would remain a presupposition after resolution, the result cannot even be interpreted since there is no interpretation for the presuppositional DRSs. Interestingly, Van der Sandt himself notes the following.

> I (...) assume the standard extensional semantics for the DRS language, which is set out well in the literature; see e.g., Kamp (1981) or Kamp & Reyle [(1993)]. One consequence is that when a 'failing' presupposition is accommodated the resulting discourse is false, and not undefined as Frege or Strawson would have it. (...) The Fregean [intuition] can, however, be restored by explicitly marking accommodated material as such and making the embedding function dependent on the status of the relevant markers.
> Van der Sandt 1992:375,fn27

In other words: accommodated, presuppositional material should be distinguished from simply asserted material. When we define Van der Sandt's theory on top of Presuppositional DRT instead of standard DRT, we can easily mark something as presuppositional, namely by representing it as a presuppositional DRS. This would call for a small change in the resolution algorithm: we accommodate the presuppositional DRS *as a presuppositional* DRS. Thus, resolving the presuppositional DRS in (DRS 6) does not result in (DRS 7), but in (DRS 8). To indicate that the presuppositional DRS has been 'resolved' it is marked with a †.[8]

---

[8]Presuppositional DRT is defined in such a way that the free occurrence of y in the condition *bald(y)* is bound by the introduction of y in the presuppositional DRS.

(DRS 8)

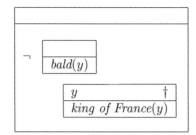

The interpretation of a presuppositional DRS will just be a dynamic version of Blamey's transplication. So, in a model where there is no king of France, (DRS 8) indeed will be undefined, as Frege and Strawson would have it.

6.2.5 Disjunctions

Consider the following presuppositional variant of the bathroom sentence discussed in Van der Sandt 1992:368, and its representation (DRS 9).

(6) Either there is no bathroom in this house, or the bathroom is in a strange place.[9]

(DRS 9)

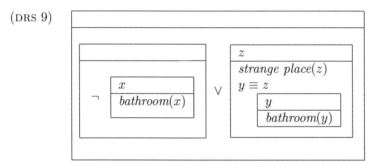

The presuppositions-as-anaphors theory, based on standard DRT, predicts that binding the presuppositional DRS $[y \mid bathroom(y)]$ is not possible, since in standard DRT a left disjunct, be it negated or not, is inaccessible for a right disjunct. Global accommodation of the presupposition triggered by *the bathroom* does not work either, since this would represent the unacceptable discourse *There is a bathroom in this house. Either there is no bathroom in this house, or it is in a strange place*: it violates the consistency constraint for sub-DRSs, since the left-hand sub-DRS of the disjunction is inconsistent with there being a bathroom in this house. As a consequence, we have to go for the least preferred way of resolving the presuppositional DRS: it is locally accommodated

---

[9]Van der Sandt's actual example is *Either John has no donkey, or his donkey is eating quietly in the stable.*

in the disjunct it originated in. This results in a reading which may be paraphrased as *Either there is no bathroom in this house, or there is a bathroom in this house and it is in strange place.* We already discussed this reading for the bathroom sentence in chapter 3 and it seems that this is not the meaning of (6): suppose that there are *two* bathrooms in this house, one which is in a strange place and one which is not. In that case (6) does not seem to be true. But the Van der Sandtian reading *is* true in that situation since the second disjunct can be verified.

Now consider the following, comparable examples (from Beaver 1995):

(7)   Either John didn't solve the problem, or else Mary realizes that the problem's been solved.

(8)   Either Mary's autobiography hasn't appeared yet, or else John must be very proud that Mary has had a book published.

Beaver points out that Van der Sandt's mechanism makes the wrong predictions for examples such as these. Let us focus on (8) and assume that *being proud that S* presupposes S, that is: the second disjunct presupposes that Mary has had a book published. Van der Sandt predicts that the most preferred reading of (8) is the one involving global accommodation. Binding is not possible (the (negated) left disjunct is again not accessible), but the global accommodation of *Mary has had a book published* is not ruled out: having published a book but not an autobiography is perfectly consistent. Nevertheless, the reading which results after global accommodation is wrong: on its most natural reading, (8) does *not* entail that Mary has had a book published.

If we interpret negation as is done in Double Negation DRT we can solve these problems. Recall that in chapter 2 we discussed the similarities between the standard DRT notion of accessibility and Karttunen's local contexts. We noted that accessibility and local contexts are calculated in a similar way, *except for disjunction.* The situation is different for Double Negation DRT, as we have seen in chapter 3. As a result of the new treatment of negation and disjunction, the modified rules for determining accessibility now entirely mirror the pattern of Karttunen's local context determination. Since Presuppositional DRT will be based on Double Negation DRT, the negated left disjunct will indeed be accessible from the right disjunct. In other words: for (6), (7) and (8) it will be predicted that the non-presuppositional (binding) reading is preferred. If we consider the Presuppositional DRT version of (DRS 9) we *can* find an antecedent when we try to resolve the presuppositional DRS; the referent x is accessible and satisfies the relevant condition. In other words, we do not need to locally accommodate the presuppositional DRS, we can simply bind it. And similarly for example (8): given the natural assumptions that an autobiography is a book and that a book which has appeared has been published, we can bind the presupposition arising in the second disjunct, and as a result it is predicted that (8) is equivalent with (9).

(9) If Mary's autobiography has appeared, John must be very proud about it.

6.2.6   Presupposition-Quantification Interaction

Van der Sandt's theory has been criticized for its treatment of presuppositions in the scope of quantifiers (see for instance Beaver 1995). A typical example is (10), due to Heim 1983b and also discussed at some length in the preceding two chapters.

(10) Every fat man pushes his bicycle.

Van der Sandt's resolution algorithm predicts that the presupposition triggered by *his bicycle* is accommodated in the scope of *every*. It cannot be accommodated in the main DRS because the discourse referent associated with the male pronoun would end up being free, which is forbidden by the trapping constraint. Since the presupposition loses its presupposition-hood it is predicted that (10) is equivalent with (11).

(11) Every fat man who has a bicycle pushes it.

The question what the exact presupposition is of sentences like (10) is hard to decide, but the alleged equivalence between (10) and (11) is not generally supported. As we shall see, Presuppositional DRT, and the assumption that presuppositions should be accommodated as presuppositions and not as assertions, may shed a new light on these examples.[10]

Summarizing

We mentioned several advantages of taking Presuppositional DRT instead of standard DRT as the foundation of the presuppositions-as-anaphors theory. Nothing significant is lost when switching to Presuppositional DRT; it is just a generalization of standard DRT. Given that we can interpret DRSs before and after resolution, various questions concerning the *meaning* of presupposition resolution suggest themselves. Later on in this chapter, we dwell on these issues. Now, let us first discuss the system of Presuppositional DRT in more formal detail.

---

[10]In fact, Geurts and Van der Sandt 1997 also assume that there is a crucial difference between presupposed and asserted material, and they subsequently argue that (10) and (11) are *only roughly* equivalent. Nevertheless they do not describe how the *difference* between presupposed and asserted material is accounted for in the usual conception of the presuppositions-as-anaphors theory.

6.3 Presuppositional DRT

The syntax of Presuppositional DRT is like the syntax of Double Negation
DRT, but with representations for *elementary* presuppositions added. In
chapter 4 we have discussed two (interdefinable) ways of adding elementary presuppositions to the language. We can either add Blamey's
binary transplication or Beaver's unary presupposition operator (∂) to
the language, and here we do the latter. Once again, we switch back and
forth between the pictorial and the linear format of DRSs. The linear
notation is used in the formalities, such as the following. The set of
terms is given by the union of Con (the set of constants) and Var (the
set of variables/discourse referents), both non-empty.

Definition 1 (Presuppositional DRT syntax)

1. If R is an n-ary predicate and $t_1, \ldots, t_n$ are terms, then $R(t_1, \ldots, t_n)$
   is a condition.

2. If t_1 and t_2 are terms, then $t_1 \equiv t_2$ is a condition.

3. If Φ and Ψ are DRSs, then $(\Phi \Rightarrow \Psi)$ is a condition.

4. If $x_1, \ldots, x_n$ are variables and $\varphi_1, \ldots, \varphi_m$ are conditions, then
   $[x_1, \ldots, x_n \mid \varphi_1, \ldots, \varphi_m]$ is a DRS (with $n, m \geq 0$).

5. If Φ and Ψ are DRSs, then $(\Phi \, ; \, \Psi)$, $\sim\!\Phi$ and $\partial\Phi$ are DRSs.

The intuition behind $\partial\Phi$ is that it says of Φ that it is an elementary presupposition. $\partial\Phi$ will be interpreted in such a way that it is supported
(True) whenever Φ is supported (True), and neither supported nor rejected otherwise. In particular: $\partial\Phi$ cannot be rejected (False). There is
one essential difference in interpretation between Double Negation DRT
and its partial counterpart under discussion here: the negative extensions are no longer defined as mere absence of truth. Let F once more
be the set of finite assignments, with Λ as the empty assignment. $g\{\vec{x}\}h$
abbreviates: assignment h extends assignment g with $\vec{x}$, as defined in
definition 2.4. Let $M = \langle D, I \rangle$ be an ordinary first-order model. For
terms the interpretation is defined as follows: $[\![t]\!]^+_{M,g} = [\![t]\!]^-_{M,g} = g(t)$
if $t \in$ Var and $t \in \mathrm{Dom}(g)$, and $[\![t]\!]^+_{M,g} = [\![t]\!]^-_{M,g} = I(t)$ if $t \in$ Con.
Since for any term t, $[\![t]\!]^+$ equals $[\![t]\!]^-$, we drop the superscript in the
interpretation of terms. If $g(x)$ is not defined, $[\![x]\!]_g$ is not defined either.
For conditions φ, we define $[\![\varphi]\!]^+_M \subseteq F$ and $[\![\varphi]\!]^-_M \subseteq F$, while for DRSs
Φ we define $[\![\Phi]\!]^+_M \subseteq F^2$ and $[\![\Phi]\!]^-_M \subseteq F^2$ as follows (in the first clause
$1 \leq i \leq n$, we drop the M-index where possible):[11]

---

[11] The interpretation of Presuppositional DRT derives from the second middle Kleene
based dynamic interpretation discussed in Krahmer 1994, definition 20. As said
above, the interpretation is closely related with the partial dynamic systems developed for the treatment of presuppositions by Beaver and by Van Eijck. This is

Definition 2 (Presuppositional DRT semantics)

1. $[\![R(t_1,\ldots,t_n)]\!]^+ = \{g \mid [\![t_i]\!]_g \text{ defined } \& \langle [\![t_1]\!]_g,\ldots,[\![t_n]\!]_g \rangle \in I(R)\}$
   $[\![R(t_1,\ldots,t_n)]\!]^- = \{g \mid [\![t_i]\!]_g \text{ defined } \& \langle [\![t_1]\!]_g,\ldots,[\![t_n]\!]_g \rangle \notin I(R)\}$

2. $[\![t_1 \equiv t_2]\!]^+ = \{g \mid [\![t_1]\!]_g, [\![t_2]\!]_g \text{ defined } \& [\![t_1]\!]_g = [\![t_2]\!]_g\}$
   $[\![t_1 \equiv t_2]\!]^- = \{g \mid [\![t_1]\!]_g, [\![t_2]\!]_g \text{ defined } \& [\![t_1]\!]_g \neq [\![t_2]\!]_g\}$

3. $[\![\Phi \Rightarrow \Psi]\!]^+ = \{g \mid \forall h(\langle g,h\rangle \in [\![\Phi]\!]^+ \Rightarrow \exists k \langle h,k\rangle \in [\![\Psi]\!]^+) \& \mathrm{DEF}_g(\Phi)\}$
   $[\![\Phi \Rightarrow \Psi]\!]^- = \{g \mid \exists h(\langle g,h\rangle \in [\![\Phi]\!]^+ \& \exists k \langle h,k\rangle \in [\![\Psi]\!]^-)\}$

4. $[\![[\vec{x} \mid \varphi_1,\ldots,\varphi_m]]\!]^+ = \{\langle g,h\rangle \mid g\{\vec{x}\}h \& h \in ([\![\varphi_1]\!]^+ \cap \ldots \cap [\![\varphi_m]\!]^+)\}$
   $[\![[\vec{x} \mid \varphi_1,\ldots,\varphi_m]]\!]^- = \{\langle g,g\rangle \mid \forall h(g\{\vec{x}\}h \Rightarrow h \in ([\![\varphi_1]\!]^- \cup \ldots \cup [\![\varphi_m]\!]^-))\}$

5. $[\![\Phi \,;\, \Psi]\!]^+ = \{\langle g,h\rangle \mid \exists k(\langle g,k\rangle \in [\![\Phi]\!]^+ \& \langle k,h\rangle \in [\![\Psi]\!]^+)\}$
   $[\![\Phi \,;\, \Psi]\!]^- = \{\langle g,g\rangle \mid \forall k(\langle g,k\rangle \in [\![\Phi]\!]^+ \Rightarrow \exists h\langle k,h\rangle \in [\![\Psi]\!]^-) \& \mathrm{DEF}_g(\Phi)\}$

6. $[\![\sim\Phi]\!]^+ = [\![\Phi]\!]^-$
   $[\![\sim\Phi]\!]^- = [\![\Phi]\!]^+$

7. $[\![\partial\Phi]\!]^+ = [\![\Phi]\!]^+$
   $[\![\partial\Phi]\!]^- = \emptyset$

Where $\mathrm{DEF}_{M,g}(\Phi)$ —'DRS Φ is dynamically defined in M with respect to g'— is defined as follows (again suppressing M).[12]

Definition 3 (DEF)

$$\mathrm{DEF}_g(\Phi) \quad = \quad \exists h\langle g,h\rangle \in [\![\Phi]\!]^+ \text{ or } \exists h\langle g,h\rangle \in [\![\Phi]\!]^-$$
$$\text{for } \Phi \text{ is } \partial\Psi \text{ or } [\vec{x} \mid \varphi_1,\ldots,\varphi_m]$$

$$\mathrm{DEF}_g(\Phi \,;\, \Psi) \quad = \quad \mathrm{DEF}_g(\Phi) \& \forall h(\langle g,h\rangle \in [\![\Phi]\!]^+ \Rightarrow \mathrm{DEF}_h(\Psi))$$

$$\mathrm{DEF}_g(\sim\Phi) \quad = \quad \mathrm{DEF}_g(\Phi)$$

We say that a DRS Φ is supported in a model M with respect to an assignment g (notation: $M,g \models_{\mathrm{PDRT}} \Phi$) iff $\exists h\langle g,h\rangle \in [\![\Phi]\!]^+_M$, and that Φ is rejected in M with respect to g (notation: $M,g \dashv_{\mathrm{PDRT}} \Phi$)

---

clearest for the system given in Van Eijck 1994b:779–780. The main difference is that Presuppositional DRT is based on Double Negation DRT, and that as a consequence negation and disjunction are treated in a different way. Other combined partial dynamic interpretations, devised for different purposes can be found in, for instance, Dekker 1993b, Piwek 1993, Van den Berg 1996a and Van den Berg 1993.

[12] In chapter 4 we have seen that the Peters/middle Kleene based version of PPL could be defined in terms of strong Kleene based PPL. This is not possible in the dynamic setting of Presuppositional DRT (at least not with the language as it is defined here), therefore 'dynamic definedness' (DEF) conditions are added on the meta-level of the interpretation.

iff $\exists h \langle g, h \rangle \in [\![\Phi]\!]_M^-$. The truth combinations can now be defined as follows.[13]

Definition 4 (Truth combinations)
Let Φ be proper DRS. In a model M, we say that

Φ is True	iff	$M, \Lambda \models \Phi$
Φ is False	iff	$M, \Lambda \dashv \Phi$
Φ is Neither	iff	$M, \Lambda \not\models \Phi$ and $M, \Lambda \not\dashv \Phi$

It is easily shown that no DRS is both True and False, and that every DRS which does not contain presuppositions is either True or False. Two DRSs Φ and Ψ are said to be equivalent iff for all models M: $[\![\Phi]\!]_M^+ = [\![\Psi]\!]_M^+$ and $[\![\Phi]\!]_M^- = [\![\Psi]\!]_M^-$. Notice that the interpretation of atomic conditions 'triggers' a presupposition to the effect that the relevant terms are defined. Obviously, this presupposition is satisfied by any proper DRS. We introduce the following abbreviations.

Definition 5 (Abbreviations)

$\Phi_{\langle \Psi \rangle}$	abbreviates	$\partial(\Psi) \, ; \Phi$
$\Phi \vee \Psi$	abbreviates	$\sim\!\Phi \Rightarrow \Psi$
$\top$	abbreviates	$[\,|c \equiv c]$, for some $c \in$ Con
$\bot$	abbreviates	$\sim\!\top$
$\star$	abbreviates	$\partial\bot$

The first abbreviation defines (a dynamic version of) transplication in terms of the unary presupposition operator. It is this operation which is our linear alternative for the presuppositional DRSs discussed in the previous section. The abbreviation results in the following interpretation for $\Phi_{\langle \Psi \rangle}$:

$$[\![\Phi_{\langle \Psi \rangle}]\!]^+ = \{\langle g, h \rangle \mid \exists k(\langle g, k \rangle \in [\![\Psi]\!]^+ \ \& \ \langle k, h \rangle \in [\![\Phi]\!]^+)\}$$
$$[\![\Phi_{\langle \Psi \rangle}]\!]^- = \{\langle g, g \rangle \mid \exists k \langle g, k \rangle \in [\![\Psi]\!]^+ \ \& $$
$$\forall k(\langle g, k \rangle \in [\![\Psi]\!]^+ \Rightarrow \exists h \langle k, h \rangle \in [\![\Phi]\!]^-)\}$$

The second abbreviation once again establishes the link between disjunction and implication, argued for in chapter 3. We have chosen for an asymmetric treatment of disjunction, although here too we could have defined disjunction in a symmetric fashion (see chapter 3 for discussion). The last three abbreviations correspond with the three truth combinations, True, False and Neither respectively. We can use them when checking that Presuppositional DRT follows the middle Kleene pattern.

---

[13]'Properness' is defined for Presuppositional DRT as it was for standard DRT. See page 166.

This is done by calculating the various combinations of $\top$, $\bot$ and $\star$. For instance, $\sim\top$ is equivalent with $\bot$, $\sim\star$ is equivalent with $\star$ and $\sim\bot$ is equivalent with $\top$. In words, $\sim$ maps True to False, Neither to Neither and False to True. Similarly, all the ; combinations ('sequencings') of the truth combinations can be checked and it is easily seen that the resulting truth table is that of middle Kleene conjunction. Observe that a DRS $[x \mid \varphi]$ also follows the Kleene pattern: it is True if φ is True for some assignment to x and False if φ is False for all assignments to x. We mention the following equivalences.

Fact 1 *(Equivalences)*

1. $\sim\sim\Phi$ *is equivalent with* Φ
2. $\Phi \,;\, (\Psi \,;\, \Upsilon)$ *is equivalent with* $(\Phi \,;\, \Psi) \,;\, \Upsilon$
3. $\Phi \Rightarrow [\,|\Psi \Rightarrow \Upsilon]$ *is equivalent with* $(\Phi \,;\, \Psi) \Rightarrow \Upsilon$
4. $\Phi_{\langle \pi_1 \langle \pi_2 \rangle \rangle}$ *is equivalent with* $\Phi_{\langle \pi_2 ; \pi_1 \rangle}$

The first equivalence states that the law of double negation still holds in its full, dynamic form. The second equivalence is about associativity, while the third relates sequencing with implication. The last one expresses that we can rewrite nested presuppositions using a single presuppositional DRS, where the deepest embedded presupposition comes first. For a proof of fact 1 the reader is referred to the appendix.

We have only marginally complicated the language of Double Negation DRT, and as a result the notion of accessibility differs only a little from the notion defined in chapter 3.[14] We begin with defining active and passive discourse referents.

Definition 6 (Active and Passive DRs)

1. $\mathsf{ADR}([x_1, \ldots, x_n \mid \varphi_1, \ldots, \varphi_m]) = \{x_1, \ldots, x_n\}$
   $\mathsf{PDR}([x_1, \ldots, x_n \mid \varphi_1, \ldots, \varphi_m]) = \emptyset$

2. $\mathsf{ADR}(\Phi \,;\, \Psi) = \mathsf{ADR}(\Phi) \cup \mathsf{ADR}(\Psi)$
   $\mathsf{PDR}(\Phi \,;\, \Psi) = \emptyset$

3. $\mathsf{ADR}(\sim\Phi) = \mathsf{PDR}(\Phi)$
   $\mathsf{PDR}(\sim\Phi) = \mathsf{ADR}(\Phi)$

4. $\mathsf{ADR}(\partial\Phi) = \mathsf{ADR}(\Phi)$
   $\mathsf{PDR}(\partial\Phi) = \emptyset$

Observe that $\mathsf{ADR}(\Phi_{\langle\Psi\rangle}) = \mathsf{ADR}(\Psi) \cup \mathsf{ADR}(\Phi)$, while $\mathsf{PDR}(\Phi_{\langle\Psi\rangle}) = \emptyset$. Accessibility can now be defined as follows. Initially, we set $\mathsf{ACC}(\Phi') = \emptyset$,

---

[14]The only addition is the presupposition operator ∂.

where Φ' is the main DRS, and compute the accessible discourse referents of subDRSs and subconditions with the help of the following rules.[15]

Definition 7 (Accessibility)

1. If $\text{ACC}(\Phi \Rightarrow \Psi) = X$, then $\text{ACC}(\Phi) = X$ and $\text{ACC}(\Psi) = X \cup \text{ADR}(\Phi)$.

2. If $\text{ACC}([x_1, \ldots, x_n \mid \varphi_1, \ldots, \varphi_m]) = X$, then $\text{ACC}(\varphi_i) = X \cup \{x_1, \ldots, x_n\}$. $(1 \leq i \leq m)$

3. If $\text{ACC}(\Phi \, ; \Psi) = X$, then $\text{ACC}(\Phi) = X$ and $\text{ACC}(\Psi) = X \cup \text{ADR}(\Phi)$.

4. If $\text{ACC}(\sim\Phi) = X$, then $\text{ACC}(\Phi) = X$.

5. If $\text{ACC}(\partial\Phi) = X$, then $\text{ACC}(\Phi) = X$.

6. If $\text{ACC}(\Phi_{\langle\Psi\rangle}) = X$, then $\text{ACC}(\Psi) = X$ and $\text{ACC}(\Phi) = X \cup \text{ADR}(\Psi)$.

7. If $\text{ACC}(\Phi \vee \Psi) = X$, then $\text{ACC}(\Phi) = X$ and $\text{ACC}(\Psi) = X \cup \text{PDR}(\Phi)$.

Notice once again that there is a strong connection between the clauses for the determination of accessibility and Karttunen's top-down specification of local contexts.[16] An occurrence of x in an atomic condition φ in Φ is said to be *free* in Φ iff $x \notin \text{ACC}(\varphi)$. An occurrence of x in an atomic condition φ in a condition ψ is free in ψ iff it is free in $[\,\mid \psi]$. A DRS is *proper* if it does not contain any free discourse referents, and a proper DRS is *totally proper* when it introduces no referent twice. The Revised Construction Algorithm (discussed in section 6.4) will produce only totally proper DRSs. Before we move on to the applications, note that we have a restricted version of the Merging Lemma.

Fact 2 *(Merging Lemma)*
$[\vec{x} \mid \vec{\varphi}] \, ; [\vec{y} \mid \vec{\gamma}]$ *is equivalent with* $[\vec{x}, \vec{y} \mid \vec{\varphi}, \vec{\gamma}]$,
provided no referent in $\vec{y}$ is free in any of $\vec{\varphi}$, and $[\vec{x} \mid \vec{\varphi}]$ is presupposition free.

Another lemma from chapter 3 which will turn out to be handy is the Single Negation Lemma.

---

[15]To be precise: $\text{ACC}(\Phi)$ calculates accessibility for an *occurrence* of Φ in some given DRS Φ'. Since this Φ' can be determined from the context we shall keep it hidden in the definition. See section 2.2.2 (on standard DRT) and section 3.3 (on Double Negation DRT) for discussion.

[16]These were the Karttunen conditions (given in chapter 2, definition 10):

1. If $\text{LC}(not \ S) = C$, then $\text{LC}(S) = C$.
2. If $\text{LC}(if \ S \ then \ S') = C$, then $\text{LC}(S) = C$ and $\text{LC}(S') = C \cup \{ \ S \ \}$.
3. If $\text{LC}(S \ and \ S') = C$, then $\text{LC}(S) = C$ and $\text{LC}(S') = C \cup \{ \ S \ \}$.
4. If $\text{LC}(S \ or \ S') = C$, then $\text{LC}(S) = C$ and $\text{LC}(S') = C \cup \{ \ not \ S \ \}$.

Fact 3 *(Single Negation Lemma)*
Define standard negation $\neg\Phi$ as $\Phi \Rightarrow \bot$, and let Υ be an arbitrary atomic DRS. *Then:*

$$
\begin{array}{lll}
\Phi\,;\sim\!\Upsilon & \textit{is equivalent with} & \Phi\,;[\,|\,\neg\Upsilon] \\
\sim\!\Upsilon\,;\Phi & \textit{is equivalent with} & [\,|\,\neg\Upsilon]\,;\Phi \\
\Phi \Rightarrow \sim\!\Upsilon & \textit{is equivalent with} & \Phi \Rightarrow [\,|\,\neg\Upsilon] \\
\sim\!\Upsilon \Rightarrow \Phi & \textit{is equivalent with} & [\,|\,\neg\Upsilon] \Rightarrow \Phi
\end{array}
$$

6.4 Applications

In chapter 3 the DRT Construction Algorithm was revised a little to enhance the treatment of double negations and disjunctions. Here we shall sketch a slight revision of this Revised Construction Algorithm to make it suitable for the purposes of the present chapter.[17] First of all, every NP is represented by a separate DRS which is immediately prefixed to the DRS in which it originated. Here is the rule for indefinites.

Indefinite Descriptions Rule

Upon encountering an NP of the form 'a(n) α', replace it with a new discourse referent x and prefix the current DRS

with $\boxed{\begin{array}{c} x \\ \hline x\,\alpha \end{array}}$

Here '$x\ \alpha$' comes from 'a(n) α' by replacing the indefinite determiner for x. When α is an atomic predicate we shall write this as $\alpha(x)$. The rule for universally quantified NPs is modified in a similar way. As far as definite descriptions are concerned we add the following rule to the construction algorithm, which is just a presuppositional variant of the rule for indefinites.

Definite Descriptions Rule

Upon encountering an NP of the form 'the α', replace it with a new discourse referent x and prefix the current DRS

with $\partial\,\boxed{\begin{array}{c} x \\ \hline x\,\alpha \end{array}}$

Ultimately we want to treat *all* definite NPs (definite descriptions, pronouns, names and possessives) in this way (see the next chapter), but

---
[17]Contrary to Van der Sandt we shall construct our DRSs in the DRT tradition, that is: top-down rather than bottom-up.

to keep things simple we stick closer to standard DRT for now. So, a pronoun is still replaced by a suitable, accessible discourse referent. As a first example of how this 'Revision of the Revised Construction Algorithm' works, consider example (12).

(12) The king with the wig ruled.

This sentence contains two presupposition triggers, one contained within the other. We start with placing the (syntactic analysis of this) sentence in a box, thus turning it into a proto-DRS, and combining it with the initial (empty) DRS, resulting in (DRS 10). The first rule which can be applied is our new-fangled definite descriptions rule, which outputs (DRS 11). The only reducible condition is found inside the representation of the definite description. We invoke our definite descriptions rule again, plus some standard construction rules, with (DRS 12) as a result. Notice that the sequencing of the empty DRS with $\partial\Phi$ is equivalent with $\partial\Phi$.

(DRS 10) $\square$; $\boxed{\text{The king with the wig ruled.}}$

(DRS 11)

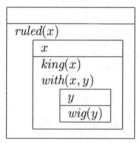

(DRS 12)

By definition 5, we can rewrite this DRS as follows.

(DRS 13)

As we shall see below, this DRS presupposes the existence of a king with a wig.

In chapters 4 and 5 we encountered two examples which could not be dealt with in a static system like PPL, because they involved presuppositional variants of typical 'dynamic' phenomena like sentence-sequencing (13) and donkey-sentences (14).

(13) A fat man pushes his bicycle. It is broken.

(14) Every man who serves his king will be rewarded by him.

According to (13), the bicycle which went into smithereens is the one belonging to the fat man, and according to (14) each man is rewarded by the king he serves. Let us begin with example (13). The Revised Construction Algorithm starts again from the empty DRS, and conjoins it with a proto-DRS containing the first sentence of (13):

(DRS 14) $\boxed{}$; $\boxed{\text{A fat man pushes his bicycle.}}$

The rule for indefinite descriptions is the first which can be applied. It introduces a new discourse referent, say x, and adds the condition that x is a fat man. This gives (DRS 15), after applying the Merging Lemma to $[\,|\,]\,;[x\,|\,fat\ man(x)]$.

(DRS 15)

$$\begin{array}{|c|} \hline x \\ \hline fat\ man(x) \\ \hline \end{array} \quad ; \quad \boxed{x \text{ pushes his bicycle}}$$

Next we come to the definite NP *his bicycle*, which we shall treat as an abbreviation of *the bicycle he owns*. This complex description introduces a new discourse referent y, while *he* picks up an accessible, suitable referent. Obviously, this will have to be x. The rest is standard DRT, and the result is (DRS 16), which may be abbreviated as (DRS 17). Notice that the Merging Lemma (which is about atomic DRSs) does not apply.

(DRS 16)

$$\begin{array}{|c|} \hline x \\ \hline fat\ man(x) \\ \hline \end{array} \quad ; \quad \partial \quad \begin{array}{|c|} \hline y \\ \hline bicycle(y) \\ of(x,y) \\ \hline \end{array} \quad ; \quad \boxed{push(x,y)}$$

(DRS 17)

$$\begin{array}{|c|} \hline x \\ \hline fat\ man(x) \\ \hline \\ \hline \end{array} \quad ; \quad \begin{array}{|c|} \hline push(x,y) \\ \begin{array}{|c|} \hline y \\ \hline bicycle(y) \\ of(x,y) \\ \hline \end{array} \\ \hline \end{array}$$

Since there are no more reducible conditions in this last DRS, the Revised Construction Algorithm allows adding a new box which only contains the second sentence of (13). The result is given in (DRS 18). The question is whether we can replace *it* with the intended antecedent y. We can, if y is an element of ACC($\boxed{\text{It is broken}}$). By definition ACC(DRS 18) = $\emptyset$, so — by clause 3 of definition 7— we have to check whether y is an element of the set of active discourse referents of the representation of the first sentence (that is: ADR(DRS 17)), which is defined as ADR($[x\,|\,fat\ man(x)]$)$\cup$ ADR($[y\,|\,bicycle(y),of(x,y)]$) $\cup$ ADR($[\,|\,push(x,y)]$) = $\{x,y\}$. And this means that y is indeed accessible. Which is as should be: when we replace *it* with y, this occurrence is 'bound' by the introduction of y in the presuppositional DRS.

(DRS 18)

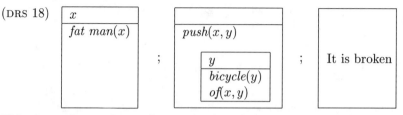

This shows that as far as dynamics is concerned, Presuppositional DRT is able to account for pronominal reference to presupposed material from previous sentences. This brings us to the presuppositional donkey-sentence (14). We treat *his king* as short for '*the king of him*'. At a crucial point in the construction of a DRS for this sentence we arrive at (DRS 19).

(DRS 19)

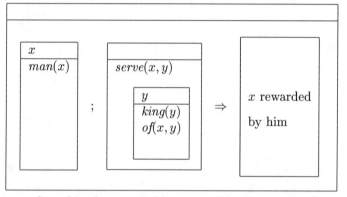

We want to replace *him* by a suitable, accessible discourse referent. Clearly, y is suitable, but is it also accessible? To find out, we have to calculate ACC($\boxed{x \text{ is rewarded by him}}$). By definition, ACC(DRS 19) = ∅. Which means —by the first clause of definition 7— that y is accessible for *him* if y is an element of the set of active discourse referents of the DRS representing the antecedent. And since this set of active discourse referents is the union of *all* sub-DRSs, which is easily seen to be $\{x, y\}$ as well, we may substitute y for *him*. The result is (DRS 20).

(DRS 20)

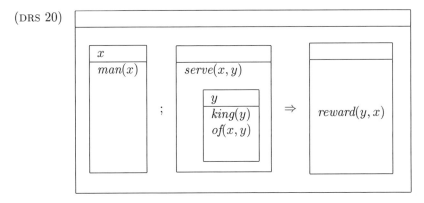

So, Presuppositional DRT can account for anaphoric reference in donkey-like presuppositional constructions such as example (14). In this respect it marks a true departure from the static analyses of presuppositions discussed in the previous two chapters. But what is presupposed by these DRSs, (DRS 17) and (DRS 20)? Since Presuppositional DRT is compatible with *two* theories of presupposition, we can give two answers to this question. According to Van der Sandt both presuppose nothing: the presuppositions are said to be 'trapped'.[18]

To determine the *semantic* presuppositions, we digress a little to discuss a general method to determine the presuppositions of an arbitrary DRS.

6.5 Determining Semantic Presuppositions

An attractive feature of Van Eijck's Error-state Semantics for DPL is that it is associated with an axiomatization, which allows for the calculation of the maximal presupposition of some DPL formula ϕ (see Van Eijck 1993, 1994b, 1996). For this purpose, Van Eijck generalizes a method from Van Eijck and De Vries 1992, in which it is shown that one can use Pratt's QDL to reason about DPL (see also Groenendijk & Stokhof 1991:83). If ϕ is a DPL formula, then the QDL formula $\langle\phi\rangle\top$ gives ex-

---

[18]To see that this is indeed the case, the reader is invited to construct a DRS for the following variant of example (13):

It is not the case that a fat man pushes his bicycle.

If we interpret the indefinite *a fat man* in a non-specific fashion (thus, it does not take scope over the negation), then the presupposition triggered by the definite *his bicycle* is not able to take scope over the negation (that is: it is not projected to the main DRS), because it is 'trapped' by the introduction of the discourse referent for *a fat man*.

actly the states with respect to which ϕ is true.[19] To generalize this to
the Error-state Semantics for DPL, Van Eijck also calculates $[\phi]\bot$, which
gives exactly the states with respect to which ϕ fails. The disjunction of
these two QDL formulae gives the conditions under which ϕ is either true
or false. And as we discussed in chapter 4, the disjunction of truth- and
falsity-conditions of a formula can be seen as its (maximal) presupposition. Here we shall discuss a similar method to calculate such semantic
presuppositions for Presuppositional DRT.

In chapter 2 we have seen an easy way to calculate truth of a DRS Φ,
namely by looking at its 'weakest existential precondition' (WEP$(\Phi, \top)$,
in Van Eijck's formulation $\langle\Phi\rangle\top$). This produces a formula of Predicate
Logic which is true whenever the DRS Φ is true. In chapter 3 this method
was generalized to deal with the distinction between support and rejection in Double Negation DRT. There, WEP$^+$ played the role of WEP in
standard DRT, while WEP$^-$ gave a Predicate Logical formula which is
true just in case the relevant DRS is false. In chapter 4 we looked at TR$^+$
and TR$^-$, which mapped Partial Predicate Logic to classical (presupposition free) Predicate Logic. It is readily observed that WEP$^\pm$ strips
a DRS of its dynamic potential, while TR$^\pm$ strips a PPL formula of its
partiality. The following WEP-calculus for Presuppositional DRT can be
seen as a combination of these two, and strips a DRS of *both* its partiality
and its dynamic potential, in such a way that WEP$^+(\Phi, \top)$ gives a PL
formula which is true when the DRS Φ is True, and WEP$^-(\Phi, \top)$ gives a
PL formula which is true when the DRS Φ is False. Using these two, we
can define the (maximal) presupposition of a DRS Φ —once more abbreviated as PR(Φ)— as WEP$^+(\Phi, \top) \vee$ WEP$^-(\Phi, \top)$. Recall from chapters
2 and 3 that we defined the WEP-calculi for the respective versions of
DRT interpreted in terms of total assignments. Here we do the same and
switch for the time being to the 'total assignments' version of definition
2 (which is obtained by replacing the set of finite assignments F for the
set of total assignments G, and replacing $g\{\vec{x}\}h$ for $g[\vec{x}]h$). It should be
stressed that this is completely harmless since the Revised Construction
Algorithm still only produces DRSs which are totally proper (see chapter
2 for discussion). Define TR$^\pm(\varphi)$, where φ is a condition, WEP$^\pm(\Phi, \chi)$,
where Φ is a DRS and χ a PL formula, and $\overline{\text{DEF}}(\Phi)$, where Φ is again a
DRS, as follows:

---

[19]In this chapter $\top$ does double duty as the DRS which is always supported and the
traditional verum, the tautological proposition. Here the latter is meant.

Definition 8 (WEP-calculus)

1. $\mathsf{TR}^+(\varphi) = \varphi$, for atomic φ
   $\mathsf{TR}^-(\varphi) = \neg\varphi$, for atomic φ

2. $\mathsf{TR}^+(\Phi \Rightarrow \Psi) = \neg\mathsf{WEP}^+(\Phi, \neg\mathsf{WEP}^+(\Psi, \top)) \wedge \overline{\mathsf{DEF}}(\Phi)$
   $\mathsf{TR}^-(\Phi \Rightarrow \Psi) = \mathsf{WEP}^+(\Phi, \mathsf{WEP}^-(\Psi, \top))$

3. $\mathsf{WEP}^+([\vec{x} \mid \varphi_1 \ldots \varphi_m], \chi) = \exists\vec{x}(\mathsf{TR}^+(\varphi_1) \wedge \ldots \wedge \mathsf{TR}^+(\varphi_m) \wedge \chi)$
   $\mathsf{WEP}^-([\vec{x} \mid \varphi_1 \ldots \varphi_m], \chi) = \forall\vec{x}(\mathsf{TR}^-(\varphi_1) \vee \ldots \vee \mathsf{TR}^-(\varphi_m)) \wedge \chi$

4. $\mathsf{WEP}^+(\Phi \, ; \Psi, \chi) = \mathsf{WEP}^+(\Phi, \mathsf{WEP}^+(\Psi, \chi))$
   $\mathsf{WEP}^-(\Phi \, ; \Psi, \chi) = \neg\mathsf{WEP}^+(\Phi, \neg\mathsf{WEP}^-(\Psi, \top)) \wedge \overline{\mathsf{DEF}}(\Phi) \wedge \chi$

5. $\mathsf{WEP}^+(\sim\Phi, \chi) = \mathsf{WEP}^-(\Phi, \chi)$
   $\mathsf{WEP}^-(\sim\Phi, \chi) = \mathsf{WEP}^+(\Phi, \chi)$

6. $\mathsf{WEP}^+(\partial\Phi, \chi) = \mathsf{WEP}^+(\Phi, \chi)$
   $\mathsf{WEP}^-(\partial\Phi, \chi) = \mathsf{WEP}^-(\top, \chi)$[20]

7. $\overline{\mathsf{DEF}}(\Phi) = \mathsf{WEP}^+(\Phi, \top) \vee \mathsf{WEP}^-(\Phi, \top)$, if Φ is $\partial\Psi$ or $[\vec{x} \mid \varphi_1, \ldots, \varphi_m]$

8. $\overline{\mathsf{DEF}}(\sim\Phi) = \overline{\mathsf{DEF}}(\Phi)$

9. $\overline{\mathsf{DEF}}(\Phi \, ; \Psi) = \overline{\mathsf{DEF}}(\Phi) \wedge \neg\mathsf{WEP}^+(\Phi, \neg\overline{\mathsf{DEF}}(\Psi))$

To illustrate this calculus let us first work out a simple example. Consider (15) and its representation (DRS 21).

(15) The king sings.

(DRS 21)

(DRS 21) is an abbreviation of $\partial[x \mid king(x)] \, ; [\mid sings(x)]$. We first calculate $\mathsf{WEP}^+((\text{DRS } 21), \top)$:

$\mathsf{WEP}^+(\partial[x \mid king(x)] \, ; [\mid sings(x)], \top) \Leftrightarrow$

$\mathsf{WEP}^+(\partial[x \mid king(x)], \mathsf{WEP}^+([\mid sings(x)], \top)) \Leftrightarrow$

$\mathsf{WEP}^+([x \mid king(x)], \mathsf{WEP}^+([\mid sings(x)], \top)) \Leftrightarrow$

$\exists x(\mathsf{TR}^+(king(x)) \wedge \mathsf{WEP}^+([\mid sings(x)], \top)) \Leftrightarrow$

---

[20] The intuition here is that the DRS $\top$ (which abbreviates $[\mid c \equiv c]$) is rejected whenever the presuppositional DRS $\partial\Phi$ is: never.

$$\exists x(\mathsf{TR}^+(king(x)) \wedge (\mathsf{TR}^+(sings(x)) \wedge \top)) \Leftrightarrow$$

$$\exists x(king(x) \wedge sings(x))$$

In words: (DRS 21) is True if there is a king who sings. Next, let us see when it is False. For this purpose, we determine $\mathsf{WEP}^-((\text{DRS } 21), \top)$:

$$\mathsf{WEP}^-(\partial[x \mid king(x)]\,;[\mid sings(x)], \top) \Leftrightarrow$$

$$\neg\mathsf{WEP}^+(\partial[x|king(x)], \neg\mathsf{WEP}^-([\mid sings(x)], \top)) \wedge \overline{\mathsf{DEF}}(\partial[x \mid king(x)]) \Leftrightarrow$$

$$\neg\exists x(king(x) \wedge \neg\neg sings(x)) \wedge \exists x(king(x)) \Leftrightarrow$$

$$\forall x(king(x) \to \neg sings(x)) \wedge \exists x(king(x))$$

In words: (DRS 21) is False if there is a king, but no king sings. The disjunction of $\mathsf{WEP}^+((\text{DRS } 21), \top)$ and $\mathsf{WEP}^-((\text{DRS } 21), \top)$ gives the presupposition of (DRS 21), and it is easily seen that this presupposition is that there is a king. In general, the following fact can be proven about these five functions.

Fact 4 *(From Presuppositional DRT to PL)*
For all models M and assignments g:

1. $g \in [\![\mathsf{TR}^+(\varphi)]\!]^{\mathrm{PL}}_M \Leftrightarrow g \in [\![\varphi]\!]^+_M$
   $g \in [\![\mathsf{TR}^-(\varphi)]\!]^{\mathrm{PL}}_M \Leftrightarrow g \in [\![\varphi]\!]^-_M$

2. $g \in [\![\mathsf{WEP}^+(\Phi,\chi)]\!]^{\mathrm{PL}}_M \Leftrightarrow \exists h(\langle g, h\rangle \in [\![\Phi]\!]^+ \ \& \ h \in [\![\chi]\!]^{\mathrm{PL}}_M)$
   $g \in [\![\mathsf{WEP}^-(\Phi,\chi)]\!]^{\mathrm{PL}}_M \Leftrightarrow \exists h(\langle g, h\rangle \in [\![\Phi]\!]^- \ \& \ h \in [\![\chi]\!]^{\mathrm{PL}}_M)$

3. $g \in [\![\overline{\mathsf{DEF}}(\Phi)]\!]^{\mathrm{PL}}_M \Leftrightarrow \mathrm{DEF}_{M,g}(\Phi)$

Where $[\![\varphi]\!]^{\mathrm{PL}}_M$ is again the Groenendijk & Stokhof formulation of the Tarskian semantics of Predicate Logic (see chapter 2, definition 17). Recall also that we relate PL to the version of Presuppositional DRT defined in terms of total assignments. For a proof of fact 4 the reader is referred to the appendix. We define what it means for a DRS Φ to presuppose, in the Strawsonian sense, a PL formula ψ as follows:

Definition 9 (Presuppose)
Φ presupposes ψ iff for all models M and assignments g:

$$(M,g \models_{\mathrm{PDRT}} \Phi \text{ or } M,g \dashv_{\mathrm{PDRT}} \Phi) \Rightarrow M,g \models_{\mathrm{PL}} \psi$$

Given that $\mathsf{PR}(\Phi)$ abbreviates $\mathsf{WEP}^+(\Phi, \top) \vee \mathsf{WEP}^-(\Phi, \top)$, it is easily seen that the following fact holds.

Fact 5
Φ *presupposes* $\mathsf{PR}(\Phi)$, *for any DRS Φ*

In fact, we can prove something stronger, namely that Φ presupposes $\mathsf{PR}(\Phi)$ *and* that whenever $\mathsf{PR}(\Phi)$ is true, Φ is defined. In other words,

$\mathsf{PR}(\Phi)$ is indeed the maximal presupposition of Φ.[21] Regarding $\mathsf{PR}(\Phi)$ we can easily show the following fact.

Fact 6 *(Presupposition Projection)*

1. $\mathsf{PR}(\sim\!\Phi) \Leftrightarrow \mathsf{PR}(\Phi)$
2. $\mathsf{PR}(\partial\Phi) \Leftrightarrow \mathsf{WEP}^+(\Phi, \top)$
3. $\mathsf{PR}([\vec{x} \mid \vec{\varphi}]) \Leftrightarrow \exists \vec{x}\ \mathsf{TR}^+(\vec{\varphi}) \vee \forall \vec{x}\ \mathsf{TR}^-(\vec{\varphi})$
4. $\mathsf{PR}(\Phi\,;\,\Psi) \Leftrightarrow \mathsf{WEP}^+(\Phi\,;\,\Psi, \top) \vee \mathsf{WEP}^-(\Phi\,;\,\Psi, \top)$

The first two equations are basic, and differ only qua terminology from what we saw in chapter 4: negation is a hole for presupposition projection, and $\partial\Phi$ presupposes the Truth of Φ. The clause for atomic DRSs mirrors the one for PPL existential quantification. The clause for sequencing generalizes the one for atomic DRSs: it is the disjunction of an existential truth-condition and a universal falsity-condition. Presuppositions in disjunctions and implications display similar projection behavior. In general, every standard DRS (a DRS free of elementary presuppositions) presupposes nothing.[22] Finally, when we assume that Φ triggers no presuppositions, then

$$\mathsf{PR}(\Phi_{\langle\Psi\rangle}) \Leftrightarrow \mathsf{WEP}^+(\Psi, \top)$$

In other words, $\Phi_{\langle\Psi\rangle}$ presupposes the Truth of Ψ. Here is the semantic presupposition of (DRS 13):

$\mathsf{PR}(\partial(\partial[y \mid wig(y)]\,;\,[x \mid king(x), with(x,y)])\,;\,[\,\mid ruled(x)]) \Leftrightarrow$

$\mathsf{WEP}^+(\partial(\partial[y \mid wig(y)]\,;\,[x \mid king(x), with(x,y)]), \top) \Leftrightarrow$

$\mathsf{WEP}^+(\partial[y \mid wig(y)], \mathsf{WEP}^+([x \mid king(x), with(x,y)], \top)) \Leftrightarrow$

$\exists y(wig(y) \wedge \mathsf{WEP}^+([x \mid king(x), with(x,y)], \top)) \Leftrightarrow$

$\exists y(wig(y) \wedge \exists x(king(x) \wedge with(x,y)))$

So, as we announced above, it is predicted that (DRS 13) presupposes the existence of a wig and a king to match. Here is the presupposition of (DRS 17).

---

[21]Here is the proof. Assume that $M, g \models_{\mathsf{PDRT}} \Phi$ or $M, g \dashv_{\mathsf{PDRT}} \Phi$. By definition, this is the same as saying: $\exists h\langle g, h\rangle \in [\![\Phi]\!]_M^+$ or $\exists h\langle g, h\rangle \in [\![\Phi]\!]_M^-$. By fact 4: $g \in [\![\mathsf{WEP}^+(\Phi, \top)]\!]_M^{\mathsf{PL}}$ or $g \in [\![\mathsf{WEP}^-(\Phi, \top)]\!]_M^{\mathsf{PL}}$. In terms of PL support: $M, g \models_{\mathsf{PL}}$ $\mathsf{WEP}^+(\Phi, \top) \vee \mathsf{WEP}^-(\Phi, \top)$, which by definition of PR means: $M, g \models_{\mathsf{PL}} \mathsf{PR}(\Phi)$.

[22]It should be noted that on the interpretation of Presuppositional DRT as given in definition 2 a non-proper DRS presupposes that its free variables are defined. This presupposition is not generated by the calculus given above, since it is based on the version of Presuppositional DRT defined in terms of total assignments. See section 2.2.4 for discussion.

PR(DRS 17) $\Leftrightarrow$

WEP$^+$([x | $fat\ man(x)$] ; $\partial[y$ | $bike\text{-}of(y, x)$] ; [| $push(x, y)$], $\top$)$\lor$
WEP$^-$([x | $fat\ man(x)$] ; $\partial[y$ | $bike\text{-}of(y, x)$] ; [| $push(x, y)$], $\top$) $\Leftrightarrow$

$\exists x(fat\ man(x) \land \exists y(bike\text{-}of(y, x) \land push(x, y)))\lor$
$\forall x(fat\ man(x) \rightarrow \exists y(bike\text{-}of(y, x) \land \forall y(bike\text{-}of(y, x) \rightarrow \neg push(x, y))))$

In words: either there is a fat man who has a bicycle which he pushes or every fat man doesn't push the bike(s) he owns. Presuppositional DRT does not have the Karttunen & Peters binding-problem when presupposition and quantification interact, and neither does it predict Heim's overly strong presuppositions in these cases. In fact, we end up with essentially the same predicted presupposition for the first sentence of example (13) as middle Kleene based PPL does, which is compatible with the conclusion of chapter 4 that no dynamics is needed to deal with these examples. Of course, (DRS 17) has dynamic potential, and this means that the second sentence of (13) does not pose problems, as we have illustrated above. That Presuppositional DRT does not predict a universal, Heimian presupposition for examples such as (14) is easily seen by checking WEP$^-$((DRS 20), $\top$), which may again be compared with the middle Kleene based PPL outcome.

WEP$^-$((DRS 20), $\top$) $\Leftrightarrow$

$\exists x(man(x) \land \exists y(king\ of(y, x) \land serve(x, y) \land \neg reward(y, x)))$

6.6 Again: Presuppositions-as-Anaphors

In the last three sections we have discussed Presuppositional DRT: the system, the applications, and the (semantic) presuppositions. Presuppositional DRT turns out to be a relatively straightforward combination of Double Negation DRT with middle Kleene based PPL. The syntax of Presuppositional DRT is just like the syntax of Double Negation DRT, but with a Beaver-style unary presupposition operator added. Using this operator a dynamic version of Blamey's transplication was defined. The semantics of Presuppositional DRT was defined in terms of support and rejection, and can be seen as a dynamic generalization of middle Kleene based PPL. We discussed a Van Eijck-style method to determine the semantic presupposition of an arbitrary DRS, and we observed that as far as presupposition projection is concerned there is not much difference between Presuppositional DRT and the middle Kleene system of PPL. The main differences arise when we look at anaphoric expressions referring back to discourse referents introduced in presuppositional DRSs, as illustrated by examples (13) and (14). Given that the *syntax* of Presuppositional DRT is perfectly compatible with the representations used in Van der Sandt's presuppositions-as-anaphors approach, we can also feed our representations to his presupposition resolution algorithm, which indeed means that we can associate two different approaches to presupposition with a single system, namely Presuppositional DRT. In section 6.2 we also claimed that Van der Sandt's theory could actually benefit from defining the resolution algorithm on top of Presuppositional DRT instead of ordinary DRT. To back-up this claim, let us briefly re-discuss the advantages.

First, Presuppositional DRT indeed allows for the interpretation of presuppositional DRSs. This entails that the constraints on accommod-ation (which refer to semantic concepts such as satisfaction and consist-ency) can be applied on the spot, even though other presuppositional DRSs are still unresolved. In this way, the procedural version of the resol-ution algorithm can stop when it has found a solution, which by the very nature of the method sketched in section 6.2 will be the most preferred one. Once again, this does not mean that we cannot continue looking for other acceptable resolutions. It only means that it is no longer necessary to compute all logical possibilities. We *can* do that, but we do not *need* to.[23]

Another issue was the accommodation of failing presuppositions. Re-consider example (5), repeated here as (16), and its representation gen-erated by the present Revised Construction Algorithm, (DRS 22).

(16) It is not the case that the king of France is bald.

(DRS 22)

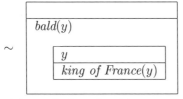

Van der Sandt's resolution-algorithm predicts that accommodating the presuppositional DRS in the main DRS is the preferred resolution. How-ever, in Van der Sandt's approach, the presuppositional DRS loses its

---

[23]It should be noted that a certain amount of backtracking is inevitable, in particular when a sentence contains two or more interdependent presuppositions. A case in point is the following example:

Either the king of France opened the exhibition or the president of France did it.

Suppose the left disjunct is resolved first; global accommodation of the presupposition that France has a king will not be blocked, although evaluation of the right disjunct will show that the presupposition should be *locally* accommodated. Of course, this kind of backtracking can be avoided when actually implementing Van der Sandt's resolution algorithm, for instance by using a rule of thumb which first determines which presuppositions are interdependent.

'presuppositionhood' in the process, and as a result the output DRS is false in any model where the French have no king. Yet intuitively, as Kracht 1994 puts it, an accommodated presupposition should still be a presupposition. Van der Sandt himself notes that the Strawsonian intuition that a failing presupposition leads to undefinedness can be modeled by 'explicitly marking accommodated material as such'. In Presuppositional DRT this is an easy matter: we accommodate the presuppositional DRS *as a presuppositional* DRS and not as an ordinary DRS. Schematically, global accommodation of Ψ in $\sim (\Phi_{\langle\Psi\rangle})$ results in $(\sim\Phi)_{\langle\Psi\rangle}$ (recall that this is just an abbreviation of $\partial\Psi ; \sim\Phi$), and not in $\Psi ; \sim\Phi$. Modulo the Single Negation lemma, this means that the (slightly modified) presupposition resolution algorithm delivers (DRS 23) when applied to (DRS 22) (where † again indicates that the presuppositional DRS has 'landed': is resolved).

(DRS 23)

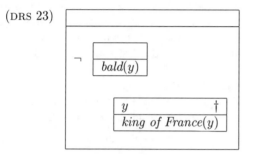

It is readily seen that (DRS 23) presupposes the existence of a French monarch (just calculate PR(DRS 23)), so this DRS is indeed be undefined when the presupposition that there is a king of France is not satisfied.[24]

---

[24]But what about the second reading of (16)? Consider:

(†) It is not the case that the king of France is bald, since there is *no* king of France.

This example does not presuppose the existence of a king of France (see chapter 4). Van der Sandt accounts for this reading by *locally* accommodating the presupposition. If we locally accommodate the presupposition *as a presupposition*, the resulting DRS still ends up being undefined in a model without a French monarch, which is plainly wrong. One option would be to only accommodate a presupposition as a presupposition if it is globally accommodated (and thus, projected). A more principled possibility is the following: we *always* accommodate a presupposition as a presupposition, but in certain specially marked contexts where global accommodation would lead to a violation of the conditions on accommodation (such as *echo negations* like (†), see Van der Sandt n.d.) the presupposition operator is 'neutralized' by the *presupposition wipe-out device* (going back to Bochvar (1939)'s *meta-assertion* operator) discussed in Beaver & Krahmer (1995) and chapter 4. Such a *dynamic* floating $\mathcal{A}$ theory could look as follows. We ground the definition of Presuppositional DRT on weak Kleene instead of middle Kleene PPL (see Krahmer 1994 for discussion on the dynamics of weak Kleene). Define $[\![\mathcal{A}\Phi]\!]^+ = [\![\Phi]\!]^+$ and $[\![\mathcal{A}\Phi]\!]^- = \{\langle g, g\rangle \mid \neg\exists h\langle g, h\rangle \in [\![\Phi]\!]^+\}$.

An advantage of the fact that Presuppositional DRT is based on Double Negation DRT has to do with the treatment of disjunction. In standard DRT (the footing of Van der Sandt's theory) it is predicted that the left disjunct is not accessible for anaphoric elements in the right disjunct. In Double Negation DRT things are different: the *negation* of the left disjunct is accessible for the right disjunct. Re-consider the relevant examples (6) and (8), repeated here as (17) and (18).

(17) Either there is no bathroom in this house, or the bathroom is in a strange place.

(18) Either Mary's autobiography hasn't appeared yet, or else John must be very proud that Mary has had a book published.

Both examples intuitively presuppose nothing. On the preferred reading, (17) does not presuppose that there is a bathroom, and similarly (18) does not presuppose that Mary has had a book published. Van der Sandt's theory accounts for (17), but only by appealing to local accommodation. However, for the second example Van der Sandt's algorithm predicts that the global accommodation reading is the most preferred one (that is, the 'presuppositional' reading, where the proposition that Mary has had a book published is placed in the main DRS). Intuitively, both examples should be rendered in terms of binding and this is exactly what happens when Van der Sandt's resolution mechanism is applied to Presuppositional DRT. Here is the schematic representation of the two examples under discussion.

(DRS 24)

$$\boxed{\quad\quad\quad\quad \atop \boxed{\sim\!\Phi \vee \Psi_{\langle\Upsilon\rangle}}}$$

Where Φ represents 'there is a bathroom in this house/Mary's autobiography has appeared', Υ represents the elementary presupposition 'there is a bathroom/Mary has had a book published' and Ψ 'it is in a strange place/John must be very proud of it'. Given the calculation of accessibility, it is easily seen that the passive discourse referents of $\sim\!\Phi$ are accessible for the presuppositional DRS Υ. And since the passive discourse referents of $\sim\!\Phi$ are the *active* discourse referents of Φ, both the bathroom and the autobiography are accessible for the presuppositions in Υ: binding is possible and preferred in both cases. The resulting reading of the original bathroom-sentence (17) can now be paraphrased as:

(19) If there is a bathroom in this house, then it is in strange place.

From here we can proceed as in chapter 4. Notice that in a dynamic floating $\mathcal{A}$ theory no weak presuppositions will be predicted.

Notice that in the situation discussed above (two bathroom in this house, one in strange place and one not), (19) is not true.

Finally, as far as presupposition-quantification interaction is concerned, note that in Presuppositional DRT it is no longer predicted that (20) and (21) are equivalent.

(20) Every fat man pushes his bicycle.

(21) Every fat man who has a bicycle pushes it.

The presupposition triggered by *his bicycle* in (20) is still accommodated in the scope of *every*, but in the process remains presuppositional, and this destroys the equivalence.

6.7   Discussion: Comparing the Two Approaches

In this chapter we have discussed Presuppositional DRT: a combination of Double Negation DRT (chapter 3) and Peters/middle Kleene based PPL (chapter 4). We have seen that presuppositions can be studied using Presuppositional DRT in *two*, rather different ways. Given some DRS Φ we can either calculate PR(Φ) and find the semantic presupposition, or we can feed Φ to Van der Sandt's resolution algorithm. It was shown that the presuppositions-as-anaphors approach actually benefits from the partial interpretation of Presuppositional DRT, even though the algorithm itself can remain essentially as Van der Sandt developed it. This picture suggests various interesting questions, and in the present section we discuss some of them.

Given that we can interpret DRSs before *and* after resolution, a natural question to ask is whether resolving presuppositions preserves meaning. Notice that this also tells us something about the relationship between the two approaches. Every time a resolution preserves meaning, the two approaches make the same predictions. To illustrate this: consider some DRS Φ. The semantic presupposition of Φ is given by PR(Φ). Feeding Φ to Van der Sandt's resolution algorithm produces a DRS Φ'. If Φ and Φ' are equivalent (thus: the resolution preserves meaning), then PR(Φ') must be equivalent to PR(Φ) as well. So, when the resolution preserves meaning, this tells us something about the *similarities* between the two approaches. And when it does not, this tells us something about the *differences* between the two (some of which were already alluded to above).

As we shall see below, the differences mainly arise when the Van der Sandtian resolution implies *moving* the presuppositional DRS from one place to another, thus: when the source-DRS is different from the target-DRS. To some extent, this points to a weakness in the *interpretation* of Presuppositional DRT, and in 6.7.3 a new interpretation is given which overcomes this. However, this new interpretation will only prove helpful in certain, 'short-distance' cases. In general, 'long-distance' cases of presupposition movement will still not be meaning preserving, and often these are the cases which Van der Sandt's theory handles better than its main competitor, the contextual satisfaction approach of Karttunen, Heim, Beaver, Van Eijck and others. Nevertheless, even though the empirical predictions of Van der Sandt's approach are good, his accommodation operation remains a 'hard' notion to grasp: it is difficult to relate it to the behavior of anaphors on the one hand, and it is unlike any other operation in DRT on the other. In fact, this may be due to a wrong perspective on accommodation. In section 6.7.4 we briefly discuss a different, proof-theoretic perspective, and argue that Van der Sandt-style accommodation is a more natural operation from this perspective.

6.7.1 Does Binding Preserve Meaning?

So consider binding: is binding a presuppositional DRS a meaning-preserving operation? Perhaps surprisingly the initial answer is no. (DRS 2) is not equivalent with its resolution (DRS 3). They do not even share their truth-conditions:

$$\mathsf{WEP}^+((\mathrm{DRS}\ 2), \top) \Leftrightarrow$$
$$\mathsf{WEP}^+([\ |\ [x\ |\ koF(x)] \Rightarrow [\ |\ bald(y)]_{\langle [y\ |\ koF(y)] \rangle}], \top) \Leftrightarrow$$
$$\neg \exists x(koF(x)) \vee \exists y(koF(y) \wedge bald(y))$$

$$\mathsf{WEP}^+((\mathrm{DRS}\ 3), \top) \Leftrightarrow$$
$$\mathsf{WEP}^+([\ |\ [x\ |\ koF(x)] \Rightarrow [\ |\ bald(x)]], \top) \Leftrightarrow$$
$$\forall x(koF(x) \to bald(x))$$

However, here the problem resides in the representation of the elementary presupposition. In terms of Van der Sandt's theory: the representation itself does not do justice to the intuition that the presupposition is actually an anaphor looking for an *antecedent*. This intuition is visualized in some (early) versions of the presuppositions-as-anaphors approach, were elementary presuppositions like those triggered by *the king* are represented as in (DRS 25).

(DRS 25)

y
$king(y)$
$y \equiv ?$

In words: the presuppositional DRS introduces a new referent y standing-in for a king, but y has to satisfy an additional constraint, namely that it is equivalent with a previously introduced referent.[25]

---

[25]Kracht 1994 observes that such a DRS is intuitively equivalent with $[\ |\ king(y)]$. Probably, Van der Sandt does not employ this notation because it would complicate

There is an interesting, alternative way to interpret a presuppositional DRS from an anaphoric angle: we can define a DRT counterpart to the notion of *contextual quantification* due to Weterståhl 1985.[26] So let us extend the language of Presuppositional DRT with *contextual DRSs*. Such contextual DRSs can introduce new discourse referents, but these referents have to be related to elements of some *context set* C. Thus we may represent (DRS 25) as follows:

(DRS 26) C
$$\begin{array}{|l|} \hline y \\ \hline king(y) \\ \hline \end{array}$$

A context set C is just a possibly empty set of variables (discourse referents). Thus if $x_1, \ldots, x_n$ are variables, then $\{x_1, \ldots, x_n\}$ is a context set. The idea is to let C be the set of accessible discourse referents. For (26) this means that y is a new discourse referent, but it should refer to some previously introduced, accessible referent.[27] The use of Contextual DRSs is nothing more than a handy method of allowing for the possibility of introducing new discourse referents referring to previously introduced objects, which is useful for an anaphoric interpretation of presuppositional DRSs. Now we can represent example (1) not as (DRS 2) but as (DRS 27).

---

the definition of accommodation; if $[\,|\,king(y)]$ cannot be bound, then it certainly cannot be accommodated (y will always remain free). Another observation which is relevant here is due to Zeevat 1992. Zeevat compares the resolution of a presupposition with answering a 'query' in PROLOG, requiring the instantiation of a variable.
[26] Weterståhl introduced context sets to deal with the context sensitivity of the definite determiner (see also Van Deemter 1992 for —a different use of— contexts sets in DRT).
[27] Thus: in general a contextualized DRS looks as follows: $\mathrm{C}\,[\vec{x}\,|\,\varphi_1, \ldots, \varphi_m]$ where C is some context set and $[\vec{x}\,|\,\varphi_1, \ldots, \varphi_m]$ is an ordinary DRS. The interpretation of a context set C with respect to an assignment g is given by: $[\![\mathrm{C}]\!]_g = \{g(v) \mid v \in \mathrm{C}\}$. Contextualized DRSs are interpreted as follows:

$$[\![\,\mathrm{C}\,[\vec{x}\,|\,\varphi_1, \ldots, \varphi_m]\,]\!]^+ =$$
$$\{\langle g, h\rangle \mid g\{\vec{x}\}h\ \&\ h(\vec{x}) \in [\![\mathrm{C}]\!]_g\ \&\ h \in ([\![\varphi_1]\!] \cap \ldots \cap [\![\varphi_m]\!]^+)\}$$

$$[\![\,\mathrm{C}\,[\vec{x}\,|\,\varphi_1, \ldots, \varphi_m]\,]\!]^- =$$
$$\{\langle g, g\rangle \mid \forall h((g\{\vec{x}\}h\ \&\ h(\vec{x}) \in [\![\mathrm{C}]\!]_g) \Rightarrow h \in ([\![\varphi_1]\!]^- \cup \ldots \cup [\![\varphi_m]\!]^-))\}$$

Here $h(\vec{x}) \in [\![\mathrm{C}]\!]_g$ abbreviates $h(x_1) \in [\![\mathrm{C}]\!]_g\ \&\ \ldots\ \&\ h(x_n) \in [\![\mathrm{C}]\!]_g$. Let me note that, as with Weterståhl's original proposal, this does not lead to an increase of logical power, since $\mathrm{C}\,[x_1, \ldots, x_n\,|\,\vec{\varphi}]$ is equivalent with $[x_1, \ldots, x_n\,|\,\vec{\varphi}, \mathrm{C}(x_1), \ldots, \mathrm{C}(x_n)]$, where $\mathrm{C}(x)$ is interpreted like an atomic condition which is supported if the value of x is an element of the relevant interpretation of C.

(DRS 27)

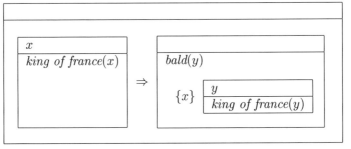

The contextualized presuppositional DRS is equivalent with the standard DRS $[y \mid king\ of\ France(y), y \equiv x]$ (see footnote 27), and as a result (DRS 27) is equivalent with (DRS 3). So for this case we can construct presuppositional representations in such a way that binding can be understood as a meaning preserving operation, and it seems that similar examples can be reformulated in a similar way. A comparable conclusion can be drawn on the basis of Zeevat 1992's reformulation of Van der Sandt's approach in Update Semantics. Yet it should be noted that there are also examples for which things are less clear. Above we mentioned that Van der Sandt allows for the possibility that a presuppositional DRS matches only partially with an antecedent,[28] and it is also possible that there are several suitable antecedents on the same level. Such cases generate a certain amount of *ambiguity*, and Van der Sandt argues that this is as it should be (Van der Sandt 1992:348-349). From the perspective of contextualized DRS this corresponds with the situation in which a context set C contains *several* suitable antecedents. In that case the best we might hope to get is that binding is meaning-preserving *per reading*.

6.7.2 Does Accommodation Preserve Meaning?

Accommodation, however, is an entirely different kettle of fish. It is easily seen that (DRS 4) and (DRS 5), to give but one example, are not equivalent, and —unsurprisingly— there is also no easy way to remedy this. In particular, the addition of context-sets in the way we did

---

[28] An example is the following:

If John has an oriental girlfriend, then his girlfriend won't be happy.

Van der Sandt argues that this sentence displays a genuine ambiguity between a binding reading (paraphrasable as *If John has an oriental girlfriend, then she won't be happy*) and an accommodation reading (*John has a_i girlfriend, and if he has an oriental girlfriend (as well), then she_i won't be happy*). Even though we agree with this intuition, it is interesting to note that this ambiguity is not actually predicted by Van der Sandts own algorithm, which assigns a general preference of binding over accommodation. In fact, this problem can be overcome by modifying Van der Sandt's basic algorithm (for more details we refer to Krahmer and Deemter 1997).

above will not help. In general, accommodation *only* preserves meaning if the source- and target-DRS are identical: the DRS in which the presuppositional DRS was triggered is the same one as the DRS in which the presuppositional DRS is accommodated (hence, the presuppositional DRS has not moved).

Since accommodation is not a meaning preserving operation in general, differences between the two approaches arise. This is one of the major points where Van der Sandt's theory positively distinguishes itself from other, purely semantic approaches to presuppositions, which (as we have seen) predict *weaker* presuppositions in these cases.

Why is accommodation not meaning-preserving? In one sense this is just what we would expect. After all, Lewis 1979 describes accommodation as the phenomenon that missing information simply 'springs into existence': the representation of the foregoing is altered in such a way that the presupposition is satisfied after all. And it is no surprise that this changes the meaning.

On the other hand, consider (DRS 22), which is of the form $\sim(\Phi_{\langle\Psi\rangle})$. If we feed this DRS to the (slightly adapted) resolution algorithm, the presuppositional DRS will be accommodated as a presuppositional DRS and the result is (DRS 23), which is of the form $(\sim\Phi)_{\langle\Psi\rangle}$ (that is: *before* application of the Single Negation Lemma). These two DRSs differ in their *dynamic* meaning (thus, they are not equivalent), and hence even this form of accommodation is not entirely meaning-preserving. Yet, we could reasonably expect the accommodation to preserve meaning in this case. In chapter 4 we saw that in static partial logics $\neg(\varphi_{\langle\psi\rangle})$ is equivalent with $(\neg\varphi)_{\langle\psi\rangle}$ and, in general, negation is simply predicted to be a hole for presupposition projection. In fact, this points to a weakness in the *interpretation* of Presuppositional DRT.

6.7.3 An Alternative Interpretation

What is the problem here? Recall that in dynamic semantics, a single negation is understood as a plug with respect to anaphoric reference. Therefore, *no* discourse referent which originates in the scope of a negation can be referred back to. So, in $\sim(\Phi_{\langle\Psi\rangle})$ any referent introduced in either Φ or Ψ is inaccessible outside the scope of the negation. In $(\sim\Phi)_{\langle\Psi\rangle}$ things are different; referents introduced in the main universe of Ψ *are* available for future reference. We would expect presuppositions to be totally insensitive to negation, and that this is not the case for the interpretation of Presuppositional DRT given in definition 2 (nor for the related interpretations of Kinematic Predicate Logic and Error-state Semantics for DPL) is an artefact of the dynamic interpretation of single negations.[29] What we want is the following: a single negation should be a *plug* for anaphoric reference to non-presupposed discourse referents (like those representing indefinites), but at the same time it should be a *hole* for anaphoric reference to presupposed discourse referents (like those representing definite descriptions). Compare:

(22) a. John didn't bake the pie for Mary's birthday. It was huge and rather tasty.

   b. John didn't bake a pie for Mary's birthday. # It was huge and rather tasty.

The phenomenon of a logical connective which should act as both a plug *and* a hole with respect to anaphoric reference is by no means restricted to negation. Consider:

(23) a. If an inhabitant of France is bald, he will wear a curled wig. # He is a dedicated follower of fashion.

   b. If the king of France is bald, he will wear a curled wig. He is a dedicated follower of fashion.

Again, we want to block anaphoric reference to an indefinite NP in the antecedent of a conditional, but not to a definite one in the same position. Can we do something about this?

Intuitively a presupposition is a proposition which should hold beforehand. In what sense, does $\Phi_{\langle\Psi\rangle}$ conform to this intuition? If we evaluate $\Phi_{\langle\Psi\rangle}$ with respect to an assignment g, then the presuppositional DRS Ψ is supported if there is an assignment h such that $\langle g, h\rangle \in [\![\Psi]\!]^+$; presupposition is a matter of *successors*. Now consider the following alternative definition:[30]

Definition 10 ($\Phi_{\langle\Psi\rangle}$ (re-)defined)
$$[\![\Phi_{\langle\Psi\rangle}]\!]^+ = \{\langle g, h\rangle \mid \exists k \langle k, g\rangle \in [\![\Psi]\!]^+ \ \& \ \langle g, h\rangle \in [\![\Phi]\!]^+\}$$
$$[\![\Phi_{\langle\Psi\rangle}]\!]^- = \{\langle g, h\rangle \mid \exists k \langle k, g\rangle \in [\![\Psi]\!]^+ \ \& \ \langle g, h\rangle \in [\![\Phi]\!]^-\}$$

Arguably this definition comes closer to the intuition of a presupposition as something which holds already. Definition 10 supports the following fact, as the reader can easily verify.

Fact 7
$\sim(\Phi_{\langle\Psi\rangle})$ *is equivalent with* $(\sim\Phi)_{\langle\Psi\rangle}$

This means that if we interpret presuppositional DRSs as in definition 10, the resolution of (DRS 22) yielding (DRS 23) *does* preserve meaning. And,

---

[29] By comparison: $\sim\sim(\Phi_{\langle\Psi\rangle})$ *is* equivalent with $(\sim\sim\Phi)_{\langle\Psi\rangle}$ in the present set-up.

[30] Notice that this interpretation of $\Phi_{\langle\Psi\rangle}$ is not definable in terms of sequencing and *any* alternative interpretation of ∂, since $[\![\partial\Psi \ ; \ \Phi]\!]^-$ will always be a subset of Δ ($= \{\langle g, h\rangle \mid g = h\}$).

moreover, the treatment of (22.a) *and* (22.b) has become possible for the semantic account as well. Now re-consider example (23.b). The first sentence is represented as follows, according to our Revised Construction Algorithm.

(DRS 28)

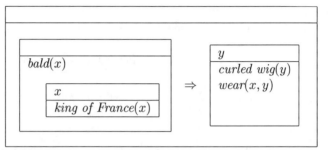

Van der Sandt's resolution algorithm predicts that the most preferred reading is given by accommodation in the main DRS. Once again accommodating the presupposition as a presupposition yields (DRS 29).

(DRS 29)

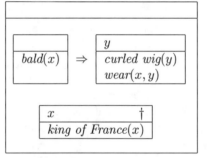

On the new interpretation of $\Phi_{\langle\Psi\rangle}$ this is also a meaning preserving operation. If we add a DRS containing the second sentence of (23.b) to (DRS 29), it is easily seen that we may replace *he* with x. The introduction of x in the presuppositional DRS of (DRS 29) will bind the representation of the pronoun. In general, the following fact holds.

Fact 8

$[\,|\,\Phi_{\langle\Psi\rangle} \Rightarrow \Upsilon]$ *is equivalent with* $[\,|\,\Phi \Rightarrow \Upsilon]_{\langle\Psi\rangle}$

To accommodate the 'looking-back' character of the new presupposition operator some minor modifications are needed. We have to generalize the notion of 'domain-extension': $g\{\vec{x}\}h$ now comes to mean 'assignment h extends assignments g *at least* with $\vec{x}$ '.[31] Otherwise, the interpretation of Presuppositional DRT remains as it was. Of course, more work

---

[31] Formally: $g\{\vec{x}\}h$ abbreviates $\mathsf{Dom}(g) \cup \{\vec{x}\} \subseteq \mathsf{Dom}(h)$ & $\forall y \in \mathsf{Dom}(g) : g(y) = h(y)$. Notice that now we have to be careful that a new variable really *is* a new

needs to go in the properties of this system. Nevertheless, this seems to be an interesting line for future research. The alternative definition given here makes it possible to bridge part of the 'accommodation-gap' between the two approaches discussed in this chapter. Notice that the new interpretation does not lead to a *strengthening* of the predicted semantic presuppositions. Reconsider (3), here repeated as (24).

(24) If a farmer owns a donkey, he gives it to the king of France.

Van der Sandt's presupposition resolution mechanism predicts —correctly— that the most preferred reading is given by accommodating the elementary presupposition at the level of the main DRS: thus, the presupposition that there is a king of France is projected. The semantic notion of presupposition, based on the new interpretation of Presuppositional DRT, still predicts the weaker presupposition *if a farmer owns a donkey, then there is a king of France* (see the end of section 6.2.1).[32]

It should be noted that in Beaver 1993 it is argued that there are also some cases where we *do* want the weak presupposition. Here is one of Beaver's examples:

(25) If Spaceman Spiff lands on Planet X, he will be bothered by the fact that his weight is higher than it would be on earth.

Van der Sandt's resolution algorithm predicts that the elementary presupposition triggered by the *fact that* construction, that Spiff's weight is higher than it would be on earth, is accommodated in the main DRS, since it cannot be bound in the antecedent. Yet example (25) does not seem to presuppose that Spaceman Spiff's weight is higher than it would be on earth. Arguably, the predicted semantic presupposition, which may be paraphrased as *if Spaceman Spiff lands on Planet X, his weight is higher than it would be on earth*, is more intuitive. So, the purely semantic account predicts weak presuppositions for conditionals as desired for (25) but not for (24), while Van der Sandt's account predicts that the elementary presuppositions arising in the consequents of (24) and (25) are accommodated at top level, which is desired for the first but not for the last case.

6.7.4 Presupposition Projection as Proof Construction

As the foregoing discussion illustrated, the predictions of Van der Sandt tend to differ from those of the contextual satisfaction camp when presuppositions are accommodated in another DRS than the one in which the presupposition was triggered in the first place. It is precisely this

---

variable in the semantics. One way to guarantee this is by adding a semantic novelty-condition on indefinites, see chapter 7.

[32]But see footnote 24.

view on accommodation as transformation which positively distinguishes Van der Sandt's theory from the competing theories. However, Van der Sandt's treatment of accommodation is also hard to grasp conceptually. Perhaps we can get a better understanding of accommodation by looking at it from a proof-theoretic perspective, as noted by Krause 1995, see also Krahmer & Piwek 1997.

In Ahn and Kolb 1990 an embedding of standard DRT in *Constructive Type Theory* (CTT, see for instance Martin-Löf 1984, Barendregt 1992) is presented. CTT differs from other proof systems in that for each proposition which is proven, CTT also delivers a proof-object which shows *how* the proposition was proven. In Krahmer and Piwek 1997 the presuppositions-as-anaphors theory of Van der Sandt is rephrased in terms of CTT. Starting point is Ahn & Kolb's embedding of DRT in CTT, which is extended to include presuppositional DRSs. Now suppose we want to evaluate (the CTT representation of) a presuppositional DRS $\Phi_{\langle\Psi\rangle}$ in a context Γ (a set of premises). Then we first try to *derive* Ψ from Γ. If this succeeds, the presupposition can be bound. However, if we are *unable* to derive Ψ, this means that our context Γ is not rich enough. In that case, we can *strengthen* Γ by extending it with Ψ (that is: Ψ is globally accommodated). Krause 1995 observes that from this viewpoint (global) accommodation is nothing more than *abductive inference* (Peirce 1870, Hobbs et al. 1993).

Interestingly, rephrasing Van der Sandt's theory in terms of CTT not only provides an interesting view on accommodation as abduction. It also has some additional benefits. In particular, CTT contexts Γ typically contain *more* information than has been conveyed by the preceding discourse, and there is a formal interaction between this 'background knowledge' and the representation of the current discourse. In Krahmer and Piwek 1997 it is shown that this paves the way for a formal treatment of the influence of world-knowledge on presupposition projection, which is needed, for example, for the correct treatment of Beaver's example (25). As Beaver observes , example (25) is typically uttered when Spiff is hanging somewhere in space. When the context Γ models the background knowledge that in space one is weightless, the global accommodation of the elementary presupposition (*Spiff's weight is higher than it would be on earth*) can be blocked: adding the presupposed proposition to the context Γ will lead to an inconsistency (given some other fairly common pieces of information, such as 'on earth one is not weightless'). Hence, the global accommodation reading is correctly blocked. For a more detailed analysis we refer to Krahmer and Piwek 1997.

Let us briefly recapitulate. In this chapter we have discussed Presuppositional DRT and we have seen that presuppositions can be studied using Presuppositional DRT in *two*, rather different ways. Given some DRS Φ we can either calculate $PR(\Phi)$ and find the semantic presupposition, or we can feed Φ to Van der Sandt's resolution algorithm. It was shown that Van der Sandt's presupposition resolution algorithm actually benefits from the partial interpretation of Presuppositional DRT, even though the algorithm itself remains essentially as Van der Sandt developed it. In this long discussion section we have seen that Presuppositional DRT also enhances the comparison between Van der Sandt's presuppositions-as-anaphors approach and its main competitor, the 'contextual satisfaction' approach.

Given that we can interpret DRSs before and after resolution, we can answer the question whether resolving presuppositions preserves meaning, which also serves to compare predicitions of the two approaches. We found that binding a presupposition generally preserves meaning, provided that we give the presuppositional DRS a slightly different (and independently motivated) interpretation. We also found that resolution does *not* preserve meaning when the presuppositional DRS in question is accommodated in a different DRS than the one it was triggered in, thus when its source-DRS is different from its target-DRS.

We concluded that this might be attributed in part to the interpretation of Presuppositional DRT: presuppositional DRSs did not do justice to the intuition that presuppositions should look back rather than forward. Therefore an alternative interpretation was explored in which presupposition is indeed a matter of 'predecessors'. However, at best, this only solves part of the problem. In general, 'long-distance' cases of accommodation are still not meaning preserving, and even though there are apparent counterexamples such as (25), the 'long distance' cases are the ones which Van der Sandt's theory handles better than the main competitor; the 'contextual satisfaction' approach of Karttunen, Heim, Beaver, Van Eijck and others. Nevertheless, Van der Sandt's accommodation operation remains a 'hard' notion to grasp: it is difficult to relate it to the behavior of anaphors, and it is unlike any other operation in DRT. We have suggested that this might be due to a wrong perspective on accommodation. We briefly discussed a different, proof-theoretic perspective, and saw that Van der Sandt-style accommodation makes perfect sense from this perspective: it is abductive inference.

Appendix

In this appendix some of the facts from this chapter are proved.

Fact 1 *(Equivalences)*

1. $\sim\sim\Phi$ *is equivalent with* Φ
2. $\Phi \, ; (\Psi \, ; \Upsilon)$ *is equivalent with* $(\Phi \, ; \Psi) \, ; \Upsilon$
3. $\Phi \Rightarrow [\, |\Psi \Rightarrow \Upsilon]$ *is equivalent with* $(\Phi \, ; \Psi) \Rightarrow \Upsilon$
4. $\Phi_{\langle \pi_1 \langle \pi_2 \rangle \rangle}$ *is equivalent with* $\Phi_{\langle \pi_2 ; \pi_1 \rangle}$

Proof. Recall that Φ and Ψ are equivalent iff for all models M, $[\![\Phi]\!]_M^+ = [\![\Psi]\!]_M^+$ and $[\![\Phi]\!]_M^- = [\![\Psi]\!]_M^-$. That the law of double negation holds in Presuppositional DRT is easily shown. The second, associativity equivalence is more interesting. The positive part of this equivalence, $[\![\Phi \, ; (\Psi \, ; \Upsilon)]\!]_M^+ = [\![(\Phi \, ; \Psi) \, ; \Upsilon]\!]_M^+$, is easily established. As for the negative case:

$[\![\Phi \, ; (\Psi \, ; \Upsilon)]\!]^- \Leftrightarrow$

$\{\langle g, g \rangle \mid \forall k (\langle g, k \rangle \in [\![\Phi]\!]^+ \Rightarrow \exists h \langle k, h \rangle \in [\![\Psi \, ; \Upsilon]\!]^-) \ \& \ \mathrm{DEF}_g(\Phi)\} \Leftrightarrow$

$\{\langle g, g \rangle \mid \forall k (\langle g, k \rangle \in [\![\Phi]\!]^+ \Rightarrow \exists h [k = h \ \& \ \forall m (\langle k, m \rangle \in [\![\Psi]\!]^+ \Rightarrow$
$\qquad \exists l \langle m, l \rangle \in [\![\Upsilon]\!]^-) \ \& \ \mathrm{DEF}_k(\Psi)]) \ \& \ \mathrm{DEF}_g(\Phi)\} \Leftrightarrow$

[by: $\varphi \to (\psi \wedge \chi) \Leftrightarrow (\varphi \to \psi) \wedge (\varphi \to \chi), \forall x (\varphi \wedge \psi) \Leftrightarrow \forall x \varphi \wedge \forall x \psi$]

$\{\langle g, g \rangle \mid \forall k (\langle g, k \rangle \in [\![\Phi]\!]^+ \Rightarrow \forall m (\langle k, m \rangle \in [\![\Psi]\!]^+ \Rightarrow \exists l \langle m, l \rangle \in [\![\Upsilon]\!]^-)) \ \&$
$\qquad \forall k (\langle g, k \rangle \in [\![\Phi]\!]^+ \Rightarrow \mathrm{DEF}_k(\Psi)) \ \& \ \mathrm{DEF}_g(\Phi)\} \Leftrightarrow$

[by: prenex, $\varphi \to (\psi \to \chi) \Leftrightarrow (\varphi \wedge \psi) \to \chi, \mathrm{DEF}$]

$\{\langle g, g \rangle \mid \forall k \forall m (((\langle g, k \rangle \in [\![\Phi]\!]^+ \ \& \ \langle k, m \rangle \in [\![\Psi]\!]^+) \Rightarrow \exists l \langle m, l \rangle \in [\![\Upsilon]\!]^-) \ \&$
$\qquad \mathrm{DEF}_g(\Phi \, ; \Psi)\} \Leftrightarrow$

[by: prenex]

$\{\langle g, g \rangle \mid \forall m (\exists k (\langle g, k \rangle \in [\![\Phi]\!]^+ \ \& \ \langle k, m \rangle \in [\![\Psi]\!]^+) \Rightarrow \exists l \langle m, l \rangle \in [\![\Upsilon]\!]^-) \ \&$
$\qquad \mathrm{DEF}_g(\Phi \, ; \Psi)\} \Leftrightarrow$

$\{\langle g, g \rangle \mid \forall m (\langle g, m \rangle \in [\![\Phi \, ; \Psi]\!]^+ \Rightarrow \exists l \langle m, l \rangle \in [\![\Upsilon]\!]^-) \ \& \ \mathrm{DEF}_g(\Phi \, ; \Psi)\} \Leftrightarrow$
$[\![(\Phi \, ; \Psi) \, ; \Upsilon]\!]^-$

Using the first two equivalences of fact 1 and the fact that $\Phi \Rightarrow [\, | \Psi \Rightarrow \Upsilon]$ is equivalent with $\neg\neg\sim(\Phi \, ; \sim\sim(\Psi \, ; \sim\Upsilon))$, the third equivalence of fact 1 is easily proved. The fourth equivalence, finally, is proved thus:

$[\![\Phi_{\langle \pi_1 \langle \pi_2 \rangle \rangle}]\!]^+ \Leftrightarrow [\![\partial(\pi_1 \langle \pi_2 \rangle) \, ; \Phi]\!]^+ \Leftrightarrow [\![\partial(\partial(\pi_2) \, ; \pi_1) \, ; \Phi]\!]^+ \Leftrightarrow$

$\{\langle g, h \rangle \mid \exists k (\langle g, k \rangle \in [\![\partial(\partial(\pi_2) \, ; \pi_1)]\!]^+ \ \& \ \langle k, h \rangle \in [\![\Phi]\!]^+)\} \Leftrightarrow$

$\{\langle g, h \rangle \mid \exists k (\exists l (\langle g, l \rangle \in [\![\pi_2]\!]^+ \ \& \ \langle l, k \rangle \in [\![\pi_1]\!]^+) \ \& \ \langle k, h \rangle \in [\![\Phi]\!]^+)\} \Leftrightarrow$

$\{\langle g, h \rangle \mid \exists k (\langle g, k \rangle \in [\![\partial(\pi_2 \, ; \pi_1)]\!]^+ \ \& \ \langle k, h \rangle \in [\![\Phi]\!]^+)\} \Leftrightarrow$

$[\![\partial(\pi_2 \, ; \pi_1) \, ; \Phi]\!]^+ \Leftrightarrow [\![\Phi_{\langle \pi_2 ; \pi_1 \rangle}]\!]^+$

$[\![\Phi_{\langle \pi_1 \langle \pi_2 \rangle \rangle}]\!]^- \Leftrightarrow [\![\partial(\partial(\pi_2) \, ; \pi_1) \, ; \Phi]\!]^- \Leftrightarrow$

$\{\langle g, g \rangle \mid \forall k (\langle g, k \rangle \in [\![\partial(\partial(\pi_2) \, ; \pi_1)]\!]^+ \Rightarrow \exists h \langle k, h \rangle \in [\![\Phi]\!]^-) \ \&$
$\qquad \mathrm{DEF}_g(\partial(\partial(\pi_2) \, ; \pi_1))\} \Leftrightarrow$

$\{\langle g, g \rangle \mid \forall k (\langle g, k \rangle \in [\![\pi_2 \, ; \pi_1]\!]^+ \Rightarrow \exists h \langle k, h \rangle \in [\![\Phi]\!]^-) \ \& \ \mathrm{DEF}_g(\partial(\partial(\pi_2) \, ; \pi_1))\} \Leftrightarrow$
$[\mathrm{DEF}_g(\partial(\partial(\pi_2) \, ; \pi_1)) \Leftrightarrow$

$\exists h \langle g, h \rangle \in [\![\partial(\partial(\pi_2) ; \pi_1)]\!]^+$ or $\exists h \langle g, h \rangle \in [\![\partial(\partial(\pi_2) ; \pi_1)]\!]^- \Leftrightarrow$
$\exists h \langle g, h \rangle \in [\![\pi_2 ; \pi_1]\!]^+$ or $\exists h \langle g, h \rangle \in \emptyset \Leftrightarrow$
$\exists h \langle g, h \rangle \in [\![\partial(\pi_2 ; \pi_1)]\!]^+$ or $\exists h \langle g, h \rangle \in [\![\partial(\pi_2 ; \pi_1)]\!]^- \Leftrightarrow$
$\mathrm{DEF}_g(\partial(\pi_2 ; \pi_1))] \Leftrightarrow$
$\{\langle g, g \rangle \mid \forall k (\langle g, k \rangle \in [\![\partial(\pi_2 ; \pi_1)]\!]^+ \Rightarrow \exists h \langle k, h \rangle \in [\![\Phi]\!]^-) \ \& \ \mathrm{DEF}_g(\partial(\pi_2 ; \pi_1))\} \Leftrightarrow$
$[\![\partial(\pi_2 ; \pi_1) ; \Phi]\!]^- \Leftrightarrow [\![\Phi_{\langle \pi_2 ; \pi_1 \rangle}]\!]^-$

$\square$

Fact 4 *(From Presuppositional* DRT *to* PL*)*
For all models M and assignments g:

1. $g \in [\![\mathsf{TR}^+(\varphi)]\!]_M^{\mathrm{PL}} \Leftrightarrow g \in [\![\varphi]\!]_M^+$
   $g \in [\![\mathsf{TR}^-(\varphi)]\!]_M^{\mathrm{PL}} \Leftrightarrow g \in [\![\varphi]\!]_M^-$

2. $g \in [\![\mathsf{WEP}^+(\Phi, \chi)]\!]_M^{\mathrm{PL}} \Leftrightarrow \exists h (\langle g, h \rangle \in [\![\Phi]\!]^+ \ \& \ h \in [\![\chi]\!]_M^{\mathrm{PL}})$
   $g \in [\![\mathsf{WEP}^-(\Phi, \chi)]\!]_M^{\mathrm{PL}} \Leftrightarrow \exists h (\langle g, h \rangle \in [\![\Phi]\!]^- \ \& \ h \in [\![\chi]\!]_M^{\mathrm{PL}})$

3. $g \in [\![\overline{\mathsf{DEF}}(\Phi)]\!]_M^{\mathrm{PL}} \Leftrightarrow \mathrm{DEF}_{M,g}(\Phi)$

Proof. By induction. Consider arbitrary M and g.

1. $g \in [\![\mathsf{TR}^+(R(t_1, \ldots, t_n))]\!]^{\mathrm{PL}} \Leftrightarrow g \in [\![R(t_1, \ldots, t_n)]\!]^{\mathrm{PL}} \Leftrightarrow$
   $\langle [\![t_1]\!]_g, \ldots, [\![t_n]\!]_g \rangle \in I(R) \Leftrightarrow g \in [\![R(t_1, \ldots, t_n)]\!]^+$

   $g \in [\![\mathsf{TR}^-(R(t_1, \ldots, t_n))]\!]^{\mathrm{PL}} \Leftrightarrow g \in [\![\neg R(t_1, \ldots, t_n)]\!]^{\mathrm{PL}} \Leftrightarrow$
   $\langle [\![t_1]\!]_g, \ldots, [\![t_n]\!]_g \rangle \notin I(R) \Leftrightarrow g \in [\![R(t_1, \ldots, t_n)]\!]^-$
   (and similar for $t_1 \equiv t_2$.)

2. $g \in [\![\mathsf{TR}^+(\Phi \Rightarrow \Psi)]\!]^{\mathrm{PL}} \Leftrightarrow$
   $g \in [\![\neg\mathsf{WEP}^+(\Phi, \neg\mathsf{WEP}^+(\Psi, \top)) \wedge \overline{\mathsf{DEF}}(\Phi)]\!]^{\mathrm{PL}} \Leftrightarrow [\mathrm{IH}]$
   $g \in [\![\neg\mathsf{WEP}^+(\Phi, \neg\mathsf{WEP}^+(\Psi, \top))]\!]^{\mathrm{PL}} \ \& \ \mathrm{DEF}_g(\Phi) \Leftrightarrow [\mathrm{IH}]$
   $\neg\exists h (\langle g, h \rangle \in [\![\Phi]\!]^+ \ \& \ h \in [\![\neg\mathsf{WEP}^+(\Psi, \top)]\!]^{\mathrm{PL}}) \ \& \ \mathrm{DEF}_g(\Phi) \Leftrightarrow [\mathrm{IH}]$
   $\neg\exists h (\langle g, h \rangle \in [\![\Phi]\!]^+ \ \& \ \neg\exists k (\langle h, k \rangle \in [\![\Psi]\!]^+ \ \& \ k \in [\![\top]\!]^{\mathrm{PL}})) \ \& \ \mathrm{DEF}_g(\Phi) \Leftrightarrow$
   $\forall h (\langle g, h \rangle \in [\![\Phi]\!]^+ \Rightarrow \exists k \langle h, k \rangle \in [\![\Psi]\!]^+) \ \& \ \mathrm{DEF}_g(\Phi) \Leftrightarrow$
   $g \in [\![\Phi \Rightarrow \Psi]\!]^+$

   $g \in [\![\mathsf{TR}^-(\Phi \Rightarrow \Psi)]\!]^{\mathrm{PL}} \Leftrightarrow$
   $g \in [\![\mathsf{WEP}^+(\Phi, \mathsf{WEP}^-(\Psi, \top))]\!]^{\mathrm{PL}} \Leftrightarrow [\mathrm{IH}]$
   $\exists h (\langle g, h \rangle \in [\![\Phi]\!]^+ \ \& \ h \in [\![\mathsf{WEP}^-(\Psi, \top)]\!]^{\mathrm{PL}}) \Leftrightarrow [\mathrm{IH}]$
   $\exists h (\langle g, h \rangle \in [\![\Phi]\!]^+ \ \& \ \exists k (\langle h, k \rangle \in [\![\Psi]\!]^- \ \& \ k \in [\![\top]\!]^{\mathrm{PL}})) \Leftrightarrow$
   $\exists h (\langle g, h \rangle \in [\![\Phi]\!]^+ \ \& \ \exists k \langle h, k \rangle \in [\![\Psi]\!]^-) \Leftrightarrow$
   $g \in [\![\Phi \Rightarrow \Psi]\!]^-$

3. $g \in [\![\mathsf{WEP}^+([\vec{x} \mid \varphi_1, \ldots, \varphi_m], \chi)]\!]^{\mathrm{PL}} \Leftrightarrow$
   $g \in [\![\exists \vec{x}(\mathsf{TR}^+(\varphi_1) \wedge \ldots \wedge \mathsf{TR}^+(\varphi_m) \wedge \chi)]\!]^{\mathrm{PL}} \Leftrightarrow$
   $\exists h (g[\vec{x}]h \ \& \ h \in ([\![\mathsf{TR}^+(\varphi_1)]\!]^{\mathrm{PL}} \cap \ldots \cap [\![\mathsf{TR}^+(\varphi_m)]\!]^{\mathrm{PL}}) \ \& \ h \in [\![\chi]\!]^{\mathrm{PL}}) \Leftrightarrow [\mathrm{IH}]$
   $\exists h (g[\vec{x}]h \ \& \ h \in ([\![\varphi_1]\!]^+ \cap \ldots \cap [\![\varphi_m]\!]^+) \ \& \ h \in [\![\chi]\!]^{\mathrm{PL}}) \Leftrightarrow$
   $\exists h (\langle g, h \rangle \in [\![[\vec{x} \mid \varphi_1, \ldots, \varphi_m]]\!]^+ \ \& \ h \in [\![\chi]\!]^{\mathrm{PL}})$

   $g \in [\![\mathsf{WEP}^-([\vec{x} \mid \varphi_1, \ldots, \varphi_m], \chi)]\!]^{\mathrm{PL}} \Leftrightarrow$

$g \in \llbracket \forall \vec{x}(\mathsf{TR}^-(\varphi_1) \vee \ldots \vee \mathsf{TR}^-(\varphi_m)) \wedge \chi \rrbracket^{\mathrm{PL}} \Leftrightarrow$
$\forall k(g[\vec{x}]k \Rightarrow k \in (\llbracket \mathsf{TR}^-(\varphi_1) \rrbracket^{\mathrm{PL}} \cup \ldots \cup \llbracket \mathsf{TR}^-(\varphi_m) \rrbracket^{\mathrm{PL}})) \ \& \ g \in \llbracket \chi \rrbracket^{\mathrm{PL}} \Leftrightarrow [\mathrm{IH}]$
$\forall k(g[\vec{x}]k \Rightarrow k \in (\llbracket \varphi_1 \rrbracket^- \cup \ldots \cup \llbracket \varphi_m \rrbracket^-)) \ \& \ g \in \llbracket \chi \rrbracket^{\mathrm{PL}} \Leftrightarrow$
$\exists h(g = h \ \& \ \forall k(g[\vec{x}]k \Rightarrow k \in (\llbracket \varphi_1 \rrbracket^- \cup \ldots \cup \llbracket \varphi_m \rrbracket^-)) \ \& \ h \in \llbracket \chi \rrbracket^{\mathrm{PL}}) \Leftrightarrow$
$\exists h(\langle g, h \rangle \in \llbracket [\vec{x} \mid \varphi_1, \ldots, \varphi_m] \rrbracket^- \ \& \ h \in \llbracket \chi \rrbracket^{\mathrm{PL}})$

4. $g \in \llbracket \mathsf{WEP}^+(\Phi \, ; \Psi, \chi) \rrbracket^{\mathrm{PL}} \Leftrightarrow$
   $g \in \llbracket \mathsf{WEP}^+(\Phi, \mathsf{WEP}^+(\Psi, \chi)) \rrbracket^{\mathrm{PL}} \Leftrightarrow [\mathrm{IH}]$
   $\exists h(\langle g, h \rangle \in \llbracket \Phi \rrbracket^+ \ \& \ \exists k(\langle h, k \rangle \in \llbracket \Psi \rrbracket^+ \ \& \ k \in \llbracket \chi \rrbracket^{\mathrm{PL}})) \Leftrightarrow$
   $\exists k(\langle g, k \rangle \in \llbracket \Phi \, ; \Psi \rrbracket^+ \ \& \ k \in \llbracket \chi \rrbracket^{\mathrm{PL}})$

   $g \in \llbracket \mathsf{WEP}^-(\Phi \, ; \Psi, \chi) \rrbracket^{\mathrm{PL}} \Leftrightarrow$
   $g \in \llbracket \neg \mathsf{WEP}^+(\Phi, \neg \mathsf{WEP}^-(\Psi, \top)) \wedge \overline{\mathsf{DEF}}(\Phi) \wedge \chi \rrbracket^{\mathrm{PL}} \Leftrightarrow [\mathrm{IH}]$
   $g \in \llbracket \neg \mathsf{WEP}^+(\Phi, \neg \mathsf{WEP}^-(\Psi, \top)) \rrbracket^{\mathrm{PL}} \ \& \ \mathrm{DEF}_g(\Phi) \ \& \ g \in \llbracket \chi \rrbracket^{\mathrm{PL}} \Leftrightarrow [\mathrm{IH}]$
   $\neg \exists k(\langle g, k \rangle \in \llbracket \Phi \rrbracket^+ \ \& \ \neg \exists l(\langle k, l \rangle \in \llbracket \Psi \rrbracket^- \ \& \ l \in \llbracket \top \rrbracket^{\mathrm{PL}})) \ \& \ \mathrm{DEF}_g(\Phi) \ \&$
   $\qquad g \in \llbracket \chi \rrbracket^{\mathrm{PL}} \Leftrightarrow$
   $\forall k(\langle g, k \rangle \in \llbracket \Phi \rrbracket^+ \Rightarrow \exists l \langle k, l \rangle \in \llbracket \Psi \rrbracket^-) \ \& \ \mathrm{DEF}_g(\Phi) \ \& \ g \in \llbracket \chi \rrbracket^{\mathrm{PL}} \Leftrightarrow$
   $\exists h(\langle g, h \rangle \in \llbracket \Phi \, ; \Psi \rrbracket^- \ \& \ h \in \llbracket \chi \rrbracket^{\mathrm{PL}})$

5. $g \in \llbracket \mathsf{WEP}^+(\sim \Phi, \chi) \rrbracket^{\mathrm{PL}} \Leftrightarrow g \in \llbracket \mathsf{WEP}^-(\Phi, \chi) \rrbracket^{\mathrm{PL}} \Leftrightarrow [\mathrm{IH}]$
   $\exists h(\langle g, h \rangle \in \llbracket \Phi \rrbracket^- \ \& \ h \in \llbracket \chi \rrbracket^{\mathrm{PL}}) \Leftrightarrow \exists h(\langle g, h \rangle \in \llbracket \sim \Phi \rrbracket^+ \ \& \ h \in \llbracket \chi \rrbracket^{\mathrm{PL}})$

   $g \in \llbracket \mathsf{WEP}^-(\sim \Phi, \chi) \rrbracket^{\mathrm{PL}} \Leftrightarrow g \in \llbracket \mathsf{WEP}^+(\Phi, \chi) \rrbracket^{\mathrm{PL}} \Leftrightarrow [\mathrm{IH}]$
   $\exists h(\langle g, h \rangle \in \llbracket \Phi \rrbracket^+ \ \& \ h \in \llbracket \chi \rrbracket^{\mathrm{PL}}) \Leftrightarrow \exists h(\langle g, h \rangle \in \llbracket \sim \Phi \rrbracket^- \ \& \ h \in \llbracket \chi \rrbracket^{\mathrm{PL}})$

6. $g \in \llbracket \mathsf{WEP}^+(\partial \Phi, \chi) \rrbracket^{\mathrm{PL}} \Leftrightarrow g \in \llbracket \mathsf{WEP}^+(\Phi, \chi) \rrbracket^{\mathrm{PL}} \Leftrightarrow [\mathrm{IH}]$
   $\exists h(\langle g, h \rangle \in \llbracket \Phi \rrbracket^+ \ \& \ h \in \llbracket \chi \rrbracket^{\mathrm{PL}}) \Leftrightarrow \exists h(\langle g, h \rangle \in \llbracket \partial \Phi \rrbracket^+ \ \& \ h \in \llbracket \chi \rrbracket^{\mathrm{PL}})$

   $g \in \llbracket \mathsf{WEP}^-(\partial \Phi, \chi) \rrbracket^{\mathrm{PL}} \Leftrightarrow g \in \llbracket \mathsf{WEP}^-(\top, \chi) \rrbracket^{\mathrm{PL}} \Leftrightarrow [\mathrm{IH}]$
   $\exists h(\langle g, h \rangle \in \llbracket \top \rrbracket^- \ \& \ h \in \llbracket \chi \rrbracket^{\mathrm{PL}}) \Leftrightarrow \exists h(\langle g, h \rangle \in \llbracket \partial \Phi \rrbracket^- \ \& \ h \in \llbracket \chi \rrbracket^{\mathrm{PL}})$

7. (Let Φ be of the form $\partial \Psi$ or $[\vec{x} \mid \varphi_1, \ldots, \varphi_m]$)
   $g \in \llbracket \overline{\mathsf{DEF}}(\Phi) \rrbracket^{\mathrm{PL}} \Leftrightarrow$
   $g \in \llbracket \mathsf{WEP}^+(\Phi, \top) \vee \mathsf{WEP}^-(\Phi, \top) \rrbracket^{\mathrm{PL}} \Leftrightarrow$
   $g \in \llbracket \mathsf{WEP}^+(\Phi, \top) \rrbracket^{\mathrm{PL}} \text{ or } g \in \llbracket \mathsf{WEP}^-(\Phi, \top) \rrbracket^{\mathrm{PL}} \Leftrightarrow [\mathrm{IH}]$
   $\exists h(\langle g, h \rangle \in \llbracket \Phi \rrbracket^+ \ \& \ h \in \llbracket \top \rrbracket^{\mathrm{PL}}) \text{ or } \exists h(\langle g, h \rangle \in \llbracket \Phi \rrbracket^- \ \& \ h \in \llbracket \top \rrbracket^{\mathrm{PL}}) \Leftrightarrow$
   $\exists h \langle g, h \rangle \in \llbracket \Phi \rrbracket^+ \text{ or } \exists h \langle g, h \rangle \in \llbracket \Phi \rrbracket^- \Leftrightarrow$
   $\mathrm{DEF}_g(\Phi)$

8. $g \in \llbracket \overline{\mathsf{DEF}}(\sim \Phi) \rrbracket^{\mathrm{PL}} \Leftrightarrow g \in \llbracket \overline{\mathsf{DEF}}(\Phi) \rrbracket^{\mathrm{PL}} \Leftrightarrow [\mathrm{IH}] \mathrm{DEF}_g(\Phi) \Leftrightarrow \mathrm{DEF}_g(\sim \Phi)$

9. $g \in \llbracket \overline{\mathsf{DEF}}(\Phi \, ; \Psi) \rrbracket^{\mathrm{PL}} \Leftrightarrow$
   $g \in \llbracket \overline{\mathsf{DEF}}(\Phi) \wedge \neg \mathsf{WEP}^+(\Phi, \neg \overline{\mathsf{DEF}}(\Psi)) \rrbracket^{\mathrm{PL}} \Leftrightarrow$
   $g \in \llbracket \overline{\mathsf{DEF}}(\Phi) \rrbracket^{\mathrm{PL}} \ \& \ g \in \llbracket \neg \mathsf{WEP}^+(\Phi, \neg \overline{\mathsf{DEF}}(\Psi)) \rrbracket^{\mathrm{PL}} \Leftrightarrow [\mathrm{IH}]$
   $g \in \llbracket \overline{\mathsf{DEF}}(\Phi) \rrbracket^{\mathrm{PL}} \ \& \ \neg \exists h(\langle g, h \rangle \in \llbracket \Phi \rrbracket^+ \ \& \ h \in \llbracket \neg \overline{\mathsf{DEF}}(\Psi) \rrbracket^{\mathrm{PL}}) \Leftrightarrow$
   $g \in \llbracket \overline{\mathsf{DEF}}(\Phi) \rrbracket^{\mathrm{PL}} \ \& \ \forall h(\langle g, h \rangle \in \llbracket \Phi \rrbracket^+ \Rightarrow h \in \llbracket \overline{\mathsf{DEF}}(\Psi) \rrbracket^{\mathrm{PL}}) \Leftrightarrow [\mathrm{IH}]$
   $\mathrm{DEF}_g(\Phi) \ \& \ \forall h(\langle g, h \rangle \in \llbracket \Phi \rrbracket^+ \Rightarrow \mathrm{DEF}_h(\Psi)) \Leftrightarrow$
   $\mathrm{DEF}_g(\Phi \, ; \Psi)$

$\square$

7

Presupposition and Determinedness

7.1 Introduction

Let us now turn to the question what the meaning is of the most frequently used word in English: *the* (Bolinger 1975).

In the previous chapter we have extended the language of Double Negation DRT with presuppositional DRSs, and revised the Revised Construction Algorithm from chapter 3 accordingly. One of the additional rules concerned definite descriptions, and it is this rule which plays a central role in the present chapter. The construction rule for definite descriptions looked as follows:

Definite Descriptions Rule
Upon encountering an NP of the form 'the α', replace it with a new discourse referent x and prefix the current DRS with ∂ $\boxed{\begin{array}{c} x \\ \hline x\ \alpha \end{array}}$

α is the Common Noun (*CN*) part of the definite description. When α is entirely processed, the semantic result is the 'property' attributed to x. When no rules from the construction algorithm can be applied to α (α is a single, simple noun), we write $\alpha(x)$ instead of $x\ \alpha$.

This rule represents definite descriptions as triggers of an existential presupposition. Let us discuss the effects of this in a little more detail by looking at some examples.[1] First, consider example (1).

---

[1] Recall from the previous chapter that we can associate two different approaches to presupposition with Presuppositional DRT. In this chapter we opt for the semantic approach unless otherwise indicated. It should be stressed that nothing hinges on this choice. For the purposes of this chapter it is immaterial which of the two approaches is chosen, since this chapter is not concerned with projection predictions, but with the *contents* of the elementary presuppositions triggered by definite descriptions.

(1)   The king of France is bald.

The Revised Construction Algorithm (sketched in section 6.4) produces the following DRS for this sentence.[2]

(DRS 1)

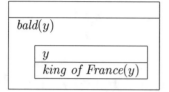

According to (DRS 1), sentence (1) presupposes the existence of a king of France, but it fails to capture another aspect commonly associated with examples like (1): the *uniqueness effect*. Consider (2).

(2)   The king of France is bald. # Another king of France told me so.

A mere existence presupposition cannot account for the oddity of the second sentence of (2). After all, it does not rule out the existence of other kings. Another, related aspect of example (1) is that it can be used at the beginning of a discourse. In particular, it does not need any preceding sentences to 'license' the definite description. This is different for the second sentence of the following two-sentence discourse.[3]

(3)   A man and a boy walk in the street. The man whistles.

The Revised Construction Algorithm first operates on the first sentence, which results in (DRS 2).

(DRS 2)

$$x, y$$
$$man(x)$$
$$walk(x)$$
$$boy(y)$$
$$walk(y)$$

Since this DRS is fully reduced the next sentence is processed, for which the algorithm outputs (DRS 3), which is sequenced with (DRS 2)

---

[2] Recall that this is an abbreviation of $\partial[y \mid \textit{king of France}(y)] ; [\mid \textit{bald}(y)]$.

[3] In the first sentence a second indefinite was added to make the use of the definite description in the second sentence more natural. If there was only one possible antecedent, the description would probably be replaced by a suitable pronoun. This is explained by the Gricean maxims, which oblige the speaker to be as informative as necessary. A particularly interesting study in this respect is Gundel et al. 1993, where the use of an NP is related to a universal 'givenness hierarchy', consisting of various cognitive statuses each corresponding with a particular kind of NP.

(DRS 3)

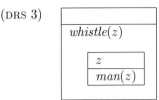

(DRS 3) again triggers an existential presupposition, but in this case the representation fails to capture the intuition that the man which is the subject of the second sentence, and whose existence is presupposed in (DRS 3), is the same man who was mentioned in the first sentence, and introduced in (DRS 2).[4] After all, the presuppositional DRS merely requires the existence of *some* man; no identification needs to be established. Notice that this example intuitively does not display a uniqueness effect: continuing (3) with (4) is not semantically marked.[5]

(4)   Another man quietly follows them.

Finally, consider the following variant of example (3).

(5)   A man and a boy walk in the street. The man's wife follows them in secret.

These two sentences are represented as the sequencing of (DRS 2) with (DRS 4).[6]

(DRS 4)

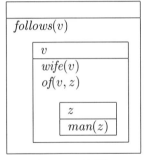

---

[4]Of course this intuition is discounted into Van der Sandt's resolution mechanism. See section 7.3 below.

[5]Kadmon 1990 has a different intuition (as does Evans 1977): she claims that examples such as (3), without additional context, give rise to absolute uniqueness: the man who walks in the street has to be unique in *all* models. We agree with Heim 1982 however, who claims that anaphoric definites do not give rise to any systematic uniqueness predictions.

[6]Since we do not discuss plurality in this book, we shall ignore the plural pronoun *them*. It is not relevant for our present purposes. Note that it poses no problems for the version of DRT presented in Kamp and Reyle 1993, where a complex discourse referent is introduced which is the *summation* of the two referents standing in for a boy and a man respectively.

Here again, the intuition is that *the man* is understood as the man mentioned in the first sentence. The man is not felt to be unique, but his wife is.

So, the existence presupposition triggered by the definite descriptions rule yields predictions which are too weak for the examples we discussed so far. The source of this weakness varies: for (1) no uniqueness effect is predicted, for (3) no link with the previous sentence, and for (5) neither. Since the rule for definite descriptions fails for different reasons, the possibility presents itself of replacing it for several rules; say, one corresponding with the 'unique' use and one corresponding with the 'anaphoric' use, giving rise to different representations in each case. This is an unattractive option, however, since the definite article itself is not felt to be ambiguous in this way; in fact it has been argued that *the* is not ambiguous at all. Perhaps the strongest claim in this respect was formulated by Löbner. He writes:[7]

The definite article has one and the same meaning in all its uses. This applies to count noun as well as mass noun cases, and for singular and plural likewise. (Löbner 1986:280)

Following Löbner's claim, we treat the definite article as unambiguous. As a consequence we assume that there is a single construction rule which applies to *all* definite descriptions. To achieve this, an extra condition is added to the presuppositional representation of a definite description, namely that it is *determined* (to use a relatively neutral term, proposed by Krámský 1976). This results in the following modified construction rule:

---

[7]Even though we agree with this claim, we will not be able to do full justice to it in the present chapter. First, the formal, dynamic analysis of plurals and mass nouns falls outside the scope of this book. We do intend the proposals made in this chapter to be applicable to plural and mass definites as well however. This means that we would need discourse referents for such complex entities (see for instance Link 1983, Bunt 1985, and in a dynamic framework, Van den Berg 1989, 1996b and Kamp and Reyle 1993). A *usage* of the definite article we will not discuss is the generic use. However, it is nowadays often accepted that generic readings are a property of sentences, rather than of NPs (see, for instance, De Swart 1994). Therefore generic readings are often attributed to a (possibly implicit) sentential quantifier (like *usually*). When genericity is not a property of NPs, we do not have to account for the generic reading of definite descriptions in the interpretation of *the*. In De Swart 1994, the generic operator is treated roughly as an unselective quantifier, binding all free variables in its scope, where a special operator is used to disclose quantified variables. Such an analysis seems compatible with the proposals in this chapter.

Definite Descriptions Rule — Modified

Upon encountering an NP of the form 'the α', replace it
with a new discourse referent x and prefix the current DRS

with ∂

x
$x\ \alpha$
Determined $(x, \boxed{x\ \alpha})$

Abusing notation a little bit, $\boxed{x\ \alpha}$ will be the set of conditions on x introduced by the *CN* α.[8] When no more construction rules can be applied,
$\boxed{x\ \alpha}$ has been turned into a DRS Φ in which x occurs free. If Φ does not
introduce new discourse referents, we just write $\mathsf{Determined}(x, \vec{\varphi})$ instead
of $\mathsf{Determined}(x, \Phi)$, where $\vec{\varphi}$ are the conditions of Φ.[9] It is not difficult
to see how the revision of the definite descriptions rule influences the
DRSs for the examples we discussed above. For (1) we now derive (DRS
5) instead of (DRS 1).

(DRS 5)

$bald(y)$	
	y
	$king\ of\ France(y)$
	$\mathsf{Determined}(y, king\ of\ France(y))$

In this case the determinedness condition should do justice to the uniqueness implication and to the related fact that the description does not
require an antecedent. For the second sentence of (3) the new Revised
Construction Algorithm generates (DRS 6) instead of (DRS 3).

---

[8]'Abusing': if α contains material which is moved out of the presuppositional DRS
by the Revised Construction Algorithm, it is also moved out of the determinedness
condition.

[9]$\boxed{x\ \alpha}$ triggers the introduction of a new discourse referent when α contains an
indefinite. The treatment of such embedded indefinites is rather complicated (some
should be read specific and seek widest possible scope or require direct 'anchoring' in
the model, while other embedded indefinites should stay were they originated), and
we do not discuss it here.

(DRS 6)

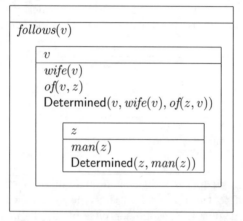

Example (3) is now represented as (DRS 2 ; DRS 6). Here the determinedness condition has to account for the anaphoric relation between *a man* and *the man*. Finally, in example (5) the two types of definite descriptions occur in a single, complex description. Here is the new DRS for this example.

(DRS 7)

Notice that Φ, the representation of the CN, plays an important role in Determined(x, Φ). As Löbner puts it: '*The definite article is just the indication of a certain way of using the noun it is attached to*' (Löbner 1986:281). A concept which will turn out to be useful in this respect is that of a *value set*. Given that Φ is a DRS representing the properties expressed by the CN and attributed to a free variable x, we are interested in the set of possible values of x: the set of objects to which the description is applicable. Define Val$(x, [\![\Phi]\!]_{M,g})$ (the set of objects which have the properties attributed to it by Φ in a model M and with respect to an assignment g) as follows:

Definition 1 (Value set)
Val$(x, [\![\Phi]\!]_{M,g}) = \{d \in D \mid M, g[x/d] \models \Phi\}$

Recall that $M, g \models \Phi$ (Φ is supported in M with respect to g) abbreviates $\exists h \langle g, h \rangle \in [\![\Phi]\!]_M^+$. Assignment $g[x/d]$ is again the assignment which is exactly like g, except that $g[x/d]$ maps x to d. The $g[x/d]$ index takes care of any free variables different from x in Φ. Here is an example.

$$\mathsf{Val}(x, [\![\,[\ |\ king(x), bald(x)]\,]\!]_{M,g}) = \{d \in D \mid d \in I(king)\ \&\ d \in I(bald)\}$$

In words, the value set of x given the DRS $[\ |\ king(x), bald(x)]$ in a model M is the set of bald kings in M. We use $|\mathsf{Val}(x, [\![\Phi]\!])|$ for the cardinality of the value set. Informally, we say that $\mathsf{Val}(x, [\![\Phi]\!]_{M,g})$ is a UD (*unique* or *upperclass denotator*) if x can only refer to a single, unique object in M and that $\mathsf{Val}(x, [\![\Phi]\!]_{M,g})$ is an LD if it can refer to more than one object in M. Notice that a UD in a model M can be an LD in a model M'. Formally:

Definition 2 (UDs and LDs)

1. $\mathsf{Val}(x, [\![\Phi]\!]_{M,g})$ is a UD if and only if $|\mathsf{Val}(x, [\![\Phi]\!]_{M,g})| = 1$
2. $\mathsf{Val}(x, [\![\Phi]\!]_{M,g})$ is an LD if and only if $|\mathsf{Val}(x, [\![\Phi]\!]_{M,g})| \geq 2$

Now a definite description presupposes existence and determinedness. But, what *is* determinedness? That is the main question we address in this chapter. We discuss four possible answers to this question. We first consider two more or less classical answers, which have been studied extensively in the semantic literature; namely *uniqueness* (section 7.2) and *anaphoricity* (section 7.3). We shall argue that neither is satisfactory, and proceed to discuss two other answers, to wit: *familiarity* (section 7.4) and *salience* (section 7.5). These suggestions can also be found in the literature on definites, although usually only in an informal manner. In this chapter we attempt to formalize these concepts in a dynamic framework, and study the effects. A complicating factor, and perhaps the main reason for the enormous attention definite descriptions have received from linguists and logicians in this century, is the large amount of phenomena which appear to have an influence on the meaning of descriptions. As said, we subscribe to Löbner's claim that the definite article is unambiguous, and hence we assume that the interpretation of the determinedness condition has to be the same for all these 'kinds' of definite descriptions. Therefore, we occasionally also ponder over the interaction between the determinedness condition and the various phenomena involving definite descriptions.[10],[11]

---

[10]But in order not to lose track of the main subject of this chapter (the determinedness condition), we shall confine these considerations mainly to the footnotes.

[11]There are several interesting recent studies of definite descriptions from the perspective of discourse semantics which discuss issues related to those discussed in the present chapter. For example, in Van Eijck 1993 definite descriptions are analysed in terms of uniqueness presuppositions using the Error-state Semantics for DPL (see also chapter 4). Groenendijk et al. 1995 employ context sets in the treatment of anaphoric descriptions in dynamic semantics. Chierchia 1995 focusses on the relation

7.2   Is Determinedness Uniqueness?

The most classical of classic approaches to definite descriptions dates back to the work of Frege and Russell, as discussed in chapter 4. Both argue that definite descriptions are about unique individuals, although they have different intuitions about the status of the uniqueness condition. Here we follow the Fregean (and Strawsonian) line, and treat it as a presupposition. So, assume that a definite description presupposes existence and uniqueness. That is: we read the Determined(x, Φ) condition in the modified construction rule for definite descriptions as Unique(x, Φ) (x is the unique Φ-er), and define:[12]

Definition 3 (Unique)
$$\llbracket \text{Unique}(x, \Phi) \rrbracket^+ = \{g \mid |\text{Val}(x, \llbracket \Phi \rrbracket_g)| = 1\}$$
$$\llbracket \text{Unique}(x, \Phi) \rrbracket^- = \{g \mid |\text{Val}(x, \llbracket \Phi \rrbracket_g)| \neq 1\}$$

This analysis essentially produces the second treatment of descriptions in Van Eijck 1993. Reconsider (DRS 5), with Determined interpreted as Unique. The new rule for definite descriptions has an obvious influence on the *content* of the elementary presupposition but not on its projection behavior. This means that (DRS 5) now presupposes the existence of a unique king of France and as a consequence the existence of another king (as in example (2)) is excluded. The situation is different for example (3). If we interpret the Determined condition in (DRS 6) in terms of uniqueness we *do* get the required co-reference. After all, the uniqueness presupposition triggered by *the man* can only be supported in a model with exactly one man, so this has to be the same man as the one introduced in the first sentence. But this means that we predict a

---

between dynamic semantics and the theory of grammar, and their influence on definite descriptions. Chierchia treats descriptions as (partial) functions from properties (plus, possibly, contextual parameters) to unique objects. Dekker 1997 argues that dynamic semantics —combined with a seperate, independently motivated, pragmatic component— sheds a new light on the referential interpretation of definite descriptions. In Von Heusinger 1995 a system of dynamic semantics is defined using choice functions (a device which goes back to the ϵ operator of Hilbert and Bernays 1939), and definite descriptions are interpreted using a choice function which selects the most salient object satisfying the descriptive content of the description. While a more detailed comparison with all these proposals with the proposals made in this chapter would certainly be interesting, it has to await a different occassion.

[12]Notice that the existence requirement is superfluous in combination with the uniqueness requirement. That is: the DRS $[x \mid \vec{\varphi}, \text{Unique}(x, \vec{\varphi})]$ is equivalent with $[x \mid \text{Unique}(x, \vec{\varphi})]$. It would be nice if we could define Unique(x, Φ) in terms of Presuppositional DRT, and in fact we can. In general, $[x \mid \vec{\varphi}, \text{Unique}(x, \vec{\varphi})]$ is equivalent with

$$[x \mid \vec{\varphi}, [y \mid \{y/x\}\vec{\varphi}] \Rightarrow [\mid x \equiv y]].$$

$\{y/x\}\vec{\varphi}$ is the simultaneous substitution of all free occurrences of x in φ for y.

uniqueness effect for this example as well. Adding a DRS for sentence (4) to (DRS 6) inevitably leads to a contradiction, which is rather unintuitive. The problem here is that 'pure' uniqueness is too strong for certain classes of definite descriptions.

7.2.1 Restricting the Uniqueness Prediction

> It sounds like a grammatical mistake —
> *happy enough*, like *rather unique*
>
> Julian Barnes, *Flaubert's parrot*

Various solutions have been proposed to weaken uniqueness predictions. Often these weakenings are based on the observation that many lexical items are restricted in their interpretation by the context. Hence, it is argued, it is only natural to add such contextual restrictions to the interpretation of descriptions as well (see Neale 1990, for example). One of the most explicit studies of context sets for descriptions is Westerståhl 1985. He writes (using X instead of C):

> (...) 'the' is not a DET but a context indicator which signals the presence of a context set C in such a way that 'the A' denotes $C \cap A$, a subset of A. (Westerståhl 1985:60)

In the discussion of the previous chapter we briefly discussed how context sets can be added to Presuppositional DRT (see page 183). So let C be some context set. We can weaken Unique by restricting the uniqueness to this C. Define $\mathsf{Unique}^C(x, \Phi)$:

Definition 4 (Unique^C)
$$[\![\mathsf{Unique}^C(x, \Phi)]\!]^+ = \{g \mid |\mathsf{Val}(x, [\![\Phi]\!]_g) \cap [\![C]\!]_g| = 1\}$$
$$[\![\mathsf{Unique}^C(x, \Phi)]\!]^- = \{g \mid |\mathsf{Val}(x, [\![\Phi]\!]_g) \cap [\![C]\!]_g| \neq 1\}$$

In the previous chapter we considered the option to let C range over the previously introduced, accessible discourse referents. This works nicely for example (3). Assume, for simplicity's sake, that this example occurs at the beginning of a discourse: C is still empty, by assumption. Then the indefinite *a man* introduces a discourse referent standing in for a man into C and the definite *the man* refers to this unique, previously introduced man.[13] Unfortunately, we cannot treat example (1) in this way; the description *the king of France* does not need context for its

---

[13] Notice that anaphoric descriptions are still associated with a (limited) form of uniqueness on this account. Problems arise when there are several alternative elements in the context set. Consider the following example, based on an example from Haddock 1987. A magician says:

> Here I have two rabbits and two hats. I put one rabbit in a hat. And now ... I will make *the rabbit in the hat* disappear.

interpretation. If we interpret example (1) with respect to an empty context set (modelling the situation in which there are no sentences preceding (1)), the restricted uniqueness presupposition incorrectly leads to presupposition failure. Thus, this way of using context sets is only useful for anaphoric definites. There are two options at this point: either the definite determiner is ambiguous or the context set is not the set of previously introduced objects. The first option is not available since, following Löbner, we assume that the definite article is not ambiguous. The second option *is* a possibility, but immediately raises a different problem: what *are* the elements of a context set? In De Swart 1994, context sets are said to contain all objects which are 'relevant' at a certain point. But this sounds like *begging the question*: what *are* the relevant objects in a given context?

It is quite impossible to discuss all proposals for realistic uniqueness in a couple of paragraphs, but it seems that they run into similar complications. Either a form of ambiguity is required (treating the definite determiner in example (1) different from the one in example (3)) or a complex, non-uniform mechanism is required to guarantee uniqueness after all. An example of the latter is the treatment of uniqueness developed in Kadmon 1987, 1990. Kadmon allows for the addition of '*implicated, accommodated and contextually supplied material*' (Kadmon 1990:286) to the current DRS in order to guarantee that uniqueness is satisfied.[14] We agree with Kadmon that uniqueness is a relevant concept for the analysis of definite NPs, but disagree that it is the fundamental property underlying *all* definite NPs. In this respect we are in full agreement with Heim 1982, where a systematic analysis of definites in terms of uniqueness is rejected and uniqueness only plays a secondary, derived role. In fact, Heim's analysis of definite NPs is an example of the second classic approach we want to discuss.

7.3   Is Determinedness Anaphoricity?

Another classical approach to definite NPs says that they essentially behave as anaphors. We have encountered several variants of this idea in the preceding chapters. In File Change Semantics (FCS) all definites are treated as anaphors. Van der Sandt's presuppositions-as-anaphora theory can be seen as a generalization of this approach to all presupposition

---

The context set contains two rabbits and two hats, so neither *the hat* nor *the rabbit* can select a unique, previously introduced hat or rabbit.

[14]This would allow her to treat descriptions like *the rabbit in the hat* in footnote 13. On the other hand, she still is committed to the claim that *the man* in (3) has to be the single, unique man walking in the street in all models (Kadmon 1990:284). See also footnote 21.

triggers. Let us look in more detail at the way in which Heim's FCS deals with definite NPs. In chapter 2 we discussed the Novelty/Familiarity Condition, repeated below.

Definition 5 (Novelty/Familiarity Condition)

A Logical form φ is *well-formed* iff for every NP_n in φ it holds that

∘　if NP_n is [+ def], it is preceded by an NP_n

∘　if NP_n is [− def], it is not preceded by an NP_n

The Novelty/Familiarity Condition operates on Logical forms; if an Lf contains a definite NP (an NP labeled [+ def]) with index n, then it has to be preceded at the level of Lf by an NP with the same index. In other words: a definite NP has to be anaphoric. Semantically speaking, a definite has to pick up a previously introduced discourse referent. As noted in chapter 2, Heim ultimately argues for her *Extended* Novelty/Familiarity Condition, which is essentially a condition on Logical forms but with the additional semantic requirement that a definite NP presupposes the existence of an object satisfying the descriptive content. Thus, according to the Extended NFC, a definite description presupposes existence and anaphoricity. In terms of the present chapter: the definite description is determined if it is anaphoric. So, let us introduce a condition Anaphoric(x, Φ) (*x is an anaphoric Φ-er*), and give it the following interpretation.

Definition 6 (Anaphoric)

$[\![\mathsf{Anaphoric}(x, \Phi)]\!]^+ = \{g \mid [\![x]\!]_g \text{ defined }\}$

$[\![\mathsf{Anaphoric}(x, \Phi)]\!]^- = \{g \mid [\![x]\!]_g \text{ not defined }\}$

It is easily seen that the anaphoricity condition on x is satisfied iff the variable x has already been introduced and is accessible. To make this work we have to alter the modified construction rule for descriptions: we do not introduce a new discourse referent but pick up an old one. Since determinedness/anaphoricity is only a matter of variable *names*, the descriptive content Φ does not play any role here.[15]

This anaphoricity analysis of definites works fine for the two-sentence discourse (3), which is represented as the sequencing of (DRS 2) and (DRS 6). In this last DRS, the determinedness condition is now interpreted in terms of Anaphoric. Picking up the discourse referent x introduced by the

---

[15]In fact, the anaphoricity condition is essentially built into the interpretation of Presuppositional DRT. In particular, every variable which occurs free in $\vec{\varphi}$ has to be defined (and hence previously introduced) anyway. Thus, $\partial[\ |R(x), \mathsf{Anaphoric}(x, R(x))]$ is equivalent with $\partial[\ |R(x)]$. So, again the effect of the determinedness condition can be achieved in terms of the language of Presuppositional DRT as well.

indefinite *a man* satisfies the existence and anaphoricity presupposition. On the other hand, this approach to definites will not work for example (1): descriptions of this type are not used anaphorically. The situation may be compared with Unique^C. In fact, Westerståhl relates his context sets to Heim's 'file-cards':

> The contextual reference of 'the' is basic in her [*Heim's*, EK] treatment (...) and she accounts for it by means of free individual variables, rather similarly to our set variables. Finally she not only gives a formal framework, but also attempts to explain how values are given to the variables. (Westerståhl 1985:70,fn3)

Notice that restricted uniqueness *à la* Unique^C is still a form of uniqueness, while uniqueness is alien from Heim's anaphoricity notion. As an aside, notice that Heim's Novelty Condition can also be modeled semantically in terms of Presuppositional DRT, by defining:

$$\mathsf{Novel}(x, \Phi) = \neg[\; | \; \mathsf{Anaphoric}(x, \Phi)]$$

Hence $\mathsf{Novel}(x, \Phi)$ is supported when x has not been introduced before. As a result, the condition predicts that an example such as the following is fine (which it is not, in general) as long as a *new* discourse referent is introduced.

(6)   # A tallest Frenchman would like to have a new XXXXL T-shirt.

The generalization here seems to be that a true UD requires a definite determiner.

7.3.1 Accommodating Missing Antecedents

Heim was well aware of the limitations of her analysis of definites, and she proposed a mechanism to deal with them: *accommodation*. Accommodation is a strong mechanism and the way Heim uses it has its roots in Lewis 1979. He writes:

> Say something that requires a missing presupposition, and straightaway that presupposition springs into existence, making what you said acceptable after all. (Lewis 1979:339)

This leads Lewis to define his *Rule for accommodation for presuppositions*:

> If at time t something is said that requires presupposition P to be acceptable, and if P is not presupposed just before t, then —*ceteris paribus* and within certain limits— presupposition P comes into existence at t.

Obviously this process has to be restricted, and one of the restrictions Heim proposes is a *cross-reference constraint*. Informally, this constraint can be paraphrased as follows: we only accommodate an antecedent for a definite NP if it is not entirely novel. A proto-typical example is the two-sentence discourse (5). The description *the man's wife* is partly novel and partly anaphoric: there is an antecedent for the man, but not for his wife. But, because this wife is not entirely novel (she is anaphorically related to the man mentioned in the first sentence), we are allowed to accommodate an antecedent for her. Exactly how this process can be formalized need not concern us here. The point is that this method of accommodation does not work for non-anaphoric definites, of which (1) contains an example. A description referring to a unique object simply does not need to be 'licensed' by a linguistic antecedent.

One might argue that Heim uses the wrong kind of accommodation. After all, the way accommodation is employed by Van der Sandt is also restricted by conditions, but these are of a different nature than the cross-reference constraint. Yet, intuitively, as Zeevat has remarked, certain classes of definites simply do not seem to participate in accommodation since '(...) *their content is already sufficient to yield a referent without any contextual dependency*' (Zeevat 1992:407).

Let us take stock. In the introduction we argued that definite descriptions presuppose existence and something we have called determinedness, and raised the question of what this 'something' is. We discussed two classical answers: uniqueness and anaphoricity. We have seen that they work well for disjoint sets of examples, and that is not easy to extend the coverage of the respective analyses. Below, we propose two alternatives with their roots in the linguistic tradition. In the next section, we discuss the notion of *familiarity* as it was proposed in the structuralist literature. This is the notion on which Heim bases her version of familiarity, but it will turn out that Heim's version models only a restricted notion of familiarity. We shall formalize the wider notion in terms of Presuppositional DRT and discuss its merits. In the section thereafter, we discuss another notion which was introduced in connection with definite NPs: *salience*. We shall also attempt to formalize a salience condition in the present framework, and discuss its pros and cons.

7.4 Determinedness is Familiarity

The notions of familiarity and novelty are not new; they have a long tradition in the linguistic literature. The concept of familiarity which emerges from Heim's sources turns out to be more involved than plain anaphoricity. In this section we will see what the intuition behind this notion of familiarity is, and how it can be formalized in terms of Presuppositional DRT.

It is often suggested that Christopherson 1939 is the reference where familiarity originates, but in fact the concept is much older.[16] Already in Miklosich 1874 a treatment of descriptions in terms of familiarity is argued for, and also in Sweet 1898 one can find such a claim. Zubatý 1917 writes:

> It is just only the familiarity of the subject in the broadest sense of the word which is indicated by the [*definite*, EK] article.

Gamillscheg 1937 writes that the definite article is an indication to the hearer that:

> (...) was nun folgt, ist dir, dem Hörenden, in seinem Wesen bekannt.[17]

In Christopherson 1939 we find the familiarity theory which both Heim 1982 and Löbner 1986 claim as a source of inspiration. Krámský summarizes Christopherson's theory as follows:

> The definite article causes that to the potential meaning of a unit-word [a *singular count noun*, EK] a certain association with the earlier knowledge is added from which it can be concluded that only one individual is meant. (...) Our familiarity with the indicated subject may be quite small but important is that we feel that the word stands for a certain individual. (page 26)

Christopherson realized that this 'association' may be indirect, his example is *the author*:

> (...) as each book has its author, the knowledge of the book automatically implies a certain author. (page 26)

This quote shows that Christopherson was well aware of this phenomenon, and that he did not see it as an exception to his familiarity thesis. About 'unique' nouns (which may be understood as those nouns which are represented as UDs), Krámský attributes Christopherson the following observation:

> Familiarity presupposes delimination and definiteness. Both these qualities are present in unique nouns. (page 27)

What is meant exactly with the words 'delimination' and 'definiteness' need not concern us here, but what is important is that Christopherson

---

[16]Krámský 1972 is particularly interesting from this point of view. He discusses various approaches to definites which have been proposed in the linguistic literature. The quotes in this paragraph come from his book, unless otherwise indicated.

[17]'(...) what follows now is in its essence familiar to you, the hearer.'

takes it for granted that UDs ('unique' nouns) satisfy the familiarity constraint. About indefinites and UDs we read the following:

> It is evident that it [*the indefinite article*, EK] cannot be used with absolute "uniques". Of course, there are only very few genuine "uniques". It is quite possible to say *a sun* but this deprives the word of its uniqueness. (page 27)

In other words, the indefinite determiner in example (6) should be ruled out, at least as long as *tallest Frenchman* is assumed to be a genuine "unique".

We cannot draw any strong conclusion from this short historical intermezzo, but it seems safe to say that Heim's interpretation leads to a somewhat restricted notion of familiarity. Put differently: familiarity is more than plain anaphoricity. Assuming that the definite article indicates that the CN it precedes is familiar, let us consider the following hypothesis, to be formalized below: *A (singular) CN satisfies the familiarity condition (use of the definite determiner is correct) when a single object can be selected to which the CN applies.*[18] How can we single out one object from a whole set of objects on the basis of some properties? One possibility is that there *is* only one object to which the description can refer. In that case it is easy, and the familiarity is immediately satisfied. But suppose that the CN is applicable to more than one individual, even though it is preceded by the definite article, which by assumption indicates familiarity. In that case, we should be able to select one individual on the basis of the context. For now, let us restrict our attention to the *linguistic* context. In short: we can say that the familiarity is satisfied if the set of objects which have the property denoted by the CN is a singleton (it is a UD), or consists of at least two elements (it is an LD) but one of them can be selected on the basis of the context.[19] Notice that this linguistically motivated concept of familiarity subsumes both the uniqueness (selecting one object on the

---

[18]This hypothesis may be compared with the theory of definiteness proposed in Löbner 1986. In this interesting paper, Löbner argues that the 'determinedness' in the analysis of definites should be interpreted as non-ambiguity (or preferably: *eindeutigkeit*). The main part of Löbner 1986 is devoted to the ways in which non-anaphoric uses of descriptions can be understood in terms of non-ambiguity.

[19]Interestingly, this is close to the way the definite article is used according to Strawson:

> We use 'the' either when a previous reference has been made, and when 'the' signalizes that the same reference is being made; or when, in the absence of a previous indefinite reference, the context (including the hearer's assumed knowledge) is expected to enable the hearer to tell *what* reference is being made. (Strawson 1950:49)

basis of model-theoretic properties) and the anaphoricity (selecting one
element from the linguistic context) discussed in the previous sections.
This leads to a single familiarity condition, even though the familiarity
of an object can be satisfied in different ways. Below we discuss the
consequences of this approach. First, let us formulate it in terms of
Presuppositional DRT.

We consider the analysis in which a definite description presupposes
existence and familiarity; that is, we interpret determinedness as familiarity. Introduce a condition $\mathsf{Familiar}(x, \Phi)$ (x *is the familiar* Φ-*er*) and
interpret it as follows:

Definition 7 (Familiar)
$[\![\mathsf{Familiar}(x, \Phi)]\!]^{+} =$
$\qquad \{g \mid |\mathsf{Val}(x, [\![\Phi]\!]_g)| = 1 \text{ or } \exists v \in \mathsf{Dom}(g)(v \neq x \,\&\, g(v) = g(x))\}$
$[\![\mathsf{Familiar}(x, \Phi)]\!]^{-} =$
$\qquad \{g \mid |\mathsf{Val}(x, [\![\Phi]\!]_g)| \neq 1 \,\&\, \forall v \in \mathsf{Dom}(g)(v \neq x \Rightarrow g(v) \neq g(x))\}$

So the familiarity of an object x with property Φ is supported in a model
M with respect to an assignment g if either the value set of x in Φ given
M, g is a singleton, or there is a previously introduced object, which
(by the existence presupposition) has the right properties. It is rejected
if the value set of x in Φ is not a singleton and there is no previously
introduced object with the right properties.[20]

How does this work for the examples discussed in section 7.1? First
re-consider example (1) and suppose that we interpret its representation
(DRS 5) (with Determined read as Familiar) in a model with a unique
king of France. In that case, the new discourse referent y introduced by
the definite description has to refer to that particular object and both
the existence and the familiarity requirements are met. When there is
no king of France in the model neither the existence nor the familiarity
condition can be supported and presupposition failure is the result. If
there were several kings of France in the model, presupposition failure
would also be the result: the existence condition can be satisfied, but
the familiarity condition not. After all, there are no preceding sentences
which would allow one of the French monarchs to be singled out. As for
example (3) and its representation (DRS 2 ; DRS 6): suppose that a model
contains several men. The indefinite *a man* introduces a discourse referent referring to a male individual (not deterministically!) and in each
case the familiarity constraint connected with *the man* applies to that
particular male individual. So, the familiarity condition is satisfied *per*

---

[20] When we add contextual DRSs (as defined in section 6.7) to the language, we can
define $\mathsf{Familiar}(x, \Phi)$ in Presuppositional DRT as $[\, |\mathsf{Unique}(x, \Phi)] \vee (C/x)\,[v \mid v \equiv x]$,
where $[\![C/x]\!]_g = \{g(z) \mid z \in (C - \{x\})\}$.

possible extension. Notice that the definite description still introduces a new discourse referent. The familiarity condition merely requires the interpretation of this new referent to be previously 'discussed'. Finally, mixed cases as found in (5) pose no problems either. The embedded description *the man* is treated just like the description in (3). Then it is checked whether or not the wife of this man is familiar *per* choice of man. So, either the man in question has a single wife and the presupposition is satisfied, or the man in question does not have a single wife and the presupposition is not satisfied (since the linguistic context (= the first sentence of example (3)) does not mention any spouses).[21] So, interpreting Determined as Familiar indeed enables us to deal with examples (1), (3) and (5). Notice that we can define novelty of an object as non-familiarity:[22]

Definition 8 (Novel)
$\mathsf{Novel}(x, \Phi) = \neg[\ |\mathsf{Familiar}(x, \Phi)]$

---

[21] Above we observed that the value set of a DRS can be a UD in one model and an LD in another. It is generally assumed that the 'mental state' of a hearer is not represented by a single model, but rather consists of a *set* of (preferably partial) models, called *epistemic alternatives* in Beaver 1992. To make the present proposal fit in with this wider perspective, we need to generalize it into something like the following: the familiarity of the representation of a CN is satisfied if it is either a UD in all epistemic alternatives, or an LD in all epistemic alternatives and in that case the context is invoked. Notice that the situation in which the representation is a UD in one epistemic alternative and an LD in another, corresponds with the situation in which it is not 'known' whether or not the relevant property is unique. The restriction to epistemic alternatives would also allow us to make sense of Kadmon's claim that a definite can only refer to an object which is unique in *all models*, by restricting the quantifier '*all*' to epistemic alternatives.

[22] Notice that this treatment of indefinites is again related to the way we use indefinites according to Strawson 1950:49.

> We use 'a' either when these conditions [*the conditions cited in footnote 19*, EK] are not fulfilled, or when, although a definite reference *could* be made, we wish to keep dark the identity of the individual to whom, or to which, we are referring.

The novelty condition defined here only does justice to the first disjunct of Strawson's characterization: *specificity* of indefinites is beyond the scope of this book. Notice, incidentally, that there is also another possibility, not mentioned by Strawson: the speaker uses an indefinite NP since he assumes that the object he refers to is not familiar to the *hearer*. This does not mean that the *speaker* is not familiar with the object. An attractive possibility, which we will not pursue here, is to equate specific uses of an indefinite with an indefinite which is familiar for the speaker but novel for the hearer. This is in line with the analysis of specific indefinites proposed by Ludlow and Neale 1990. They argue that an indefinite can be either weakly or strongly specific. In both cases the speaker utters a sentence with a particular individual in mind, but he assumes that the hearer will not realize that it is about a single individual (weakly specific) or he intends or suspects that the hearer will not be able to deduce who this particular individual is (strongly specific).

If we translate the indefinite determiner using a novelty presupposition, then we predict that example (6) leads to presupposition failure in any model in which there is only one tallest Frenchman.[23] This tallest Frenchman is familiar and, by assumption, the definite article should have been used.

We started this section with a brief historical survey into the linguistic notion of familiarity from which it became clear that it is more involved than Heim's version of it. A formalization of this wider notion of familiarity was presented which turned out to subsume both the uniqueness and the anaphoricity analyses discussed before. In this way, the examples from the introduction could all be dealt with, without invoking restricted uniqueness or accommodation of missing antecedents.

Above we argued against an ambiguity for the definite article, but one could say that even though Familiar is a single condition encompassing several subcases, the ambiguity in some sense returns via the back-door at a lower level. After all, the positive extension of Familiar(x, Φ) contains a disjunction. Did we miss a generalization?

7.5 Determinedness is Salience

There is an informal discussion in Lewis 1979 concerning the treatment of descriptions.[24] Lewis suggests that a definite description refers to the *most salient* element satisfying the descriptive content (Lewis 1979:348–350). Lewis mentions the following example:

(7)   The pig is grunting, but the pig with the floppy ears is not grunting.

This sentence can be uttered without any linguistic context, for instance, when the speaker is walking past a piggery. So, the definite descriptions are not used anaphorically. For (7) to be true, there have to be at least *two* pigs, one of which is grunting, one of which is not. So, the definite descriptions cannot be interpreted using (some contextual weakening) of uniqueness. According to Lewis, (7) is true if *the pig* refers to the most salient pig (and this most salient pig is grunting) while *the pig with the floppy ears* refers to the most salient pig *with floppy ears* (and this pig is not grunting). Lewis does not mention descriptions which refer to unique objects, but it is not a major effort to see that they can also

---

[23]The assumption that novelty is a presupposition has the following consequences for non-denoting indefinites: they give rise to presupposition failure. So, as things stand, both *a square circle* and *the square circle* cause presupposition failure. An alternative is to treat novelty not as a presupposition, but as part of the assertion. In that case, 'non-existing' indefinites give rise to falsity, which is more in line with classical approaches to indefinites.

[24]Lewis' discussion of definite descriptions in terms of salience goes back to Lewis 1973:111–117, and McCawley 1979.

be understood in terms of salience. After all, if there is only one object with the right properties, it *has* to be the most salient one with these properties. In this section, we present a full, dynamic characterization of salience. The funny thing is that this results in a condition which is closely related to Familiar *qua* predictions, even though there are some subtle, but important, differences.

We assume that each object in the domain of discourse has a 'salience weight', and that a definite description refers to the object which has the highest salience weight among the objects with the relevant properties at that point. In the initial situation (say, the beginning of a discourse) all objects are equally salient by assumption. One central question is how an object increases in salience. Heim 1982, in a discussion of Lewis' suggestion, offers the following possibility:[25]

A necessary condition of an utterance of a sentence S to promote an object x to maximal salience is that S contain either an NP that refers to x or a singular indefinite whose predicate is true of x. (Heim 1982:21)

Since indefinites are interpreted non-deterministically in Presuppositional DRT, the increase of salience weight is done *per case* (assignment). This marks an important departure from Lewis' idea. He discusses the following example:

(8)   A cat is on the lawn.

And writes in a remark:

---

[25] A notion of salience increase based entirely on model-theoretic properties is attractive, but will not work. Heim points to Partee's marble sentences.

(†) a. I dropped ten marbles and found all of them, except for one.
       It/The marble is probably under the sofa.
    b. I dropped ten marbles and found only nine of them.
       # It/The marble is probably under the sofa.

In (†.a) the description *the marble* can easily refer to the missing marble (even though a pronoun, as in Partee's example, is more natural) since the first sentence contains an NP (*one*) referring to it. In (†.b) (the first sentence of which is semantically equivalent with the first sentence of (†.a)) this is not unproblematic. That a description like *the missing marble* is possible in both cases is a different matter: such associative/anaphoric cases are discussed later on (notice that there is a most salient *missing* marble). Another relevant pair of examples, derived from Quine and cited in Evans 1977:159 is the following:

(‡) a. John owns a donkey. He beats it/the donkey.
    b. John is a donkey-owner. # He beats it/them/the donkey(s).

In (‡.a) *it/the donkey* refers to the donkey mentioned in the first sentence, but in the (‡.b) such a link is not easily established, even though the two first sentences are semantically equivalent.

What I said was an existential quantification; hence, strictly speaking, it involves no reference to any particular cat. Nevertheless, it raises the salience of the cat that made me say it. (...) Thus although indefinite descriptions —that is, idioms of existential quantification— are not themselves referring expressions, they may raise the salience of particular individuals in such a way as to pave the way for referring expressions that follow. (Lewis 1979:350)

The version of salience defined below in no way requires an indefinite to be used in such a way that there is a specific individual to which the indefinite refers. This means that examples such as the following provide no problems for the present version of salience:

(9)   If a farmer has a farm-hand, then *the farm-hand* will feed the animals.

Assume that the indefinites *a farmer* and *a farm-hand* are represented by discourse referents x and y respectively. On the Presuppositional DRT interpretation of a conditional with respect to some assignment g, all extensions h such that $g\{x,y\}h$ and such that $h(x)$ is a farmer which has $h(y)$ as farm-hand are relevant. So, in general, a range of values of x and y are considered (that is: on the assumption that a given model contains several farmers and several farm-hands). With respect to each assignment h, the objects $h(x)$ and $h(y)$ become more salient, where the duration of this increase in salience coincides with the life-span of the referents. Given each extension of h, the discourse referent introduced in the representation of the definite description *the farm-hand* is required to refer to the most salient object which is a farm-hand, and without additional context this is $h(y)$.

One way to model salience in Presuppositional DRT is as follows. We extend the set of variables Var with a function-variable sw ('salience weight'), interpreted with respect to an assignment g as $g(sw) \in \mathbb{N}^D$. That is: $g(sw)$ is some total function from D into the natural numbers. Let me note immediately that there are also other, perhaps more elegant, methods to mark salience. We can, for instance, impose some orderings on the relevant objects. But since we are primarily interested in the *effects* of a salience condition we stick to the simple addition of sw here. We now interpret Presuppositional DRT with respect to all finite assignments whose domain includes sw. That is, we replace F (the set of finite assignments, mapping finite subsets of Var to D) with F^{sw}, where $F^{sw} = \{f \in F \mid sw \in \mathsf{Dom}(f)\}$. To keep things simple, let us assume that in the beginning of a discourse all objects are equally salient. This corresponds with the element Λ^{sw} of F^{sw}, where $\mathsf{Dom}(\Lambda^{sw}) = \{sw\}$ and $\Lambda^{sw}(sw)$ is the constant function mapping every element of D to 1.

How does an object get more salient? Let us make the minimal assumption (following Heim's quoted suggestion) that introducing a new discourse referent leads to a re-assignment of sw. Thus, when we introduce a new referent x given some assignment g, we not only move to an assignment h such that $g\{x\}h$,[26] but we also change the interpretation of sw in such a way that:[27]

- $h(sw)(h(x)) = g(sw)(h(x)) + 1$
  (the value of the new referent, $h(x)$, rises in salience) and,

- $\forall d \in D(d \neq h(x) \Rightarrow h(sw)(d) = g(sw)(d))$
  (all other elements of the domain remain as salient as they were).

Finally, we define the determinedness condition as $\mathsf{Salient}(x, \Phi)$ (x is the most salient Φ-er), with the following interpretation.

Definition 9 (Salient)
$[\![\mathsf{Salient}(x, \Phi)]\!]^+ =$
$\quad \{g \mid \forall d \in \mathsf{Val}(x, [\![\Phi]\!])\ (d \neq g(x) \ \Rightarrow\ g(sw)(d) < g(sw)(g(x)))\}$
$[\![\mathsf{Salient}(x, \Phi)]\!]^- =$
$\quad \{g \mid \exists d \in \mathsf{Val}(x, [\![\Phi]\!])\ (d \neq g(x) \ \& \ g(sw)(d) \geq g(sw)(g(x)))\}$

So, $\mathsf{Salient}(x, \Phi)$ is supported in a model M with respect to an assignment g iff $g(x)$ is more salient than all other elements in the value set $\mathsf{Val}(x, [\![\Phi]\!]_{M,g})$ (that is: more salient than the other objects which satisfy the descriptive content Φ), it is rejected if there is an object d which satisfies the descriptive content Φ and is at least as salient as $g(x)$.

Let us now illustrate this definition, once again for the examples discussed in the introduction, beginning with (1) together with its representation (DRS 5), repeated below as (10) and (DRS 8) respectively (and with Determined interpreted as Salient).

(10)   The king of France is bald.

---

[26]Which now abbreviates: $\mathsf{Dom}(g) = \mathsf{Dom}(h) \cup \{x\}$ & $\forall y \in \mathsf{Dom}(g) - \{sw\} : g(y) = h(y)$, thus allowing re-assigning values to sw.

[27]Naturally, this is a simplification, but for the present purposes this simple version will do. We would like to stress, however, that the fact that the determination of salience weights is independent of the salience interpretation of determinedness, makes it easier to investigate the usefulness of more fine-grained definitions of sw. For example, it is an easy exercise to define the updating of sw in such a way that the main claims of *centering theory* are incorporated, which would entail, for instance, that an entity referred to in subject position is more salient than one referred to in object position (Grosz et al. 1995:214).

(DRS 8)

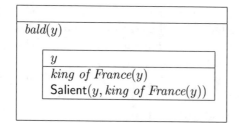

Let us assume once more that we interpret this DRS in a model M with a unique king of France —call him l— and at the beginning of a discourse. Thus, *king of France* is an UD in M and at the moment of interpretation all objects are equally salient by assumption. In that case, y can only refer to this l, and since l is the currently most salient king of France, the existence and salience presuppositions are satisfied. If the model represented the situation in which France has no king, neither the existence nor the salience condition would be supported and presupposition failure would be the result. Similarly, if the model represented the situation in which France has several kings. In that case the existence condition would be satisfied, but the salience condition would not, since —by assumption— all these kings of France would be equally salient.[28]

Now re-consider example (3) and its representation (DRS 2 ; DRS 6), repeated below as (11) and (DRS 9) respectively (again with Determined interpreted as Salient).

(11) A man and a boy walk in the street. The man whistles.

(DRS 9)

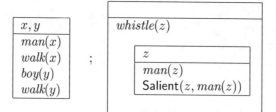

Let us assume that example (11) marks the beginning of a discourse (thus, all objects are equally salient by assumption), and that we interpret (DRS 9) in a model M which contains two men, call them a and b (thus, *man* in an LD in M). The indefinite *a man* introduces a referent x, and this x can refer to either a or b. Thus, once we have interpreted the first sub-DRS of (DRS 9) we have to consider two output-assignments:[29]

---

[28]According to the intuitions of Lewis 1973:116, however, example (10) would be false in this situation.

[29]Ignoring *the boy*, which was only added to avoid pronominal reference, see footnote 3 above.

$$h_a: \quad x \to a$$
$$h_b: \quad x \to b$$

A side-effect of these assignments is the increase in salience of the referent of x. More specifically, h_a maps sw to a function which maps a to a higher salience weight than b ($h_a(sw)(a) > h_a(sw)(b)$) and *vice versa* for h_b ($h_b(sw)(b) > h_b(sw)(a)$). Now we interpret the second sub-DRS with respect to these output-assignments (recall that ; is interpreted as relational composition). The presupposition triggered by the definite *the man* introduces a fresh referent z standing for a man, and again z can refer to either a or b. This means that we evaluate the salience condition with respect to essentially four relevant assignments:

$$\begin{aligned}
h_{aa}: &\quad x \to a, \quad z \to a \\
h_{ab}: &\quad x \to a, \quad z \to b \\
h_{ba}: &\quad x \to b, \quad z \to a \\
h_{bb}: &\quad x \to b, \quad z \to b
\end{aligned}$$

Consider first h_{aa}. Does z refer to the most salient man with respect to this assignment? The answer is *yes*, since z refers to a and this man has been referred to previously and as a consequence $h_{aa}(sw)(a) > h_{aa}(sw)(b)$. Using this line of reasoning it is easily seen that the salience presupposition is only satisfied with respect to the assignments h_{aa} and h_{bb}. Put differently, the salience presupposition is only satisfied if x and z refer to the same man, and in this way the anaphoric link between *a man* and *the man* is accounted for. The reader is invited to check that example (5) poses no problems for the salience analysis either.

Salient(x, Φ) is closely related to Familiar(x, Φ). Either the value set Val$(x, [\![\Phi]\!])$, corresponding with the CN under consideration, is a singleton (it is a UD) and in that case the element of that singleton is both familiar and the most salient one. Or the value set is not a singleton, but consists of at least two elements instead (it is an LD). Then the preceding linguistic context is needed: there must be an (indefinite) antecedent to guarantee satisfaction of the familiarity as well as the salience condition. We can also define an '*inconspicuous*' constraint on indefinites, which says that an indefinite has to refer to an inconspicuous (not salient) individual. In this way, the use of an indefinite determiner in an example like (6) is blocked.[30]

Differences between Familiar and Salient arise in the case of an LD for which *several* antecedents are available. An example is (12).

(12) A black Chihuahua and a white one walk in the park. #The Chihuahua barks.

---

[30] Again, specificity is beyond the scope of this condition. See footnote 22.

If the Determined presupposition triggered by *the Chihuahua* is interpreted as Familiar, the presupposition is satisfied as the reader can easily check. However, the Salient condition is not, since neither the black nor the white chihuahua is more salient than the other, thus correctly predicting the oddity of the second sentence. A general advantage of Salient over Familiar is that it is more flexible, since other relevant factors like discourse structure and topic/focus distinctions can be dealt with by 'fine-tuning' the notion of salience increase. Above we assumed, following the qouted suggestion from Heim, that an object becomes more salient if it has been referred to. However, one can easily imagine ways in which salience increase is dealt with in a more fine-grained manner. We already alluded to the insights from Centering Theory which state, among other things, that objects in grammatical subject position are more salient than objects in grammatical object position. In a similar vein, one can imagine that focus-shifts promote the new focus to maximal salience.[31] The main point of this section, however, is that interpreting Determined as Salient yields an intuitive and uniform interpretation of the presupposition triggered by definite descriptions.

7.6 Discussion: Extending the Analysis

We started this chapter with the assumptions that (i) definite descriptions are unambiguous and (ii) trigger existence and determinedness presuppositions. We raised the question how this determinedness presupposition should be interpreted and discussed four possible answers: uniqueness, anaphoricity, familiarity and salience. We presented formalizations of these concepts in terms of Presuppositional DRT and saw that neither the uniqueness nor the anaphoricity interpretation does full justice to the behavior of definite descriptions. In particular, the first interpretation has problems with 'anaphoric descriptions', the second with 'unique descriptions'. We then presented a formalization of the traditional notion of familiarity which looked promising, but arguably did not fully meet the non-ambiguity assumption. We then turned to the salience interpretation. The formalization of this concept in Presuppositional DRT does justice to our assumptions, and can deal with both descriptions which are used anaphorically and descriptions referring to unique objects. Moreover, in the case that there are several equally prominent objects, the salience presupposition is not met (which seems correct) while the familiarity presupposition is satisfied. A further advantage of the salience condition over the familiarity one is that it is

---

[31] For details on the precise formulation of such conditions see Grosz et al. 1995 and the references cited therein.

more flexible. In particular, the seperate assignment of salience weights makes it possible to take factors like recency and topic-shifts into account without touching on the salience condition as such.[32]

So far all we have done is define a semantic notion of determinedness underlying the analysis of definite descriptions. It is still a long way from here to a realistic analysis of the semantics of definite NPs in discourse. But, the salience condition seems to provide an excellent starting-point for developing such an analysis. In this final discussion section we back-up this claim by describing three extensions of the salience approach. In section 7.6.1 we discuss non-identity anaphora, with the emphasis on bridging, and argue that these pose no specific problems for the salience approach as such. Thereafter, we argue that the salience condition applies *mutatis mutandis* to all kinds of definite NPs (section 7.6.2). And in section 7.6.3 we show that the salience condition is also perfectly compatible with the *deictic* usage of definites.

7.6.1 Dependencies and Non-identity Anaphora

As far as anaphoric uses of definite descriptions are concerned, we have only been looking at *identity anaphora*: the relation between the anaphoric description and its antecedent was one of referential identity. In fact, we only looked at a specific *kind* of referential identity: namely the case in which the description does not introduce new 'information' about its antecedent. Thus, in example (3) *a man* and *the man* refer to one and the same man, and the definite description itself adds no new information about this man.

Nevertheless, anaphoric descriptions can sometimes add information, and this might pose problems for the present proposal. A well-known type of example is the following, quoted from Zeevat 1992:407.

---

[32]The salience condition has one shortcoming which we have not discussed and which arguably also plagues the other conditions. When Lewis 1979 introduced the notion of salience, he immediately noted "(...) *the possibility that something might be highly salient in one of its guises, but less salient in another.*" Consider the following example (without additional context):

A man and his son walk in the street. The man whistles.

Under the assumption that every son is a man, the value of the referent introduced for *his son* will be an element of the value set of *man* as well. In other words: there are *two* equally salient male objects. Nevertheless, intuitively it is obvious to which one *the man* refers. The point is that *a man* should raise the salience of an object *as a man* and not as a son, while *his son* should raise the salience of an object *as a son* and not as a man. Lewis 1979 writes: "*Possibly we really need to appeal to a salience ranking not of individuals but rather of individuals-in-guises — that is, of individual concepts.*"

(13) A man died in a car crash yesterday evening. The Amsterdam
father of four was found to have been drinking.

When the time has come to interpret the second sentence of (13), there
does not seem to be a 'most salient' *Amsterdam father of four*, so the
presupposition might fail. Zeevat notes that examples such as these
could be analyzed by distinguishing between the core, restrictive material of the description —which in this case is like a male pronoun,
and notice that there *is* a most salient male person example (13)— and
the rest, which should be seen as '*an adjectival non-restrictive modifier*'
(Zeevat 1992:411).[33] So it seems that such 'informative' anaphors pose
no problems for the salience condition as such.

It is well known, however, that identity anaphora is only one of the
possible species of anaphora.[34] Consider the following examples, from
Heim 1982 and Hintikka and Kulas 1985 respectively.

(14) a. John read a book about Schubert. He wrote a letter to the
author.

b. In every group, the unit-element commutes with any other
elements.

In (14.a) *the author* is anaphoric (in the sense that it depends on
its interpretation) on the book mentioned in the first sentence, but
clearly the relation is not one of identity. In (14.b) *the unit-element*
is anaphoric (in the same sense) on *group*, but again we do not want
to equate the unit-element with the mathematical structure it is part
of. Such anaphora have been called *bridging anaphors* (Clark 1977,
Clark and Haviland 1977) or *associative anaphors* (Hawkins 1978), since
an additional 'bridge' or 'association' is needed to account for the ana-

---

[33]It should be noted that such examples are limited in their occurrences. For instance, they cannot easily be embedded in conditionals:

If a man died in a car crash yesterday evening, then the Amsterdam father of
four was found to have been drinking.

An attractive hypothesis is that an anaphoric definite can only *add* information if the
antecedent is interpreted specifically. In Krahmer and Van Deemter 1997:89 this is
captured by the INFORMATIVE ANAPHORS HYPOTHESIS: *A potential antecedent with
a non-specific interpretation, which is less informative than the anaphor under consideration, does not qualify as a suitable antecedent for the anaphor, provided that
the relation between anaphor and potential antecedent is one of identity.* A second
kind of identity anaphora which could be said to add some form of information about
their antecedent are so-called *epithets*, of which *the bastard* and *the jerk* are relatively
decent examples. Here as well, there is some evidence that epithets are a kind of *emo-
tionally dressed-up pronouns* (see Geurts 1994:47, Krahmer and Deemter 1997:102).
We shall not discuss the deviate use of these descriptions here.
[34]For a radical perspective on anaphora see Van Deemter 1991, 1992. Van Deemter
generalizes the notion of anaphora to include essentially all cohesion in text.

phoric relation: books tend to be written by authors, and groups have a unit-element. As we have seen, Christopherson was well aware of such examples and did not see them as a problem for his familiarity thesis. But as things stand in the present chapter, no interpretation of the determinedness condition results in the right reading. The problem is that the links between books and authors, and groups and unit-elements, are not taken into account. What is needed is a general theory of *dependencies* (as Kracht 1994 calls it) and here the claim is that given such a theory, the salience condition takes care of the rest.

What a dependency theory looks like and how it is constructed are not questions which need to be answered by the semanticist, but obviously such a theory has to model the knowledge that books are written by authors, that groups contain a unit-element, but also that mothers have children, that restaurants have waiters and so on and so on. The semanticist *does* have to say something about the interaction between such dependencies and the semantic representation. Without wanting to commit ourselves to it, let us discuss one proposal found in the semantic literature to account for such dependencies, namely by using implicit arguments.[35] On this approach, the semantic representation of nouns like *author* and *unit-element* contains a hidden argument (for the book written by the author and for the group containing the unit-element). Such hidden arguments can be seen as a kind of meaning-postulates which are discounted into the lexicon. Explicit complements (like (author) *of a book about Schubert* or (unit-element) *of the group of positive rational numbers with multiplication*) act as modifiers of the nouns, 'disclosing' and restricting the interpretation of the hidden argument.

Let us consider the following possibility: the definite article can optionally trigger disclosure of the hidden argument and require it to be salient as well. Reconsider example (14.a). Schematically, the combination of the article *the* with the CN *unit-element [of a group]*, produces *the unit-element of the group*.[36] That is: the result is a complex description containing two presupposition triggers: for a group and for a unit-element for that group. From here things can proceed as sketched above for *the man's wife*.

The problem with an approach using hidden arguments of CNs is that it rests on the assumption that we can actually build our knowledge of dependencies into the lexicon. For cases like *unit-element* this is defend-

---

[35]See De Bruyn and Scha 1988 and —in a dynamic framework— Dekker 1993a, 1993b and Van Deemter 1991, 1992. A different, more general analysis of hidden arguments can be found in Visser and Vermeulen 1996.

[36]This process should be optional, since for identity-anaphora (*a unit-element... the unit-element*) the hidden argument has to remain hidden.

able, but for ordinary non-mathematical words things are not so clear. Another strategy might be to seperate world-knowledge (that books usually have authors, that groups have a unit-element) from the lexicon, and use some kind of inference mechanism to derive dependencies.[37] Whether or not dependencies can and need to be modeled as hidden arguments remains to be seen, but for the present purposes it does not really matter. The point is that once dependencies are taken into account, the salience condition is fully applicable again.

7.6.2 Definites and Salience

So far we have only discussed definite descriptions, but ultimately we want to treat *all* definite NPs in this way. That is: we want to replace the definite descriptions rule by the following general rule-scheme applying to all definite NPs (and with Determined interpreted as Salient).

Definite NPs Rule — Scheme

Upon encountering a definite NP of the form 'α', replace it with a new discourse referent x and prefix the current DRS

$$\text{with } \partial \quad \boxed{\begin{array}{l} x \\ \hline \alpha'(x) \\ \text{Salient } (x, \boxed{\alpha'(x)}) \end{array}})$$

Here $\alpha'(x)$ is the representation of the definite α with a free occurrence of x. In general: a definite NP triggers a presupposition which requires existence and salience. In this chapter we have seen how this works for definite descriptions and possessives (where α's β is treated as *the β of α*). What about other definites?

The new rule treats a pronoun like *he* as presupposing the existence of a salient male individual; *he* is analyzed analogously to *the male individual*.[38] On the assumption that a model contains more than one male individual, it is predicted that a pronoun like *he* is always used in a context-dependent fashion, and refers to the most salient male individual at that point. In this way the standard DRT rule ('pick up an accessible, previously introduced discourse referent') is replaced by the somewhat more specific 'introduce a new discourse referent referring

---

[37] This is done in, for instance, Piwek and Krahmer 1998, where the proof-theoretic perspective to presupposition projection discussed in the previous chapter is used to tackle some of the problems associated with bridging anaphors.

[38] This is in contrast with Evans' *E-type pronouns*, which are treated as descriptions in disguise, but with a different description for each occurrence of a pronoun, depending on the context it occurs in. See, for instance, Evans 1977, Heim 1990, Neale 1990, Van der Does 1994 and Van Rooy 1997a for discussion.

to the currently most salient object which is of the right gender and number'.

A PN like *Louis* presupposes the existence of a salient individual having that name. In this way the PN rule in traditional DRT ('introduce a new discourse referent as high as possible') is replaced by a rule which treats PNs like all other definite NPs. A PN is represented by a presupposition at the level where it originates (as argued for in Zeevat 1991): it introduces a new discourse referent which has to refer to the currently most salient individual bearing that name. This seems to be a reasonable approximation of the way PNs are actually used. Usually the combination of someone's first name and surname is enough to identify a person uniquely, and in that case no context is needed. But since someone's first name is not unique in general, the context is needed to satisfy the salience condition in those cases.

Demonstratives can be understood as *marked* descriptions. The use of a demonstrative determiner like *this* or *that* instead of the definite article *the* usually indicates something (although demonstratives also occur as stylistic variants of definite descriptions, see Maes 1991). It can indicate contrast, especially when accompanied by a pitch accent. Another typical use of a demonstrative determiner is to instruct the hearer to look around and locate the relevant object, in particular when combined with a 'demonstration' ($\nearrow$), as in (15).

(15) $\nearrow$ That man is looking at you.

An initial hypothesis might be that a demonstrative NP semantically behaves like a definite description, and that additional means (pointing, intonation, etc.) lead to additional constraints on the meaning.

These remarks can be seen as a first step in the direction of a full-fledged, uniform approach to definite NPs in discourse. Of course they are informal and inconclusive, but at least they do show that the salience condition is applicable to other definites as well.

7.6.3 Surroundings: The Dynamics of Pointing

So far, we only considered the *linguistic* context (the preceding discourse) but of course there is also a *non-linguistic* context. Here we briefly discuss the connection between the salience condition and the non-linguistic context, or *surrounding* as we shall call it. From a semantic perspective we have to take care that there is a relation between the surrounding and the semantical interpretation. Proposals to achieve this can be found in Montague 1974a, Lewis 1979 and Kaplan 1989. We follow the last mentioned here, and define a surrounding S as follows:

Definition 10 (Surroundings)
If s is a speaker, a an addressee, $\delta_1, \ldots, \delta_n$ are objects which are 'apt for pointing', t is a time and p is a place, then a surrounding S is defined as:

$$S = \langle s, a, (\delta_1, \ldots, \delta_n), t, p \rangle$$

We assume that $\delta_1, \ldots, \delta_n$ are also elements of the domain of interpretation. The interpretation of Presuppositional DRT is modified by the addition of S as a second semantic parameter to both $[\![.]\!]^+_M$ and $[\![.]\!]^-_M$. This means that $[\![\Phi]\!]^\pm_{M,S}$ gives the set of pairs of assignments which support/reject Φ in a model M and a surrounding S. To refer to S we also extend the language of Presuppositional DRT: we add *i, you, here* and *now* to the set of terms, and when x is a variable, then $(\nearrow^\delta x)$ is a DRS. These extensions are interpreted as follows (recall that terms are interpreted polarity-insensitive).

Definition 11

1. $[\![i]\!]_S = s$, $[\![you]\!]_S = a$, $[\![now]\!]_S = t$, and $[\![here]\!]_S = p$
2. $[\![\nearrow^\delta x]\!]^+_S = \{ \langle g, h \rangle \mid g\{x\}h \ \& \ h(x) = \delta \}$
   $[\![\nearrow^\delta x]\!]^-_S = \{ \langle g, g \rangle \mid \forall h(g\{x\}h \Rightarrow h(x) \neq \delta) \}$

Notice that $\nearrow^\delta x$ is interpreted as a *specific assignment* (chapter 2, definition 20); a specific value (namely δ) is assigned to a variable x. These additions make it possible to deal with sentences like the following:

(16)   a.   I am telling you about $\nearrow$ *that man* here and now.
     b. $\nearrow$ *That man* is bald. He wears a wig.

Let us look at the second example in somewhat more detail. The Revised Construction Algorithm produces the following DRS for this sentence, on the assumption that the act of pointing precedes the representation of the demonstrative NP. Although this obviously is an idealization, it seems plausible in the sense that intuitively the demonstrative NP cannot be interpreted without the accompanying demonstration.

(DRS 10)

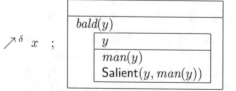

The act of pointing $\nearrow$ in (16.b) is represented as $\nearrow^\delta x$, where x is a new discourse referent and δ is the object which is pointed at. If we assume that *man* is an LD (the value set is not a singleton), then the context is needed to guarantee that the salience condition is satisfied. In this case there is only possibility: δ has to be a man. This means that when the speaker points to an object which is not of the male species, the salience presupposition is not satisfied and presupposition failure follows.[39] This indicates that the salience condition works for both the linguistic and the non-linguistic context.

Another potential use of surroundings is for examples like the following.

(17)   The queen dislikes gossip-magazines.

Even though the predicate *queen* is applicable to a handful of women in the world, it can be used as a UD in certain 'surroundings'. In the Netherlands, (17) is probably about Beatrix, while in Britain it is more likely to concern Elizabeth. *Queen* is not a one-place predicate but a three-place one, with additional arguments for a country and a period. The use of the definite determiner in examples like (17) seems to invoke a default which uses the surrounding to fill in the missing arguments: the queen is interpreted as *the queen of the here and now*; the present queen of the Netherlands for instance.

In sum, it seems fair to say that the determinedness presupposition, interpreted in terms of salience is not only applicable to 'ordinary' definite descriptions, but also paves the way for a more general theory of definites. In this discussion section we have seen that bridging and deixis

---

[39]This touches on the distinction drawn in Donnellan 1966 between *attributive* and *referential* uses of definites. The analyses of definite descriptions we pursued so far all involve the attributive use: the relevant property is attributed to a certain individual. According to Donnellan descriptions can also be used in a directly referential way, an example is the following:

↗ The man with the glass of vodka is looking at you.

The referential usage is especially prominent when the man in question is in fact drinking water (and the hearer knows this). According to Donnellan the attributed property is not really relevant in such cases: the hearer has no difficulty in finding out to whom the speaker refers. Notice that in Presuppositional DRT this example would lead to presupposition failure when the man actually holds a glass of water. Does this mean that we have to postulate an attributive-referential ambiguity for *the*? In Kripke 1977 it is argued that this is not necessary. Kripke takes the attributive use as basic, and argues that a form of pragmatic reasoning is used to generate the referential use (see also Neale 1990 and Dekker 1997). In the present set-up this might go as follows. In the above situation the example leads to presupposition failure, but the hearer will reason roughly as follows: 'there is no man with a vodka, but there is one holding a glass of water in the region the speaker is indicating, and since water and vodka are visually indistinguishable (even though their taste is a little different) the speaker probably refers to the man with the glass of water.' We conclude that the phenomenon of referential usage does not provide an insurmountable counterexample to the analysis of descriptions in terms of salience.

pose no problems for the salience condition as such, and that the salience presupposition seems applicable to other definites besides descriptions.[40]

---

[40]Various puzzling examples remain. One of those is the following example, due to Löbner 1986.

(†) He put his hand on her knee.

Neither *his hand* nor *her knee* needs to be related to a unique object or preceded by an indefinite reference; presupposition failure seems inevitable. Nevertheless, this example is perfectly natural. Things change when we shift our attention to other body-parts. For example:

She broke his tooth in return.

Here *his tooth* really has to refer to a salient tooth. Consider also:

(‡) After that, they went to the cinema.

In this example, *the cinema* can be used without a salient cinema in the context. But, this is different for:

They should have gone to the restaurant.

Here we do have the feeling that a contextually salient restaurant is meant. Example such as (†) and (‡) have bothered various people (for instance Löbner, Kadmon). Perhaps they are best treated as exceptions.

8

Concluding Remarks

In this book we have studied presuppositions and anaphors. Both phenomena have their proper place somewhere in the twilight zone between *semantics* and *pragmatics*, and as a result they have been studied from both angles. Nowadays, the traditional distinction between semantics and pragmatics is becoming increasingly blurred. One reason for this tendency may be the fact that phenomena such as those addressed in this book appear to resist analysis in purely semantic or purely pragmatic terms. But perhaps the distinction is somewhat arbitrary in the first place. This seems to be indicated, for instance, by the fact that it is notoriously difficult to define what 'semantics' is and what 'pragmatics', and to give a precise demarcation of the division of labour between these two aspects of meaning.

In Levinson 1983 one can find an intriguing discussion of the problems encountered when trying to give a precise definition of pragmatics. He notes that such a definition should at least cover *context-dependent aspects of meaning* (Levinson 1983:9). It is interesting to note that one important way in which dynamic semantics differs from traditional (truth-conditional) semantics is precisely its emphasis on meanings in context.[1]

It is no coincidence then, that dynamic semantics forms the backbone of most of the work in this book. A second recurring theme of this book is the usefulness of techniques from partial logic in the analysis of the phenomena under consideration. The use of partiality can be

---

[1]Groenendijk et al. 1996a contains a good, informal discussion of the importance of context change and the dynamic approach to meaning. They note that the real novelty is not so much the emphasis on meanings in context, but the fact that the construction of contexts is incorporated within a formal framework. They write in the conclusion: *The bite of it does not lie in metaphors, such as the slogan that meaning is information change potential, but in providing logical tools to implement and analyze these ideas.*

directly traced back to the Strawsonian definition of presupposing, which says that the question of truth and falsity does not arise for a sentence containing a failing presupposition.

In section 8.1 of this concluding chapter, we summarize the main results of this book. In the preceding chapters, we have mentioned many interesting points for future research. Rather than repeating all of them, we single out the most important ones and briefly expand on them. We end this chapter, and the book as well, with a final discussion (section 8.2).

8.1 Summary

8.1.1 Anaphora

Theories of Anaphora in Discourse We started our investigations in chapter 2, by looking at a number of approaches to anaphora in discourse which have been proposed in the past decades, and we have given special attention to the way they relate to each other. For example, we defined a meaning preserving map from the Logical forms of File Change Semantics (FCS) to the Discourse Representation Structures of Discourse Representation Theory (DRT), thereby showing that FCS can be embedded in DRT. Additionally, this map can be seen as an alternative, linguistically motivated method for constructing DRSs. Special attention was paid to the quest for *the* theory of discourse semantics. On the basis of our findings, combined with results from the literature, we arrived at a systematic overview of some of the relevant possibilities.

A Solution for the Negation and Disjunction Problems All the systems we discussed in chapter 2 do justice to most of the generalizations in Karttunen 1976 about discourse referents and their life-span, but none does justice to all of them. In particular, all the systems discussed have problems with *umbrella-* and *bathroom-sentences*, of which (1) and (2) are examples:

(1)   It is not true that John didn't bring an umbrella. It was purple and it stood in the hallway.

(2)   Either there is no bathroom in this house, or it's in a funny place.

All theories discussed in chapter 2 predict that the *it* pronouns cannot have (an umbrella or bathroom as) an antecedent, which is clearly not borne out by the facts. In chapter 3 it is argued that the problems connected with negation and disjunction can be solved in one go, if the classical law of double negation is restored in the dynamic set-up. We have presented a system which does precisely that: *Double Negation* DRT. Its main departure from standard DRT(-like) formalisms is that discourse referents which are introduced in the scope of *two* negations remain accessible for future reference. In this way, single negations remain a plug for anaphoric binding, while double negations now act as a hole for anaphoric reference. This is desirable for the treatment of umbrella-sentences. This new treatment of negation paves the way for re-defining disjunction, allowing discourse referents introduced in a negated disjunct to be picked up in the other disjunct, thus enabling a treatment of bathroom-sentences. The interpretation of Double Negation DRT uses some standard techniques from partial logic: in particular the distinction between positive and negative extensions (corresponding with 'active' and 'passive' occurrences of discourse referents) and the flip-flop operation assigned to negation.

8.1.2 Presupposition

PARTIAL LOGIC AND PRESUPPOSITION The central question we raised in chapter 4 concerned the role of partial logic in the treatment of presuppositions. In recent years, a lot of attention has been paid to examples involving the interaction between quantifiers and presuppositions. Prime examples are (3) and (4), due to Karttunen and Peters 1979 and Heim 1983b respectively.

(3)   Somebody managed to succeed George V on the throne of England.

(4)   Every man who serves his king will be rewarded.

Recent work on presupposition has shown that the *binding-problems* which Karttunen and Peters 1979 and Heim 1983b encounter with such examples, can be solved within combined partial-dynamic systems. In chapter 4 we have shown that these problems can also be solved in a *static* system with a partial interpretation. We started from a static, strong Kleene based interpretation of *Partial Predicate Logic* (PPL) with Blamey's presupposition-operator (transplication) added. In terms of this *mother of all partial logics*, two other systems were defined: Bochvar/weak Kleene based PPL and Peters/middle Kleene based PPL. On the propositional level, each of these systems corresponds with a 'traditional' approach to presuppositions. It was shown that none of these PPL interpretations suffers from the binding-problem arising in Karttunen and Peters 1979. Moreover, all three systems could handle the quantificational examples discussed in Heim 1983b, predicting appropriate, weak presuppositions in each case. In other words: the examples which play a central role in the recent dynamic-semantic approaches to presuppositions can be dealt with in a static partial logic. There is no immediate reason to 'go dynamic'. To be sure: this is not to say that the move to dynamic semantics is not necessary for other reasons, for, as we have seen in chapter 2, there *are* such other reasons.

We discussed two question related to this outcome. First, can we use these results to construct a satisfactory, classical Montague grammar for a fragment of English containing presupposition triggers? And second, if we take it that the partial element in the analysis of presupposition is still highly relevant, then as a consequence, so is the critique on it: can we do something about this critique?

PARTIALITY AND FLEXIBILITY To begin with the latter question: one general and often recurring point of criticism is that the partial approach to presuppositions lacks *flexibility*. For example, the following pair of examples illustrates that a presupposition triggered in the consequent of a conditional projects, unless the presupposed proposition is asserted in the antecedent. Thus, example (5.a), but not example (5.b), presupposes that France has a king.

(5)　a.　If baldness is hereditary, then the king of France is bald.
　　　b.　If France has a king, then the king of France is bald.

However, once we give implication an interpretation in partial logic we fix the projection predictions: a weak Kleene interpretation implies always predicting that elementary presuppositions project from the consequent, while a strong or middle Kleene interpretation implies never predicting projection from the consequent.

To show that it *is* possible for an approach using partial logic to achieve the required flexibility, a *presupposition wipe-out device* dating back to Bochvar was discussed: the $\mathcal{A}$ operator. It was shown how this operator can be used in a 'floating $\mathcal{A}$ theory'. We have seen that this approach allows us to give an account of cancellation of presuppositions in the scope of a negation by throwing away inconsistent readings, and that it helps in giving an account of cancellation in conditionals (such as (5.b)) by throwing away readings which violate the informativity constraint.

Thus, we can use partial logic as the starting point for a flexible account of presupposition projection, where the machinery of partial logic does the hard work, and general, well-defined pragmatic constraints filter out unwanted readings. In this way it gives a straightforward and intuitive interpretation of the claim found in, for instance, Martin 1979 and Link 1986, that semantics and pragmatics should be 'mutually supportive'.

The main point of the floating $\mathcal{A}$ theory is to show that it *is* possible to construct a theory of presupposition on the basis of a standard partial logic which makes flexible predictions about presupposition projection without postulating any *ad hoc* ambiguities for the logical connectives. We have developed this account in as much detail as required to make this point. There is a lot of room for fine-tuning, and one important line for future research is the full development of such a theory, in particular concerning the preference order and the constraints. With respect to the latter, and following Stalnaker and Van der Sandt, we have only defined an informativity and a consistency constraint. In chapter 4 we conjectured that more conditions besides these two have an influence on presupposition projection. Of course, this is just as true for the floating $\mathcal{A}$ theory as it is for, say, Van der Sandt's presuppositions-as-anaphors approach. It would be very interesting to find and formalize these conditions and investigate their interplay with the underlying partial logic. The floating $\mathcal{A}$ theory bears a certain resemblance with Van der Sandt's presuppositions-as-anaphors theory. For the sake of comparison it might be interesting to 'dynamify' the floating $\mathcal{A}$ theory, which can be done in two ways: either by following the recipe given in section 5.4.3 for dynamifying the static and partial version of Presuppositional Montague Grammar, or by constructing the translation set for a given sentence from its representation in Presuppositional DRT as discussed briefly in section 6.6. A final point for future research with respect to the floating $\mathcal{A}$ theory we would like to mention is the following. It might be interesting to replace the translation *set* by a single *underspecified* representation which subsumes the possible readings. A particularly interesting theory of underspecification from the current perspective is the one developed in Muskens 1995a, in which an underspecified version of classical Montague Grammar is presented which is perfectly compatible with the Presuppositional Montague Grammar of chapter 5.

Presuppositions and Montague Grammar Another issue which we addressed is the following. If the binding problem does not arise in a more or less standard logic, albeit a partial one, then why do Karttunen and Peters run into this binding problem? In chapter 5 we argued that this might be due to the lack of proper partializations of Montague Grammar at that time. Karttunen and Peters 1979 do not need partiality since they switch to an essentially *two-dimensional* approach in which each sentence of the fragment is translated into *two* expressions of Montague's Intensional Logic: one representing what is *expressed* (asserted) and one what is *conventionally implicated* (presupposed). But, as Karttunen and Peters themselves note, this two-dimensionality is the very source of their binding problem. In chapter 4 we concluded that standard Partial Predicate Logic is a suitable vehicle for the semantic treatment of presuppositions, even when they occur under the scope of quantifiers. Combined with the first decent Partial Montague Grammar, developed in Muskens 1989, this paves the way for a presuppositional extension of classical Montague Grammar, which combines technical clarity with a decent analysis of presupposition. Such a *Presuppositional Montague Grammar* was given in chapter 5, once again with the emphasis on presupposition-quantification interaction. Presuppositional Montague Grammar not only provides compositional derivations of the translations used in chapter 4, it also indicates what the Montagovian presupposition-theories of Hausser 1976, Cooper 1983 and Karttunen and Peters 1979 might have looked like if they could have used a clean partialization of classical Montague Grammar. Moreover, an easy recipe was presented to *dynamify* the system, thus bringing it completely up to date.

8.1.3 Anaphora and Presupposition

Two Theories of Presupposition in DRT In chapter 6 we introduced *Presuppositional* DRT. The language of Presuppositional DRT is the result of adding DRSs representing elementary presuppositions to the language of Double Negation DRT. The interpretation of Presuppositional DRT is a relatively straightforward combination of the interpretation of Double Negation DRT and the middle Kleene based interpretation of PPL.

We believe that the resulting system is interesting for various reasons. To begin with, it offers a single framework in which two rather different approaches to presupposition can be modelled. On the level of representations, Presuppositional DRT is perfectly compatible with the representations used by Van der Sandt in his presuppositions-as-anaphors approach. On the level of interpretation, Presuppositional DRT is comparable with the combined partial and dynamic approaches to presuppositions in the Karttunen and Heim tradition of Beaver and —in particular— Van Eijck, be it that Presuppositional DRT embodies a different treatment of negation and disjunction. We have seen that presuppositions can be studied using Presuppositional DRT in two different ways. We can continue in the Karttunen/Heim tradition and compute the presuppositions of a DRS Φ by calculating PR(Φ), that is by looking at the cases when Φ is either True of False. On this method, Presuppositional DRT and middle Kleene based PPL make comparable predictions, which should come as no surprise in the light of our findings in chapter 4. On the other hand, since the representations of Presuppositional DRT are perfectly compatible with those employed by Van der Sandt's presuppositions-as-anaphors theory, we can also feed our DRSs to Van der Sandt's presupposition resolution algorithm.

The fact that we can associate two rather different approaches to presupposition with a single system enhances comparison between the two approaches. However, Presuppositional DRT is not only beneficial for the sake of comparison, it actually leads to an *improvement* of Van der Sandt's theory. It was shown that merely defining Van der Sandt's theory on top of Presuppositional DRT, and not on standard DRT as usual, has various advantages. In particular, it enables the interpretation of presuppositional DRSs. As a result, the conditions on accommodation (consistency, informativity) can be checked on the spot even if there are still other unresolved presuppositions. As a result, there is no need to calculate *all* logical possibilities (as done in Van der Sandt 1992), and in many cases this leads to a reduction of the search space. Moreover, we can restore the Strawsonian intuition that presupposition failure leads to undefinedness by accommodating elementary presuppositions *as* presuppositions. The different treatment of disjunction embodied in Double Negation DRT simplifies the presuppositions-as-anaphors theory and improves its predictions, since presuppositions which arise in a right-hand disjunct can now be bound to passive discourse referents of the left-hand disjunct. Finally, as far as presupposition-quantification interaction is concerned, we saw that in Presuppositional DRT it is no longer predicted that (6) and (7) are equivalent.

(6)   Every fat man pushes his bike.

(7)   Every fat man who has a bike pushes it.

The presupposition triggered by *his bike* in (6) is still accommodated in the scope of *every*, but in the process remains presuppositional, and this destroys the equivalence.

DETERMINEDNESS AND SALIENCE In chapter 7 we zoomed in on a specific kind of presupposition triggers: definite descriptions. Usually it is assumed that definite descriptions presuppose existence, but it has often been argued that this presupposition is too weak to capture the behavior of definite descriptions. We therefore hypothesized that definites presuppose existence and something else: *determinedness*. We discussed four possible interpretations of this determinedness presupposition, in terms of uniqueness, anaphoricity, familiarity and salience. Formalizations of these four concepts in terms of Presuppositional DRT were presented and each was judged on its merits. One central condition is that the determinedness condition should apply to *all* definite descriptions alike, following Löbner's claim that the definite article is unambiguous. We argued that the salience interpretation of determinedness is our best bet. On this view, a definite description *the CN* triggers the presupposition that there is an object d which has the properties expressed by CN and moreover that this d is the currently most salient object with these properties. The salience weight of objects is modelled using a function variable sw, which refers to a function mapping objects in the domain to natural numbers. As an object becomes more salient (for instance because it was referred to by an NP), its salience weight increases. It was shown that this works well for definite descriptions referring to inherently unique objects as well as for anaphoric definites.

Of course, defining a determinedness presupposition for definite descriptions in terms of salience is one thing, developing a general theory of definites based on this notion is quite another. To work from the salience notion towards such a theory, there are two general lines for future research. The first concerns the notion of salience itself. In his discussion of salience, Lewis 1979:348 mentions two complications without the intention to overcome them. What happens if there is no most salient object satisfying the descriptive content or if there are two? And what if something is highly salient under one of its guises, but less salient under another? In the previous chapter, the first question was answered (this leads to presupposition failure), but the second was not addressed. In fact, we take it that one important line for future research would be to try and define salience not on individuals but on 'individuals under roles'. For this move, the work of Landman 1989 seems highly relevant. A somewhat related point for future work connected to the notion of salience itself is the determination of salience weights. For the sake of simplicity we merely followed the minimal suggestion from Heim 1982 that an object increases in salience when it has been referred to by an NP. Of course, in reality the assignment of salience weights is subject to many different factors. Fortunately the literature contains a lot of work in this direction (Grosz et al. 1995 seems a good starting point) and moreover, the separate definition of sw can easily be adjusted without touching on the fundamentals of the salience presupposition. The second general line of future research concerns the overall applicability of the salience presupposition. As noted in chapter 7, it is our intention to take the salience condition as starting point for a general, uniform theory of definite NPs. In this respect, it was argued in the discussion section of the previous chapter that the salience presupposition carries over *mutatis mutandis* to definite NPs in general, and we also saw that the salience condition is perfectly compatible with the deictic usage of definite descriptions. We only hinted at the interaction between the salience condition and bridging, but we take it that the work of Piwek and Krahmer 1998 on the interaction between world-knowledge and presupposition projection provides a promising starting point for a full-fledged account of bridging, which is perfectly compatible with the salience approach.

It has been observed that a general problem with any theory of definites is that it really should be a theory of everything. After all, as Neale 1990:10 observes, there is hardly a part of semantic theory which has *no* influence on the behavior of definites. We have tried to separate the presuppositional content of definites from all the rest, and thereby were able to give a general interpretation to the salience condition. We have illustrated that this condition seems applicable to all kinds of definite NPs and to many of their uses. We feel certain that future work along the lines mentioned above will not require significant changes to the salience interpretation as such.

8.2 Discussion: Rounding Off

In this book, we have discussed a considerable number of approaches to discourse anaphora and presupposition projection based on the partial and/or dynamic view on meaning. It has not been our intention to add completely new theories to the already considereable gamut of existing theories. Rather we have been inspired by existing approaches which aim at accounting for the behavior of presuppositions and/or anaphors, making improvements where necessary and comparing the results, and this led to a number of interesting insights. If this book contains a single moral, then it is presumably this: a century after Frege introduced the notion of presupposition and connected it with truth-value gaps, partial logic still has a lot to recommend for itself. We have seen that techniques from partial logic are the key to solving the negation and disjunction problems of DRT and related theories, that the notorious binding problems of Karttunen and Peters and Heim can be solved in an ordinary, static partial logic, and that Van der Sandt's theory of presuppositions-as-anaphors can benefit from partializing his representation language. While one could argue that the use of partiality in Double Negation DRT is merely a technicality to model the distinction between active and passive discourse referents, the partiality plays a key-role in our treatment of presupposition, motivated by our wish to stick close to the Strawsonian intuition. The fact that the problems encountered when presuppositions and quantifiers interact can be solved in static partial logic, can be taken as an indication that, at least for such examples, there is no immediate need to turn to a dynamic framework. Additionally, the discussion of Bochvar's $\mathcal{A}$ operator has shown that the traditional misconception that partial approaches to presupposition lack flexibility can be overcome. The outline of a floating $\mathcal{A}$ theory shows that we can use standard static partial machinery as the foundation of a simple and flexible theory of presupposition with a well-defined inter-action with pragmatic conditions, which bears a certain resemblance to the presuppositions-as-anaphors theory of Van der Sandt.

Bibliography

Ahn, R., and H-P. Kolb. 1990. Discourse Representation meets Construct-ive Mathematics. In *Papers from the Second Symposium on Logic and Language*, ed. L. Kálmán and L. Pólos. 105–124. Budapest: Akademiai Kiado.

Asher, N. 1993. *Reference to Abstract Objects in Discourse*. Dordrecht: Kluwer Academic Publishers.

Asher, N., and A. Lascarides. 1997. Bridging. In *From Underspecification to Interpretation*, ed. R. Van der Sandt, R. Blutner, and M. Bierwisch. IBM Deutschland, Heidelberg. Working Papers of the Institute for Logic and Linguistics.

Asher, N., and H. Wada. 1989. A Computational Account of Syntactic, Semantic and Discourse Principles for Anaphora Resolution. *Journal of Semantics* 6:309–344.

Barendregt, H.P. 1992. Lambda Calculi with Types. In *Handbook of Logic in Computer Science*, ed. S. Abramsky, D. Gabbay, and T. Maibaum. Oxford: Oxford University Press.

Barnes, J. 1984. *Flaubert's Parrot*. London: Picador.

Barwise, J. 1987. Noun Phrases, Generalized Quantifiers and Anaphora. In *Generalized Quantifiers*, ed. P. Gärdenfors. 1–29. Dordrecht: Reidel.

Barwise, J., and R. Cooper. 1981. Generalized Quantifiers and Natural Language. *Linguistics and Philosophy* 4:159–219.

Barwise, J., and J. Perry. 1985. Shifting Situations and Shaken Attitudes. *Linguistics and Philosophy* 8:103–161.

Beaver, D. 1992. The Kinematics of Presupposition. In *Proceedings of the Eight Amsterdam Colloquium*, ed. P. Dekker and M. Stokhof. 17–36. Amsterdam: ILLC.

Beaver, D. 1993. What Comes First in Dynamic Semantics. Technical report. Amsterdam: ILLC Report LP-93-15.

Beaver, D. 1994. When Variables Don't Vary Enough. In *Proceedings from Semantics and Linguistic Theory IV*, ed. M. Harvey and L. Santelman, 35–60. Ithaca, NY. Cornell University.

Beaver, D. 1995. *Presupposition and Assertion in Dynamic Semantics*. Doctoral dissertation, University of Edinburgh. To appear with CSLI Publications.

Beaver, D. 1997. Presupposition. In *Handbook of Logic and Language*, ed. J. van Benthem and A. ter Meulen. Chap. 17, 939–1008. Amsterdam/Cambridge, MA: Elsevier/MIT Press.

Beaver, D., and E. Krahmer. 1995. Back to the Future. Amsterdam/Tilburg.

Belnap, N. 1979. A Useful Four Valued Logic. In *Modern Uses of Multiple-Valued Logics*, ed. J. Dunn and G. Epstein. 8–37. Dordrecht: Reidel.

Blamey, S. 1986. Partial Logic. In *Handbook of Philosophical Logic*, ed. D. Gabbay and F. Guenthner. 1–70. Dordrecht: Reidel.

Blok, P. 1993. *The Interpretation of Focus*. Doctoral dissertation, Rijksuniversiteit Groningen.

Bochvar, D. A. 1939. Ob Odnom Trehznachom Iscislenii i Ego Primeneii k Analizu Paradoksov Klassicskogo Rassirennogo Funkcional'nogo Iscislenija'. *Mathematicheskii Sbornik* 4:287–308. English translation (1981): 'On a Three-valued Logical Calculus and Its Applications to the Analysis of the Paradoxes of the Classical Extended Functional Calculus,' in: *History and Philosophy of Logic* 2:87–112.

Bolinger, D. 1975. *Aspects of Language*. New York: Harcourt Brace Jovanovich. 2nd edition.

Bos, J., P. Buitelaar, and M. Mineur. 1995. Bridging as Coercive Accommodation. In *Edinburgh Conference on Computational Logic & Natural Language Processing*, ed. E. Klein, S. Manandhar, W. Nutt, and J. Siekmann. Edinburgh. HCRC.

Bos, J., E. Mastenbroek, S. McGlashan, S. Millies, and M. Pinkal. 1994. A Compositional DRS-based formalism for NLP Applications. In *Proceedings of the International Workshop on Computational Semantics*, ed. H. Bunt, R. Muskens, and G. Rentier, 21–31. ITK, Tilburg.

Bouchez, O., J. Van Eijck, and O. Istace. 1993. A Strategy for Dynamic Interpretation: A Fragment and an Implementation. In *Proceedings of the Sixth Conference of the EACL*, 61–70. Utrecht.

Brink, C., and R. Schmidt. 1992. Subsumption Computed Algebraically. *Computers Math. Applic.* 23(2–5):329–342.

Bunt, H. 1985. *Mass Terms and Model-Theoretic Semantics*. Cambridge: Cambridge University Press.

Bunt, H. 1988. Towards a Dynamic Interpretation Theory of Utterances in Dialogue. In *Working Models of Human Perception*, ed. B. Elsendoorn and H. Bouma. 419–455. New York: Academic Press.

Bunt, H. 1990. DIT Dynamic Interpretation in Text and Dialogue. In *Papers from the Second Symposium on Logic and Language*, ed. L. Kálmán and L. Pólos. Budapest: Akademiai Kiado.

Chierchia, G. 1992. Anaphora and Dynamic Logic. *Linguistics and Philosophy* 15:111–183.

Chierchia, G. 1995. *The Dynamics of Meaning: Anaphora, Presupposition and the Theory of Grammar.* The University of Chicago Press.

Chomsky, N. 1981. *Lectures on Government and Binding.* Dordrecht: Foris.

Christopherson, P. 1939. *The Articles. A Study of Their Theory and Use in English.* London: Oxford University Press.

Church, A. 1940. A Formulation of the Simple Theory of Types. *Journal of Symbolic Logic* 5:56–68.

Clark, H. 1977. Bridging. In *Thinking: Readings in Cognitive Science.* 411–420. Cambridge University Press.

Clark, H., and S. Haviland. 1977. Comprehension and the Given-New Contrast. In *Discourse Production and Comprehension,* ed. R. Freedle. 1–40. Norwood, NJ: Ablex.

Cooper, R. 1983. *Quantification and Syntactic Theory.* Dordrecht: Reidel.

De Bruyn, J., and R. Scha. 1988. The Interpretation of Relational Nouns. In *Proceedings of the 26th ACL.* Buffalo. State University of New York.

De Jong, F. 1987. The Compositional Nature of (In)definiteness. In *The Representation of (In)definiteness,* ed. E.Reuland and A.ter Meulen, 270–285. Cambridge, MA. MIT Press.

De Rijke, M. 1993. *Extending Modal Logic.* Doctoral dissertation, ILLC/University of Amsterdam. ILLC Dissertation Series, no. 4.

De Swart, H. 1994. Definite and Indefinite Generics. In *Proceeding of the Ninth Amsterdam Colloquium,* ed. P. Dekker and M. Stokhof. 625–644. Amsterdam: ILLC.

Dekker, P. 1993a. Existential Disclosure. *Linguistics and Philosophy* 17:561–587.

Dekker, P. 1993b. *Transsentential Meditations — Ups and Downs in Dynamic Semantics.* Doctoral dissertation, ILLC Dissertation Series, no. 1, Amsterdam.

Dekker, P. 1994. Predicate Logic with Anaphora. In *Proceedings Semantics and Linguistic Theory IV,* ed. M. Harvey and L. Santelman, 79–95. Ithaca, NY. Cornell University.

Dekker, P. 1996. The Values of Variables in Dynamic Semantics. *Linguistics and Philosophy* 19:211–257.

Dekker, P. 1997. On Denoting Descriptions. In *De Dag: Proceedings of the Workshop on Definites,* ed. P. Dekker, J. van der Does, and H. de Hoop. Utrecht Institute of Linguistics OTS, LEd.

Donnellan, K. 1966. Reference and Definite Descriptions. *Philosophical Review* 75:281–304.

Dowty, D., R. Wall, and S. Peters. 1981. *Introduction to Montague Semantics.* Synthese Language Library 11. Dordrecht: Reidel.

Evans, G. 1977. Pronouns, Quantifiers and Relative Clauses (1 & 2). *Canadian Journal of Philosophy* 7:467–536, 777–797.

Feferman, S. 1984. Towards Useful Type Free Theories I. *Journal of Symbolic Logic* 49:75–111.

Fernando, T. 1992. Transition Systems and Dynamic Semantics. In *Logics in AI*. LNCS 633, (subseries LNAI). Berlin: Springer-Verlag.

Fernando, T. 1994a. Generalized Quantifiers as Second-Order Programs – 'Dynamically Speaking, Naturally. In *Proceeding of the Ninth Amsterdam Colloquium*, ed. P. Dekker and M. Stokhof. 249–268. Amsterdam: ILLC.

Fernando, T. 1994b. Translations in the Dynamic Analysis of Presuppositions. In *Proceedings of the 5th Symposium on Logic and Language*.

Fernando, T. 1994c. What is a DRS? In *First International Workshop on Computational Semantics*, ed. H. Bunt, R. Muskens, and G. Rentier. Tilburg. ITK.

Frege, G. 1879. *Begriffsschrift*. Halle: Verlag L. Nebert.

Frege, G. 1892. Über Sinn und Bedeutung. *Zeitschrift für Philosophie und philosophische Kritik* 100:25–50. English translation (1960): 'On Sense and Reference'. In *Philosophical Writing of Gottlob Frege*, ed. P. Geach and M. Black. Basil Blackwell, Oxford.

Gallin, D. 1975. *Intensional and Higher-Order Modal Logic*. Amsterdam: North-Holland.

Gamillscheg, E. 1937. Zum Romanischen Artikel und Possessivpronomen. *Supplementheft XV der Zeitschrift für Französische Sprache und Literatur*.

Gamut, L.T.F. 1991. *Logic, Language and Meaning, Vol. 2, Intensional Logic and Logical Grammar*. Chicago: The University of Chicago Press.

Gazdar, G. 1979. *Pragmatics: Implicature, Presupposition and Logical Form*. New York: Academic Press.

Geach, P. 1962. *Reference and Generality*. Ithaca: Cornell University Press.

Geurts, B. 1994. *Presupposing*. Doctoral dissertation, University of Osnabrück.

Geurts, B. 1997. Dynamic Dido and Commutative Aeneas. In *From Underspecification to Interpretation*, ed. R. van der Sandt, R. Blutner, and M. Bierwisch. IBM Deutschland, Heidelberg. Working Papers of the Institute for Logic and Linguistics.

Geurts, B., and R. Van der Sandt. 1997. Domain Restriction. In *Focus: Linguistic, Cognitive and Computational Perspectives*, ed. P. Bosch and R. van der Sandt. Cambridge. Cambridge University Press. (to appear).

Geurts, B. and R. Van der Sandt. 1997. Presuppositions and Backgrounds. In *The Proceedings of the 11th Amsterdam Colloquium*, ed. P. Dekker, M. Stokhof, and Y. Venema, 37–42. Amsterdam. ILLC.

Gilmore, P. 1974. The Consistency of Partial Set Theory Without Extensionality. In *Axiomatic Set Theory, Proceedings of Symposia in Pure Mathematics*. Providence. AMS.

Goldblatt, R. 1982. *Logics of Time and Computation*. CSLI Lecture Notes. Stanford: CSLI Publications.

Groenendijk, J., and M. Stokhof. 1984. *Studies on the Semantics of Questions and the Pragmatics of Answers*. Doctoral dissertation, University of Amsterdam.

Groenendijk, J., and M. Stokhof. 1988. Context and Information in Dynamic Semantics. In *Working Models of Human Perception*, ed. B. Elsendoorn and H. Bouma. 457–488. New York: Academic Press.

Groenendijk, J., and M. Stokhof. 1990. Dynamic Montague Grammar. In *Papers from the Second Symposium on Logic and Language*, ed. L. Kálmán and L. Pólos. 3–48. Budapest: Akademiai Kiado.

Groenendijk, J., and M. Stokhof. 1991. Dynamic Predicate Logic. *Linguistics and Philosophy* 14:39–100.

Groenendijk, J., M. Stokhof, and F. Veltman. 1995. Coreference and Contextually Restricted Quantification. In *Proceedings from Semantics and Linguistic Theory V*, ed. M. Simons and T. Galloway, 112–129. CLC Publications, Ithaca, NY.

Groenendijk, J., M. Stokhof, and F. Veltman. 1996a. Changing the Context. Dynamic Semantics and Discourse. In *IATL3: Proceedings of the 11th Annual Conference and of the Workshop on Discourse*, ed. E. Doran and S. Wintner, 104–128. Israel Association for Theoretical Linguistics, Jerusalem.

Groenendijk, J., M. Stokhof, and F. Veltman. 1996b. Coreference and Modality. In *The Handbook of Contemporary Semantic Theory*, ed. S. Lappin. 179–214. Blackwell.

Groenendijk, J., M. Stokhof, and F. Veltman. 1996c. Coreference and Modality in Multi-Speaker Discourse. In *Proceedings of the Workshop on Context-Dependence in the Analysis of Linguistic Meaning*, ed. H. Kamp and B. Partee. IMS, Stuttgart.

Grosz, B., A. Joshi, and S. Weinstein. 1995. Centering: A Framework for Modeling the Local Coherence of Discourse. *Computational Linguistics* 21(2):203–225.

Gundel, J., N. Hedberg, and R. Zacharski. 1993. Cognitive Status and the Form of Referring Expressions in Discourse. *Language* 69(2):274–307.

Haddock, N. 1987. Incremental Interpretation and Combinatory Categorial Grammar. In *Proceedings of IJCAI*.

Harel, D. 1984. Dynamic Logic. In *Handbook of Philosophical Logic*, ed. D. Gabbay and F. Hunter. Dordrecht: Reidel.

Hausser, R. 1976. Presuppositions in Montague Grammar. *Theoretical Linguistics* 3:245–280.

Hawkins, J.A. 1978. *Definiteness and Indefiniteness; A study in Reference and Grammaticality Prediction*. London: Croom Helm.

Heim, I. 1982. *The Semantics of Definite and Indefinite Noun Phrases*. Doctoral dissertation, University of Massachusetts, Amherst.

Heim, I. 1983a. File Change Semantics and the Familiarity Theory of Definites. In *Meaning, Use and Interpretation of Language*, ed. R. Bäuerle, C. Schwarze, and A. von Stechow. Berlin: De Gruyter.

Heim, I. 1983b. On the Projection Problem for Presuppositions. In *Proceedings of the Second West Coast Conference on Formal Linguistics*, ed. M. Barlow. 114 – 125. Stanford: Stanford University.

Heim, I. 1990. E-type Pronouns and Donkey Anaphora. *Linguistics and Philosophy* 13:137–178.

Heim, I. 1991. Artikel und Definitheit. In *Semantik/Semantics, ein Internationales Handbuch der Zeitgenössischen Forschung*, ed. A. von Stechow and D. Wunderlich. 487 – 535. Berlin: Walter de Gruyter.

Heim, I. 1992. Presupposition Projection and the Semantics of Attitude Verbs. *Journal of Semantics* 9(3):183–221.

Hendriks, H. 1993. *Studied Flexibility, Categories and Types in Syntax and Semantics*. Doctoral dissertation, ILLC Dissertation Series, no. 5, Amsterdam.

Herzberger, H. 1973. Dimensions of Truth. *Journal of Philosophical Logic* 2(4):535–556.

Hilbert, D., and P. Bernays. 1939. *Grundlagen der Mathematik*. Springer Verlag, Berlin.

Hintikka, J., and J. Kulas. 1985. *Anaphora and Definite Descriptions*. Dordrecht: Reidel.

Hobbs, J., M. Stickel, D. Appelt, and P. Martin. 1993. Interpretation as Abduction. *Artificial Intelligence* 63:69–142.

Horn, L. 1985. Metalinguistic Negation and Pragmatic Ambiguity. *Language* 61:121–174.

Janssen, T. 1986. *Foundations and Applications of Montague Grammar*. CWI Tracts 19/28. Amsterdam: Centre for Mathematics and Computer Science.

Kadmon, N. 1987. *On Unique and Non-Unique Reference and Asymmetric Quantification*. Doctoral dissertation, University of Massachusetts, Amherst.

Kadmon, N. 1990. Uniqueness. *Linguistics and Philosophy* 13:273–324.

Kamp, H. 1981. A Theory of Truth and Semantic Interpretation. In *Formal Methods in the Study of Language*, ed. J. Groenendijk, T. Janssen, and M. Stokhof. 277–322. Mathematical Centre Tracts 136. Amsterdam. Reprinted (1984). In *Truth, Interpretation and Information*, ed. J. Groenendijk, T. Janssen, and M. Stokhof. 1–41. Foris Publications, Dordrecht.

Kamp, H. 1990. Comments on: J. Groenendijk and M. Stokhof: Dynamic Predicate Logic. In *Partial and dynamic semantics I*, ed. J. Van Benthem. DYANA BR 3175.

Kamp, H., and U. Reyle. 1993. *From Discourse to Logic: Introduction to Modeltheoretic Semantics of Natural Language, Formal Logic and Discourse Representation Theory*. Dordrecht: Kluwer Academic Publishers.

Kamp, H., and C. Rohrer. 1983. Tense in texts. In *Meaning, Use and Interpretation of Language*, ed. R. Bäuerle, C. Schwarze, and A. von Stechow. Berlin: De Gruyter.

Kanazawa, M. 1994. Weak vs. Strong Readings of Donkey Sentences and Monotonicity Inference in a Dynamic Setting. *Linguistics and Philosophy* 17:109–158.

Kaplan, D. 1989. Demonstratives: An Essay on the Semantics, Logic, Metaphysics, and Epistemology of Demonstratives and Other Indexicals. In *Themes from Kaplan*, ed. J. Almog, J. Perry, and H. Wettstein. 481–614. New York: Oxford University Press.

Karttunen, L. 1973. Presuppositions of Compound Sentences. *Linguistic Inquiry* 4:167–193.

Karttunen, L. 1974. Presupposition and Linguistic Context. *Theoretical Linguistics* 1:181–194.

Karttunen, L. 1976. Discourse Referents. In *Syntax and Semantics, Vol 7: Notes from the Linguistic Underground*, ed. J. McCawley. 363–385. New York: Academic Press.

Karttunen, L., and S. Peters. 1979. Conventional Implicature. In *Syntax and Semantics, Vol 11: Presupposition*, ed. C. Oh and D. Dinneen. 1 – 56. New York: Academic Press.

Keenan, E. 1972. On Semantically Based Grammar. *Linguistic Inquiry* 3:413–462.

Kleene, S. 1938. On a Notation for Ordinal Numbers. *Journal of Symbolic Logic* 3:150–155.

Kleene, S. 1945. On the Interpretation of Intuitionistic Number Theory. *Journal of Symbolic Logic* 10:109–124.

Kracht, M. 1994. Logic and Control: How They Determine the Behaviour of Presuppositions. In *Logic and Information Flow*, ed. J. Van Eijck and A. Visser. 89–111. Cambridge, MA: MIT Press.

Krahmer, E. 1993. Donkeys Galore, Approaches to Discourse Semantics. Technical report. ITK memo # 17.

Krahmer, E. 1994. Partiality and Dynamics. In *Proceedings of the Ninth Amsterdam Colloquium*, ed. P. Dekker and M. Stokhof. 391–410. Amsterdam.

Krahmer, E., and K. Van Deemter. 1997. Presuppositions as Anaphors: Towards a Full Understanding of Partial Matches. In *De Dag: Proceedings of the Workshop on Definites*, ed. P. Dekker, J. van der Does, and H. de Hoop. Utrecht Institute of Linguistics OTS, LEd.

Krahmer, E., and R. Muskens. 1994. Umbrellas and Bathrooms. In *Proceedings from Semantics and Linguistic Theory IV*, ed. M. Harvey and L. Santelman, 179–194. Ithaca, NY. Cornell University.

Krahmer, E., and R. Muskens. 1995. Negation and disjunction in Discourse Representation Theory. *Journal of Semantics* 12:357–376.

Krahmer, E., and P. Piwek. 1997. Presupposition Projection as Proof Construction. In *Computing Meanings: Current Issues in Computational Semantics*, ed. H. Bunt and R. Muskens. Dordrecht. Kluwer Academic Publishers. (to appear).

Krámský, J. 1972. *The Article and the Concept of Definiteness in Language.* The Hague: Mouton.

Krámský, J. 1976. Some Ways of Expressing the Category of Determinedness. In *Papers in General Linguistics.* 181–197. The Hague: Mouton.

Krause, P. 1995. Presupposition and Abduction in Type Theory. In *Edinburgh Conference on Computational Logic & Natural Language Processing,* ed. E. Klein, S. Manandhar, W. Nutt, and J. Siekmann. Edinburgh. HCRC.

Krifka, M. 1992. Presupposition and Focus in Dynamic Interpretation. *Journal of Semantics* 10(4):269–300.

Kripke, S. 1977. Speaker Reference and Semantic Reference. In *Contemporary Perspectives in the Philosophy of Language,* ed. P. French, T. Uehling Jr., and H. Wettstein. 6–27. Minneapolis: University of Minnesota Press.

Kripke, S. n.d. Presupposition and Anaphora: Remarks on the Formulation of the Projection Problem. Princeton University.

Landman, F. 1989. Groups (I and II). *Linguistic and Philosophy* 12:559–605, 723–744.

Langendoen, D., and H. Savin. 1971. The Projection Problem for Presuppositions. In *Studies in Linguistic Semantics,* ed. C. Fillmore and D. Langendoen. 55–60. New York: Holt.

Langholm, T. 1988. *Partiality, Truth and Persistence.* CSLI Lecture Notes 15. Stanford: CSLI Publications.

Larson, R., and G. Segal. 1995. *Knowledge of Meaning.* MIT Press.

Levinson, S. 1983. *Pragmatics.* Cambridge: Cambridge University Press.

Lewis, D. 1973. *Counterfactuals.* Blackwell.

Lewis, D. 1979. Scorekeeping in a Language Game. *Journal of Philosophical Logic* 8:339–359.

Link, G. 1983. The Logical Analysis of Plural and Mass Terms: a Lattice-theoretical Approach. In *Meaning, Use and Interpretation of Language,* ed. R. Bäuerle, C. Schwarze, and A. von Stechow. Berlin: De Gruyter.

Link, G. 1986. Prespie in Pragmatic Wonderland or: the Projection Problem for Presuppositions Revisited. In *Foundations of Pragmatics and Logical Semantics,* ed. J. Groenendijk, D. de Jongh, and M. Stokhof. Dordrecht: Foris.

Löbner, S. 1986. Definiteness. *Journal of Semantics* 4:279–326.

Ludlow, P., and S. Neale. 1990. Indefinite Descriptions: In Defence of Russell. *Linguistics and Philosophy* 13:171–202.

Maes, F. 1991. *Nominal Anaphors.* Doctoral dissertation, Tilburg University.

Martin, J. 1979. Some Misconceptions in the Critique of Semantic Presupposition. *Theoretical Linguistics* 6:235–282.

Martin-Löf, P. 1984. *Intuitionistic Type Theory.* Naples: Bibliopolis.

May, R. 1977. *The Grammar of Quantification.* Doctoral dissertation, MIT, Cambridge, MA.

McCawley, J. 1979. Presupposition and Discourse Structure. In *Syntax and Semantics, Vol 11: Presupposition*, ed. C. Oh and D. Dinneen. New York: Academic Press.

Miklosich, F. 1874. *Vergleichende Grammatik der Slavischen Sprache IV*. Vienna.

Milsark, G. 1977. Towards an Explanation of Certain Pecularities in the Existential Construction in English. *Linguistic Analysis* 4:1–30.

Montague, R. 1974a. Pragmatics. In *Formal Philosophy, Selected Papers of Richard Montague*, ed. R. Thomason. 95–118. New Haven: Yale University Press.

Montague, R. 1974b. The Proper Treatment of Quantification in Ordinary English. In *Formal Philosophy, Selected Papers of Richard Montague*, ed. R. Thomason. 247–270. New Haven: Yale University Press.

Morrill, G. 1994. *Type-Logical Grammar*. Amsterdam: Kluwer.

Muskens, R. 1989. *Meaning and Partiality*. Doctoral dissertation, University of Amsterdam. Reprinted (1995) by CSLI Publications, Stanford (Studies in Logic, Language and Information).

Muskens, R. 1990. Montague Grammar without Tears. lecture notes, Tilburg.

Muskens, R. 1991. Anaphora and the Logic of Change. In *JELIA '90, European Workshop on Logics in AI*, ed. J. Van Eijck. 414–430. Springer Lecture Notes. Berlin: Springer Verlag.

Muskens, R. 1994a. Categorial Grammar and Discourse Representation Theory. In *Proceedings of COLING 94*, 508–514. Kyoto.

Muskens, R. 1994b. A Compositional Discourse Representation Theory. In *Proceeding of the Ninth Amsterdam Colloquium*, ed. P. Dekker and M. Stokhof, 467–486. Amsterdam. ILLC.

Muskens, R. 1995a. Order Independence and Underspecification. In *Ellipsis, Underspecification, Events and More in Dynamic Semantics*, ed. J. Groenendijk. DYANA deliverable R2.2.C.

Muskens, R. 1995b. Tense and the Logic of Change. In *Lexical Knowledge in the Organization of Language*, ed. U. Egli, P. Pause, C. Schwarze, A. von Stechow, and G. Wienold. 147–183. Amsterdam/Philadelphia: John Benjamins.

Muskens, R. 1996. Combining Montague Semantics and Discourse Representation. *Linguistics and Philosophy* 19:143–186.

Muskens, R., J. Van Benthem, and A. Visser. 1997. Dynamics. In *Handbook of Logic and Language*, ed. J. van Benthem and A. ter Meulen. Chap. 10, 587–648. Amsterdam/Cambridge, MA: Elsevier/MIT Press.

Neale, S. 1990. *Descriptions*. Cambridge, Massachusetts: MIT Press.

Partee, B. 1973. Some Structural Analogies between Tenses and Pronouns in English. *Journal of Philosophy* 70:601–609.

Partee, B with H. Hendriks. 1997. Montague Grammar. In *Handbook of Logic and Language*, ed. J. van Benthem and A. ter Meulen. Chap. 1, 5–92. Amsterdam/Cambridge, MA: Elsevier/MIT Press.

Paustovskij, K. 1970. *Verre Jaren.* Amsterdam: Arbeiderspers.

Peirce, C. S. 1870. Description of a Notation for the Logic of Relatives, Resulting from an Amplification of the Conceptions of Boole's Calculus of Logic. *Mem. Amer. Acad.* 9:317–378.

Pelletier, J., and L. Schubert. 1989. Generically Speaking. In *Properties, Types and Meaning,* ed. G. Chierchia, B. Partee, and R. Turner. Dordrecht: Kluwer.

Peters, S. 1979. A Truth-Conditional Formulation of Karttunen's Account of Presupposition. *Synthese* 40:301–316.

Piwek, P. 1993. Partiële Discourse Representatie Theorie voor Neutrale Perceptieverslagen. Master's thesis, Tilburg University.

Piwek, P. 1998. *Logic, Information and Conversation.* Doctoral dissertation, IPO, Eindhoven University of Technology.

Piwek, P., and E. Krahmer. 1998. Presuppositions in Context: Constructing Bridges. In *Formal and Linguistic Aspects of Context,* ed. P. Brézillon and M. Cavalcanti. Dordrecht. Kluwer Academic Publishers. (to appear).

Pratt, V. 1976. Semantic Considerations on Floyd-Hoare Logic. In *Proceedings of the 17th IEEE Symposium on Foundations of Computer Science.* 109–121.

Quine, W.V.O. 1952. *From a Logical Point of View.* Cambridge, MA: Harvard University Press.

Reinhart, T. 1976. *The Syntactic Domain of Anaphora.* Doctoral dissertation, MIT, Cambridge, MA.

Rescher, N. 1969. *Many-Valued Logic.* New York: McGraw-Hill Book Co.

Roberts, C. 1987. *Modal Subordination, Anaphora and Distributivity.* Doctoral dissertation, University of Massachusetts, Amherst.

Roberts, C. 1989. Modal Subordination and Pronominal Anaphora in Discourse. *Linguistics and Philosophy* 12:683–721.

Rooth, M. 1985. *Association with Focus.* Doctoral dissertation, University of Massachusetts, Amherst, MA.

Rooth, M. 1987. Noun Phrase Interpretation in Montague Grammar, File Change Semantics, and Situation Semantics. In *Generalized Quantifiers,* ed. P. Gärdenfors. 237 – 268. Dordrecht: Reidel.

Rooth, M. 1992. A Theory of Focus Interpretation. *Natural Language Semantics* 1:75–116.

Russell, B. 1905. On Denoting. *Mind* 14:41–56.

Russell, B. 1959. Mr. Strawson on Referring. In *My Philosophical Development.* London: George Allen and Unwin.

Sæbø, K. 1996. Anaphoric Presuppositions, Accommodation, and Zero Anaphora. *Linguistics and Philosophy* 19:187–209.

Saurer, W. 1993. A Natural Deduction System for Discourse Representation Theory. *Journal of Philosophical Logic* 22:249–302.

Segerberg, K. 1982. A Completeness Theorem in the Modal Logic of Programs. In *Universal Algebra and Applications*, ed. T. Traczyk. 31–46. Banach Centre Publications 9, PWN. Warsaw: Polish Scientific Publishers.

Seuren, P. 1985. *Discourse Semantics*. Oxford: Blackwell.

Soames, S. 1979. A Projection Problem for Speaker Presuppositions. *Linguistic Inquiry* 10(4):623–666.

Soames, S. 1989. Presupposition. In *Handbook of Philosophical Logic*, ed. D. Gabbay and F. Hunter. Dordrecht: Reidel.

Stalnaker, R. 1979. Assertion. In *Syntax and Semantics, Vol 9: Pragmatics*, ed. P. Cole. 315–332. New York: Academic Press.

Strawson, P. F. 1950. On Referring. *Mind* 59:21–52.

Strawson, P. F. 1964. Identifying Reference and Truth-Values. *Theoria* 29:96–118.

Sweet, H. 1898. *A New English Grammar, Logical and Historical II – Syntax*. Oxford University Press.

Thijsse, E. 1992. *Partial Logic and Knowledge Representation*. Doctoral dissertation, Tilburg University, Eburon Publishers, Delft.

Urquhart, A. 1986. Many-Valued Logic. In *Handbook of Philosophical Logic*, ed. D. Gabbay and F. Guenthner. 71–116. Dordrecht: Reidel.

Van Benthem, J. 1991. *Language in Action: Categories, Lambdas and Dynamic Logic*. Studies in Logic, No. 130. North Holland.

Van Deemter, K. 1991. *On the Composition of Meaning*. Doctoral dissertation, University of Amsterdam.

Van Deemter, K. 1992. Towards a Generalization of Anaphora. *Journal of Semantics* 9:27–51.

Van den Berg, M. 1989. A Dynamic Predicate Logic for Plurals. In *Proceedings of the Seventh Amsterdam Colloquium*, ed. M. Stokhof and L. Torenvliet. University of Amsterdam.

Van den Berg, M. 1993. Full Dynamic Predicate Logic. In *Proceedings of the 4th Symposium on Logic and Language*, ed. K. Bimbó and A. Máté. Budapest: Eötvös University.

Van den Berg, M. 1994. A Direct Definition of Generalized Dynamic Quantifiers. In *Proceedings of the Ninth Amsterdam Colloquium*, ed. P. Dekker and M. Stokhof. 121–140. Amsterdam.

Van den Berg, M. 1996a. Dynamic Generalized Quantifiers. In *Quantifiers, Logic, and Language*, ed. J. Van der Does and J. Van Eijck. 63–94. CSLI Lecture Notes Number 55. Stanford: CSLI Publications.

Van den Berg, M. 1996b. *The Internal Structure of Discourse*. Doctoral dissertation, ILLC/University of Amsterdam. ILLC Dissertation Series 1996-3.

Van der Does, J. 1992. *Applied Quantifier Logics: Collectives, Naked Infinitives*. Doctoral dissertation, ILLC/University of Amsterdam.

Van der Does, J. 1994. Formalizing E-type Anaphora. In *Proceeding of the Ninth Amsterdam Colloquium*, ed. P. Dekker and M. Stokhof, 229–248. Amsterdam. ILLC.

Van der Sandt, R. 1988. *Context and Presupposition*. London: Croom Helm. English translation of *Kontekst en Presuppositie*. 1982. Doctoral dissertation, Nijmegen.

Van der Sandt, R. 1989. Presupposition and Discourse Structure. In *Semantics and Contextual Expression*, ed. R. Bartsch, J. van Benthem, and P. van Emde Boas. Dordrecht: Foris Publications.

Van der Sandt, R. 1992. Presupposition Projection as Anaphora Resolution. *Journal of Semantics* 9:333–377.

Van der Sandt, R. n.d. Discourse Semantics and Echo-Quotation. To appear in *Linguistics and Philosophy*.

Van der Sandt, R., and B. Geurts. 1991. Presupposition, Anaphora and Lexical Content. In *Text Understanding in LILOG*, ed. O. Herzog and C.-R. Rollinger. 259–296. Springer Lecture Note. Berlin: Springer Verlag.

Van Eijck, J. 1983. Discourse Representation Theory and Plurality. In *Studies in Model-Theoretic Semantics*, ed. A. ter Meulen. Dordrecht: Foris Publications.

Van Eijck, J. 1993. The Dynamics of Description. *Journal of Semantics* 10:239–267.

Van Eijck, J. 1994a. Axiomatizing Dynamic Predicate Logic with Quantified Dynamic Logic. In *Logic and Information Flow*, ed. J. Van Eijck and A. Visser. Cambridge, MA: MIT Press.

Van Eijck, J. 1994b. Presupposition Failure — A Comedy of Errors. *Formal Aspects of Computing* 6A:766–787.

Van Eijck, J. 1996. Presuppositions and Information Updating. In *Quantifiers, Deduction and Context*, ed. M. Kanazawa, C. Piñon, and H. de Swart. 87–110. CSLI Lecture Notes No. 57. CSLI Publications.

Van Eijck, J., and G. Cepparello. 1994. Dynamic Modal Predicate Logic. In *Dynamics, Polarity and Quantification*, ed. M. Kanazawa and C. Piñon. 251–276. CSLI Lecture Notes No. 48. Stanford: CSLI Publications.

Van Eijck, J., and H. Kamp. 1997. Representing Discourse in Context. In *Handbook of Logic and Language*, ed. J. van Benthem and A. ter Meulen. Chap. 3, 179–238. Amsterdam/Cambridge MA: Elsevier/MIT Press.

Van Eijck, J., and F.-J. De Vries. 1992. Dynamic Interpretation and Hoare Deduction. *Journal of Language, Logic and Information* 1:1–44.

Van Riemsdijk, H., and E. Williams. 1986. *Introduction to the Theory of Grammar*. Cambridge, Massachusetts: MIT Press.

Van Rooy, R. 1995. A Two-dimensional Account of Presuppositions in Quantified Contexts. In *The Blaubeuren Papers, Proceedings of the Workshop on Recent Developments in the Theory of Natural Language Semantics*, ed. F. Hamm.

Van Rooy, R. 1997a. *Attitudes and Changing Contexts*. Doctoral dissertation, Institut für Maschinelle Sprachverarbeitung der Universität Stuttgart.

Van Rooy, R. 1997b. Descriptive Pronouns in Dynamic Semantics. In *The Proceedings of the 11th Amsterdam Colloquium*, ed. P. Dekker, M. Stokhof, and Y. Venema, 265–270. Amsterdam. ILLC.

Veltman, F. 1996. Defaults in Update Semantics. *Journal of Philosphical Logic* 25:221–261.

Vermeulen, C.F.M. 1993. Sequence Semantics for Dynamic Predicate Logic. *Journal of Logic, Language and Information* 3:217–254.

Vermeulen, C.F.M. 1994. *Explorations of the Dynamic Environment*. Doctoral dissertation, Utrecht University.

Vermeulen, C.F.M. 1995. Merging without Mystery, or: Variables in Dynamic Semantics. *Journal of Philosophical Logic* 35:405–450.

Verschuur, L. 1994. Dynamic Semantics in HPSG. In *First International Workshop on Computational Semantics*, ed. H. Bunt, R. Muskens, and G. Rentier. Tilburg. ITK.

Visser, A. 1984. Four Valued Semantics and the Liar. *Journal of Philosophical Logic* 13:181–212.

Visser, A., and C.F.M. Vermeulen. 1996. Dynamic Bracketing and Discourse Representation. *Notre Dame Journal of Formal Logic* 37:321–365.

Von Heusinger, K. 1995. Reference and Salience. In *Choice Functions in Natural Language Semantics*, ed. U. Egli and K. von Heusinger. 21–40. University of Konstanz.

Westerståhl, D. 1985. Determiners and Context Sets. In *Generalized Quantifiers in Natural Language*, ed. J. van Benthem and A. ter Meulen. 45–71. Dordrecht: Foris Publications.

Whitehead, A., and B. Russell. 1927. *Principia Mathematica*. Cambridge: Cambridge University Press. 2nd edition.

Williams, E. 1981. On the Notion 'Lexically Related' and 'Head of a Word'. *Linguistic Inquiry* 12.

Zeevat, H. 1989. A Compositional Approach to Discourse Representation Theory. *Linguistics and Philosophy* 12:95–131.

Zeevat, H. 1991. *Aspects of Discourse Semantics and Unification Grammar*. Doctoral dissertation, University of Amsterdam.

Zeevat, H. 1992. Presupposition and Accommodation in Update Semantics. *Journal of Semantics* 9:379–412.

Zubatý, J. 1917. Ten. *Naše řeč* 1(10).

Zucchi, A. 1995. The Ingredients of Definiteness and the Definiteness Effect. *Natural Language Semantics* 3:33–78.

Subject Index

abductive inference, 188
accessibility
  double negation DRT, 76
  presuppositional DRT, 166
  standard DRT, 38
accommodation, 117, 149, 152,
    153, 157, 158, 183, 204
active discourse referents
  double negation DRT, 75
  presuppositional DRT, 165
  standard DRT, 38
alpha-conversion, 130
anaphoric loop, 156
anaphoricity, 202–205
assertion operator, 113
associative anaphor, 218
attributive description, 223

beta-reduction, 130
binary presupposition operator,
  96
binding, 152, 181
binding problem, 14
black hole negation, 12, 111
bridging anaphor, 218

Categorial Grammar, 126
categorical restrictions, 5
categories, 55, 144
category-to-type rule, 55, 145
centering theory, 213, 232
change of state verbs, 5

Church-Rosser property, 130
classical DRT, 36
clefts, 4
common ground maintenance, 117
conditions, 36
consistency constraint, 115, 154
construction algorithm, 77
  definite descriptions rule, 167,
    193
  definite NPs rule, 220
  indefinite descriptions rule, 167
  negation rule, 77
  proper name rule, 77
constructive type theory, 188
context change potential, 15
context set, 182, 201, 204
contextual quantification, 181
contextual satisfaction approach,
  149
contextual DRS, 182
conventional implicature, 140
cross-reference constraint, 204
cross-sentential anaphors, 1
cumulative hypothesis, 107

definedness, 98
deixis, 23
demonstrative, 221
denial, 4
dependencies, 217
determinedness, 23, 196, 199
dialogue, 62

diamond-property, 130
discourse referents, 1, 30, 35, 65
Discourse Representation
    Structures (DRS), 36
  constructed from Logical forms,
    37
  construction algorithm, 36, 77
Discourse Representation Theory
    (DRT), 35–46, 59
  total assignment version, 43, 44
disjunction problem, 68
domain-extension, 34
donkey sentence, 28
double negation problem, 65
double negation DRT, 74–76, 150
downdate problem, 50, 60
dynamic binding, 51
dynamic floating A theory, 179,
    229
Dynamic Intensional Logic, 52
Dynamic Montague Grammar, 52
dynamic negation, 75, 79
Dynamic Predicate Logic (DPL),
    49–52, 60
dynamics, 3

E-type pronoun, 84, 220
echo negation, 12, 178
eindeutigkeit, 207
elementary presupposition, 5, 9,
    94, 96, 162, 185
eliminative DPL, 60, 92
epistemic alternative, 209
error-state semantics for DPL, 18,
    22, 150, 171
eta-conversion, 130
even, 147
extended middle Kleene, 121
Extended Novelty/Familiarity
    Condition, 203

factives, 5
familiarity, 23, 32, 205–210
file card, 30, 35, 204
File Change Semantics (FCS),
    30–35, 42–43

filter, 6
finite assignment, 34
first commandment, 28
floating A theory, 110–118, 179,
    228, 229
focus sensitive particles, 139
four-valued two-sorted type
    theory (TY_2^4), 143
functional application, 132

generalized quantifier theory, 62
generics, 196
global accommodation, 153
Government and Binding, 31
guarded assignments, 60
guises, 217

Head-driven Phrase Structure
    Grammar, 126
hidden argument, 219
hole, 5
horizontal, 113

implicatives, 4
implicit argument, 219
inconspicuous constraint, 215
individual concept, 54
individuals under roles, 217, 232
inference, 83
informativity constraint, 115, 154
intensional logic, 127
intermediate accommodation, 154
internal matrices, 113

Kinematic Predicate Logic, 22,
    150

lambda-conversion, 54, 130
lexical restrictions, 5
local accommodation, 154
local context, 16, 39, 166
logic of conventional implicature
    (CIL), 120
Logical form, 30, 31

many-valued logic, 9
mass nouns, 196

merging lemma, 37
  double negation DRT, 76
  presuppositional DRT, 166
merging DRSs, 36, 41
middle Kleene, 10, 98, 99
modal subordination, 63
modality test, 4
Montague Grammar, 27

negation rule, 77
negation test, 3
non-identity anaphors, 23, 217
non-linguistic context, 221
non-representationalism, 46
novelty, 32, 209
Novelty/Familiarity Condition,
    32, 203
NP presupposition scheme, 137
NP-indexing, 31
NP-prefixing, 31

partial logic, 9
partial match, 152, 183
Partial Predicate Logic (PPL),
    94–100
  middle Kleene, 99, 150
  strong Kleene, 97
  weak Kleene, 100
partial type theory, 127
passive discourse referents
  double negation DRT, 75
  presuppositional DRT, 165
Peirce product, 42
plug, 6, 66
plurality, 62, 196
pointing, 221
polarity item, 4
possessive, 220
potential presupposition, 5
pragmatics, 225
Predicate Logic (PL), 44–46
prenex normal form, 29
presuppose
  in presuppositional DRT, 174
  in presuppositional MG, 133
  in PPL, 101

Strawsonian concept of, 89
presupposition resolution
    algorithm, 152, 156
presupposition trigger, 4
presupposition wipe-out device,
    21, 114
Presuppositional Montague
    Grammar, 130–137,
    144–147
presuppositional normal form, 102
presuppositional DRS, 149, 156,
    162
presuppositional DRT, 162–167
presuppositions-as-anaphors, 13,
    39, 150–161, 176–180, 229
principle of the excluded middle,
    8, 88, 95
programs, 46
projection line, 153
projection problem for
    presupposition, 5, 90
proper name, 221
proper name rule, 77
proper DRS, 40, 46, 166
proto-DRS, 36, 156
PTQ, 27, 130, 131, 145

Quantificational Dynamic Logic
    (QDL), 46–49
Quantifier construal, 31
quantifier raising, 31
quantifying-in, 28, 29, 134
questions, 7

random assignment, 47
referent systems, 42, 61
referential description, 223
relative clause formation, 136
representationalism, 30
restricted uniqueness, 201
revised construction algorithm,
    77, 167
revised extended standard theory,
    31
right-hand head rule, 33

salience, 23, 210–216, 220, 232
salience weight, 212
satisfaction theory, 149
semantic presupposition, 13, 89, 149
sequence valued assignments, 60
sequencing, 47
sequencing DRSs, 36
single negation lemma
    double negation DRT, 81
    presuppositional DRT, 166
source DRS, 153
specific assignment, 47, 222
specificity, 209
standard DRT, 36
static negation, 81
store, 54
strong determiner, 137
strong Kleene, 95–97
strong specificity, 209
strongest existential postcondition, 42
strongest presupposition, 101
suitability, 152
summation, 195
surrounding, 221
symmetric disjunction, 80
syntactic trees, 144

target DRS, 153
tense, 62
tertium non datur, 95
test, 47, 50
text formation, 27, 141
three-valued two-sorted type theory (TY_2^3), 127–130
too, 140, 147
total assignment, 43
totally proper DRS, 40, 166
trace, 28
transplication, 9, 96, 162
trapping constraint, 154
truth combinations
    in presuppositional DRT, 164
    in PPL, 95, 97
two-dimensional logic, 119, 125

two-sorted type theory (TY_2), 52, 53, 127
types, 127

unary presupposition operator, 96
underspecification, 229
unique denotator (UD), 199
uniqueness, 83, 84, 200–202
uniqueness effect, 194
unselective binding lemma, 57
Update Semantics, 61, 150
upperclass denotator (UD), 199

value set, 198

weak donkey sentences, 63
weak Kleene, 100
weak presupposition, 11, 105, 155, 184, 187
weak specificity, 209
weakest existential preconditions
    double negation DRT, 82
    presuppositional DRT, 173
    standard DRT, 44
world-time pairs, 128

Name Index

Ahn, R., 188
Asher, N., 52, 68, 117
Barendregt, H., 188
Barnes, J., 201
Barwise, J., 21, 46, 62, 125
Beaver, D., 4, 7, 13, 15, 18, 21,
   22, 52, 91–93, 96, 110, 113,
   115, 117, 119, 126, 130,
   140, 155, 160, 161, 187,
   188, 209
Belnap, N., 95
Berman, S., 69
Bernays, P., 200
Blamey, S., 9, 94
Blok, P., 12, 117
Bochvar, D.A., 93, 100, 113
Bolinger, D., 193
Bos, J., 52, 117
Bouchez, O., 52
Brink, C., 42
Buitelaar, P., 117
Bunt, H., 62, 196
Cepparello, G., 62
Chierchia, G., 37, 62, 63, 66, 199
Chomsky, N., 2, 31
Christopherson, P., 23, 206
Church, A., 52
Clark, H., 218
Cooper, R., 21, 24, 62, 101, 119,
   125, 126, 132, 230
De Bruyn, J., 219
De Jong, F., 137

De Rijke, M., 42
De Swart, H., 196, 202
De Vries, F.-J., 44, 52, 62, 171
Dekker, P., 22, 52, 60, 62, 79, 83,
   92, 163, 200, 223
Donnellan, K., 223
Dowty, D., 27, 130
Evans, G., 19, 28, 68, 84, 195,
   211, 220
Feferman, S., 101
Fernando, T., 36, 41, 42, 48, 60,
   62, 150
Frege, G., 3, 87, 88, 93, 113, 200
Gallin, D., 127, 130
Gamut, L., 27, 54, 131
Gazdar, G., 14, 107
Geach, P., 2, 28
Geurts, B., 13, 22, 63, 73, 83, 84,
   117, 139, 140, 151, 155,
   161, 218
Gilmore, P., 101
Goldblatt, R., 47, 48
Groenendijk, J., 2, 3, 29, 40, 45,
   46, 48, 50, 52, 58, 59,
   61–63, 66, 79, 83, 96, 99,
   127, 171, 199, 225
Grosz, B., 213, 216, 232
Gundel, J., 194
Haddock, N., 201
Harel, D., 48

Hausser, R., 21, 24, 105, 119, 125, 126, 132, 135, 137–140, 143, 230
Haviland, S., 218
Hawkins, J., 218
Hedberg, N., 194
Heim, I., 3, 7, 14–17, 20, 22–24, 30, 31, 34, 84, 90, 92, 108–110, 133, 135, 139, 150, 161, 195, 202, 211, 218, 220, 227, 232
Hendriks, H., 27, 126
Herzberger, H., 119
Hilbert, D., 200
Hintikka, J., 218
Hobbs, J., 188
Horn, L., 12
Istace, O., 52
Janssen, T., 52
Joshi, A., 213, 216, 232
Kadmon, N., 84, 195, 202
Kamp, H., 2, 3, 29, 35–38, 40, 42, 44, 58, 62, 66, 68, 69, 77, 156, 195, 196
Kanazawa, M., 63
Kaplan, D., 221
Karttunen, L., 1, 5, 6, 13–17, 21, 24, 25, 30, 39, 65, 66, 80, 89–91, 101, 105–109, 119, 121, 122, 125, 126, 131, 137, 138, 143, 147, 149, 226, 227, 230
Keenan, E., 137
Kleene, S.C., 95, 137
Kolb, H.-P., 188
Krámský, J., 23, 196, 206
Kracht, M., 93, 102, 178, 181, 219
Krause, P., 188
Krifka, M., 140
Kripke, S., 39, 140, 223
Kulas, J., 218
Löbner, S., 23, 196, 198, 206, 207, 224
Landman, F., 232
Langendoen, D., 5, 107

Langholm, T., 101
Larson, R., 7
Lascarides, A., 117
Levinson, S., 4, 225
Lewis, D., 23, 30, 184, 204, 210, 212, 214, 217, 221, 232
Link, G., 20, 93, 116, 196, 228
Ludlow, P., 209
Maes, F., 221
Martin, J., 93, 100, 228
Martin-Löf, P., 188
May, R., 31
McCawley, J., 210
Miklosich, F., 23, 206
Milsark, G., 137
Mineur, A., 117
Montague, R., 27, 125, 127, 130, 131, 134, 136, 145, 221
Morrill, G., 126
Muskens, R., 21, 29, 34, 37–39, 44, 45, 48, 49, 52, 54, 55, 57, 62, 95, 125–130, 141, 143, 144, 229, 230
Neale, S., 7, 201, 209, 220, 223, 233
Partee, B., 19, 27, 62, 68, 85, 126, 211
Paustovskij, K., 28
Peirce, C.S., 42, 188
Pelletier, J., 63
Perry, J., 21, 125
Peters, S., 10, 14, 17, 21, 24, 25, 27, 66, 89–91, 93, 98, 101, 105–109, 119, 121, 122, 125, 126, 130, 131, 137, 138, 143, 147, 227, 230
Piwek, P., 22, 117, 163, 188, 220, 232
Pratt, V., 46, 171
Quine, W.V.O., 9, 89, 211
Reinhart, T., 2
Rescher, N., 137
Reyle, U., 2, 29, 35, 36, 38, 40, 44, 62, 66, 68, 69, 77, 156, 195, 196

Roberts, C., 19, 63, 68, 69, 71
Rohrer, C., 62
Rooth, M., 46, 52, 62, 63, 140
Russell, B., 6–8, 87, 88, 200
Saurer, W., 84
Savin, H., 5, 107
Scha, R., 219
Schmidt, R., 42
Schubert, L., 63
Segal, G., 7
Segerberg, K., 44
Seuren, P., 12, 111
Soames, S., 4, 12, 20, 89, 112,
    113, 140
Stalnaker, R., 155
Stokhof, M., 2, 3, 29, 40, 45, 46,
    48, 50, 52, 58, 59, 61–63,
    66, 79, 83, 96, 99, 127, 171,
    199, 225
Strawson, P.F., 7, 8, 89, 200, 207,
    209
Sweet, H., 23, 206
Sæbø, K., 151
Tarski, A., 45, 82
Thijsse, E., 95
Urquhart, A., 9
Van Benthem, J., 34, 39, 44
Van Deemter, K., 137, 182, 183,
    218
Van den Berg, M., 22, 62, 79, 83,
    163
Van der Does, J., 58, 62, 220
Van der Sandt, R., 4, 7, 12, 13,
    22, 39, 90, 93, 94, 113, 115,
    117, 140, 149, 151, 152,
    155, 156, 158, 159, 161,
    178, 183, 205, 231
Van Eijck, J., 6, 18, 20, 22, 37,
    42, 44, 52, 62, 92, 126, 163,
    171, 199, 200
Van Riemsdijk, H., 31
Van Rooy, R., 83, 84, 122, 220
Veltman, F., 22, 29, 61, 62, 199,
    225
Vermeulen, K., 42, 60, 61, 219

Verschuur, L., 126
Visser, A., 34, 39, 44, 121, 219
Von Heusinger, K., 200
Wada, H., 68
Wall, R., 27, 130
Weinstein, S., 213, 216, 232
Westerståhl, D., 182, 201, 204
Whitehead, A., 88
Williams, E., 31, 33
Zacharski, R., 194
Zeevat, H., 22, 41, 46, 139, 150,
    155, 182, 205, 217, 218, 221
Zubatý, J., 206
Zucchi, A., 137

University of Michigan Museum of Art, 1948/1.333

The lithograph on the cover of the paperback edition of this book is *Dynamic Force of the Cyclist*, ca. 1914, by Umberto Boccioni, Italian, 1882–1916, from the collecton of the University of Michigan Museum of Art. Lithograph: H. 29.5 cm.; W. 38.4 cm.